TRANSACTION MAN

Traders, Disrupters, and the Dismantling of Middle-Class America

NICHOLAS LEMANN

Picador
Farrar, Straus and Giroux
New York

Picador
120 Broadway, New York 10271

Originally published in 2019 by Farrar, Straus and Giroux as *Transaction Man:
The Rise of the Deal and the Decline of the American Dream*
First Picador paperback edition, 2020

The Library of Congress has cataloged the Farrar, Straus and Giroux
hardcover edition as follows:
Names: Lemann, Nicholas, author.
Title: Transaction man : the rise of the deal and the decline of the American dream /
Nicholas Lemann.
Description: First Edition. | New York : Farrar, Straus and Giroux, [2019] | Includes index.
Identifiers: LCCN 2019020255 | ISBN 9780374277888 (hardcover)
Subjects: LCSH: Corporations—United States—History. | United States—Economic
conditions—20th century. | United States—Economic policy—20th century. | United
States—Politics and government—1945–1989.
Classification: LCC HD2785 .L456 2019 | DDC 330.973—dc23
LC record available at https://lccn.loc.gov/2019020255

Picador Paperback ISBN: 978-1-250-75795-1

Designed by Jonathan D. Lippincott

For Alan Brinkley

CONTENTS

Prologue   3

1. Institution Man   23

2. The Time of Institutions   70

3. Transaction Man   100

4. The Time of Transactions: Rising   136

5. The Time of Transactions: Falling   182

6. Network Man   222

Afterword: An Attempt to Use a Tool   252

Notes   269

Acknowledgments   287

Index   291

TRANSACTION MAN

PROLOGUE

There are moments in history when everything seems calm, when there isn't obvious, bitter contention about big questions. It takes some effort now to remember that the dawn of the new millennium was like that, at least to the minds of fortunate people in the United States. As the portentous date approached, it was possible to believe that a happy age had begun. The great struggle over the Soviet Union's ambitions during the last half of the twentieth century had ended. There was no evident argument regarding the rightness of capitalism as the dominant economic system and democracy as the dominant political system; surely the places where they did not prevail would soon be brought into their warm embrace. The world was peaceful and prosperous, relatively speaking. American influence in every aspect of life, from banking and technology to movies and sneakers, had spread everywhere. The miraculous advent of the Internet was making instantaneous global communication and commerce possible.

Everything seemed calm and settled—and then, boom, it wasn't. The two decades since the millennium have brought a series of unpleasant surprises wildly at odds with the way things seemed to be going. First came the September 11 attacks and the endless wars that followed from them; then the sudden collapse of the supposedly invulnerable financial system; then, substantially as a result of that collapse, a similarly unexpected disintegration of political consensus, leading to the rise to power of right-wing nativist politicians in the United States and many other places in the world. It wasn't long before every item on the optimists' old checklist, including the most important ones—confidence in the future of capitalism and democracy—had begun to seem misguided.

Economics and politics usually operate together as a society's main organizing principles. Somehow the connection between them broke. Dramatic events made its brokenness evident, but those events were effects, not causes. To find out what happened requires looking under the surface. Headline-making news is easy to see; the rules that shape our everyday lives are not. Obviously they changed, a great deal. When did that happen, and who did it, and why? As a result, who has more power now and who has less? Whose interests are taken care of and whose are ignored? What can you do to provide yourself with some security and hope, and what would be fruitless? These are the kinds of questions people often talk about at seminars and conferences—usually people who are not directly on the receiving end of what happened. To understand the urgency of these questions, it may help to meet some of the people for whom they are not interesting and abstract, but concrete and terrifying.

■

On May 15, 2009, FedEx dropped off an ominously slender package from General Motors at the parts department at D'Andrea Buick, on the South Side of Chicago. Okay, maybe the FedEx guy didn't know what was in the package, but it was typical that nobody thought to make sure it went to the main office. The parts department got the package to Nick D'Andrea, the owner, a strutting bantam rooster with a broad chest, a head of curly white hair, and sharp eyes that moved around, taking everything in. He tore it open and found that he was out of business.

What was happening? The world was falling apart. It had been falling apart gradually for quite a while, from Nick D'Andrea's point of view, and now it was falling apart quickly. General Motors, the Gibraltar of the American economy as far as Nick was concerned—"the General!"—had gone bankrupt. It meant that the whole dense, built-up web of arrangements that gave some protection to a small one-store auto dealer like Nick was null and void. President Barack Obama had appointed a "car czar," a guy from Wall Street who didn't know the car business, and he had decreed that in exchange for its $50 billion in government bailout money, GM, along with Chrysler, which was also bankrupt, would have to close more than a thousand dealerships all over the country. D'Andrea Buick was one of them. The letter told Nick to sell his inventory and close his store in a month.

Nick had lived his whole life in Chicago. He thought he knew how life was supposed to work: it was far from perfect, but at least it was understandable. Showing loyalty, being straight with people, and maintaining connections was everything. If you did all that and something still went wrong, it meant that somebody somewhere didn't wish you well or had some kind of deal going that you were on the wrong side of. GM used to send a guy around to visit D'Andrea Buick every so often—a good guy, who could see how well Nick was running the dealership. Then the Internet came along, and the visits were replaced by teleconferences. At one of the teleconferences it was announced that GM was going to start combining several brands into single dealerships; Buick was going to be put together with Pontiac and GMC trucks.

GM started putting heavy pressure on Nick to absorb a nearby Pontiac dealership that wasn't doing well. He resisted like hell, but in 2007 the company gave him an ultimatum: do this, or your business will be in jeopardy, because we control your supply of cars and, in the end, the franchise that lets you operate as a GM dealer. So Nick, who'd been proud to operate a debt-free dealership, borrowed money—from GM's credit company, GMAC—and bought out the Pontiac dealer. Then he had to get a "floor plan"—another loan, also from GM—to stock his dealership with new Pontiacs. And he had to renovate the building, using a GM-approved architect, again with money borrowed from GM. By the time he reopened, he was in debt to GM for close to a million dollars, with heavy monthly payments to meet, and he had mortgaged both the dealership and his house.

Nick started selling Pontiacs along with Buicks in August 2008. In September, the financial crisis hit. On the South Side of Chicago, everybody buys cars with borrowed money—but suddenly you couldn't borrow, because the credit markets had frozen. The Pontiacs were just sitting there. Then, in October, Nick got a letter from GM saying that in a few months it was going to terminate Pontiac as a brand. (What had saved Buick? It was a status brand in China.) So he was fighting for his survival even before the termination letter arrived in May.

Nick's grandfather was an immigrant from a village in Southern Italy who had found work in Chicago as a pick-and-shovel guy, digging sewers and subway tunnels. His father was a maintenance electrician for Kodak. The family lived in an Italian neighborhood, went to church, sent its kids to Catholic schools, and served as foot soldiers in the mighty Chicago Democratic political machine. Experts can say what they want about the importance of "civil society" in neighborhoods like the one on the West Side of Chicago where Nick grew up, but that concept over-complicates things: it was really just church (Catholic) and state (the machine) that had been the dominant forces in the lives of poor Italians for centuries. The police were Irish, and there was no love lost between them and the Italians, but as Nick liked to say, if you needed a cop, you called a cop and you got a cop. The local alderman was Vito Marzullo, a legendary, all-powerful Chicago politician. If you wanted something or if you had a problem, you went to your precinct captain and he went to Marzullo and made the case. Otherwise you kept your mouth shut. Your economic life was essentially an offshoot of your political life. Jobs, from the Chicago neighborhood perspective, came not from abstract concepts such as economic growth or innovation or entrepreneurship, but from Marzullo: either they were patronage jobs with the city or the county, or they were quasi-patronage jobs with large, stable corporate employers who knew it was a good idea to be on friendly terms with the machine. And on election day you repaid your debts by delivering votes for the Democratic Party.

As soon as Nick was into his teens, his father began to get him little jobs here and there by asking the precinct captain. Nick finished high school, started college, then left school and went to work full-time. He worked in a hardware store. He operated a hot dog stand for a few years. Then he got a call from a friend asking him if he'd like to try selling used cars. That was how he started at what eventually became his dealer-ship. He was a salesman for a few years, then a manager, then a part owner, and, finally, more than twenty years in, the sole owner. Back in the days when he was still a salesman, a shy, composed young woman wearing a crucifix around her neck, Amy Vorberg, who was a divorced single mother with two young children, came into the store to look at

Buicks. She wound up buying a car, and then she kept finding occasions to bring it back to have something looked at, and pretty soon she and Nick were married.

D'Andrea Buick stood at the corner of Seventy-First Street and Western Avenue, in a neighborhood called Chicago Lawn. When Nick first started working there in the late 1970s, that section of Western Avenue was an automobile row for miles, with one dealership after another, plus repair shops, used-car lots, tire shops, and parts supply stores. At least in the memories of Chicago Lawn old-timers, the cars glistened in the sun, practically emanating optimism. If a thriving automobile row is one of the jewels of a neighborhood, you know the neighborhood is nothing fancy, but to Nick and Amy D'Andrea (whose father, a Greek immigrant, operated a candy store in Chicago Lawn for years) it gleams in memory as, to use Nick's word, *Eden*. That meant a Sears, Roebuck store so big that it operated a charm school where Amy sent her daughters; block after block of neat beige brick bungalows with tiny, fanatically well-tended patches of front lawn; rows of small owner-operated shops and white-ethnic restaurants (Lithuanian, Polish, Italian) along the main thoroughfares; a skyline dominated by church spires (St. Rita of Cascia, St. Nicholas of Tolentine) and factory smokestacks (Nabisco, General Foods); and quasi-religious customer devotion to General Motors cars.

Chicago Lawn was one of the last places in Chicago, maybe *the* last, to switch from white to black during the long, barely controlled chaos of changing racial geography in the last half of the twentieth century. In 1990 it was still just over half white; by 2000 it was just over half black. The whites left mainly for neighborhoods to the south and west (Nick and Amy lived in Orland Park, a close-in suburb). Most people in Chicago Lawn were first-time homeowners who had no tangible assets except their house and their car. Panicked, or induced to panic by Realtors, many of the whites sold quickly and too cheaply. Sometimes people would go to bed next to an occupied house and wake up to find it abandoned. The new black residents arrived mainly from neighborhoods to the east, such as Englewood, that had become dangerous and partly abandoned. Many of these people were frightened, too, and had let themselves be talked into buying places at prices far above what the fleeing whites had sold for. Most of the factories left. The big stores left. The little shops and restaurants closed down.

But Nick stayed. He had an overwhelmingly black clientele, a black manager, and a union shop with lots of black employees. He wasn't selling as many cars as he used to, but he was still making decent money. Let's face it—he wasn't going to have a lot of other opportunities set before him as good as this, and he knew how to make the most of the one he had. He'd learned how to size up a customer's ability to repay a loan, not just by his credit score, but by the way he looked at you. Maybe he'd "been to college," as Nick liked to say (meaning a spell at Joliet state prison), but you'd known his family and sold them cars for years, and you trusted him to keep up on his loan. Sometimes you carried a car loan yourself. You knew not to get greedy and try to get terms that would only wind up with your having to summon a repo man to get the car back. You beefed up your used-car business. You put up a basketball hoop on your lot so the neighborhood kids could play there. You bought seats at the neighborhood fund-raising dinners. You got to know your alderman well enough (campaign contributions helped with this) to get a little break, sometimes, on this or that dumb requirement the city was imposing on businesses. You supported the archdiocese, and sometimes one of the nuns from St. Casimir's came in and bought a Buick. You learned to keep your blood pressure under control when Buick sent you the same old Rivieras and LeSabres every year, at higher prices, while the Japanese car companies were introducing new models. Nick liked to tell a story about a customer who asked him why the car he was looking at cost so much. Nick explained that there had been trouble with the paint job on the previous year's models, so Buick had bought robots to paint the cars and had passed the cost along to customers. "Who's gonna pay for my car?" the customer said. "The robot? I don't have a job anymore."

After the FedEx package from GM arrived, Nick started making calls. He called GM—nobody was available to speak with him. Because of a redistricting, the alderman he'd put time into cultivating a relationship with had retired, and the new alderman didn't return his calls. Nick called his congressman, Bobby Rush. He called the Illinois state's attorney, Lisa Madigan, who had grown up in Chicago Lawn. He called Father Michael Pfleger, a celebrated activist Catholic priest whose parish, St. Sabina, was just a few blocks away. Nobody would see him. He told his employees they had lost their jobs, worked the phones to help them get new ones, and negotiated the end of his union contracts. By the middle of June everybody was gone, but Nick was still on the hook for his loans, the property, and his inventory of unsold cars. Once, he saw President Obama on television explaining that GM had gone bankrupt because it had been making cars nobody wanted to buy—and Nick still owned a bunch of those cars. How did anybody expect him to sell them? He and Amy had the feeling that they were tiny, inconsequential specks swept away in a vast catastrophe they couldn't comprehend. Somebody, without warning them, had changed the rules they'd lived by all their lives. Amy was often up at night, crying. Nick told his friends that he felt as if one day he went to sleep in America, and the next day he woke up in . . . someplace else. Iran, maybe.

One of Amy's daughters, Elaine Vorberg, was a lawyer who, fortunately for the D'Andreas, had recently become a mother, left her firm, and gone into practice for herself—so she could get as involved in the family crisis as she wanted, and she wanted to be very involved. She told Nick not to sign anything, and she started calling and emailing people at GM. Nobody responded. Finally she got a GM lawyer on the phone. I have a client I'm representing for free, she said, and he's my stepfather, so I have all the time in the world to devote to his case. But you'll have to hire an expensive lawyer to spend hundreds of hours fighting me. So here's what I want: I want GMAC to take back the cars on the lot and cancel our floor plan loan. We'll sell the property and pay off that loan when we do. And then we'll be done.

Elaine had heard about an energetic auto dealer in Maryland, named Tamara Darvish, who was organizing a national protest by as many of the terminated dealers as she could find. The dealers organized a "fly-in" at the Capitol building in Washington: hundreds of them, from all over the country, each wearing a badge bearing the number of employees at their terminated stores, would come and make as much of a fuss as they possibly could, to the press, politicians, and whomever else they could get to listen to them. Aggressive collective lobbying works. Members of Congress started badgering the White House on behalf of the dealers. On July 13, the day before the fly-in, the car czar, Steven Rattner, announced his resignation. When the D'Andreas were in Washington for the fly-in, they and the other terminated dealers from Illinois who had

come to town were able to set up a meeting with one of the top aides of
Senator Richard Durbin, whose mother was a Lithuanian from Chicago
Lawn. He promised to help.

Before long, GM had settled with the D'Andreas, and Congress had
passed a law called the Automobile Dealer Economic Rights Restora-
tion Act, which set up a way for dealers to challenge their terminations
before an arbitrator. Nick sold his store and paid off the loan. The building was demolished. The lot stood empty for several years. Nick found
work selling cars at other dealerships for a while, first Hondas and then
Fords, but it wasn't the same. After a few years he retired, his finances
in decent shape. He bought a Lexus, as a sign that he no longer felt
bound by the old social compact, now that it was clear that the people in
charge, whoever they were, didn't feel bound by it either. He still couldn't
understand what had happened. He liked to say that he felt like collateral damage—but from what?

The only time Chicago Lawn ever made the national news, it was for
something terrible. In 1966 Martin Luther King, Jr., decided to bring
the civil rights movement north, to show that discrimination and segregation didn't exist only in the Jim Crow South. He and his lieutenants
moved to Chicago and began staging protests. In August that year they
traveled to Chicago Lawn to march down Kedzie Avenue and into the
broad, flat expanse of the neighborhood's one open space, Marquette
Park, to call attention to housing discrimination in the white sections of
the South Side. In those days, if you were black, you were taking your
life in your hands if you ventured west of Western Avenue; being able
to buy one of the pleasant brick bungalows in Chicago Lawn was inconceivable. As with many of King's activities, you could view his coming
to Chicago Lawn in one of two ways: as a means of calling attention to
the most obvious flaw in an unforgivable American system, or as a way
of creating the opportunity for black people to have access to life inside
the web of institutions that gave people like the D'Andreas what they
had in those days.

That march was one of the great disasters of the civil rights movement. Chicago Lawn has always been a neighborhood of first-time homeowners, intensely tribal and provincial. For the Italians, Lithuanians, and

Irish who lived there, the houses they had struggled to buy and maintain were all they had in the world. They had seen Englewood, to the east, go from white to black and lose its stable property values and its sense of order, and that was a terrifying prospect. That terror was readily exploitable: the American Nazi Party and the Ku Klux Klan had both recently opened recruiting offices in Chicago Lawn.

On the day of the march, many of the owners of Chicago Lawn's copious taverns left boxes of empty beer bottles outside on the sidewalk so that the neighborhood's young men could bring them to the march. King's marchers were greeted by a large, violent crowd that spat at them, called them niggers, held up hand-lettered signs that said WHITE POWER, and pelted them with bottles and bricks. A brick hit King in the head—it was the worst violent attack on him by whites until his assassination, in 1968—and he had to be rushed away. The marchers dispersed, many of them injured, and tried to escape to the safety of a black church in Englewood. Unlike some of the violent white reactions to the movement in the South, this did not lead to new federal legislation; the Fair Housing Act stalled in Congress until after King's death, and the results of the 1966 elections—in Chicago Lawn and places like it all over the country—gave birth to the term "white backlash."

One of the marchers at Marquette Park was a sixteen-year-old girl named Ann Collier. Around the time Nick D'Andrea's family was leaving the West Side and moving to the suburbs, Ann Collier's family arrived in Chicago. Ann was born on the rural outskirts of Jackson, Mississippi, in 1950. Her family moved to Jackson a few years later, and to Chicago in 1960 as part of the last wave of the Great Migration of African Americans from the rural South to the urban North and West. Two of her uncles had moved earlier and had sent word that the rest of the family should come north for a better way of life. Ann's father moved first and then sent for his wife and five children. Both parents quickly found jobs in small factories, and they settled in a neighborhood on the West Side called East Garfield Park, which during the 1950s had changed from all white to all black. For Ann's parents, the neighborhood was an almost unimaginable improvement on what they had known as a domestic servant and a junk collector in the South, but within a few years the neighborhood had begun to change for the worse. East Garfield Park lost almost a quarter of its population in the 1960s because of rising crime, departing jobs, and deteriorating housing stock. Ann's father started drinking more—he'd get paid on Friday and not come home, sometimes, until Sunday or even Monday, and when he did, there would be a fight with her mother. By the time Ann was into her teens, her parents were breaking up; her mother was going from lower working class to poor; and Ann herself was leaving high school to get married and have a baby with a boy from the neighborhood.

Just at this time Martin Luther King, Jr., had rented an apartment on the West Side, not far from where Ann lived, and Ann's father began bringing her to meetings at a church in the neighborhood, where she encountered King and his lieutenants. She listened as people in King's circle planned demonstrations at the offices of slumlords who didn't maintain their apartments and at banks that wouldn't lend to black people. It wasn't clear at the time that these neighborhood meetings with a group of pleasant young ministers from the South—King, Jesse Jackson, Andrew Young—would be Ann's one direct experience with something historically extraordinary, but it was a good cause, and it kept her in touch with her father. For her father, participating in the movement with his daughter was a positive counterpoint to the rest of his life and a way to do something about the disaster that was unspooling around him. They marched together in picket lines all over the West Side.

On the day of the Marquette Park march, Ann and her father drove down from the West Side. That put them among a small minority of marchers who arrived with a visible possession: a car. After they parked and got out, some of the young men in the mob spotted the car, pushed it into a shallow lagoon, doused it with kerosene, and set it on fire while Ann and her father watched, wondering what would happen to them next. The only way they escaped unharmed was that the man who had driven the gospel singer Mahalia Jackson to the rally saw them, hustled them into his car, and drove them out of the neighborhood. After that, they didn't march anymore.

For Ann, the years following the march were hard ones. Deeply religious, meticulously neat and organized, wearing her sense of dignity like an enfolding cloak, she was lucky and determined enough to find a steady job as a back-office clerk at the big Montgomery Ward store in the Loop. For her, as for Nick D'Andrea, that one minor link to the large-scale American system was a blessing, gratefully received. Otherwise her life often felt like a procession of disasters. In the two decades after her family arrived, East Garfield Park lost more than half of its population and took on an abandoned look: boarded-up houses, empty storefronts, cash exchanges and liquor stores encased in wire mesh, groups of men standing on the corners not doing much. Her father moved back to Mississippi, had a religious conversion, and became a minister. Her mother struggled to keep food on the table, often just beans and salt pork, and to resist the temptation to save some money by moving into one of Chicago's all-black, all-poor high-rise housing projects, which she didn't consider to be a good environment for her family. Men treated Ann badly. As a teenager, she was, as she put it, molested, touched, and misused by a variety of relatives and men who were seeing her mother—and her marriage proved to be no escape. She was beaten. She had a gun pointed at her. She had to work endlessly to keep her two children fed, clothed, and in church and school. Finally, after fifteen years, she called the police during one evening's fight, had her husband taken away, and filed for divorce.

Ann's life got a lot better after 1985, when, in her mid-thirties, she met her second husband, Richard Neal, a machinist who also had moved from the South to the West Side. Both of them had steady jobs that connected them to the protective structures of big companies and labor unions, and that meant they could afford to join the thousands of people from East Garfield Park who were leaving the neighborhood for someplace safer. In 1988 they bought their first house—in, of all places, Chicago Lawn, not far from where Ann had spent that terrifying day in Marquette Park as a teenager, and just a few blocks from D'Andrea Buick. The color line had moved a few miles west since 1966. Their block, the 6400 block of South Artesian Avenue, was about half black and half white when they moved in; one of the white neighbors came over and told the Neals that they should go back to where they came from. Within a few years, there were almost no white families left on the block.

More than thirty years later, the Neals are still in the same house. Outside is a black metal fence with a gate that locks, an impeccably neat small garden with a fountain, an American flag, and a NO LOITERING sign. The front steps lead to a porch with an old easy chair, where Ann often sits, chatting with people who pass by. Inside, the living room has a vast collection of small figurines that Ann has collected, plus photographs of her children and stepchildren—all educated, working in white-collar jobs, and out of the neighborhood—and, in a corner, a photographic shrine to the Obama family. Ann is retired. Aside from being active in her church and taking care of her ailing mother, her life is mainly about trying to maintain order on her block, and that hasn't been easy.

Chicago Lawn, nowhere near the prosperous sections of Chicago, has never represented anything grander than the first step above working-poor apartment life for whoever is moving in from a fresh-off-the-boat ethnic neighborhood. That step is a big one, though; it makes the neighborhood worth fighting for, and it makes the danger of falling back palpably real, especially for someone like Ann, who had lived through the vertiginous fall of another neighborhood. In the years after the Neals arrived in Chicago, a lot of the factories and stores in Chicago Lawn shut down. That was a big blow. Then, beginning in the 1990s, Chicago tore down most of its high-rise housing projects and some of the residents moved into rental housing in Chicago Lawn. At least to Ann's way of thinking, that introduced gangs, drugs, and guns to the life of the neighborhood. And then, aggressive peddlers of mortgage loans, set in motion by mysterious faraway developments in the financial system, appeared in Chicago Lawn and devoted themselves to trying to persuade financially unsophisticated people that they could afford a second mortgage or a refinancing at an interest rate that started low and quickly zoomed upward. That soon led to foreclosures and then to empty houses on the block that gangs would occupy.

Ann, a small woman with a sweep of gray hair and the careful, clear elocution and relentlessly positive attitude of a devoted church-goer, could sit on the porch and name every person who walked past, or could give the history of every house. The man who had told her to go back home when she first arrived—he was still there, the last remaining white person, and now they were friends because Ann had helped him when his wife was sick. The two-decker house across the street was the site of the block's one murder—the result of a horrific dispute between a mother and son in the upstairs apartment that ended with her stabbing him in the neck with a house key—and of a shooting at the door of the downstairs apartment that Ann had watched from her porch, whose victim had survived. She knew who took care of their home and who didn't, and if they didn't, she was not shy about letting them know how she felt about that. She had once called the police on a neighbor who was ignoring her entreaties to stop blaring loud music from his house. He had to spend the night in jail, and after that the loud music stopped. She knew which young men were in what gangs, which ones had been in prison, and which of those had since turned their lives around. She wasn't afraid of anybody. As president of the 6400 South Artesian block club, she had put up signs at either end of the block, listing the club's by-laws: no loud music, no ball playing, no vandalism, no drugs, no littering, no loitering, no abandoned cars. The 6300 block of South Artesian, just to the north, was run by gangs, and you wouldn't go there if you could avoid it. Sixty-Third Street, Chicago Lawn's main commercial strip, was full of graffiti-adorned, metal-grated abandoned stores. But the 6400 block was run by Ann and her allies, and because she always chose to be optimistic, she was certain that it was at the very least stable, and probably on the way up.

Like Nick D'Andrea, Ann felt that she was fighting against something very big and pervasive, some great social deterioration that had made itself powerfully felt in Chicago Lawn but hadn't originated there. What she understood it to be was hatred—not just white racism directed at black people, but also the hatred that motivated people in the neighborhood to shoot each other, and the hatred that showed itself in the language used by political leaders. Unlike Nick, she did not believe the hatred was too powerful for people in the neighborhood to resist successfully. By now, there were murders every year in the neighborhood. In 2011 a pregnant seventeen-year-old girl was murdered a few blocks away from Ann's house. In 2014 a fifteen-year-old fatally shot a sixteen-year-old through the window of his bedroom on the 6700 block of South Artesian. A nineteen-year-old college student returning home on the Sixty-Third Street bus was killed for his cell phone. Officers from the 8th Police District, which occupies the largest new building in Chicago Lawn, were responsible for the notorious murder of seventeen-year-old Laquan McDonald in 2014. At the same time, Ann spent most of her life with black people who worked, owned homes, and went to church, and she often saw politicians and commentators on television—in particular President Donald Trump, who had a special preoccupation with violence on the South Side of Chicago—speaking about black America as if the tragedies in her neighborhood were the norm and people like her were the exception. They talked as if, to their minds, black people hadn't had to fight against anything, hadn't achieved anything. So, to Ann, talking obsessively about crime in black neighborhoods, with no context, was hatred too. Watching these people speak, she felt as if someone were cutting at her heart with the edge of a sharp sword. How could a country that was supposed to have put hatred behind it have embraced it now as both the local reality and the official national culture? What happened?

■

If you drove south on Western Avenue about twenty-five miles from where D'Andrea Buick used to be, you'd get to Park Forest, a modest suburb built by real estate developers just after the Second World War to house veterans and their families. Today Park Forest is a black-majority town, full of people who moved out of the South Side, but what it's famous for is having been, back when it was all white, the exemplary location in *The Organization Man*, a 1956 book by William H. Whyte, a reporter for *Fortune* magazine. *The Organization Man* was one of the best of a whole shelf's worth of books published in the 1950s and 1960s that identified domination by large, bureaucratic institutions—especially business corporations—as the characteristic malaise of postwar American society. It wasn't the institutions themselves that were the worst of the problem; it was the way in which they appeared to have altered the national character itself, such that Americans' former independence and individualism had been snuffed out. Whyte introduced his social type this way: "They are the ones of our middle class who have left home, spiritually as well as physically, to take the vows of organization life, and it is they who are the mind and soul of our great self-perpetuating institutions." And as for Park Forest: "This is the new suburbia, the packaged villages that have become the dormitory of the new generation of organization men."

Whyte was writing under the heavy influence of David Riesman's *The Lonely Crowd*, published in 1950, which was too theoretical to use specific vivid examples but shared the same diagnosis of what was wrong with America. Riesman, a sociologist, believed that there had been a great and unfortunate transition in the typical American's character, from "inner-directed" to "other-directed"; Whyte's version was that we had abandoned the Protestant ethic for the Social ethic. He used words like *belongingness, togetherness,* and—the great bogeyman term of liberal intellectuals in the 1950s—*conformity* to capture the traits he disapproved of. For example, he was alarmed by the thickness of the Organization Man's community life in Park Forest: "He has plunged into a hotbed of Participation. With sixty-six adult organizations and a population turnover that makes each one of them insatiable for new members, Park Forest probably swallows up more civic energy per hundred people than any other community in the country." Whyte ended his book with a ringing charge to his subject: "He must *fight* The Organization. Not stupidly, or selfishly . . . But fight he must, for the demands for his surrender are constant and powerful, and the more he has come to like the life of organization the more difficult does he find it to resist these demands, or even recognize them."

Neither Whyte nor Riesman, nor most of the other social critics in their line, felt the need to produce hard evidence in support of their argument. For them, the Organization Man was the representative American—like the nineteenth-century frontiersman or yeoman farmer—the exemplar of the national culture at that moment, the person you'd think about if you wanted to understand America. In the same way, though it may not have been the formal employer of most middle-class Americans, the specific organization where you could assume the Organization Man worked was the corporation, a place like (to use some of Whyte's examples) General Electric, General Motors, and IBM. These companies would come to college campuses, recruit budding Organization Men, and turn them into lifetime employees who obediently accepted their orders to transfer to a new location every few years and finally retired at age sixty-five with a handsome company pension and health benefits, the expectation of which served to extinguish whatever occasional forbidden impulses to leave and do something more creative may have arisen along the way.

Today what you'd notice first about Whyte's description of typical American life is what isn't there: though ardently liberal, he hardly mentions race relations, or the state of the economy (besides noting that it's prosperous), or the role of women except as housewives. These turned out to be, in a way, self-correcting omissions, because later writers found ways to introduce new concerns into the same overall picture of a stiflingly organization-dominated country. Tom Hayden's *Port Huron Statement* (1962) and Betty Friedan's *The Feminine Mystique* (1963), for example, made new claims on behalf of college students and women, respectively, but with copious references to corporations, suburbs, and conformity as the main locus of the problem. Books like these were popular and influential, and they only strengthened the idea of the national character's being slowly crushed under the oppressive weight of large organizations.

But there was another liberal vision of American society in competition with that of Whyte and Riesman, one in which large organizations were, or at least could be, an essential element in a good society. This vision began with a fundamentally different view of human nature in which people naturally and inevitably operated in society as members of groups, not as individuals. As the political scientist David Truman put it, "Men, wherever they are observed, are creatures participating in those established patterns of interaction we call groups . . . We do not, in fact, find individuals otherwise than in groups." (Whyte and Riesman thought of group membership as a malign corruption of the individualistic best in American society.) When groups matured into organizations, that was positive too, because organizations have rules and structures and ongoing lives rather than operating according to personal whim. And organizations from various parts of the society—corporations, labor unions, political parties, ethnic organizations, religious denominations—could meet at the bargaining table and together find their way to a good society. That was how, for example, corporations had decided to offer their supposedly constraining benefits and pensions, which their employees were grateful to receive.

The writers who wrote sympathetically about organizations and groups were almost all professors, prominent in their world, but not known to the public; an exception was John Kenneth Galbraith, whose 1952 book *American Capitalism* promoted the organization-based idea of a liberal society based on "countervailing power," but it was only with his later books that he became a bestselling author and public figure. Still, the idea was a reality in people's lives, not just an academic abstraction. As working-class city dwellers who didn't have college degrees, people like Nick D'Andrea and Ann Neal, aside from being a generation too young, may appear not to have fit the model of the Organization Man, but they were happy to occupy places in the outer reaches of that social order. Nick was a small businessman, not a corporate employee, but he sold only GM products and, at least until the arrival of that fateful FedEx package in 2009, considered himself part of the GM family. Ann worked for much of her career for what was then a big, prominent corporation, though not as a briefcase-toting manager. And the larger system of big organizations that coexisted with the corporation—unions, the Chicago machine, their churches—was usually a positive force in their lives, not a soul-extinguishing burden.

Who won in this contest of visions—the side that valued a structured, organization-based society or the side that saw it as profoundly unhealthy? The anti–Organization Man view won, without question, if the field of battle was a term Galbraith made popular, "the conventional wisdom." Its victory was so thorough, and so consequential, that today the representative figure of our age is an almost completely opposite character, whom we can call Transaction Man. Transaction Man (who may be a woman, of course) often works in a job that is literally transactional, in such fields as trading financial instruments, private equity, venture capital, and hedge funds—parts of American culture and the American economy that writers like Whyte didn't even bother to mention, because they seemed so inconsequential at the time. The Organization Man dutifully followed orders at the serene, secure big corporation that was his lifetime employer. Transaction Man is often in the business of breaking corporations apart and rearranging them in ways that have made it just about impossible for anybody these days to be an Organization Man. The idea of a corporation, or any other institution, providing generous guaranteed benefits and career-long job security is at odds with the way Transaction Man thinks the world should work. It's too static, too traditional, too constraining of creativity.

William Whyte noted that the Organization Man could be found applying his set of attitudes all over America, not just in the corporations and suburbs that were his primary home, and the same is true of Transaction Man. What really matters about Transaction Man is the way he thinks, not specifically what he does. Professionally, Transaction Man can perform any function that involves arriving in the middle of a complicated situation and, at least in his own mind, finding a solution that has eluded the participants: strategic consulting, global philanthropy, education reform. He is confident, not cautious; change-embracing, not change-resisting. Transaction Man thinks of himself as an idealist, someone whose work will benefit humanity. He'll alleviate poverty, help conquer disease, give opportunity to the underprivileged, make markets function better. Although he does well for himself, he doesn't see any self-interest in what he's doing—only an improving instinct.

Transaction Man is fundamentally skeptical about institutions and organizations, especially long-existing ones. He believes they are stodgy, bureaucratic, stuck in the past, and too beholden to traditions and arrangements that have built up over time. He'd use terms like "innovation," "disruption," and "breaking down silos" to describe healthy social processes, and "incumbents" or "rent-seekers" or "special interests" to describe those who are standing in the way of them. He believes there is a rational, efficient solution to every big problem, and that it can usually be achieved by bypassing or even eliminating existing structures and replacing them with something more fluid and unconstrained. Anything that throws sand in the gears, that delays what looks like progress, that involves negotiation and compromise, that gets in the way of the obvious solution—labor unions, local governments, legal constraints, interest groups that make particular claims—is problematic. Transaction Man is suspicious of politics and of provincial concerns; his perspective is global and based on what he regards as universal principles. He likes to do things quickly and forcefully. The idea that bargaining among groups is the way to achieve the best solution strikes him as fundamentally wrongheaded, not to mention boring.

If you were to go looking for a specific place to find Transaction Man, it would certainly not be Park Forest, Illinois. Wall Street and Silicon Valley, which have become far more powerful and wealthy over the last generation or two, would be more like it. These are new, or newly altered, locations that exemplify the rising spirit of the time, just as Park Forest did for its time—but now the spirit is about speed, not stodginess; individual expression, not conformity; undoing restrictions, not adhering to them. Like the spirit of the previous age, ours has its characteristic flaws. The transactional society has become one where wealth and power are increasingly concentrated, and where public life, rather than being contained inside a narrow band of acceptable thought, is much more fraught with anger and contention. That is because, paradoxically, our suspicion of institutions has brought us a new set of institutions (because institutions are an inescapable part of human life, and the real question is what form they will take) that are fewer, but larger and more dominant, than the set of institutions that preceded them. The most important ones are clustered in a few areas, such as finance and technology, and in a few places geographically, mainly the East and West Coasts. The ecosystem is out of balance: the institutions responsible for maintaining democracy and ensuring a good life for ordinary people are badly outmatched. All over the world, through their political and cultural behavior, people are showing how they feel about that.

Social changes of this magnitude are too large to have occurred just because of a shift in the atmosphere. They have a history in which events generated ideas, ideas generated actions, and actions changed the structure of society. This book aims to lay out the history of our move from an institution-oriented to a transaction-oriented society. This is not a matter of one set of values succeeding another for no particular reason. It's a more specific story, which begins with Americans of the early twentieth century confronting the powerful new reality of concentrated economic power and debating how to constrain it. This was an intense, all-consuming, highly consequential battle, fought not just here but worldwide. Out of these intense dissatisfactions and disagreements and conflicts, the institution-based order, with a much bigger national government and the corporation at its anchors, emerged. Then another set of dissatisfactions and disagreements, this time directed against government and corporations, produced another set of big changes, which, in turn, created the new transaction-based order. And today, a third vision, of a society based on Internet-enabled networks—which might restore some of what the age of transactions destroyed—is emerging. A handful of companies based on this vision have become the largest in the world, and networks have created instant ways for people to connect. We are only just beginning to see this vision's large effects on how work, economic life, and politics are organized and on how power is distributed. After laying out institutions, transactions, and networks as successive master organizing principles for society, this book finally will suggest another way entirely of thinking about our future, one that would give more honor to people like Nick D'Andrea and Ann Neal, who live at a great distance from the country's centers of power.

For each succeeding period—institutions, transactions, networks—we will meet an exemplary figure, someone who put forth sweeping new ideas about how the world should work and who had a far more real, immediate impact than people who have big ideas usually do. These people were caught up in their times, as people always are, but they helped shape their times too. They are Adolf Berle, who as a member of Franklin Roosevelt's Brain Trust was one of the architects of the New Deal; Michael Jensen, an economist who supplied some of the crucial principles and techniques that led to the dramatic rise to power of the financial world during the last decades of the twentieth century; and Reid Hoffman, one of the founders of online social networks, in particular one that aims to redefine what work means, away from traditional employment. All three of these people have been primarily concerned with how business works and how capital is allocated; the premise of this book is that these economic arrangements, as they are altered, profoundly reshape the way most people live and work, even if they are not in business strictly speaking. To demonstrate that, the book will revisit such places as Chicago Lawn, Wall Street, and Silicon Valley, and such institutions as General Motors and the federal government, and show how they have changed as the governing ideas of the times have changed.

This is a history, told as a story that moves forward through time. Stories are dramatizing, but also, in this case, clarifying, because they can make it clear that arrangements that seem natural or automatic were actually made. The form of the world we live in now was not inevitable. It isn't the result of inexorable processes that were too powerful to resist. Instead, it came from a series of choices that we, or at least America's business and political elites, made. Everything, always, could have turned out differently from the way it did. Only by understanding the choices that created our world—who was arguing for them and why, what forces were arrayed around them, and what the alternative, bypassed choices were—is it possible to imagine fully what choices we can make now. The familiarity of the present is a trap. It narrows our vision. Understanding how we got here is the first step out of the trap.

1

INSTITUTION MAN

Some of history's great consequential events are easy to take in, even many years later: wars, the creation of new nations, the triumphs of social movements. One that isn't so easy, but was no less consequential, was the sudden and unexpected rise of big business to a position of great economic and political power in the decades following the Civil War. The founding ideas of the United States concerned the power of the state, not of private economic interests, because it was hard to imagine that those interests could ever become full rivals to the national government. But now here they were, dominating nearly every aspect of the life of the country. Industrial capitalism gave rise not only to extremes of wealth and poverty but also to big cities, mass immigration, political machines, and other developments that upended everyone's assumptions about how the country worked. For two or three generations, what to do about big business was the central question of American life.

In 1911, Justice John Marshall Harlan of the U.S. Supreme Court, who was born in 1833 and was only a few months away from the end of his life, wrote an opinion in the case that affirmed the government's breakup of John D. Rockefeller's Standard Oil Company. He recalled the situation, two decades earlier, that led to the country's first major law limiting the power of big business, the Sherman Act:

All who recall the condition of the country in 1890 will remember that there was everywhere, among the people generally, a deep feeling of unrest. The nation had been rid of human slavery—fortunately, as all now feel—but the conviction was universal that the country was in real danger from another kind of slavery . . . namely, the slavery that would result from aggregations of capital in the hands of a few individuals and corporations controlling, for their own profit and advantage exclusively, the entire business of the country, including the production and sale of the necessaries of life.

It was into this situation that Adolf Augustus Berle, Jr., was born, in 1895. Solving the problem of big business would be the dominant concern of his life. Berle was an overwhelmingly ambitious man who spent his long career jousting with the major figures of his time over the business question, wanting to be recognized as the one who had come up with the best solution to the most vexing problem of the twentieth century. How, exactly, could concentrated economic power be counteracted in a way that preserved freedom and prosperity and offered a decent life to most people? He felt that he was competing, at home and abroad, and before and after the early New Deal period that represented the peak of his political influence, with socialists and communists, with fascists and free marketeers, with antitrusters and economic technicians. By the time he died, in 1971, Berle, who was never modest, felt that he had, indeed, solved the problem. The solution was the corporation, which for Berle's generation represented an astonishing new kind of economic institution, the advent of which, at least to Berle's mind, rivaled in importance the earlier advents of the church and the state. Initially all-powerful and threatening, the corporation, Berle felt, had by the middle of the twentieth century been tamed by government to the point that it could play the central role in a good society dominated by large, stable institutions that would provide people's material needs, protect them from economic shocks, and generate cohesion. That was what he saw as his life's achievement.

Berle's father, also named Adolf Augustus Berle, was born in 1866, the son of a German immigrant who died of the long-term effects of wounds he had suffered as a soldier under the command of Ulysses S. Grant in the Union Army. A physically tiny man with no inherited resources or connections, the elder Berle had somehow by his early adulthood, in the closing years of the nineteenth century, acquired a superpowered personal force and drive. As a student at Oberlin College in Ohio, he met and married Mary Augusta Wright, the daughter of one of the most renowned members of the faculty, George Frederick Wright, a Congregationalist minister and professor of religion who was also, improbably, an accomplished geologist. Berle himself studied theology, first at Oberlin and then at Harvard Divinity School, and became a Congregationalist minister. The Berles had four children. Adolf Jr. was the second, their first son.

Adolf Berle, Sr., was a brilliant man with a very grand conception of his place in the world. This meant, on one hand, that he regularly alienated the congregations of the churches over which he presided, so he wound up moving around, never having long-term control of a major pulpit; on the other hand, he somehow knew everybody worth knowing, especially if the person was a prominent liberal. Vastly ambitious for his children, he taught them all at least the rudiments of Latin, Greek, and Hebrew, plus some mathematics, at the age of three. Years later, after the children had grown, Berle used them as instructors in a summer school he operated at his house in New Hampshire, which promised "to instruct a small number of superior children in such a way as will make them natural companions of knowledge." He also wrote a book called *The School in the Home* and another called *Teaching in the Home: A Handbook for Intensive Fertilization of the Child Mind for Instructors of Young Children*, both meant to make his prodigy-producing techniques widely available.

Adolf Jr. was admitted to high school at the age of nine and to Harvard College at the age of thirteen (his father didn't think he was quite ready then, so he actually enrolled at fourteen). As a small child, he was taken to meet the most celebrated social reformer in the United States, Jane Addams, a friend of his father's, at Hull House in Chicago. At eighteen, through another friend of his father's, he had an audience at the White House with President Taft. By the age of twenty-one he had acquired three Harvard degrees: a bachelor's, a master's in history, and a law degree, the last of which made him the second-youngest graduate in the history of Harvard Law School. Then he got a job in the Boston law office of another of his father's exalted friends, Louis D. Brandeis, the crusading lawyer and future Supreme Court justice, who was the only person to have graduated from Harvard Law School at twenty—at an even younger age than Berle. A few years later, the elder Berle testified at Brandeis's Senate confirmation hearing, conferring the blessing of a Christian man of the cloth on the first Jewish justice.

When the United States entered the First World War, Adolf Jr. enlisted in the army. At twenty-three, still in uniform, he managed to get himself assigned to the American delegation at the peace talks in Paris that followed the armistice ending the war. He arrived in Paris in December 1918, having crossed the Atlantic on a converted cattle boat, but within a day he was staying at the Hotel Crillon, "a palatial palace with Marie-Antoinette furnishings" (he wrote in his diary) whose lobby was filled with "hosts of minor retainers, gold-plated secretaries swaggering in splendid and unused uniforms . . . Many are intriguing for themselves, but most are endeavoring to find themselves in a rather inchoate mess." During his first week in Paris, Berle witnessed President Woodrow Wilson being greeted by a cheering throng as he entered the Place de la Concorde and took in "a naughty show" at a burlesque house. He also had an opportunity to encounter some of the most brilliant young men of his generation who were serving as junior staff members at the peace conference: John Maynard Keynes, the British economist; Walter Lippmann and William Bullitt, the American journalists; Samuel Eliot Morison, the historian; and the Dulles brothers, John Foster, the future secretary of state, and Allen, the founding director of the Central Intelligence Agency.

Soon Berle was in a more modest hotel but with a definite assignment—he would join the American delegation's Russian section, which was charged with deciding what stance the peace treaty would take toward the newly empowered Bolshevik regime headed by V. I. Lenin. By the spring of 1919 Berle had become thoroughly disillusioned with the negotiations, which to his mind had strayed a great distance from the inspiring Fourteen Points that Wilson had put forth in advance as the basis for peace. On Russia, he thought his superiors were too unwilling to work with the Bolsheviks and too caught up in the idea that some form of the old regime could be restored. The broader terms of the armistice, he felt, were too punitive toward Germany, too generous toward France, and too unwilling to guarantee the rights of the Jews of Eastern Europe, the Latvians and Lithuanians, and other oppressed people. The result would be, he believed, that in a few years Germany and Russia might "start the whole game of competitive armaments on a bigger scale than ever."

In May 1919 Berle, assuming the stagy veneer of cynicism of a disappointed crusader, wrote his father, "I have come to the conclusion that no statement of ideals by anybody will ever get any reaction from me again. If I can trust myself I shall be happy; if I trust anyone else I shall be a fool." And then, a few days later, "The quiet intoxication of a really big row is stealing over me, and I should like nothing better than to tell the truth about the peacemaking to the Senate Committee [that would have to ratify the Versailles treaty]; after which I could retire for life." And a few days after that, Berle and a group of his young colleagues resigned from the delegation in protest. When he was back in the United States, Berle—still only twenty-four—wrote a stinging article in *The Nation*, "The Betrayal at Paris," in which he called the treaty an "abortion of compromise and hate" that "pointed the world back to the path of terror and tears." This was not, of course, the work of someone who was renouncing public life forever.

Berle settled in New York and became a corporation lawyer on Wall Street, first in the office of yet another friend of his father's, then, beginning in 1924, in a firm of his own. Today this would be the safe career for a young lawyer, but Berle didn't see it that way; large corporations were new, the coming thing, and he thought that by understanding how they worked, he could hold the key to shaping the country's future. He was being relentlessly prodded to do something important by his domineering and personally disappointed father, the semi-itinerant minister, who dreamed that Adolf Jr. might become president of the United States one day. What he chose to do was not meant to be safe, but to propel him into the stratosphere. Berle always projected complete confidence, veering into arrogance, but privately there was a measure of desperation in the way he experienced his father's aggressively asserted expectations. One miserable day in the fall of 1922 he wrote in his diary,

For the ghastly fact is that our family . . . is being wrecked by my Father's curious egomania which takes the most brutal form and is mainly directed (God forgive) against my mother. When it began to be acute in 1919 she spoke of possible euthanasia suicide as a remedy. Now that is possible; or desertion is possible; I have thought myself that by sacrificing two lives I might free my mother for quiet evening years and liberate my sister . . . Father of course is convinced that he is an aggrieved vicar of God.

Besides practicing law, Berle was frequently publishing articles in such prominent liberal magazines as *The Nation* and *The New Republic*, and in the leading law reviews; he was expanding his impressive array of well-known friends; and he was actively engaged in a number of social reform movements. Dressed in the elegant double-breasted suits he had begun wearing, his hair neatly parted and slicked down, he commuted to Wall Street from an apartment next door to the Henry Street Settlement on the Lower East Side, whose director, Lillian Wald, became a mentor of his. His job was part of, not separate from, a life dedicated to liberal reform.

■

The Industrial Revolution did not fully arrive in the United States until after the Civil War, so it was not until the last quarter of the nineteenth century that Americans began thinking seriously about what it meant to live in a world of big businesses, big cities, and, for a few people, vast personal fortunes. The country's founding documents did not envision such things. The census of 1880 was the first to show that the United States had a city, New York, with a population of more than a million. In 1890 Congress passed the Sherman Act. In 1896 the Democratic Party nominated a presidential candidate of populist inclinations, William Jennings Bryan of Nebraska (whom it nominated again in 1900 and 1908), on a platform of hostility to unbridled capitalism.

Educated middle-class people such as the young Adolf Berle had been raised on the idea that American civilization was at heart one of small-town merchants and independent farmers. Now, as the historians Charles and Mary Beard put it,

the isolated establishment under the ownership of a single master or a few masters had surrendered to the corporation. At the end of the century three-fourths of the manufactured products came from factories owned by associations of stockholders; in each great industry was a network of federated plants under corporate direction; by 1890 combination was the supreme concept of the industrial magnate.

It wasn't just Americans who were noticing the magnitude of this sudden change in the national economy. In 1903 Liang Qichao, a pioneering Chinese journalist and intellectual, visited New York and reported to his countrymen about the trusts: "In essence, this monster, whose power far exceeds that of Alexander the Great or Napoleon, is the one and only sovereign of the twentieth-century world."

Berle's generation was heavily influenced by the historian Frederick Jackson Turner's ominous declaration in 1890 that the opportunity-providing American frontier had closed and so the essential nature of the society had to be remade (Berle was a student, and then a research assistant, of Turner's at Harvard). How to do that, especially in light of the sudden and unexpected dominance of big business, was the great career-defining question for reform-minded Progressives. One answer was the conservative one: celebrate capitalism. Berle was uncomfortable with that. Another was to import European socialism to the United States. Berle was uncomfortable with that too. For people like him, the real choice was a narrower but highly consequential one between two varieties of liberalism. This choice was most obviously on display in the 1912 presidential campaign, when Berle was a precocious college student, in the difference between Theodore Roosevelt's economic program, which he called the New Nationalism, and Woodrow Wilson's, which he called the New Freedom. These are terms that don't communicate much today, so let's give them more vivid and cinematic names: Clash of the Titans liberalism and Middle-earth liberalism.

The combative, wealthy, power-loving Roosevelt was naturally drawn to the idea of the federal government's assuming enough new force and size to be able to fight big business as an equal. His historic reputation as a "trustbuster" is misleading; he was not against large economic units per se, only against their excesses. Government's job was to check the excesses, not to break up the businesses. Roosevelt expanded government's power to regulate railroads, food, and medicine, but it was during the presidency of his successor, Taft, that the government broke up the steel trust (a decision Roosevelt publicly opposed) and Standard Oil. Roosevelt had no patience for the traditional constitutional suspicion of concentrated state power. The urgent necessity before the U.S. government was to project its might, against private economic power at home and against hostile governments abroad.

Among the leading intellectual proponents of Roosevelt's form of liberalism were the three brilliant young founders of *The New Republic*, Herbert Croly, Walter Lippmann, and Walter Weyl—all slightly older friends of Adolf Berle's. In 1909 Croly published a Progressive Era manifesto called *The Promise of American Life*. "The net result of the industrial expansion of the United States since the Civil War," Croly wrote, "has been the establishment in the heart of the American economic and social system of certain glaring inequalities of condition and power . . . The rich men and big corporations have become too wealthy and powerful for their official standing in American life." He asserted that the way to solve the problem was to reorient the country from the tradition of Thomas Jefferson (rural, decentralized) to the tradition of Alexander Hamilton (urban, financially adept). Weyl, in *The New Democracy* (1913), wrote that the country had been taken over by a "plutocracy" that had rendered the traditional forms of American democracy impotent; government had to restore the balance and "enormously increase the extent of regulation."

To liberals of this kind, these were problems of nation-threatening severity, requiring radical modernization that would eliminate the trace elements of rural nineteenth-century America. Lippmann, in *Drift and Mastery* (1914), argued that William Jennings Bryan ("the true Don Quixote of our politics") and his followers were fruitlessly at war with "the economic conditions which had upset the old life of the prairies, made new demands on democracy, introduced specialization and science, had destroyed village loyalties, frustrated private ambitions, and created the impersonal relationships of the modern world." A larger, more powerful, more technical central government, staffed by a new class of trained experts, was the only plausible way to fight the dominance of big business. The leading Clash of the Titans liberals were from New York City, but even William Allen White, the celebrated (in part for being anti-Bryan) small-town Kansas editor who was a leading Progressive and one of their allies, wrote, in 1909, that "the day of the rule of the captain of industry is rapidly passing in America." Now the country needed "captains of two opposing groups—capitalism and democracy" to reset the balance away from the capitalists' current dominance.

The Berle family's friend Louis Brandeis was the intellectual leader of the other camp, the Middle-earth liberals. Brandeis agreed with the Rooseveltian liberals that the rise of the trusts posed a dire threat to the health of the republic, but his remedy was quite different: break up the trusts into smaller units. The idea of an economic future in which big centralized businesses battled with a big centralized government did not appeal to him. Brandeis was not a Jeffersonian, exactly—his preferred America was one where economic power was more regional than local, and where businesses that were medium-size to large, rather than either small or enormous, were at the heart of American economic life. Brandeis was focused on the rights of nonplutocratic businesses, such as local banks or stores or manufacturers that weren't part of national chains, in the new industrial economy, far more than on the rights of consumers, who in those days were not yet a category in the public debate. His best-known antitrust case involved protecting a regional railroad line from being taken over by J. P. Morgan. Most of the leaders of Brandeis's strain of liberalism were from the provinces—especially provincial cities. Most members of Congress, because they represented geographic areas, were naturally in the Brandeis camp, unless they were from New York. (It may be pertinent that around the time Brandeis was becoming preoccupied with what he liked to call "the curse of bigness," he was also, well into middle age, becoming a passionate convert to Zionism, which he saw as another form of legal protection for a vulnerable group. The elder Adolf Berle was another early Zionist.) Brandeis was an adviser to Woodrow Wilson during the 1912 presidential campaign. Trying to frame the difference between his man and Roosevelt, he wrote in a private letter to Wilson that Roosevelt "does not fear commercial power, however great, if only methods for regulation are provided," but that "we believe that no methods of regulation ever have been or can be devised to remove the menace inherent in private monopoly and overweening commercial power."

During the campaign, Wilson gave speeches that took the Brandeis approach on economic issues. He spoke on behalf of "the little man . . . crushed by the trusts." Trusts, he asserted, were by no means the natural and healthy products of market forces. They had been economically manufactured by underhanded, albeit legal, means, and they stifled competition. "I take my stand absolutely," Wilson declared, "on the proposition that private monopoly is indefensible and intolerable . . . And I know how to fight it." As president, Wilson passed the second major federal antitrust law, the Clayton Act, and established the Federal Trade Commission, a new regulatory agency meant to ensure open economic competition. When he established the country's central banking system, the Federal Reserve, it was as a system of twelve regional banks, in order to avoid the danger of the control of credit by the "money trust" in New York. And he put Louis Brandeis on the Supreme Court.

Though Adolf Berle was still a college student, and an unusually young one at that, during the 1912 campaign—too young to be a direct participant in these struggles—he entered adulthood fully persuaded that taming the power of centralized business was the overwhelming task facing the country. Playing an important role in that struggle would enable him to become the great man he desperately wanted to be. Now he would have to figure out how—and that meant deciding what kind of liberal he was.

■

The Progressives were sincere in their convictions, but they also had psychological motives for committing themselves to the cause of political reform. As the historian Richard Hofstadter put it,

> In a score of cities and hundreds of towns, particularly in the East but also in the nation at large, the old-family, college-educated class that had deep ancestral roots in local communities and often owned family businesses, that had traditions of political leadership, belonged to the patriotic societies and the best clubs, staffed the governing boards of philanthropic and cultural institutions, and led the movements for civic betterment, were being overshadowed and edged aside in the making

of basic political and economic decisions . . . They were less important, and they knew it.

That description roughly fits the Berle family and most of the upper-
middle-class people they knew; indeed, Hofstadter cited the Berles specifically as an example of the Progressive mentality. Adolf Berle's wife,
Beatrice Bishop, came from a different group, which also resented the
sudden rise to dominance of people whom the industrialization of the
United States had made rich: they were from the class that had been
rich and dominant before the rising group surpassed them.

Beatrice Berle's father, Cortlandt Bishop, whom she adored, was the
scion of a prominent New York family that had substantial real estate
holdings. A brilliant man who had earned four degrees from Columbia
University, he did not hold a job, as it was considered vulgar for a gentleman of his class to work for pay. Instead, he was an early automobile and
aviation enthusiast, bibliophile, art collector, and investor (he helped
bankroll the Wright brothers' invention of the airplane) who spent six
months of every year in France and the other six months traveling back
and forth between an estate in the Berkshires and a grand stone house
just off Fifth Avenue in New York City that housed an institution-size
private library that he had created. Beatrice's mother, Amy Bend Bishop,
whom she did not adore, was a late-to-marry society beauty, the daughter
of a former president of the New York Stock Exchange. She was supposedly the real-life model for Lily Bart, the heroine of Edith Wharton's
The House of Mirth (Wharton's house in the Berkshires wasn't far from
the Bishops', and they knew each other). The Bishops, Beatrice wrote
in her memoir, looked down on such families as the Vanderbilts and
Rockefellers as nouveau riche.

Even though it was a hundred years ago, it's hard to imagine that
Americans ever lived the way the Bishops did. They spoke French at
home—Beatrice was raised by a French governess—and dressed for
dinner every night, the men in starched collars, white tie, and tails, the
women in gowns, the food and wine always grandly French. They were
surrounded by servants. They were fantastically snobbish. Beatrice had
to fight to be permitted to go to college (Vassar, then populated exclusively by proper young ladies), for her mother thought a higher education

might give her an unacceptable tincture of the middle class. Her parents rejected, one by one, the impressive series of suitors she attracted, as each of them was below the family's standing. In one especially painful case, her mother, learning that she was seeing a young man named Carl Binger, who went on to become a prominent psychiatrist, told her, as Beatrice recorded it in her diary, "I must never invite a Jew to the house, that this house was hers and that she would never tolerate a Jew inside it." Beatrice acquiesced: "I cannot imagine happiness coming from a total break with those I have loved best so far and I believe to cause them such pain is unnecessary. It means sacrificing Carl to other people's prejudices." But even if she wanted to avoid it, the total break was coming.

Beatrice was an only child. Her mother, at least as Beatrice told the tale, had wanted a boy, partly because she had an overpowering fear of losing her husband's affection to a female rival as her looks inevitably faded, despite her copious use of treatments meant to defy aging. (Amy Bishop's fear wasn't unjustified, though directing it at her daughter was: the family had twice discovered that Cortlandt Bishop was having extramarital affairs.) In 1925, when Beatrice was in her early twenties, her mother turned violently against her and told her that she never wanted to see her again. Beatrice went to see a cousin of hers, also a neighbor in the Berkshires, Austen Riggs, a prominent psychiatrist who had founded a clinic in Stockbridge that still operates under his name. He told her that her mother had a mental disorder called paranoia and there was nothing to be done about it. Over the next year or so, Amy Bishop made it clear to her husband that he would have to choose between her and Beatrice; he chose his wife. In 1926 Beatrice received a curt note from Cortlandt Bishop: "I would like you to remove your goods and chattels and not to return to the place thereafter. Do it as quickly as possible." When she arrived at the house to take her things away, her father was not there. She never saw him again.

While this drama was unfolding, Beatrice met Adolf Berle; it's impossible not to notice the exact coincidence of the abrupt and painful loss of her relationship with her father and the start of her relationship with her husband. One of the suitors her parents had forbidden her to see was a friend of Adolf's, and he had introduced them one spring evening in Washington Square. She always remembered her first impression: "Erect, an irrepressible little wave on top of his head, rimless glasses, a small moustache . . . precise, reserved, and courteous." The three of them had gone to dinner in Greenwich Village. "Adolf spoke rapidly," she wrote later, "the ideas following each other one after another with the force and speed of a mountain brook in the spring." They talked about the Crusades, Napoleon, Columbus; economics, religion, politics. At that moment there was still enough left of her relationship with her parents that she was able to arrange for Adolf to come over for dinner as part of a small group and not as an announced beau. On Beatrice's instruction, he wore a top hat. A little later, Adolf arranged for Beatrice to meet his parents over a Jewish Sabbath dinner at the Henry Street Settlement, with Lillian Wald presiding.

Adolf had the wit not to press his case during the worst of Beatrice's family turmoil. On the day before Easter 1927, a suitable time after Beatrice and her parents' final break, they visited Vassar together. After an afternoon rain, Beatrice remembered, "we walked around the lake, and the delicious smell of wet earth and the pattern of the trees in flower, mirrored in the water through the lamplight, were suddenly obliterated as Adolf took me in his arms and murmured, *cras amet qui numquam amavit*."* They were married not long afterward in a small ceremony her parents refused to attend. They bought an old white farmhouse and forty acres of adjoining land in the Berkshires and, by way of a statement of Beatrice's intention to depart from her parents' mores, hung a tile next to the front door that read

> My house has the most noble coat of arms
> To receive without distinction rich and poor

All available evidence would indicate that the Berles had a blissful marriage. On their wedding night, as Beatrice wrote in her diary, "through the exploring and the marriage of our bodies, we reach states of bliss and ecstasy previously unimaginable. It is as when man discovered fire!" They had two daughters and a son. They bought a large town house near Gramercy Park in New York, where Beatrice installed a master bathroom with aquatic murals painted on the walls and two con-

---

*This is a line from *Pervigilium Veneris*, or *The Vigil of Venus*, an anonymous Latin poem that translates as "Let those love now who have never loved."

joined tubs—as a *New Yorker* profile of Adolf sarcastically put it, "so that she wouldn't miss any of his sudsy wisdom." And their graves, just down the road from their farm in the Berkshires, have conjoined headstones that bear the legend FORTIS ET DULCIS: strong and sweet.

Adolf encouraged Beatrice to pursue her own interests to an extent that many of their contemporaries found almost peculiar. She became a social worker and then, after the children were born, a doctor. She operated a clinic in Harlem. And she transferred to Adolf all the admiration she was unable to give to her father, or maybe more. In one characteristic diary entry she exclaimed, "He has one of the few creative minds in the domain of public affairs—and this brilliance is tempered with a great humanity." From Beatrice, Adolf got his father's sky-high expectations minus the elder Berle's oppressive need to dominate. They were mutually certain that he was going to do something remarkable, a grand intellectual achievement that would also have an effect on the world; at various times over the years, privately to Beatrice, Adolf compared himself to Shakespeare, Napoleon, Adam Smith, and Karl Marx. He wanted, Beatrice wrote, to be "a social prophet." It was just a question of exactly how and where he would find the opportunity.

One winter night early in their marriage Adolf didn't come home for dinner. Finally, at 9:30, he turned up. He explained that he had been in a law library and had lost track of time. Beatrice asked him what he'd been working on, and she found his answer puzzling because it didn't seem to be on the grand plane of Adolf's philosophical interests: the relationship between corporate executives and stockholders.

■

The liberal reaction against big business had been going strong for nearly half a century, having taken a number of different forms, but mainly it had identified its target as a coterie of men who made themselves very rich by building up the kind of business empires that people in the Progressive Era called "trusts": Cornelius Vanderbilt in railroads, Andrew Carnegie in steel, Thomas Edison in electric power, John D. Rockefeller in oil, J. P. Morgan in finance. Now, in the 1920s, these people were dead or fading. Berle's legal career on Wall Street, which put him in the middle of a lot of detailed work on stock and bond offerings, proxy votes, and so on, allowed him to come to what became the great insight of his career: the old trusts were being succeeded by corporations that did not have identifiable owners.

Business corporations had existed for a long time. What struck Berle as new and alarming was that a relatively small number of American corporations had rather suddenly become very large, very rich, and very dominant. They had outlived their founders. Although most of them had shareholders, they were really accountable to nobody. To Berle they looked like permanent, unstoppable institutions. As he wrote a few years later, "The huge corporation . . . has come to dominate most major industries if not all industry in the United States . . . There is apparently no immediate limit to its increase. It is coming more and more to be the industrial unit with which American economic, social, and political life must deal." Therefore, it was time to do something to counteract the corporation:

> The economic power in the hands of the few persons who control a giant corporation is a tremendous force which can harm or benefit a multitude of individuals, affect whole districts, shift the currents of trade, bring ruin to one community and prosperity to another. The organizations which they control have passed far beyond the realm of private enterprise—they have become more nearly social institutions.

Berle believed that they could no longer be permitted to have their way with every aspect of the country's life.

He persuaded a research organization to give him a grant to make a detailed study of the corporation, hiring an economist named Gardiner Means—someone he'd known in the army, also a Harvard-educated son of a Congregationalist minister, married to a Vassar graduate who was a friend of Beatrice Berle's—to work up statistical evidence about how big and powerful corporations had become. In 1932, when Berle was thirty-seven, the study was published: *The Modern Corporation and Private Property*, which became a classic almost instantly and still stands as the main intellectual achievement of Berle's life.

Other intellectuals besides Berle had noticed how trusts and robber barons had been succeeded by corporations that operated on an even grander scale and that aspired to permanence. The final book by the radical economist Thorstein Veblen, *Absentee Ownership: Business Enterprise in Recent Times* (1923), was mainly about corporations. So was *Main Street and Wall Street* (1927), by William Z. Ripley, a professor at Harvard Business School who was a mentor of Berle's. Both of these books were essentially hostile to corporations, focusing on the shenanigans— or, to use Ripley's memorable language, "prestidigitation, double shuffling, honey-fugling, hornswaggling, and skullduggery"—that they used to disadvantage their investors. They diluted their shares, gave sweetheart contracts to their directors, took away shareholders' voting rights, and were, as Ripley put it, "cloaked and hooded like the despicable Ku Klux Klan" when it came to issuing information about their economic performance.

What Berle brought to the subject was the combination of a much broader historical and social perspective, and detailed evidence in the form of the charts and tables that Means had worked up. And Berle's timing was better: Veblen's and Ripley's books came out when the rise of the corporation was generally seen as a great achievement and as a delirious moneymaking opportunity for the growing American middle class. *The Modern Corporation and Private Property* was published in the wake of the 1929 stock market crash, with the Great Depression under way and the country coming to the view that the economic arrangements of the 1920s had utterly failed and needed to be replaced.

The Modern Corporation and Private Property had two central arguments: first, that a relatively small number of corporations had rapidly come to dominate the American economy, and second, that because these corporations had so many shareholders (the biggest one, American Telephone and Telegraph, had more than half a million), they represented a historically new kind of economic institution that was not under the control of its owners. Means's research showed that of three hundred thousand American corporations, two hundred of them controlled half of the national wealth—and their proportionate power, being relatively new, was sure to increase in the future. They were ubiquitous and inescapable, Berle wrote:

> Perhaps . . . the individual stays in his own home in comparative isolation and privacy. What do the two hundred largest companies mean to him there? His electricity and gas are almost sure to be furnished by one of the public utility companies; the aluminum of his kitchen utensils by the Aluminum Co. of America.

His electric refrigerator may be the product of General Motors Co., or of one of the two great electric equipment companies, General Electric and Westinghouse Electric.

And so on.

What Berle called the corporate revolution was every bit as significant as the Industrial Revolution, or maybe even more so: "It involves a concentration of power in the economic field comparable to the concentration of religious power in the medieval church or of political power in the national state." And unlike the church, the state, or earlier-stage industry, the corporation had severed the tie between control and ownership. As Berle put it, "The dissolution of the atom of property destroys the very foundation on which the economic order of the past three centuries has rested." Adam Smith's conception of the market no longer applied, because the owners of businesses, the shareholders, were no longer vigorous entrepreneurs. They were passive and distant from the enterprise. Control lay in the hands of managers and directors who were not significant owners. There was not yet a theory or practice of economics or government big enough to encompass these developments. Therefore, the task ahead was clear:

> The recognition that industry has come to be dominated by these economic autocrats must bring with it a realization of the hollowness of the familiar statement that economic enterprise in America is a matter of individual initiative. To the dozen or so men in control, there is room for such initiative. For the tens and even hundreds of thousands of workers and of owners in a single enterprise, individual initiative no longer exists. Their activity is group activity on a scale so large that the individual, except he be in a position of control, has dropped into relative insignificance. At the same time the problems of control have become problems in economic government.

It would have been possible to take the same set of economic facts and arrange them differently from the way Berle did. Twenty years before *The Modern Corporation and Private Property*, Louis Brandeis wrote a searing series of articles for *Harper's Magazine*, later published as a small book called *Other People's Money and How the Bankers Use It*, that noted the widespread dispersion of ownership of stocks and bonds but treated it as a minor point. That was because, to Brandeis, it didn't matter who nominally owned shares in big companies—the real control was in the hands of the "money trust," meaning bankers, especially J. P. Morgan. They assembled the great corporations and then sat on their boards of directors and pulled the strings from there. Berle, in *The Modern Corporation and Private Property*—or for his entire life, really—barely mentioned banking and finance. His focus was on the industrial corporation.

Berle believed that the public's widespread buying of government war bonds during the First World War had greatly accelerated the habit of small-scale ownership of financial instruments. That continued during the stock market boom of the 1920s. And bankers, he thought, had become less important because, by the early 1930s, the major corporations were fully formed independent entities, so financially powerful on their own that they didn't much need bankers' help. Still, there was something almost fetishistic about his preoccupation with the corporation as the dominant element in society. In this way Berle was influential: the corporation still looms large in the liberal mind.

It wasn't entirely clear in *The Modern Corporation and Private Property* what Berle wanted to *do* with the corporation. At the end of the book he called, rather vaguely, on "the community" to "demand that the modern corporation" serve "all of society." But what did that mean? Many years later, Berle wrote a book that he wanted to be considered as major an achievement as *The Modern Corporation and Private Property*. It was called, simply, *Power*. The book didn't take hold, but the title indicates what Berle was always most interested in. What drew him to the corporation as a primary concern was that it was so powerful and was evidently free of any external control. What he wanted was for its power to be reined in.

It soon became clear to Berle that the institution by far best suited to control the corporation was the federal government. That he was wary of corporate power did not mean he was wary of power per se, in the manner of the Founders or Brandeis. He liked centralized government power just fine. At heart he was what political scientists would call a corporatist, a believer in a highly structured society in which big business would dance to a tune called by government—forced to provide economic benefits to the rest of society as the price of its extraordinary prosperity and stability. In a sense he wanted to use the power of the corporation as a pretext for a great expansion of the power of the government. Back in 1912, when Theodore Roosevelt and Woodrow Wilson were arguing between the New Nationalism and the New Freedom, Berle was too young to take sides officially. By the 1930s he had taken a side. He was a New Nationalist—a Clash of the Titans liberal.

Because Berle's intellectual milieu was a highly enclosed world in which law professors debated technical questions of corporate governance and ownership, he was not immediately understood as what he understood himself to be—a big thinker about power. The one immediate challenge to Berle's writing about corporations came from a Harvard law professor named E. Merrick Dodd. From the law review articles Berle had published before *The Modern Corporation and Private Property* was finished, Dodd got the impression that Berle's main complaint about the corporation was that its managers weren't running it solely for the economic benefit of their shareholders. He thought Berle was looking for a way to restore the shareholders' power over management—to reclaim their rights as owners. Understanding this to be Berle's position, Dodd then argued against it, saying that corporations had a broad "social responsibility" to their employees, their communities, their customers, and the public, not merely an economic responsibility to shareholders. The executives of the great new corporations should see that "they are guardians of all the interests which the corporation affects and not merely servants of its absentee owners," and the law should see to it that they be permitted to follow this impulse even if their shareholders objected.

But if Berle ever had any genuine concern for shareholders, he had moved away from it by the time he was writing *The Modern Corporation and Private Property*. Their disempowerment was merely a piece of evidence used by Berle to sound the alarm about the excessive power of the men who were running corporations—and therefore, really, the country. (It also differentiated his theories from those of the thinkers he thought of as his competition, Adam Smith and Karl Marx, since they both had posited that capital controlled capitalism; Berle was saying that was no longer the case.) He believed that the big corporation itself was the problem, and that government had to be empowered to counteract it. As early as 1929, just as he was homing in on the full extent of corporate wealth, Berle wrote to a friend, "This is a problem of government rather than finance."

Berle did disagree with Dodd, but that was because he did not believe the corporation's immense power could be exercised independently, voluntarily, and benignly for the benefit of the whole society—not because he thought shareholders were being denied their economic rights. He felt that Dodd was naïve if he believed the corporation would ever behave responsibly unless it was forced to. In a published response to Dodd's criticisms, he wrote, "The industrial 'control' does *not* now think of himself as a prince; he does *not* now assume responsibilities to the community; his bankers do *not* now undertake to recognize social claims; his lawyers do *not* advise him in terms of social responsibility. Nor is there any mechanism now in sight enforcing accomplishment of his theoretical function."

In *The Modern Corporation and Private Property*, there was no discernible remnant of the argument Dodd thought Berle was making. It was an attack on the corporation not for the way it treated its shareholders, but for the fact of its power. Shortly after it was published, the book's original publisher, a financially oriented firm called Commerce Clearing House, "discovered that they had harbored a viper in their bosom," as Berle later put it, because it did not want to be associated with dangerous sentiments like Berle's. Berle always believed that the most powerful corporation, General Motors, had somehow exercised its influence over Commerce Clearing House to put an end to the book's publication. But the publisher's unionized printers in Chicago filched the book's plates and sent them to New York, where it was republished by a trade publishing house.

After the book was finished but before it was published, Berle wrote a letter to Louis Brandeis, perhaps by way of preparing him for the news that he was just about to depart publicly from the justice's preferred solution to the power of corporations, which was to break them up into smaller parts. "Rereading your collected essays not so long ago, I was struck with your opposition to the tremendous corporate concentration," Berle wrote.

You were writing in 1915. Now the concentration has progressed so far that it seems unlikely to break up even in a period of stress. I can see nothing at the moment but to take this trend as it stands endeavoring to mold it so as to be useful. If the next phase is to be virtually a non-political economic government by mass industrial forces, possibly something can be done to make such government responsible, sensitive and actuated primarily by the necessity of serving the millions of little people whose lives it employs, whose savings it takes in guard, and whose materials of life it apparently has to provide.

It may have been that, as he wrote to Brandeis, he had taken a position at odds with the justice's simply in response to changing conditions, but his position on corporations also suited his large ambitions. A society that had been broken down into smaller units that engaged in constant mundane quarrels was much less appealing to Berle than a society devoted to grand struggles between great forces—especially if he could be a significant participant on the side of the national government, which was the only entity potentially more powerful than the biggest corporations. Now he had to find a way to do that.

■

Just as he was finishing *The Modern Corporation and Private Property,* Berle joined a group of "younger men in the statistical departments of banks" (as he put it years later) who met regularly, and secretly, to discuss the growing crisis in the financial system and what to do about it. In the spring of 1932 Berle began writing a memorandum that summarized the group's views. (Only Berle's name and that of one other man were on the memorandum; the other members of the group were afraid they would be fired if their association with it was known.) Berle called it "The Nature of the Difficulty." The combination of the economic crisis and the increasing concentration of economic power meant that "for the first time, the United States has come within hailing distance of revolution along continental European lines." Dramatic new measures were required. These included pumping more money into the economy through tax cuts; offering government guarantees of job security and of savings deposited in banks; creating a new federal agency that would regulate the stock market; developing a new system of federal old-age pensions and health and unemployment insurance; and relaxing the antitrust laws and the traditional restrictions on the size of banks in exchange for imposing greater regulation on them. To register the full meaning of reforms like these when they were still new and unfamiliar ideas, it is necessary to recall that, as Berle put it, "the then revolutionary conception was simply this: for the first time in its history the federal government had to assume responsibility for the economic condition of the country."

One weekend during the period when Berle was composing "The Nature of the Difficulty," he and Beatrice went for a walk in the woods behind their house in the Berkshires. As she remembered it later, "It was one of those rare Spring days in New England when Spring dispels Winter and has not been overtaken by Summer. Patches of snow dotted last year's brown leaves, a warming sun came through the maple trees in tiny leaf, yellow-chartreuse, banks of wild violets coming into flower lined the road." Adolf was talking nonstop in his customary low, rapid confidential mumble about how dire the situation in the country was and how important he thought his ideas were. Beatrice went on: "As Adolf was talking, I suggested that he needed a 'prince'—somebody who could make real the ideas he so freely spawned."

Providentially, not long after that conversation, the prince appeared. For the past several years Berle had been teaching corporation law part-time at Columbia. One of his faculty colleagues, a political scientist named Raymond Moley who knew about the work he had been doing, approached him to say that he had been informally advising the presidential campaign of Franklin D. Roosevelt, the governor of New York. Would Berle be willing to come with him to Albany and have dinner with the governor? At that point Berle was officially a Republican, though not firmly identified with either political party, and Roosevelt's views on what to do about the economic crisis were unknown; a previous visitor dispensing economic advice was Irving Fisher, a Yale professor about the age of Adolf Berle, Sr., who was the country's leading free-market economist. But Berle's visit to Albany in May 1932 went splendidly.

"I took my memorandum in my hot little hand and we went up there," Berle remembered years later.

I was a bit dismayed, and stopped being dismayed three minutes after I met Franklin Roosevelt. He was not a man who dismayed people. He was a man who took you into camp almost at once, and we had a pleasant dinner and went to the library, and then he said, "All right now, do you want to say something?"

I said, "I have a memorandum here and I wonder if I could make a short speech?"

The Governor said, "No, make a long one, you can't do this with a short speech."

Soon Berle, Moley, and a few other advisers were set up in a hotel suite in New York, working for the Roosevelt campaign, and Berle was often called to meet with Roosevelt in person. As Beatrice put it in her diary, "A. has been in great & constant demand at Albany and Hyde Park." She sometimes accompanied him on these trips. On one visit to the Roosevelt homestead in the Hudson Valley, Sara Roosevelt, the governor's mother, took Beatrice aside and told her that she had known both of Beatrice's grandmothers and that it was a great relief to know that her son "had one gentleman at least working for him." She asked Adolf, "Are you very radical? I hope not. I am an old conservative."

Berle may not have been a radical—if that meant being a socialist or a communist—but he knew that this was his great opportunity to see the ideas he had formed put into effect, and he was determined to take maximum advantage of it, to push as hard as he could for as much change as he could get. As he later put it, "For an intellectual this was the golden period of being able to state a case with a fair hope that if it stood up it would be adopted. Further, it was a situation in which the normal political resistance was not likely to apply. The country was too badly off. Something had to be done." In August 1932 he wrote a memorandum to Roosevelt pressing his case more insistently than he had done before. He reminded Roosevelt that even a losing presidential candidate could become a significant figure in American life, but only if he could "quite definitely become the protagonist of an outstanding policy." Otherwise he would be forgotten. It was time for Roosevelt to create such a policy. Berle ran through the major points in *The Modern Corporation and Private Property* and "The Nature of the Difficulty" and then suggested that Roosevelt propose "a policy by which the government acted as regulating and unifying agency, so that within the framework of this industrial system, individual men and women could survive, have homes, educate their children, and so forth."

Roosevelt asked Berle to draft a speech for him that would lay out this new idea. Over the next few weeks, the Berles sat at their dining room table in the Berkshires and wrote draft after draft in longhand, Beatrice rewriting Adolf's work and Adolf rewriting Beatrice's. When they had a draft they felt was ready for Roosevelt to see, Adolf, in a state of high excitement, sent off the speech text to Roosevelt's campaign train by air mail, along with a long telegram describing its contents, so that Roosevelt could get a sense of the main ideas right away. It began: "Fundamental issue today adaptation old principles to new and probably permanent change in economic conditions which can only be done by enlightened government stop."

Roosevelt delivered the speech on September 23, 1932, at the Commonwealth Club in San Francisco. It's worth bearing in mind that up to that point, Roosevelt, whose governing vision is firmly fixed in our minds today, was widely regarded as a charming and high-spirited man who didn't stand for anything in particular. He was intelligent, but not an intellectual, and he never wrote a manifesto in his own hand. People who met him were always impressed by his curiosity and his ebullience, but they rarely came away with a clear sense of what he thought. So the Commonwealth Club address stands as the best prospective blueprint for the enormous change in the American political order, which the public hadn't yet started calling the New Deal.

The address displayed the Berle touch in the way it put an argument about what needed to be done right now into the context of the broad sweep of American history, so that to question what Roosevelt was proposing now would seem to be standing in the way of progress. The Berles had Roosevelt locate himself in the political tradition of two of his party's great figures: Jefferson, the champion of democracy and enemy of centralized power, and Wilson, the opponent of big business whose agenda was left unfinished because of the exigencies of the First World War. In the early nineteenth century the United States had protected its citizens from despotic political power and had provided them with opportunity through the open frontier. Then came the Industrial Revolution. In order to develop its full potential, the country had empowered "a group of financial Titans" and had conceived of government's role as "not to interfere but to assist in the development of industry." But now the frontier was closed, the railroads and factories were built, and the great threat to the freedom and welfare of the individual was not the kind of oppressive political power the Founders had feared, but super-concentrated economic power. This had become "the despot of the twentieth century, on whom great masses of individuals relied for their safety and their livelihood, and whose irresponsibility and greed (if it were not controlled) would reduce them to starvation and penury."*

The Berles had Roosevelt note that recently, "a careful study was made of the concentration of business in the United States"—meaning *The Modern Corporation and Private Property*—whose implication was that, if nothing were done, "at the end of another century we shall have all American industry controlled by a dozen corporations, and run by perhaps a hundred men." These men would be—this was a phrase Beatrice was especially proud of having written into the speech—"not business men, but princes—princes of property." The only way to forestall the onset of this "economic oligarchy" was to develop "an economic declaration of rights, an economic constitutional order." Roosevelt's program would be a kind of sequel to the founding of the United States, in which government protected the yeoman (who was now likely to be a city dweller) from the excesses of economic power instead of the excesses of political power.

On very close inspection, the address rejected Brandeis's dismantling impulses toward business: there was a line about the impossibility of trying to "turn the clock back, to destroy the large combination and to return to the time when every man owned his individual small business." But this was easy to miss because Roosevelt so enthusiastically praised Jefferson and Wilson and so ardently held up individualism as the most sacred American value. Adolf Berle was more candid about what he had in mind for the Roosevelt administration in a letter he wrote just after election day to a friend who was a federal judge in Boston and also a friend of Brandeis's:

---

*It's worth noting that, just as it's almost impossible to imagine a Democratic presidential nominee today making such economically radical statements, it's also impossible to imagine one offering a sweeping account of the history of opportunity in the United States without ever mentioning slavery or any other instance of a group of Americans being denied the rights of citizenship.

Brandeis dreams of turning the clock backward. His constant phrase is "the curse of bigness"—who shall say he is not right?—but from the puzzled position of mid-career, I cannot see how the tide can be turned back. Like you, I am afraid we are doomed to an era of big business, and possibly even to State socialism. The line that I am working on is a vague dream that the commercial organizations which we have built up may be used, more or less as they stand, without being destroyed, in the public interest . . . It cannot be individualism, pure and simple, as we used to know it.

In a letter to another friend the next month, Berle sketched out some of the ideas he had put forth in "The Nature of the Difficulty" and, by way of putting a label on them, said, "These measures . . . give all the machinery for a controlled capitalism as against an uncontrolled capitalism."

■

In those days, presidents were not inaugurated until early March. By that time in 1933, the banking system had substantially collapsed; since the 1929 stock market crash, thousands of banks had gone out of business, and now thousands more were simply closing their doors so that the depositors could not withdraw their funds. With the banks frozen, lending to businesses and consumers, which might have put some life into the dead economy, was impossible. The best-remembered line from Roosevelt's inaugural address—"We have nothing to fear but fear itself"—was specifically meant to give people the confidence not to take their savings out of banks, and hence out of the economy, from sheer panic.

On the day before Roosevelt's inauguration, Berle attended an emergency meeting of bankers at the Fifth Avenue apartment of the incoming secretary of the Treasury, William Woodin. The Berles then took the train to Washington for the inauguration ceremony, which Beatrice remembered as being rather grim: "As for it being a good show, there was no show," she wrote in her diary. "We have lost all color and all sense of pomp and ceremony . . . There was no thrill in the crowd, only idle curiosity." Adolf went directly from the ceremony to another emergency meeting at the White House, not leaving there until late in the evening. He spent the next day, Sunday, at a second all-day meeting of bankers at the Treasury. "I never saw a more disorderly meeting in my life," he recalled later; one banker was weeping, another "drawing ladies and crescent moons" on a piece of paper. Just after midnight on Sunday night, Roosevelt ordered that all the banks in the country be closed for a few days. During that time, Congress passed emergency legislation authorizing the reopening of the stronger banks and the reorganization of the smaller ones. By the middle of March the immediate crisis had passed, and the federal government had become involved in operating the American economy as it never had been before.

William Woodin offered Berle a job in the Treasury. He considered it (Beatrice wrote that he said to her that "pulling out from the government now may be declining a place in history—shall I be Alexander Hamilton?") but decided not to take it. Berle believed he could have more influence if he was a member of Roosevelt's informal Brain Trust, not a full-time government employee with a specific job. Roosevelt presided over the executive branch in the manner of a politician, not a businessman. He liked keeping his options open until the last minute, maintaining in his head a private accounting, which was exclusively his, of who the actors were and where they stood. He consulted all sorts of people constantly about all sorts of matters that may or may not have been their official responsibility. This was an atmosphere in which somebody like Berle, whom FDR liked, could thrive. He was closer to power without a formal assignment than he would have been with one; he was one of a small group of people who had permission to telephone Roosevelt at any hour on his private line. At the same time, Berle had forged a close advisory connection to Fiorello La Guardia, who was mayor of New York during the time Roosevelt was president. Under the quaint-sounding official title of city chamberlain, Berle was a one-man Brain Trust for La Guardia's administration. As Beatrice put it in her diary, "Before the Brain Trust days I felt that he would die a disappointed man if he did not have a finger in the pie. Now he has had a finger in all the pies there are."

It would be hard to think of anyone who managed to make a tighter connection between formulating big ideas and having a big effect than Berle did in the early 1930s. As Beatrice observed, intellectual life did not satisfy him; he wanted his ideas to "govern and change the course of history . . . He was not satisfied with emitting wisdom from a distance in a detached and unemotional manner." But he lacked the temperament to obtain and exercise power in the manner of Roosevelt and La Guardia. Beatrice went on: "He is a man of unlimited ambition . . . but he is too sensitive, not sufficiently ruthless and outwardly aggressive to gratify this ambition comfortably." Therefore, and necessarily, "his great genius consists in supplying the ideas for other people." Berle was fully aware of how large, and how unlikely ever to be repeated, the opportunity before him was. As he told an interviewer many years later, "Suddenly you find yourself connected with the unlimited voltage of a government the size of the United States, when handled by as forceful and determined a man as Roosevelt was—the power became enormous."

It's necessary to keep in mind that because the country was in a state of near chaos, and because Roosevelt had a chaotic governing style anyway, nothing about the New Deal was inevitable or uncontentious. Outside of Washington, communism and fascism had more serious support than they have had before or since; inside Roosevelt's administration, fierce disagreement among the president's advisers was constant. How much power Berle had can't be calculated with mathematical precision. All we can know is what Berle wanted to happen at this great turning point in American history and what actually did happen—not the precise relation between the two.

Within the first few months of Roosevelt's presidency, three economic reforms Berle had been advocating for years became law: the legal separation of commercial and investment banking, federal insurance of the bank deposits of working-class and middle-class Americans (along with federal regulation meant to prevent the insured banks from using their depositors' money in ways that put them at risk of failure), and federal regulation of stock and bond offerings by corporations. The first of these reforms was aimed at eliminating one of the leading corrupt financial practices of the 1920s: banks lending money to companies and then ensuring that their loans would be repaid by selling stocks and bonds in these companies to unsuspecting customers. The second restored enough confidence in the safety of banks so that people would start putting their money into them again, so that banks could make loans. The third required corporations to provide prospective investors with basic financial information. During the campaign, Berle had written a speech that Roosevelt never delivered, about the problem of "masterless money." He wanted Roosevelt to exclaim, "Look about you in the whole financial system for anyone who assumes responsibility for the little man, or his little savings." Now that Roosevelt was president, the government had assumed that responsibility, no matter whether the little man's savings were deposited in banks or invested in stocks and bonds.

That left as an open question what would come next in the great enhancement of the government's role in the economy. Would Roosevelt abandon capitalism entirely or merely reform it? And what would reform mean, exactly? Berle knew what he believed: that the government should directly control the economic life of the corporation to the greatest possible extent. In those early years of the New Deal, Berle found himself in constant battle with other liberals who did not share his view. He had hoped, for example, that when the new agency regulating stocks, the Securities and Exchange Commission, was created, it would not only require public information but also regulate financial behavior— for example, banning margin trading, short selling, and the practice of banks trading stocks for their own accounts rather than those of their customers. Instead, his rivals holed up in a suite at the Mayflower Hotel to draft the SEC's charter without informing Berle, and none of that happened.

Berle enthusiastically supported the National Industrial Recovery Act, a law passed during the early days of Roosevelt's presidency that gave the federal government the power to regulate specific companies' prices, wages, and basic economic decisions, as another aspect of its new role as an economic power fully equal to the corporation. The idea of the government as grand economic planner and regulator, its power extending fully into the suites where the largest corporations made their decisions, appealed deeply to Berle. The larger the economic units, the easier it would be for the government to enact Berle's concept of controlled capitalism, so he had no sympathy for the antitrust movement. All this was the antithesis of what Brandeis believed, but Berle had kept up his respectful connection with the justice, who may not have realized how completely Berle's views had by now departed from his own.

In April 1934 Berle fired off a letter to Roosevelt. "Dear Caesar," it began. "Mr. Justice Brandeis has been revolving matters in his head and

I think requires some attention." Brandeis did not feel that his seat on the Supreme Court should constrain him from making his views known to the president, though he usually did so through intermediaries such as Berle. "His idea was that we were steadily creating organisms of big business which were growing in power, wiping out the middle class, eliminating small business and putting themselves in a place in which they rather than the government were controlling the nation's destinies." Brandeis wanted Roosevelt to know, Berle went on, that "unless he could see some reversal of the big business trend, he was disposed to hold the government's control legislation unconstitutional from now on"— including specifically the National Industrial Recovery Act. Roosevelt replied to Berle typically—he was charming but cryptic: "As to our friend of the highest court, I expect to have a good long talk with him within the next few days. The difficulty is that so many people expect me to travel at a rate of one hundred miles an hour when the old bus cannot possibly make more than fifty miles an hour, even when it is hitting on all eight cylinders."

Neither Berle nor Roosevelt, evidently, was shocked that a Supreme Court justice would, in effect, try to blackmail a president into changing his policies with the threat of overturning them as unconstitutional. Berle always claimed to admire Brandeis—he kept a portrait of the justice on the wall of his office for decades—and to have become opposed to Brandeis's anti-bigness liberalism only reluctantly, with sincere regret, because it had become unrealistic in the modern world. Whatever resentment of Brandeis he may have been inclined to feel, he transferred to Brandeis's chief protégé in Washington, Felix Frankfurter, who was the New Dealer Berle hated most. As enemies often are, Berle and Frankfurter were a lot alike: both of them were diminutive, brilliant former child prodigies; both were professors at Ivy League law schools; both were active liberals who liked taking controversial public positions; and both had chosen to spend the early years of the New Deal mostly out of Washington, as advisers to Roosevelt without a specific portfolio. Twenty years earlier, when Berle was an unusually young student at Harvard Law School and Frankfurter an unusually young professor, Berle took one of Frankfurter's classes and rose constantly from his seat to offer an improved version of what Frankfurter was saying; at least according to legend, the next year he appeared in the same class again, in order, he told Frankfurter, to see whether Frankfurter had corrected the errors he had pointed out the year before.

By the time of the Roosevelt administration, Berle saw Frankfurter as a highly effective schemer—operating through a web of former students he had placed in important jobs in Washington—who was somehow more allied than Berle both with Brandeis's brand of small-bore liberalism and with European socialism. (Decades later, a historian discovered that while Brandeis was on the Supreme Court, he had paid Frankfurter a retainer for receiving from him—and trying to promote—the policy views Brandeis was not permitted to express openly.) It was Frankfurter's protégés who had taken control of the design of the Securities and Exchange Commission and given it less regulatory power than Berle thought it should have. Frankfurter was also skeptical of the National Industrial Recovery Act's expansive powers. It was a bitter pill for Berle to swallow when the Supreme Court, in May 1935, unanimously declared the NIRA to be unconstitutional, with Brandeis concurring—and another bitter pill when, in 1939, Roosevelt nominated Frankfurter to join Brandeis on the Supreme Court.

Roosevelt reacted to changes in the economy and in the political atmosphere by constantly tacking this way and that on economic policy, which only inflamed the rivalries between planning- and regulation-oriented liberals like Berle and power-mistrusting liberals like Frankfurter. In 1938 Roosevelt appointed an old-fashioned crusader, Thurman Arnold, to run the antitrust division of the Justice Department in an especially aggressive way; Berle continued to believe that bigness in the corporate world was not a curse, but an occasion for empowerment of the government to involve itself deeply in corporations' affairs. In the wake of the Supreme Court decision invalidating the NIRA, he wrote to a friend in New York, perhaps a little disingenuously, "I wish I could agree that a decline in centralized economy will be possible . . . Life under a small unit society would satisfy both you and me a great deal better than life under the present system does. As someone said in dismissing Mr. Brandeis's views: I feel with sympathy for decentralization and will support it whenever I can with the hopeless feeling that all bets are the other way."

Berle was so focused on Brandeis that he failed to appreciate that a much more profound and enduring liberal challenge to his economic views had arisen. In 1936 John Maynard Keynes published *The General Theory of Employment, Interest, and Money*, proposing a new and more technical way for government to solve economic problems: by managing interest rates, the money supply, and the overall level of government spending. Berle knew Keynes slightly; they had met during the peace negotiations after the First World War, and he and Beatrice had even quoted Keynes in one of the many drafts of the Commonwealth Club speech. But he didn't take Keynes as seriously as he should have. That was partly because Berle felt he had, on his own in "The Nature of the Difficulty" memo, arrived at the key point of Keynesian economics—the way out of a depression was to give ordinary people the means to spend more. He advocated such ideas all through the New Deal. Also, Keynes was close to the hated Frankfurter, who had arranged for him to meet with Franklin Roosevelt in the White House even before the *General Theory* was published. Berle's old writing partner, Gardiner Means, who was working in one of the New Deal planning agencies, instantly recognized Keynes's importance. In the summer of 1939 Means traveled to England and spent a day conferring with Keynes at his country house in Sussex, leaving with the conviction that the two of them weren't really so different.

That was wishful thinking. Berle and Means were focused on government, as an institution, directly participating in the operations of business institutions, especially large corporations. The NIRA may have died, but Franklin Roosevelt had created dozens of other new agencies of the federal government that lived on and that told corporations what to do. The National Labor Relations Board could force corporations to negotiate with unions, the Social Security Administration could make them set aside money for their employees' retirement, the Securities and Exchange Commission could tell them whether they were permitted to issue new stock, and so on. Keynes, as a macroeconomist, was primarily concerned with the economy overall, not with specific institutions, even ones as big as the great American corporations.

Keynesian economics offered liberals in government an entirely different set of tools from the ones Berle and Means were attracted to. Keynes's American admirers were not particularly interested in the main battles of the past ten years of Berle's life: the clash between government and the corporation, and the question of whether the biggest businesses should be broken up into smaller units. When Berle and Means were writing together, the leading economics departments in universities were filled with people who studied institutions—microeconomists. Within a generation, macroeconomists, who studied economies as a whole rather than specific businesses, dominated economics, and the whole question of government's relationship to the corporation—whether to control it or break it up—began to be succeeded by what might be called Macro Liberalism, which focused on managing the economy rather than on taming big business. Berle thought of his version of liberal economics as being about power; the macroeconomists thought of their version as being about science.

As the New Deal's main attentions began to shift from economic reform to fighting the Second World War, it was still not entirely clear whose economic vision had prevailed. Keynes's followers could say that the war demonstrated the truth of their economic prescriptions: lots of new government spending finally ended the Depression. But Berle, too, had plenty of evidence at hand that he could use to show that he'd been proved right. Capitalism had survived, and so had the large corporation as its giant institution. The war had given the government the pretext to institute Berle-style policies that would have been inconceivable during the 1930s. It was directly setting the prices of consumer goods and telling General Motors and U.S. Steel and the others exactly what to produce in their factories. The results were wonderful, both for the great global struggle and for the economic well-being of ordinary Americans. Why couldn't that continue after the war?

■

In 1935 the Berles got word that Cortlandt Bishop, Beatrice's father, was dying and that he had told one of his nurses that he wanted to see his daughter. One day they drove to the grand Bishop house in Lenox, from which Beatrice had long been banished, and knocked on the door. Amy Bishop appeared, "looking like an old hag with eyes that were not there," as Beatrice remembered it, and said, "Your Father does not want to see you alive or dead." They left, and soon Cortlandt Bishop was gone. "It hurts," Beatrice wrote in her diary. "I have lived now for nine years without seeing him. I have made a home and a full life and in back of my mind I have always felt that some day I would see him again; that some day he would come to know Adolf and be proud and happy about his daughter."

Cortlandt Bishop left Beatrice nothing in his will. She and Adolf hired lawyers, went to court, and wound up succeeding in receiving some family money that her father had inherited and held in trust. This meant that the Berles no longer needed the income Adolf had been earning by practicing law on Wall Street. In 1938 he was appointed assistant secretary of state, with a special responsibility for Latin American affairs, and the family moved to Washington for the rest of the Roosevelt years. Berle had been interested in Latin America ever since he'd spent time in the Dominican Republic as a young army officer back in 1918; and by now, with war imminent, the State Department was becoming the center of the action.

The Berles lived in a series of rented mansions, entertained constantly, and knew everybody. Compared with most assistant secretaries, Adolf was hugely influential. He drafted Roosevelt's declaration-of-war message to Congress after the attack on Pearl Harbor, in addition to several other important speeches. He helped create the St. Lawrence Seaway in Canada and the modern system of commercial airline regulation. He was the person Whittaker Chambers came to see in 1939 to report that there were Communist Party spies working in government. He continued to see Roosevelt regularly. He tried to make himself part of just about everything in Washington, and sometimes he succeeded.

But Berle was never as influential as an official full-time diplomat as he had been as an informal economic adviser in the early days of the New Deal. His grandiose and earnest conception of himself, his closeness to Roosevelt, his self-promotion, and his propensity for feuding made him one of Washington's most disliked figures. In a typical incident, in 1940, annoyed about the editing of a draft of a speech he had written for Roosevelt, he gave the original version to two Washington journalists, Joseph Alsop and Robert Kintner. "Berle is always more literary, more formally eloquent, and less guarded than the President," they reported. Behind Berle's back people called him, not fondly, Little Atlas, or The Brain. *The New Yorker*'s two-part profile of him in 1943 ended by saying, "It is a big job to plot the future of the world, but Berle gives many onlookers the impression that he is up to it." Felix Frankfurter, whose appointment to the Supreme Court in no way diminished his dislike of Berle or his competition with him for Roosevelt's favor, wrote in his diary in 1942, "There is not one iota of doubt that Berle is almost pathologically anti-British and anti-Russian, and his anti-Semitism is thrown in, as it were, for good measure, though probably derived through certain personal hostilities and jealousies." Talk of that kind around Washington—along with Berle's hesitancy about the United States entering the Second World War as soon as Britain did and, later, about giving the Soviet Union a free hand on the Eastern Front—got him a reputation for being an appeaser and a too-ardent anticommunist.

After Roosevelt was elected to his fourth term, in 1944, his closest aide, Harry Hopkins, flew out to Chicago, where Berle was attending a conference, and told him his service as assistant secretary of state was over. As a consolation prize, Berle was made ambassador to Brazil. He had one final private audience with Roosevelt in the White House, to discuss the shape of the postwar world, only a little more than a month before Roosevelt died. In 1946 he resigned from government, and the Berles moved back to New York.

■

Some people start out as optimists, seeing the world as a shimmering field of unrealized possibilities, and as they age, they become pessimistic, preoccupied with everything that can go wrong. Adolf Berle had an opposite progression. In his twenties, at the peace talks in Paris, he thought he was watching the creation of arrangements that could bring civilization to an end. In his thirties, in New York, he perceived in the rise of the corporation a basic threat to American democracy. But in his fifties and sixties he believed he was living under a strong, benign, lasting social order, one he had helped to create: domestically and economically, the apotheosis of the tamed, socialized corporation; internationally, an all-powerful United States presiding over an expanding free world.

Although Berle never again experienced the kind of extraordinary confluence of the publication of *The Modern Corporation and Private Property* and his role as a key adviser to Roosevelt at the moment of his ascension to an unusually consequential presidency—who ever does?— he spent the last quarter century of his life, after he returned to New York, being treated as a liberal sage. The Berles moved back into their town house on Gramercy Park. Although both of them were conducting demanding careers, they entertained relentlessly—usually in the form of black-tie dinner parties, held once a week or even more often, with the guest lists and menus meticulously planned and recorded by Beatrice, for politicians, professors, novelists, musicians, diplomats, scientists, and whoever else struck them as prominent and interesting. At one dinner, during the period of guided discussion the Berles always initiated over the main course, a socialist guest announced, "If there is a lower class, I want to be in it!" After he had left and only the family remained, Beatrice said, "Well, if there is an upper class, I want to be in it."

Adolf Berle was a founder and longtime chairman of the Liberal Party of New York City, which tried to throw its support to whichever of the major parties was more in favor of generous government social programs while also being staunchly anticommunist. He advised Adlai Stevenson, the Democrats' presidential nominee in 1952 and 1956, and Nelson Rockefeller, the governor of New York in the 1960s and the leader of the liberal wing of the Republican Party. Adolf constantly contributed articles to prominent newspapers and magazines, gave lectures all over the country, and was often cited in books, law review articles, and judicial decisions. He served briefly as an adviser on Latin American policy to President John F. Kennedy. If there was an obvious way in which Berle's views were becoming out of date as he aged, it was on foreign policy. He didn't see any problem with the United States exerting its power maximally everywhere, and he had trouble perceiving the aspirations of left-wing movements around the world as anything but attempts by the Soviet Union to extend its influence. He supported the disastrous Bay of Pigs invasion of Cuba in 1961, which tried to depose Fidel Castro in his early years in power; the United States' military invasion of the Dominican Republic in 1965 to help the regime there put down a rebellion; and the Vietnam War. But until the end of his life—he died in 1971—*The Modern Corporation and Private Property* was treated as a classic, and his insights about the corporation, rather than being controversial as they had been when he first stated them, had become part of the way everybody thought.

What made Berle famous was his alarmed criticism of the power of the corporation, but his attitude toward this power was more complicated than pure opposition. That became clear during the New Deal, when he was battling with Brandeis and his protégés. All through the 1930s Berle argued against the kind of aggressive enforcement of antitrust laws that would entail breaking up big corporations. In 1937, when Brandeis and his allies had the idea of imposing a big new tax on corporations' profits, Berle convened a small group of powerful men—including the chairman of General Electric, a partner of J. P. Morgan's, and the presidents of the steelworkers' and mine workers' unions—to oppose the new tax and, for good measure, the Roosevelt administration's antitrust program. When Congress created a new body to study economic concentration, called the Temporary National Economic Committee, in 1938, Berle came before it to testify against antitrust actions and in favor of national economic planning. In 1949, when Congress began considering what wound up being the last major piece of American antitrust legislation, the Celler-Kefauver Act of 1950, Berle again testified in favor of keeping big corporations big. "I do not think we are going to get rid of big units," he wrote Congressman Emanuel Celler of New York, the cosponsor of the law (and, naturally, a friend of Berle's). "The real question is whether . . . we need have a real piece of work done permitting an appropriate Federal agency to do industrial planning."

To Berle, in the mid-twentieth century and as far as the eye could see into the future, the triumph of controlled capitalism was inevitable. The Nazis and the Italian Fascists had had planned economies, and so did the Soviet Union. Any thought that the United States could avoid having one was nothing but a sentimental fantasy on the part of either blindly doctrinaire free-market purists or backward-looking Brandeis-style liberals. The real fight was between the other systems and an American one that would preserve democracy and individual rights. Hadn't economic planning gotten the country out of the Depression? Hadn't an even higher level of economic planning—with Washington setting wages, prices, consumption levels of goods, and factory production schedules—won the war?

All the angry younger Berle had really wanted was to enhance the power of government to the point where it could outmatch the power of the corporation. The direness of his warnings about corporate power could obscure the fact that he actually had no quarrel with centralized power, as long as it was used for good, by the state. The drama of his career was the harnessing of the corporation, not its destruction; indeed, in order to work, his vision of a good society actually required that corporations be as big and powerful as possible. Berle's was a not quite Oedipal dream in which the corporation, the domineering father of the national economy, rather than being slain, would be civilized and made benign. Now that government was so much bigger and exercised so much more power over big business, he was discovering that he rather liked the corporation.

During the 1950s and 1960s, Berle wrote several books and essays meant to bring up to date the themes of *The Modern Corporation and Private Property*. None of these made as much noise as his first book, but they all showed that he hadn't lost his special talent for transforming the technical details of corporate law and finance into a series of large, attention-grabbing assertions that presented the advent of the modern corporation as one of the milestones of human history, ranking with the Magna Carta or the Russian Revolution. By now, though, to Berle's mind, it had become a positive development, not an alarming one. "Its aggregate economic achievement is unsurpassed," he wrote about the American corporate economy in 1954. "Taking all elements (including human freedom) into account, its system of distributing benefits, though anything but perfect, has nevertheless left every other system in human history immeasurably far behind. Its rate of progress shows no sign of slackening."

By Berle's reckoning, the economic dominance of the corporation had only increased since the 1930s: now, only 135 corporations owned 45 percent of the country's industrial assets, and 25 percent of the world's. The reason this did not trouble him as it once had was that government had become powerful enough to control the corporation; government in fact owed a debt to the corporation, for providing it (via Berle's writings) with the justification to enlarge itself. The United States now had "a mixed system in which governmental and private property are inextricably mingled . . . not the result of any creeping socialism. Rather it is a direct consequence of galloping capitalism." It had all worked out so splendidly, from the point of view of democracy and social justice, that Berle was sure that even Louis Brandeis, by now long dead, "would be the first to deal with the facts and the last to fetter his views with fiction"—meaning that Berle felt empowered to convert the justice posthumously to his form of pro-corporate liberalism.

It was unimaginable to Berle that the role of government as master planner of the economy would not increase. Already, government controlled vast regions of the economy: banking through the Federal Reserve Board, airlines through the Civil Aeronautics Board, trucking through the Interstate Commerce Commission, electric power and natural gas through the Federal Power Commission, broadcasting through the Federal Communications Commission. All in all, he estimated, about half the economy was in government's warm embrace. Surely there would be more such agencies in the future. The public would not stand for any attempt to diminish government's role in the economy, and therefore neither would politicians: to abandon planning "meant risking unemployed workers, failure of supply of consumer goods, deterioration of standard of living, possible political disorder, in brief, a step backward in civilization."

Also, the corporation had become so powerful that it could easily afford to step into the role government had forced upon it, as the "conscience-carrier of twentieth-century American society." Berle still firmly believed in the central finding of *The Modern Corporation and Private Property*: because the corporation's stockholders were so widely dispersed (by now AT&T had more than a million shareholders), there was no relationship between ownership and control. The financial markets had become irrelevant. By Berle's calculations, corporations were so profitable that they were able to pay for nearly two-thirds of their investments with their own cash, and this trend too would surely continue. One could now simply write off Wall Street, the great villain for Brandeis and other economic liberals in Berle's youth, as vestigial: "The capital is there, and so is capitalism. The waning figure is the capitalist. He has somehow vanished in great measure from the picture." Berle recalled his pre–New Deal argument with Professor Merrick Dodd of Harvard Law School and magnanimously acknowledged that Dodd had won: "Stockholders do not hold the center of the corporate stage right now." Corporations safely could, and had, become socially responsible in the way Dodd had envisioned.

Sentiments such as Berle's were everywhere in the 1950s. In 1953 David Lilienthal, former head of the Tennessee Valley Authority and the Atomic Energy Commission and a student of Frankfurter's who had converted to Berle's side in the arguments about bigness, published a book called *Big Business: A New Era*, which was a full-throated celebration of the corporation and an attack on Brandeisian sentiments. "Bigness is . . . a way of thinking," Lilienthal wrote. "We think negatively. We are pre-occupied with restraints, prohibitions, antitrust, antimonopoly, anti-this and anti-that. This should not be the mood of sanguine and confident Americans." Lilienthal one-upped Berle's declaration that Brandeis, if he were alive, would now be in favor of bigness, asserting that even Walt Whitman, if he were alive, would be an admirer of the corporation.

Another of Berle's many friends had a voice that rose above the low general murmur of assent about the corporation-dominated postwar economy, to the point of attracting real public notice—more, in fact, than Berle himself ever did. That was John Kenneth Galbraith, who was more than just a protégé of Berle's, though he was that; he was the leading champion of the liberal idea that the corporation, properly handled, could provide the economic foundation for a benign social order. Galbraith was a Canadian agricultural economist who had wound up in Washington during the Second World War, helping to run the government's Office of Price Administration—which is to say that he came of age as a government official directly intervening in the economic lives of big companies. He met and befriended both Berle and Gardiner Means. In the 1950s, as an economics professor at Harvard, Galbraith wrote a series of books (funded partly through Berle's lobbying some wealthy patrons he knew) that made him famous, all of which follow in the line of *The Modern Corporation and Private Property*—especially the first of the books, *American Capitalism*, published in 1952.

Galbraith accepted most of Berle's basic tenets. He believed that corporations completely dominated the American economy, that bankers and financiers had become irrelevant, and that using antitrust law and other Brandeisian means to weaken corporations would not be productive. Liberals should be trying to make corporations behave in socially useful ways, not to reduce their power. Writing at a time when, not so long after the Great Depression, the American economy seemed almost miraculously prosperous, Galbraith added a new dimension to the influence of the corporation: using advertising in the mass media, it could now manipulate consumer demand for its products almost at will. The corporation wasn't just protected from its owners, as Berle had been saying for years; it was also protected from its customers' whims. That made the need even more urgent for a large role for government, on behalf of the public, in the affairs of these institutions, the most powerful and unaccountable in history.

In two important ways, Galbraith's ideas about the American economy were different from those of Berle. He could see, far better than Berle did, that management of the economy along the lines of John Maynard Keynes's theories posed a threat to the government's ability to direct the specific activities of corporations, always Berle's preference. That was because the Berle method was confrontational—therefore inevitably controversial—and the Keynes method was invisible. As Galbraith put it, under Keynesian government management of the economy, "to the naked eye, the scope of private business decision remained as before. General Motors still decided what cars to produce, what prices to charge, how to advertise and sell them, when to build a new assembly plant and how many workers to employ." Keynesian economic management had no immediate natural enemies; Berle's style of planning did.

Galbraith was also a shade less comfortable than Berle with unadulterated Clash of the Titans liberalism, in which the federal government would take the field as the corporation's sole all-powerful opponent. Berle, by now, had lost whatever measure he may once have had of the traditional American mistrust of concentrated power—and anyway, it wasn't much to begin with. His objection had been to corporate power unadulterated by government power. Galbraith had somewhat more Jeffersonian instincts. The big idea he promoted in *American Capitalism* was "countervailing power," in which other organized groups—labor unions, consumers, farmers, smaller business competitors—would bring the corporation to heel, forcing it to attend to society's needs. Government had to play a part in this, because it had to create a system in which these groups could become powerful enough to take on the corporation; indeed, Galbraith wrote, "the provision of state assistance to the development of countervailing power has become . . . perhaps *the* major domestic function of government." Galbraith's ideal world was one of political bargaining and compromise, and the willingness to sacrifice the purity of a big idea like economic market efficiency (the preoccupation of most of his fellow economists) or state power (Berle's preoccupation) in order to achieve social peace and attend to the needs of smaller play-ers. But the goal was the same: accept the dominance of the corporation and find a way to turn it to the benefit of society.

■

"I find it very difficult to join with people who like to yammer about the American system," Berle told an audience of students in 1960, "because by the time you get all through yammering, you still have to recognize that it has done more for more people and it has done a better job for a great block of the population than any system in history." It's easy to imagine the identities of some of the yammerers he had in mind. On the right, there was the Austrian economist Friedrich Hayek, who had relocated to the University of Chicago after the war and had begun to attract a passionate band of followers to his view that markets did a far better job than governments of responding to changing conditions. Any major enhancement of the power of the state in response to perceived social needs wasn't just unnecessary; it represented an unpardonable step in the direction of totalitarianism. To Berle it was understandable that Hayek, who had watched the Nazis take over his country, would think this way, but there was no actual danger of this in the United States. Hadn't democracy and liberty remained strong in the decades since the coming of the New Deal? Hadn't markets failed and govern-ment succeeded during the Great Depression?

On the left, there was a group of social critics who shared Berle's preoccupation with the corporation but saw it as a kind of disease to be overcome rather than an unstoppable force to be managed. David Riesman, the lawyer turned sociologist whose 1950 book *The Lonely Crowd* was an influential bestseller, identified the fundamental shift in the American character from inner-directed to other-directed as the great national peril. The rise of the corporation had turned a country of independent individuals into one of company men for whom the need for approval was an "insatiable force." Then there was Berle's Columbia colleague C. Wright Mills, the radical sociologist who followed in Ries-man's path but raised the temperature of alarm about the corporation even higher. In *White Collar*, published in 1951, he had this to say to corporate employees:

You are the cog and the beltline of the bureaucratic machinery itself; you are a link in the chains of commands, persuasions, notices, bills, which bind together the men who make decisions and the men who make things; without you the managerial demiurge could not be. But your authority is confined strictly within a prescribed orbit of occupational actions, and such power as you wield is a borrowed thing. Yours is the subordinate's mark, yours is the canned talk. The money you handle is somebody else's money; the papers you sort and shuffle already bear somebody else's marks. You are the servant of decision, the assistant of authority, the minion of management.

All through the 1950s and 1960s, journalists, novelists, and filmmakers struck this kind of note—including of course William Whyte in *The Organization Man*. Psychologists conducted ominous experiments that showed the danger of conformity. *The Port Huron Statement* (1962), the founding document of the student radical movement of the 1960s, reads as a kind of thirty-years-later sequel to *The Modern Corporation and Private Property*, sounding again and again the alarm about the dominance a few dozen corporations had established over American society. Norman Mailer, in his 1965 novel *An American Dream*, had his hero, Stephen Rojack, interrupt a lovemaking session to pluck out and fling away his partner's diaphragm because it was a "corporate rubbery obstruction." By 1970 Charles Reich, a Yale law professor who was another popular social critic of the day, took the argument to its logical conclusion by declaring, in *The Greening of America*, that by now the United States "can be thought of as a single vast corporation, with every person as an involuntary member and employee."

Berle didn't take opinions like these seriously. The new social critics' central insight—that corporations dominated American life, economically and otherwise—was one Berle had had decades earlier. Now, all these years later, they were missing what to him was the overwhelming, undeniable main point about American society in the twentieth century—the success of the political and economic order he had helped to introduce in the early years of the New Deal. The Depression had been conquered, the Second World War had been won, and the great competition with the Soviet Union was moving toward the inevitable triumph of American capitalism. There had not been a financial crisis for decades. The standard of living for working- and middle-class people was rising, and the kind of widespread severe material deprivation Berle had seen firsthand as a young man had almost disappeared. Against all this, it was hard for him to perceive some sensed but unprovable increase in conformity as a menace to the republic.

Also, the new critics of the corporation didn't seem to have a plan, as Berle had had in his younger days. It looked as if they were dreaming of creating a neo-Jeffersonian world in which there would be no large organizations at all; they made Brandeis look hardheaded and practical. The Commonwealth Club address the Berles wrote for Roosevelt in 1932 was framed as a defense of "individualism" in the age of the corporation, but choosing that label was only a tactic, so it wouldn't seem that Roosevelt was being too radical. (Roosevelt's opponent, Herbert Hoover, often used individualism as a slogan; the Berles may have wanted to counter his monopoly on the term.) The truth was that Berle thought, back then and even more now, that the age of individualism had ended, succeeded by an age of institutions. He had no sympathy for the idea that the country should make individualism its premier value.

What would we notice now as looming challenges to the peaceable kingdom where Berle imagined himself to be living—challenges that were not so apparent to him, as they didn't originate in his immediate world of liberal politicians and professors? One was the deep dissatisfaction of the excluded. Like many white American liberals during the first two-thirds of the twentieth century, including Franklin Roosevelt, Berle, through a lifetime of producing grand, morally concerned *tours d'horizon* of the state of American democracy, almost never noticed that racism was a big problem. When the civil rights movement became inescapably apparent to people in his world, he of course supported it, but he didn't see how deeply it countered his view of the United States as a high-functioning society that provided opportunity to everybody, or how powerfully it would inspire additional social movements dedicated to other problems he didn't much notice.

Another challenge was the growing prestige and influence of Keynesian economics, which was skeptical of the kinds of economic remedies—direct regulation of the activities of corporations—that Berle and his allies had been advocating for decades. Probably the most important economics publication of the 1950s was a paper called "Existence of an Equilibrium for a Competitive Economy." Using dozens of dense mathematical formulas, its authors, Kenneth Arrow and Gerard Debreu, endeavored to demonstrate that under the right economic conditions, prices will always find their natural level—which made their findings a far cry from Berle's, Means's, and Galbraith's argument that it was a good idea for government to set prices. No one who was not an academic economist may have read the Arrow-Debreu article, but from 1948 on, millions of college students learned about economics from an introductory textbook by Arrow's relative by marriage, Paul Samuelson, which presented Keynesian economic management as gospel and was highly skeptical of Berle-style planning (and, in later editions, specifically made fun of Galbraith for being an unrigorous popularizer). After the war, academic economists, who usually thought in terms of how well markets functioned rather than how much power corporations had, had their own permanent office in the White House, the Council of Economic Advisers.

Still, the rise of the corporation was a massive, undeniable reality, and so was the government's establishment of some measure of dominion over it. After the war, President Harry Truman had proposed another major ratcheting up of government's role in American life, which he called the Fair Deal. The country was not in the kind of economic crisis that allowed for the institution of anything the president wanted, as it had been in 1933, so major elements of the Fair Deal did not materialize: national health insurance, federal funding of public education, new laws that would strengthen the hand of organized labor. The United States declined to create the kind of comprehensive welfare state most European countries had. This meant that the corporation, when it could be successfully pushed into behaving like a social institution, *was* the American welfare state, at least for its many millions of employees, their families, and to some extent the much wider circle of its small-scale suppliers, service providers, and retail outlets for its products. Liberals were the natural champions of the welfare state, but not many liberals younger and less established than Berle thought of the corporation as either a central institution in a good society or as vulnerable to attack for the social aspect it had taken on. All the grumbling about corporations made it easy to miss that they were now bearing a heavy noneconomic load, and if that changed, there wasn't a real plan for what would take their place.

In the summer of 1970, a chest X-ray picked up an "infiltration" on one of Adolf Berle's lungs. Because Beatrice Berle was a doctor and Adolf a lifelong heavy smoker, they had no illusions about what the infiltration might be. The Berles decided to forgo any aggressive medical treatment for Adolf. Instead, they would try to enjoy the time they had left together. They kept up their usual routine as much as they could: lectures, short vacation trips, holidays in the Berkshires. One morning in February 1971, in their house on Gramercy Park, as Beatrice remembered it, "Adolf and I sat down together hand in hand, enjoying a pink hyacinth brought down from the country." He was feeling better than he had recently. They had houseguests, a prominent doctor and his family visiting from Brazil. There was a lively lunch. When it was over, Adolf rose from the table and collapsed. Beatrice recorded what happened next: "I picked up his right arm, then all four limbs—they were paralyzed. I ran upstairs to get adrenaline and a needle and shot the hormone into his heart, but in ten minutes, he was gone."

There was one more challenge that Berle hadn't seen—the most significant challenge of all, as it turned out—to the corporation and to his idea of its proper role. It came from the market forces to which Berle, and most other liberal thinkers of his day, believed the corporation had become invulnerable. The biggest corporations could afford to operate large research labs; that, along with their supposedly effortless dominance of the mind of the American consumer, ensured that nobody but they could develop important and successful new products. They were not vulnerable to competition from abroad; as Berle had insisted for decades, no national government, including that of the United States, would ever permit unimpeded access to its markets by foreign companies or permit domestic companies to make their products overseas simply in order to reduce their labor costs. They were even more immune to pressure from stockholders than they had been back in the 1930s, when Berle first proposed his theory of the corporation's historic separation of ownership and control. In 1959 Edward Mason, the dean of Harvard's public policy school, published a book of essays by prominent liberals, *The Corporation in Modern Society*, which reads as a kind of collective homage to Berle (who contributed a brief foreword). In his introduction, Mason summed up the situation this way: "Innovation at the hands of the small-scale inventor and individual entrepreneur has given way to organized research. The role of government in the economy persistently increases. The rugged individualist has been supplanted by smoothly efficient corporate executives participating in the group decision. The equity owner is joining the bond holder as a functionless *rentier.*"

Adolf Berle, Sr., lived well into his mid-nineties: he was born in the 1860s and died in the 1960s, never ceasing to prod his son to offer more of the benefits of his insights to the world. Had Adolf Jr. lived as long, he would have seen the economic certainties of a lifetime—everything he was so celebrated for perceiving—blown apart. Perhaps it was better that he did not.

2

THE TIME OF INSTITUTIONS

In the summer of 1940, Peter Drucker, a young Viennese émigré in his early thirties who had fled Hitler and was now trying to establish himself in the United States as a journalist, professor, and dispenser of advice to businesses, rented a cabin for his family in northern Vermont. Not long after the Druckers arrived, they acquired an unexpected long-term houseguest: Karl Polanyi, another Viennese émigré intellectual, a generation older than Peter Drucker, who had come to the United States from London to give lectures and had been unable to return because of the rising intensity of the war.

At that moment it wasn't just Adolf Berle who was drawn to thinking grandly about the future of civilization. It was a kind of sweepstakes, with many contestants—the times demanded it. People like Drucker and Polanyi had witnessed two world wars, the Great Depression, and the rise of the Soviet Communists, the Nazis, and the Fascists (not to mention the advent of the corporation), and they had seen the thriving societies where they had been born fall into ruin. In the space of only a few years in the early 1940s Friedrich Hayek published *The Road to Serfdom*, and Joseph Schumpeter published *Capitalism, Socialism, and Democracy*; both authors were also from Vienna, and Drucker and Polanyi knew them. James Burnham, an American ex-communist, published *The Managerial Revolution*, a dire warning that professional business bureaucrats, comfortable with government regulation, were becoming the ruling class in modern society (Burnham devoted several pages to summarizing *The Modern Corporation and Private Property*). Henry Luce, who as the head of the Time-Life publishing empire was an occasional employer of Drucker's, wrote his famous essay proclaiming the arrival of "the American Century." And both Drucker and Polanyi had it in mind to write visionary books of their own about how modern society might begin to repair itself and function again if the Allies won the war. Critical questions about the future were in play; the opportunity to offer answers was not to be missed.

Drucker and Polanyi argued with each other in the cabin in Vermont that summer: Drucker, neat, organized, and ambitious, playing the conservative, and Polanyi, large, voluble, and messy, playing the socialist. Drucker was able to get Polanyi a job teaching at Bennington, a small women's college in Vermont. Polanyi rented a house of his own. Then Drucker was hired at Bennington too. Through 1941 and 1942 and into 1943 the arguments continued, especially in the winters, when Bennington was forced to cancel classes because of wartime shortages of fuel oil and both men had plenty of time to talk, as long as Drucker could make his way through the snowdrifts to Polanyi's house.

Polanyi's book, *The Great Transformation*, argued that the rise of unimpeded modern capitalism had generated a vast, long-running social disaster. "At the heart of the Industrial Revolution of the eighteenth century," he wrote, "there was an almost miraculous improvement in the tools of production, which was accompanied by a catastrophic dislocation of the lives of the common people." All the wars and malign political systems of the early twentieth century could be understood as misguided responses to this dislocation. The only possible lasting solution to the problem of capitalism was for government to make itself such a forceful presence that the economy would be made the servant of society, instead of society being the servant of the economy. Although Polanyi believed that his great intellectual opponent was Hayek, and he hardly mentioned the United States, Adolf Berle thought so highly of *The Great Transformation* that he made it assigned reading in his classes at Columbia. For Berle, Polanyi's descriptions of the widespread pain inflicted by unregulated capitalism called to mind the rough, cruel America of his youth.

Drucker's book was called *The Future of Industrial Man: A Conservative Approach*. The subtitle was apt. Drucker enthusiastically accepted Berle's idea that the corporation had become the dominant institution in the modern world and that its nominal owners, the shareholders, had no real control or power over it. But he disagreed with Polanyi—and surely would have disagreed with Berle, had they ever met—about whether it was necessary that the corporation operate under the controlling hand of the state. Drucker was absolutely opposed to the kind of government economic planning that Berle favored, which at that moment the young John Kenneth Galbraith was enacting in Washington, because Drucker thought it would lead to "centralized bureaucratic despotism." Instead, the corporation, on its own rather than under the government's direction, must invent something heretofore unknown: "a functioning industrial society."

Not long after *The Future of Industrial Man* was published, Drucker was surprised to get a call from an executive at General Motors—at that point, the ne plus ultra of corporations. How would he like to come to Detroit for a couple of years and find out how GM actually worked? Nobody had ever been offered this kind of free pass permitting the long-term observation of a corporation from the inside; Adolf Berle and other philosophers of the corporation knew all about how corporations were structured, but nothing about how they operated. Drucker had been asking other corporations for permission to study them, with no success. He eagerly accepted GM's offer, and in 1946 he published a book about what he had found there, called *Concept of the Corporation*.

Drucker was every bit as adept as Berle, or maybe even more adept, at making grand historical claims for the significance of the corporation. "The large industrial unit has become our representative social actuality," he declared, "and its social organization, the large corporation in this country, is our representative social institution." The corporation "sets the pattern and determines the behavior even of the owner of the corner cigar store who never owned a share of stock, and of his errand boy who never set foot in a mill." And: "The emergence of Big Business, i.e., the large integrated industrial unit, as a social reality during the past fifty years is the most important event in the recent social history of the Western world. It is even possible that to future generations the world wars of our time will seem to have been an incident in the rise of big-business society just as to many historians the Napoleonic wars have come to appear incidental to the industrial revolution."

Although Drucker went on to become probably the best-known management consultant in history, and although General Motors may have invited him to Detroit because it believed he might provide organizational advice, his book *Concept of the Corporation* didn't have much to say about how a corporation should be managed. It offered GM the highest praise for its system of decentralized management of its many units—Buick, Oldsmobile, Cadillac, Chevrolet, and so on—and then rather quickly moved on to Drucker's real purpose, which was to argue that the way to think of the corporation was as a "social institution" that should occupy the central role in the modern world. Like a weary Mittel-European Humbert Humbert who finds in everyday America a fresh new answer to all the old, insoluble human problems (except that he was oriented toward political theory rather than the search for true love), Drucker was entranced with the unrecognized potential of the corporation. It could be the guarantor of dignity and of equal opportunity to the great mass of people: "Only now have we realized that the large mass-production plant is our social reality, our representative institution, which has to carry the burden of our dreams. The survival of our basic beliefs and promises—the survival of the very meaning of our society—depends on the ability of the large corporation to give substantial realization of the American creed in an industrial society." Drucker praised GM's policy of keeping itself at just below half of the automobile market, lest Washington launch an antitrust suit, but he also took pains to distance himself from Justice Brandeis's old worries about bigness. In the modern world, bigness was a necessity. The corporation was the way to make society work.

Only at the end of his research at GM was Drucker given an audience with the company's chairman, Alfred P. Sloan, a starchy, formal man, by then in his late sixties and quite hard of hearing, who had been running the company for twenty years. Sloan said he hadn't supported Drucker's project—and, after *Concept of the Corporation* was published, he never said a word about it to Drucker personally or in public. It's not hard to see why. Sloan was definitely not one of the new breed of professional managers. He was a former owner of a ball-bearing factory in New Jersey that had been acquired by GM in exchange for stock, and he remained one of the company's largest individual shareholders. (That's why today there is a Sloan school, a Sloan foundation, and a Sloan hospital.) Sloan personally dominated GM, and he thought of it as a purely economic institution.

The founder of General Motors, William Durant, was a vivacious supersalesman who had pieced the company together through a series of acquisitions. But, as Sloan put it in his memoir, "Mr. Durant was a great man with a great weakness—he could create but not administer." GM's shareholders forced Durant out in 1910 because of his indiscriminate spending and borrowing, and he devoted his exile to elaborately and successfully plotting his return, which he accomplished mainly by founding Chevrolet and selling it to GM on terms that made him a major shareholder. He was back as president of GM in 1916, but out again, owing to another bout of financial imprudence, in 1920.

Sloan ran the company according to the precepts of a memorandum he wrote in 1919 called the "Organization Study," which was meant to impose order on the company's Durant-era administrative and financial chaos. GM had by then grown so big that if every decision had to be made at headquarters, nothing would ever get done. Sloan's solution was to create autonomous divisions organized around product lines, each with its own president and its own budget. Having devoted his whole career to making GM function properly as a business—his memoir has an appendix devoted to organization charts showing how the division structure worked—Sloan was not the ideal audience for the idea that it was actually a social institution. It's especially hard to imagine him agreeing with Drucker's breezy assertion that GM division managers did their jobs in a manner quite like "the reported approach of Soviet industrial managers."

Drucker had much better luck, though, with Sloan's successor, Charles Wilson, who had the title of president during the time Drucker was at GM. Posterity remembers Wilson for just one sentence, which he said during his Senate confirmation hearing to become Dwight Eisenhower's secretary of defense, in 1952: "For years I thought what was good for our country was good for General Motors, and vice versa." If you loved David Riesman's *The Lonely Crowd* and were looking for the perfect synecdoche of its main idea about what America had become, this was it. But Wilson was something more interesting and complicated than a pure company man. He had grown up in a union household in Pittsburgh, campaigned for Eugene Debs, the socialist candidate, in the 1912 presidential election, and briefly been a member of the pattern makers' union after college. He was also seriously religious—a member of the Church of God, a Pentecostal sect. According to Drucker, Wilson told him at their first meeting that Sloan's generation's task had been to develop a functioning very big business (at that point GM had almost half a million employees), but that now, "to develop citizenship and community is the task of the next generation." He and Drucker started a conversation about how to accomplish that, which continued even after Drucker had finished his book.

During the war, under urgent pressure, Wilson was in charge of converting most of GM's factories to the production of military matériel. After a couple of years of this, he had some kind of breakdown, which GM officially called a broken hip, and the company put him on leave for three months. He used the time to begin reflecting on how the company might stabilize the lives of its workers after the war. On the eve of the New Deal, Alfred Sloan's policy had been that there was no need for labor unions at General Motors; as he drily noted in his memoir, "We were largely unprepared for the change in political climate and the growth in unionism that began in 1933." As factory jobs for unskilled workers went, GM's were well paid—meaning, at the time, as much as fifty cents an hour—so it was impossible for Sloan to see the depth of the anger generated by such GM policies as relentlessly ever-moving assembly lines, no employee rights whatsoever, frequent unpaid layoffs, and unsafe working conditions.

It was only in 1937, after a series of sit-down strikes—essentially, temporary worker takeovers of factories—that GM signed its first contract with the United Auto Workers. When the war ended, demand for automobiles soared, and the end of price controls set off a large increase in inflation; GM was eager to sell cars, and the UAW members were afraid that inflation would make their incomes fall while the company's profits increased. In the winter of 1945–46, Walter Reuther, the president of the union, led its GM workers on one of the longest, largest strikes in American history—113 days, more than three hundred thousand workers—and wound up getting them a 17.5 percent wage increase.

GM's executives and the UAW leadership had spent the past decade in an atmosphere of maximum conflict, locally between labor and management and globally between the United States and totalitarian political systems. Both sides were inclined to see their negotiations as having very high stakes. During the strike, Sloan and Wilson issued a joint statement that asked, "Is America to continue as a democratic nation, based on free competition, with Government the servant of the people—or is it to become a Socialistic nation with all activities controlled and regimented, and with the people the servants of Government?" It didn't mollify them when, in 1947, thirteen thousand GM employees left work, in violation of their contract, to go to a mass demonstration protesting against the Taft-Hartley bill, a proposed piece of legislation cutting back on labor's power, which soon wound up becoming law. Sloan, furious, initiated disciplinary action against hundreds of union members who had participated in the walkout.

On the other hand, the company was not in the mood for another all-out war with the UAW. It was making substantial profits that depended on its factories turning out cars at full capacity. And Reuther had earned a measure of the company's trust, though only a measure, by expelling communists from the union's leadership. What worried GM about Reuther, aside from his ability to stop production, was that he had an expansive idea of what the union's role in GM's operations should be, including that it should help set the prices of cars at a level low enough for working people to buy them. The company's incentive to bargain was not only to keep its cars rolling out of the factories, but also to limit Reuther's authority to his members' economic condition and keep him out of comanagement of GM. Reuther, for his part, was well aware of how badly GM wanted stability and of how threatening it found the idea of relations between labor and management, or between corporations and government, changing even more than they already had.

In 1948 GM and the UAW signed a two-year contract that, for the first time, promised workers regular wage increases tied to the official rate of inflation—an idea Wilson had been toying with for several years. In 1949, with the end of that contract in sight, both sides began preparing for the next one. Wilson gave a speech as negotiations were about to start, musing that for GM's workers, there was another economic problem besides inflation: how to survive after retirement, if they needed more than the very modest amount the government's Social

Security program provided. "On a farm, when a man was young, maybe he milked twenty cows a day," he said. "When he got old, say sixty-five, maybe he would milk twelve; and when he got to be eighty, if he was still in good health, maybe he just fed the cows, but he still did something useful." It wasn't the same for a factory worker: when he was no longer able to carry a full workload, he was out. That was a problem the company should take on.

Years later, Peter Drucker reported that Wilson had confided to him that he would not send the GM team into the negotiations to offer up the ideas he had been developing. Instead, Wilson told Drucker, "I grudgingly yield to a union demand when I have to," because "the union leaders won't go along unless it's a 'demand' we resist and they 'win.'" Reuther, in the same spirit, sent the UAW's chief economist and house intellectual, Nat Weinberg, into the negotiations to deliver a long opening statement, full of references to prominent economists in universities and government, about the necessity of giving the union a role in setting both wages and prices. And while the two sides were preparing to negotiate, Reuther led the UAW into another strike against another auto company, Chrysler.

The actual mood of the GM negotiations seems to have been surprisingly peaceful. In May 1950, after only a few weeks at the bargaining table, the two sides announced an agreement that would have been unimaginable a few years earlier. The new contract between the UAW and GM would last for five years. Workers would get a cost-of-living increase every three months, plus a measure of job security, plus a company health insurance plan, plus a company-paid retirement pension—all of which was previously almost unheard-of for American factory workers. GM, in exchange for the promise of a long period of labor peace and the union's putting aside its ambitions to function as comanager of the corporation, was willing to set itself up as a comprehensive welfare state for its workers.

Both sides came out of the negotiations not only claiming victory but also believing that they had invented a new American social compact that would have an effect far beyond even the capacious boundaries of a very big corporation and a very big union. *Fortune* led its July 1950 issue with an article called "The Treaty of Detroit." The author, Daniel Bell, the magazine's young labor editor, noted that GM's profit in 1950 might be almost as much as its profit during the entire decade of the 1930s. He treated the contract as a win for both sides, but especially for GM. "General Motors may become the first to prove what has hitherto been only theory: that a corporation can be unmistakably big, powerful, and profitable, and on top of all that be widely popular," Bell wrote. He ended his report on the contract by saying, "There are lessons in this contract for most of American industry, including many units whose annual sales are smaller than General Motors' monthly profits."

Charles Wilson went to Washington shortly after the agreement to deliver a triumphant speech at the National Press Club. He said it was a way "to work out an American solution for the relations of labor and industry and not attempt to adopt the philosophy of class conflict from Europe, either from the communists and socialists on the one hand or the cartel-thinking, non-competitive reactionaries on the other." This view was more than just a momentary justification by a corporate executive. Daniel Bell, a few years later, published a book called *The End of Ideology*; the idea of an emerging, distinctively American social compact was in the air. In the 1930s the United States chose—though that word makes the process sound more organized than it actually was—to have a much bigger central government that took responsibility for the economic life of the country on behalf of ordinary people's welfare but rejected the big alternative ideas of the time: communism, socialism, and fascism. In the 1940s the country became the world's leading power and chose not to become a full-dress welfare state on the European model. Now, in the 1950s, it was settling on a system built around big corporations, with labor unions and the central government as ever-hovering presences that made sure the corporations attended to their obligations.

It wasn't as if every American child from then on was taught in civics class that the national idea ran in a straight line from the Founders to the modern corporation. Only a few people, such as Peter Drucker and perhaps Adolf Berle in his older and more satisfied period, would even have been able to articulate the vision fully, and of course many liberals reflexively thought of the corporation as the enemy. Quite a few corporate chief executives, though, began conceiving of their companies as having broad social responsibilities, with unions and government no longer their sworn adversaries. The same view pervaded business schools; Adolf Berle proudly reported in 1959 that Harvard Business School, where he had taught back in the 1920s, "for thirty years has devoted itself to making businessmen into professionals instead of privateers-men." Many graduates of these schools, and of undergraduate colleges and (if they were blue-collar workers) high schools, found the pay and benefits and security and prestige the corporations were able to offer, in exchange for loyalty, attractive enough to want to spend their lives work-ing for them. If they hadn't, social critics like William Whyte would not have been so alarmed.

Large portions of the country were excluded from the corporate so-cial compact, but its borders extended far beyond the employees of the corporations themselves. Corporations bought goods and services from thousands of smaller companies, and these companies dominated the economies of hundreds of cities and towns. Berle, after asserting in 1954 that two hundred corporations controlled half the economy, took pains to show that this impressive figure actually understated their reach:

> The impact of many corporations—for example, General Motors or the great oil companies—goes beyond the confines of their actual ownership. For example, at a rough estimate, some three billions of dollars are invested in garages and facilities owned by so-called "small" businessmen who hold agency contracts from the principal automobile manufacturers. The owners are small, independent businessmen usually trading as "corporations" but certainly not giants. They are, nominally, independent. But their policies, operations, and, in large measure, their prices, are determined by the motor company whose cars they sell. The same is true of the "small businessman" who "owns" a gasoline filling station.

Berle was thinking especially of automobile dealers. At the time he was writing, there were forty-seven thousand of them in the United States, about a third of whom were GM dealers. "We must approach this group of people with more respect than is presently accorded salesmen in current literature," Berle wrote, sounding uncharacteristically senti-mental, and a little like Linda Loman at the end of *Death of a Salesman*.

Auto dealerships were mainly family businesses in small towns, al-most never operated by people with degrees from leading universities.

They called to mind a country that early-twentieth-century Progressives, like Berle in his youth, believed to be passing away: a country of modest independent business operators who knew their customers as neighbors and whose main skills were salesmanship and horse sense. In many cases the dealers were quite literally connected to an earlier America; they traced their roots to harness shops and hardware stores and bicycle repair sheds and horse and mule auctioneers who had converted to selling cars when the automobile came along. An auto dealer was, almost inevitably, in the business not just of selling new cars, but also of running a repair shop, of buying and selling used cars, and of lending money. He had to be able to meet a customer, perform an instant, silent cold-blooded assessment of how much the car he'd driven up in was worth and how likely it was that he would keep up on his monthly loan payments, and at the same time project enough enthusiasm and trustworthiness to make that customer want to buy another car. (Politicians who grew up in the business, like Bill Clinton or Joe Biden, give off a sense that they absorbed some of the essence of what it takes to be an auto dealer.)

The big auto companies had decided early on that it was to their advantage not to try to open their own networks of thousands of retail stores all over the country, but instead to sell their cars through independent businesses. The dealers were a big collective economic anomaly: they may not have been of the managerial type that now dominated American business, but they were firmly bolted to the world of the corporation. As a dealer, you lived and died by your franchise agreement with GM or Ford or Chrysler. The company got to decide what products you sold, whether you had the right to sell them, and even how many of each model to allocate to you. (Dealers have always loved to complain about the auto companies giving them too many slow-selling cars and too few fast-selling ones.) The company sent representatives to inspect your showroom and make sure it looked the way they wanted it to. The company decided how many miles away from your store to put your competitors. The company made you buy in advance the cars you wanted to sell, and if they didn't sell, that was your problem, not theirs. Usually the way you bought them was by taking out a loan from the company—so you were not just buying cars from the company, you were making interest payments to it too. The dealers' dependence on the corporation was especially extreme in GM's case: for decades it would allow each of its dealers to operate at only a single location.

In any relationship, economic or otherwise, it's rare for all the power to be on one side. The auto companies, even the mighty GM, needed the dealers almost as much as the dealers needed them. Peter Drucker reported in *Concept of the Corporation* that even as GM embodied all the principles of a modern bureaucracy, it had a special program to train the sons of dealers to take over for their fathers—something it would never do for its own executives—because that was what the dealer business was like. In the early days of Alfred Sloan's reign at GM, he set up a private railroad car, with an office and bedrooms, and traveled around the country, in the company of an entourage of other GM executives, to visit dealers. He remembered seeing five or ten dealers every day on these trips, sitting down with each one in the office the dealer used to close a customer so he could hear how things were going. The company brought the dealers to Detroit for annual presentations of the new models and took the dealers who sold the most cars to Las Vegas for weekends of golf and floor shows.

Yet the dealers did not passively wait to receive the tender mercies of GM and the other auto companies. They formed trade associations, nationally and in all fifty states, whose power came not just from their collective economic weight but also from the contributions the dealers made to their senators, congressmen, state legislators, mayors, and aldermen. Over the years, they succeeded in getting laws passed that banned anybody except auto dealers from selling new cars directly to the public—including the manufacturers, in case they ever changed their minds about not wanting to be in the retail end of the auto business. The picture of how the country worked then shouldn't be one of a handful of corporations simply dominating everything. Life is more complicated than that. It would be closer to accuracy to say that, radiating outward from the corporations, you'd find a series of other institutions: governments, unions, related businesses like suppliers and dealers, and not obviously related business that had something to do with cars, such as oil, insurance, retailing, and banking—all politically and economically organized, all in a constant managed tension with one another over what the rules of the game would be, each element always trying to gain an advantage over the others. Nothing existed entirely out of politics, institutional strength was rewarded, and the balance of power was constantly being adjusted.

General Motors was the number one corporation in America in those days. Number two was Standard Oil of New Jersey, the company John D. Rockefeller had founded, whose prosperity was closely tied to the success of the automobile because its best-known product was gasoline. Number three was U.S. Steel, Andrew Carnegie's company: same story, because a lot of steel went into making automobiles. Corporations like these were operating all over the country, but the Upper Midwest felt like the unofficial home region of the corporation-dominated institutional order. It was where the cars were made and the steel was milled, where unions were strongest, where the white-collar managerial culture felt most culturally dominant. If you were going to be an auto dealer, you could be anywhere, but there was a centrality, a perfectness of fit for dealers in the Midwest that no other place could quite match in those days. A leading example would be the Spitzer family, in northeast Ohio.

One day early in the second decade of the twentieth century Henry Ford was riding a train from New York to Detroit. The train stopped in the small town of Grafton, Ohio, twenty-five miles west of Cleveland, to take on water. Ford—who believed that the sort of country towns that the automobile was beginning to make obsolete were the repository of national virtue—got out, walked around, and decided he liked the look of the place. When he got back to Detroit, he instructed his sales executives to plant a dealership there. Someone from Ford went back to Grafton, found a hardware store owner named George Spitzer who had a sideline in renting horses and buggies to travelers, and recruited him. Spitzer Ford opened in 1914.

By the 1950s two of George Spitzer's sons, John and Delbert, were running the business, which had expanded into a small empire of dealerships, selling not just Fords but also Chryslers, Dodges, and Chevrolets. Cleveland was a booming blue-collar city in those days, and a lot of the Spitzers' customers were factory workers who lived on the east side of Cleveland or in nearby industrial towns; they manufactured cars or auto parts during the day and came in to one of the dealerships to buy them on weekends. The Spitzer brothers made a black-and-white film called *Ten Step Sales Procedure* to show their employees and whoever else cared to watch how they had become so successful.

John, eleven years older, with dark hair and glasses, was the sober, managerial Spitzer; Del, in a blond crew cut, was the peppy supersalesman. Through most of the film they role-play—John is usually the customer, Del the salesman—with such enthusiasm that they often lose track of which of the ten steps they're covering at that moment. "My name's Del Spitzer! What's yours?" Del says, bounding onto the showroom floor and greeting John with an outstretched hand. The fundamentals are just what they were in the horse-and-buggy days: First you walk the customer back outside the store and "qualify" him, meaning, ask him a few questions and look over his trade-in. Check the trunk, check the "headliner" above the windshield, just the way George Spitzer used to check a horse's teeth and shoes. Make him feel important, listened to. Find out a few things about him. Walk him back in, guide him to the right model. Take some time with it: show him the windows, the steering system, the seats, the running boards, the engine. Tell him about all the latest features. Have him sit in the backseat, then the driver's seat. Close him.

On the South Side of Chicago, the heart of the auto dealer culture was a three-mile stretch of Western Avenue, from Fifty-First Street down to Seventy-Ninth Street, at the edge of Chicago Lawn. This wasn't a part of town a tourist would ever see. It sat in the middle of an endless brown and gray expanse of working-class and lower-middle-class neighborhoods, miles from the glamorous Loop and the lakefront; the closest thing Chicago Lawn had to a tourist attraction was a shirtless two-story-high cigar store Indian set on the roof of a tobacco shop at Sixty-Third and Pulaski, his right hand raised in a salute. All up and down Western Avenue were new-car dealers, used-car dealers, parts stores, repair shops, and purveyors of auto loans. Pretty much the only reason somebody who didn't live nearby would come to Chicago Lawn was to buy or fix a car.

Chicago Lawn got its name from the University of Chicago's sociology department, which divided the city into seventy-seven "community areas" back in the 1920s, although in the years after the Second World War, nobody called it that (they do now). People who lived there would either say they were from Marquette Park or would just give the name of the nearest street corner to their house, or they would use the

name of their Catholic parish as geographical identification: St. Mary
Star of the Sea, St. Rita of Cascia, St. Nicholas of Tolentine, St. Clare
of Montefalco, Nativity of the Blessed Virgin Mary. There wasn't much
need for the neighborhood to have a name anyway, because so many
people there never left, so why would you need to explain where you
lived? Most women didn't have paid jobs, and most men, if they could
swing it, worked at one of the factories or stores in the neighborhood,
or they owned a shop and lived upstairs, or, better yet, they worked for
the City of Chicago or for Cook County (best of all, for both the city
and the county at the same time). There were people in Chicago Lawn
who worked at Midway Airport, just a few blocks away, but had never
been on an airplane, and people who could let a year slip by without ever
going to the Loop. People didn't leave to go to college; they didn't go to
college unless they were priests and went to seminary. Everything you
needed was in the neighborhood. Running perpendicular to the automobile row on Western Avenue was a commercial strip on Sixty-Third
Street, with shops, bakeries, taverns, restaurants, movie theaters, and
even a moderately glamorous nightclub, called Club El Bianco.

When immigrants arrived in Chicago from Europe, their first stop
was usually a tenement neighborhood close to the center of the city. A
place like Chicago Lawn was a big step up, achieved after a decade or
two of hard work. Moving there meant owning a home for the first time.
In those days, people thought of Chicago Lawn as an ethnically mixed
neighborhood; you might find Irish, Italian, Polish, and Lithuanian families all living on the same block, which was inconceivable in the old slum
districts. The houses were nearly identical one-story brick bungalows
set six feet apart, with three bedrooms, one bathroom, a front porch, a
patch of lawn, and maybe a finished basement. Children were likely to
go to one of the Catholic schools operated by the parishes, where most of
the teachers were nuns, tuition was fifty dollars a year or less, and there
might be fifty kids or more in a classroom. Chicago Lawn liked to call
itself the candy capital of the world: it was where Oreos, Lorna Doones,
Cracker Jacks, and Kool-Aid were made (also Dove Bars, which were invented by Amy D'Andrea's father, a Greek immigrant named Leo Stefanos, in the kitchen of his candy shop on Sixty-Third Street). The largest
employer in the neighborhood was a vast Nabisco factory at Seventy-
Third and Kedzie, which employed two thousand people. Second larg-

est was Holy Cross Hospital, operated by the Sisters of St. Casimir, an order of Lithuanian nuns who also ran Maria High School for girls, which opened in 1952 and soon had fourteen hundred students.

It would be possible, but misleading, to see Chicago Lawn as an exemplar of the kind of small-bore civic life that observers of American society have been writing about since at least the days of Alexis de Tocqueville in the early nineteenth century. It was true that the neighborhood was all about personal connections; even at a place like the Nabisco factory, the best way to get a job was to know somebody who already worked there—a neighbor, a fellow parishioner, or, better yet, a relative. People belonged to church groups and Little League teams, they knew their neighbors, they had block parties. Yet to leave it at that misses the context. The churches were connected to the archdiocese and from there to the Vatican. Employers like Nabisco and American Can and the big Sears store at Sixty-Second and Western, not to mention the new-car dealerships, were outposts of the corporate economy. The labor unions so many people in Chicago belonged to were national organizations, which had become far more powerful since the 1930s because national labor laws had put wind in their sails. The precinct and ward politics essential to maintaining order and employment in the neighborhood were part of the Chicago machine, which was part of the national Democratic Party. As much as the culture of Chicago Lawn was intensely provincial and based on personal, family, and ethnic ties, it worked because it was connected to the big organizations that dominated American culture. Chicago Lawn had been cut in on the deal. (The black neighborhoods immediately to the east of Chicago Lawn had not.) That was one reason why people there—not far below whatever surface cynicism about big shots they chose to display—gave large, distant institutions, and authority generally, an automatic respect.

Those small, fantastically well-tended houses that were the center of every family's life in Chicago Lawn—was it true, or just a persistent myth, that some people cut their front lawns blade by blade, with a pair of scissors?—were always mortgaged, and the mortgages usually came from Talman Federal Savings. Ben Bohac, a Slovakian guy from the neighborhood, had founded Talman in 1922 in his living room. In 1957 he opened a grand block-long building at Fifty-Fifth and Kedzie that was the largest savings and loan office in the country. On Fridays after they got paid, people would go to Talman to make deposits. Alan Ehrenhalt, in his book *The Lost City*, described the scene: "Friday night in Talman was a social occasion. It was always crowded . . . There were long rows of couches all over the enormous lobby, and nearly all of the seats were occupied by people who had stopped to talk." Four times a year, Ehrenhalt reported, people would come in to Talman to have the quarterly interest payments on their savings accounts written down in their passbooks, and for these occasions Bohac would hire musicians to play in the lobby. The money Talman took in as savings from Chicago Lawn's residents was loaned out to them as home mortgages; the contrapuntal ritual to making your weekly deposit was faithfully bringing in the monthly payment on your $10,000 or $15,000 thirty-year mortgage.

This was another example of an intensely local system that took place in a not immediately visible larger context. During the period following the breakdown of the financial system that was the first crisis Franklin Roosevelt confronted as president, the federal government had created several institutions that made it possible for ordinary Americans to feel safe about putting their money into savings and loans, and for the savings and loans to feel safe issuing mortgages to them: the Federal Housing Administration, the Federal Savings and Loan Insurance Corporation, and the Federal National Mortgage Association. The government set the interest rate on passbook savings accounts, keeping it high enough to appeal to depositors and low enough to enable Talman to be profitable. (And the only reason Talman attracted deposits at all is that the government would let only savings and loans, not banks, pay interest on small customers' deposits.) After the war, the government also began guaranteeing mortgage loans to veterans. The Illinois legislature, intensely suspicious of banks because of their misdeeds during the early years of the Depression, made it illegal for any financial institution in the state to operate in more than one location, which meant that non-local banks were banned from Chicago Lawn and local ones had a captive market. All this made the glory days of Talman Savings possible.

The row of auto dealers on Western Avenue formed the eastern border of Chicago Lawn. The next neighborhood to the east was West Englewood, and the one to the east of that was Englewood. These neighborhoods were in the path of the swelling population and rising material aspirations of black Chicagoans, who, during those peak years of the

Great Migration from the South, had traditionally been confined to a narrow quadrant on the South Side. Englewood was 11 percent black in 1950, 69 percent black in 1960, and 96 percent black in 1970. West Englewood was essentially all white in 1950, 12 percent black in 1970, and 48 percent black in 1980. These were far from orderly changes. Unscrupulous Realtors flooded the neighborhoods. First they'd tell white residents that they'd better sell fast, before their houses became completely worthless. Having scooped up houses for a fraction of what they were worth, the Realtors sold them at much higher prices to unsophisticated first-time black homeowners "on contract"—meaning that the buyers could be loaded down with a variety of cockamamy fees and charges and then evicted if they didn't keep up. Then the houses wound up at best deteriorated and at worst abandoned.

Chicago Lawn in the 1950s and 1960s was all-consumingly aware that it was next in line. Its residents, when they arrived, had identified themselves with the European country their families had come from, but the proximity of black people now made them white—militantly so. It was well known in black Chicago that you'd better not venture west of Western Avenue, especially after dark. Whatever else was in their hearts and minds about race, for whites in Chicago Lawn there was first a brutal real estate calculus: the most valuable asset most of them had, often their only valuable asset and one they could barely afford, was their house, and if what had happened in Englewood and West Englewood happened in Chicago Lawn, it could become worthless almost overnight. Then what would they do? Where would they go?

Dennis Hart was born in 1950 in West Englewood. His parents were Irish; West Englewood, where they moved from Bridgeport after the war, was supposed to be where they made it to the middle class, or at least the lower middle class. Getting there was a big stretch. Dennis's father had just a seventh-grade education, having been kicked out of his school, on the grounds of guilt by family association, when one of his brothers was found there carrying a gun. At thirteen, Dennis was working full-time in the Chicago stockyards. By his forties, he was holding down two full-time jobs, one as a teamster working on a loading dock and one as a liquor control board inspector for the state of Illinois. And he was running a small delivery dispatching business out of his house on weekends. And he had to deliver his precinct for the machine, lest he lose his job with the state and maybe the one with the Teamsters too. And he'd had three heart attacks.

When blacks began moving to the neighborhood, Dennis's father was dead set against leaving—until his wife was held up one Tuesday evening on the grounds of St. Raphael Church. They sold their house, supposedly worth $16,000 in 1962, for $5,700 in 1963, and bought a bungalow at Fifty-Ninth and Talman, in Chicago Lawn, for $18,300. In 1966 Dennis's father, who'd almost never been outside the South Side of Chicago and was obsessively afraid that he'd lose everything he had, insisted on going to Martin Luther King's march in Marquette Park to let the marchers know they weren't welcome. Dennis's mother insisted that Dennis go too, to make sure his father didn't get so overwrought that he'd have another heart attack. Dennis performed the same filial duty at another of King's activities, a protest outside the office of a Realtor who wouldn't show apartments to black families, and at a speech in Marquette Park by George Lincoln Rockwell, the head of the American Nazi Party. The next year, his father died of his fourth heart attack.

■

Chicago Lawn was a distant outpost of a social order devised and controlled by people far away: corporate managers, politicians, bureaucrats, intellectuals. They imagined a tight, orderly, top-down system that balanced the powers of the major elements of the country for everyone's benefit. When they miscalculated, as in the case of their failure to notice that race was a major issue in American life, they didn't suffer the consequences, but people on the South Side of Chicago did. And when those in power underestimated the latent power of a potentially serious enemy of the system over which they presided, they didn't prepare defenses. That was the case with the supposedly quiescent financial system.

To the minds of the celebrators of the postwar apotheosis of big institutions, the United States had developed, at least in theory and maybe in practice, a new and distinctive form of capitalism—distinctive because capital, formerly the star attraction in the account of every thinker from Adam Smith to Karl Marx, was now a bit player. The corporation and its corps of salaried managers, people who were happy to extol capitalism in after-dinner speeches but didn't own more than trivial amounts of capital themselves, were now in the lead role. But if one were to go searching for actual capitalists in postwar America—if, let's say, General Motors or one of the other great industrial corporations felt the need to issue stocks or bonds and sell them to the public in order to build new factories or develop new products—the search would lead first to 2 Wall Street in New York City, where Morgan Stanley, the country's leading investment banking firm, had its office. In 1953, for example, Morgan Stanley created and sold $300 million in bonds—the largest corporation bond issue since the Depression—to finance the development of a new V-8 engine for the giant-size GM cars that the American public wanted to drive in those days. Less dramatically, Morgan Stanley was constantly creating small bond issues for the General Motors Acceptance Corporation, GM's car loan division, so that GMAC could use the proceeds to help customers finance their new cars.

Morgan Stanley was the love child—though *love* probably isn't *le mot juste*—of two of the great figures of the twentieth century: J. P. Morgan and Franklin Roosevelt. Morgan was the dominant financier of the Industrial Age, so much so that he functioned as a de facto central bank before the Federal Reserve existed. During the devastating financial panic of 1907, it was Morgan, not the government, who convened the leading bankers and industrialists and made the arrangements necessary to keep the economy functioning—extracting along the way a promise from President Theodore Roosevelt that he would exempt U.S. Steel, in which Morgan's bank was a major stockholder, from the antitrust laws. Morgan's power generated enemies. In 1912 a Louisiana congressman named Arsène Pujo held sensational hearings on the "money trust," which found that Morgan was its controlling member (Morgan and his partners together sat on the boards of seventy-two corporations). Louis Brandeis's book *Other People's Money and How the Bankers Use It* was based primarily on evidence unearthed by Pujo. Not long after enduring the indignity of testifying before Pujo's subcommittee, Morgan died. Beginning in 1932, during the time Franklin Roosevelt was running for president, there was another riveting congressional investigation into the misdeeds of financiers—called the Pecora hearings, after the investigation's counsel and chief inquisitor—during which the lengthy testimony by Morgan's son and heir, J. P. Morgan, Jr., made him into the main public villain. These hearings—along with the Depression,

Roosevelt's political skill, and the ideas that Adolf Berle and other advisers to Roosevelt had been working up for years—prepared the ground for the new banking laws that sailed through Congress at the outset of the New Deal.

The passage of the Glass-Steagall Act, which forbade banks that accepted deposits from underwriting stocks and bonds, forced the Morgan bank, previously private, nearly unregulated, and active in all forms of finance, to make a choice about its future. It chose to keep banking and stop underwriting. That was in 1934. In 1935 a small group of Morgan partners announced that they would move one block east on Wall Street and form the firm of Morgan Stanley to go into the underwriting business. The name of the new firm came from Henry Morgan, the thirty-five-year-old son of J. P. Morgan, Jr., and Harold Stanley, its chief executive, formerly a J. P. Morgan partner. In every way, Morgan Stanley wanted the world to know that, Glass-Steagall or no Glass-Steagall, it was as closely connected to the Morgan bank as it was possible to be. The announcement of its founding was at the J.P. Morgan office at 23 Wall Street; all its partners had come from J.P. Morgan; J.P. Morgan provided its start-up capital; and Morgan Stanley's clients were long-standing customers of the bank. In 1936, its first full year of operation, Morgan Stanley, with only twenty employees, created $1.1 billion in new offerings, which represented about a quarter of the entire American investment banking market.

Morgan Stanley's partners were used to banking as a completely private and unimpeded activity, and now they had to live with congressional investigations and a new federal regulatory agency, the Securities and Exchange Commission. The older partners had begun their careers when there was no income tax or Federal Reserve. From the vantage point of the twenty-first century, though, what's striking is not how much Morgan bankers' world had changed by the 1930s, but how little. The bankers themselves were formal men who came to work in three-piece suits and fedoras and sat at rolltop desks, whose idea of their defining quality was not intelligence or aggressiveness or cunning, but a gentlemanly integrity and discretion. J. P. Morgan, Jr., when he was preparing to testify at the Pecora hearings in Washington, wrote out a handwritten statement that said, "If I may be permitted to speak of the firm of which I have the honor to be the senior partner, I should state that at all times the idea of doing only first-class business, and that in a first-class way, has been before our minds." Morgan Stanley partners lived on the East Side of Manhattan or in the older and wealthier New York suburbs. They had lunch at their clubs. They were yachtsmen and golfers and fly fishermen. They had country houses in Palm Beach or Southampton or on the Maine coast. They considered themselves to be, as a group, what we would now call diverse and meritocratic, but that meant that a few of them had grown up in only moderately wealthy families; of course they were all white Protestant men who had gone to boarding schools and Ivy League colleges.

Because of the original J.P. Morgan's role in creating so many of the country's largest corporations, Morgan Stanley's clients were the great names of industrial America: General Motors and AT&T, U.S. Steel and Standard Oil of New Jersey, DuPont and General Electric. Morgan Stanley also worked for many local utility and telephone companies, for governments in the United States and abroad, and for globe-spanning institutions like the World Bank. The means by which a firm with only one office, a handful of partners, and a few million dollars of its own—capital the partners had put into the firm—could occupy such a dominant position in supplying capital to these giants was through a device called the syndicate system. If a corporation like General Motors needed capital, its treasurer and its comptroller would have a talk with the Morgan Stanley partner assigned to them. Although Morgan Stanley was small and General Motors was enormous, the treasurer and comptroller at GM were not especially high-ranking in the company, and they usually didn't come from the same kind of fancy background as the partners at Morgan Stanley, so the social deference went from the corporation to the bank, not the other way around.

The Morgan Stanley man would return to 2 Wall Street and discuss the new issue with his partners: Stocks or bonds? How many shares? How much per share? Every Morgan Stanley partner, in those days, had to offer an opinion on every new issue. Once the nature and price of the financial product was settled, Morgan Stanley—along with its equally blue-blooded law firm, Davis Polk—would approach the Securities and Exchange Commission to seek the government's approval to sell it. Although, officially, bankers don't like government regulators, this requirement had distinct advantages for Morgan Stanley. The men at the SEC

were usually just as deferential as the corporate treasurer and comptroller, and the approval process protected Morgan Stanley from competition: no other banking firm could try to become the underwriter of that
issue because the SEC could review only one firm's request at a time.
The process was so leisurely that whenever the government of Australia,
a client of the firm, wanted to issue bonds, a Morgan Stanley partner
would travel there and back by ship, which took weeks, and then file the
application with the SEC, which took more weeks, knowing that nothing could happen in all that time that might sour the bond issue.

　　As the day of SEC approval drew near, Morgan Stanley would begin to contact lesser investment houses and parcel out portions of the
new issue to them to sell to their customers. First there was the "bulge
bracket" of three other firms that would get the largest portions: Kuhn
Loeb, First Boston, and Dillon Read. Then came lesser New York firms
like Merrill Lynch and Goldman Sachs. Then the first regional bracket,
family-run investment banks in cities around the country. Then the
second regional bracket. General Motors would pay Morgan Stanley a
fee, and Morgan Stanley would keep the largest portion of the fee for
itself and apportion the rest to the other firms in the syndicate. The syndicate often had more than a hundred member firms, each of which had
committed to selling a share of the new issue. That meant that Morgan
Stanley was able to manage the issue and collect its fee without having
to own and then sell any of the stocks or bonds itself, unless it wanted
to keep a block and sell it to a few choice clients. That was how it could
get away with having no sales force, no trading desk, and very little firm
capital. It made money from the seigneurial position that its privileged
relationships with the royalty of corporate America engendered. At the
end of the process, an inscrutable all-type "tombstone ad" would appear
in *The Wall Street Journal* containing the rank-ordered names of all the
firms in the syndicate, with Morgan Stanley gloriously alone at the top.
Partners would keep miniature versions of the tombstone ads, encased
in Lucite, on their desks as mementos.

　　In 1947, in what turned out to be one of the last great campaigns by
the Brandeis tendency in American liberalism, the Department of Justice filed an antitrust suit—*United States of America v. Henry S. Morgan,
Harold Stanley, et al.*—that aimed to end the syndicate system. Morgan
Stanley, first on a list of seventeen defendants, was the primary tar-

get. The government's main witness was a Chicago investment banker named Harold Stuart, who was so upset about having been excluded from the syndicate Morgan Stanley had created for a utility company bond offering that he was willing to break ranks. As the Justice Department's lawsuit had it, Morgan Stanley and the others had devised the syndicate system back in 1915 to underwrite bonds to finance the British and French military campaigns in the First World War, and they had operated it ever since as a conspiracy that prevented true competition in investment banking. The Justice Department wanted to replace the syndicate system with sealed bids, so that if an investment bank wanted a corporation's business, it would have to commit to a price in advance, and other banks would be able to submit lower bids and get the business. This would be a disaster for Morgan Stanley: not only would it lose its primary position in investment banking, but it would also, if it won a bid, have to purchase the entire stock or bond issue up front and then resell it, and it didn't have that kind of money.

The suit landed in the court of Harold Medina, a federal judge in New York City, and it led to one of the longest trials in American history. The pretrial hearings lasted for three years; the trial itself took up 309 courtroom days, beginning in 1950 and ending in 1953, and produced more than a hundred thousand pages of documents. Medina even made a field trip, accompanied by lawyers for both sides, to Harold Stuart's office in Chicago to see firsthand how the investment banking business worked. In 1954 Medina issued a 425-page opinion that was a dyspeptic, sarcastic rebuke to the government and an almost awestruck encomium to Morgan Stanley and its way of doing business. There was no investment banking conspiracy, Medina declared. How could there be, when the business was controlled by the corporations that issued stocks and bonds, not by the banks? It was high time that "the myth of domination and control of issuers by investment bankers . . . be given a decent burial and quietly laid to rest."

Medina was especially impressed with the "absolute integrity" of Harold Stanley, who had testified at length. He had concluded, he wrote, that if Stanley said something, it could be trusted simply because it had come from him. And Stanley had insisted that if Morgan Stanley did not compete for clients with other firms in the way the Department of Justice had in mind, it was only because the firm's clients believed that "if the business is satisfactorily done, it would be fair enough to think that the fellow who has it should keep on with it." Presumably the other firms on Wall Street felt the same way about Morgan Stanley's relationships with its clients, and that was why they did not try to compete with Morgan Stanley either. (It was inconceivable in those days that someone from another banking firm would presume to enter the building in New York where the treasurer of General Motors worked and ask for GM's business.) Medina was fully persuaded: "I am told that Morgan Stanley is the ringleader of the conspiracy and Stanley its 'master mind.' It may perhaps be more reasonable to infer that the absence of any such dealings by Morgan Stanley had much to do with its reputation for integrity and for its success."

Medina's decision meant that the syndicate system and Morgan Stanley's place in it, and therefore the firm's manner of doing business— genteel, but in a way that worked powerfully to its advantage—were safe. Well into the 1970s, when a young banker at Morgan Stanley was elected to the partnership, the news was delivered in person by the aging Henry Morgan, who still came in most days for lunch, often taking a seaplane to lower Manhattan from his estate in the section of the North Shore of Long Island where *The Great Gatsby* was set. Morgan Stanley legend has it that in 1970, when Morgan called in Richard Fisher, who later became head of the firm, to tell him that he had made partner and could now buy his ownership share, Fisher, a salesman's son, confessed that he didn't have the money. Morgan, in turn, confessed that Morgan Stanley had never before elected a partner who didn't have family money—but he'd solve the problem by making a personal loan.

All through the rest of the 1950s and beyond, it was common for people to say that the head of the syndicate department at Morgan Stanley was the most powerful man on Wall Street. Morgan Stanley partners had three push buttons built into their desks, communication shortcuts to the three people they needed to be in touch with several times every day. The buttons read BOY (for the office boy), SEC (for their secretary), and SYND (for the syndicate department). In the 1970s and 1980s, the head of the syndicate department was white-haired Frederick Whittemore, scion of a family that had come to America on the *Mayflower*, whose nickname in the financial world was "Father Fred" because of the paternal authority over the other investment banks in the country that his job gave him. Patricia Beard, the author of the only full-length book about Morgan Stanley, and Whittemore's niece, described him this way: "A dry raconteur with a New England accent and a gravelly voice, Whittemore had a way of peering over his glasses, leaning back with one arm over the chair next to him, staring down his quarry, then leaning forward again, steepling his hands and tapping his fingers together, asking the provocative question." People were afraid of him, or at least afraid of crossing him, because he had the power to decide which firms got how much of every stock and bond issue led by Morgan Stanley. For every issue, he kept a card for each firm in the syndicate, which noted how much of the issue it got and how efficiently it had sold its allocation. Firms that won Whittemore's favor got more. Firms that didn't meet his standard or pestered him too insistently for a bigger allocation got less the next time around—and if they went further and crossed some invisible line, after which his displeasure was irreversible, they could get nothing.

The social critics who portrayed the corporation as all-powerful in the American economy were thinking about industrial companies, not banks or financial companies. Finance had been a principal target of liberal reformers during the period between, say, the Pujo hearings in 1912 and the Pecora hearings in 1932, but the work Adolf Berle and his colleagues had done at the outset of the New Deal had constrained banks so severely that for decades there were no financial companies on the scale of the major industrial corporations. The world over which Morgan Stanley presided was a limited one. In 1960 the total value of the new issues the firm handled was less than the total in 1935, its first full year in business. In 1970 Morgan Stanley had only 230 employees—and General Motors had more than 500,000. Entering students at Harvard Business School were required to read Alfred Sloan's memoir, *My Years with General Motors*, the summer before they arrived, on the assumption that after they graduated they would go to work in management at an industrial corporation. (In those days, Harvard Business School's course on investing was nicknamed "Darkness at Noon"; so few people wanted to take it that it was offered in a basement room at lunchtime.) In 1973, two years after Berle died, secure in the belief that his theory of the separation of ownership and control in the age of the modern corporation was eternal truth, John Kenneth

Galbraith published the last of his big books on the economy, *Economics and the Public Purpose.* He reported that Berle had actually understated the phenomenon he had discovered back in the 1920s: by now, management, not stockholders, controlled 169 of the 200 largest corporations, which, in turn, controlled most of the economic life of the country. These corporations together comprised what Galbraith called a "planning system" that could be further loaded up with social obligations by government because it was impervious to competition, price-cutting, customer dissatisfaction, antitrust attacks, and, most of all, its own supposed owners, who were entirely passive.

Someone sitting at Fred Whittemore's side as he was assembling a syndicate would not have seen anything to contradict this picture. Morgan Stanley would typically keep a portion of each new stock or bond issue and then sell it in a few big blocks to the kinds of capital pools that a partner in the firm could call from his desk: life insurance companies, private offices managing family fortunes, bank trust departments, university endowments. Morgan Stanley announced what the price of the issue was, and the buyer paid it; it was a pure case of the corporation, through Morgan Stanley, giving orders to capital, rather than capital giving orders to the corporation. Smaller versions of this scene cascaded downward through the syndicate. Local investment banks sold their stock allocations to local families and the trust departments of local commercial banks. Stockbrokers called their clients and sold their allocations. The sellers set the price and the buyers accepted it. Everyone in the syndicate made money by taking a generous percentage commission on sales, at a rate set by the Securities and Exchange Commission. People who bought bonds generally held them for years, until they matured. People who bought stocks could trade them on an exchange, but often chose not to.

Wall Street was at the other end of American society from Chicago Lawn, but like Chicago Lawn, it wasn't quite as self-contained and particular a little world as it appeared to be. It operated the way it did only because it lived inside the intricately constructed and balanced social, economic, and political ecosystem that was created in the early days of the New Deal. In any ecosystem, if one element becomes much stronger or much weaker, the balance is upset and the whole system is at risk. American capitalism, forty years after Franklin Roosevelt took office, depended not just on the size and power of the corporation and on its cold peace with the federal government, but also on the passivity of capital. And in turn, the system's ability to deliver a good life to ordinary people—at least the ones lucky enough to have positioned themselves within the system's capacious reach—also depended on the passivity of capital, because the invulnerable corporation was supposed to supply Americans with the rudiments of prosperity and security.

Adolf Berle's idea that the distinctive aspect of American capitalism was the absence of capital as a power player—in shorthand, the idea that AT&T had hundreds of thousands of small shareholders whom its executives could safely ignore—may always have been a little exaggerated. Berle liked to make grand claims. Now, as the success of the postwar American economy manifested itself in growing prosperity, Berle's picture was beginning to change, because large new accumulations of capital were beginning to appear. Pension funds and mutual funds, holding the assets of people who worked for wages and salaries, had gone from negligible during the Depression and the Second World War to holding hundreds of billions of dollars by the 1970s. These funds had managers who invested in the markets—so the control of stock in corporations wasn't so widely dispersed anymore. There is an enormous difference between a middle-class family that owns a few shares of stock—the key to Berle's model—and a fund manager, representing the collective assets of many thousands of middle-class families, who invests a large amount of capital and has a duty to try to make it grow. These managers were a new species in the ecosystem.

Peter Drucker, by now a famous man, considered to be the world's leading expert on managing the corporation, published a book in 1976 called *The Unseen Revolution*, in which he announced, with typical flair, that the United States was the first truly socialist country in world history. That was because the workers now owned the means of production through their union and company pension funds' new role in the stock and bond markets. Drucker's adopted country, he wrote, had actually achieved what "all the Marxist church fathers, saints, and apostles before Lenin had been preaching and promising, from Engels to Bebel and Kautsky, from Viktor Adler to Rosa Luxemburg, Jaures, and Eugene Debs." And who was responsible for this achievement? Drucker's old friend Charles Wilson of General Motors, through the 1950 contract with the United Auto Workers, which had been widely copied by other corporations. Drucker reported that two thousand company pension plans had been created in the hundred years preceding the Treaty of Detroit—and eight thousand in just one year afterward. Now, in the 1970s, pension funds controlled about $200 billion in assets and owned almost a third of the shares on the public stock markets. This represented "a bigger shift in ownership than any that had occurred since the end of feudalism."

You might think Drucker would see a change of this proportion as a threat to the serene and eternal dominance of the corporation in American society—but he didn't. Adolf Berle's theory, he wrote, still held true, because "the pension funds are not 'owners,' they are investors. They do not want 'control'; indeed, they are disqualified from exercising it." The funds, Drucker believed, were legally required to invest conservatively, and they had no interest in monitoring the performance of a corporation's management. As for the workers and managers whose assets were in pension funds, they thought of ownership only in terms of their houses, cars, and television sets, not of the holdings of their pension funds. As long as corporations kept feeding their profits into the pension funds, this bargain would prevail, and their executives could continue to ignore their shareholders. The United States would remain "a society in which the performance of all major social tasks is entrusted to large institutions."

One person who would have disagreed with Drucker, more on the basis of instinct and firsthand experience in the markets than of a sweeping command of intellectual history, was Robert Hayes Burns Baldwin, who in 1973 became the head of Morgan Stanley. Baldwin was a tall, thin, theatrically hard-driving man who thought of himself as not the Morgan Stanley type, although he was a product of Exeter, Princeton, and the U.S. Navy. He was more aggressive, tougher, less gentlemanly than the older partners; he would call in his own children for periodic performance reviews. Lewis Bernard, who in 1963 became the first Jewish banker hired by Morgan Stanley—a milestone made possible by his having been roommates at Princeton with the son of Frank Petito, the head of the firm's investment banking department—was, as a new hire, required to write a memo after six months at the firm and to deposit a copy on the desk of each partner. He quickly got a note back: "RHBB wants to see you immediately!" In his office, Baldwin held the memo in his hands and asked Bernard whether he had written it. Yes, sir, Bernard said. Well, Baldwin said, I have to tell you that I opposed your being hired here, because I reviewed your college transcript and I didn't approve of the courses you had taken. But now I see that I was wrong. That was about as close to offering praise as Baldwin ever got.

In 1965, frustrated with the pervasive traditionalism of Morgan Stanley, Baldwin left to become undersecretary of the navy. He returned to the firm two years later and began, with the help of some of the younger partners, pushing his way into a leadership position. He wanted to change practically everything about Morgan Stanley, but all the changes he had in mind proceeded from one big idea. Up to that point, the firm had seen itself as serving the users of capital—General Motors, AT&T, and its other corporation clients—and had felt safe in ignoring the needs of the providers of capital, the people who bought the corporations' stock and bond issues. Whatever Morgan Stanley offered on behalf of the users of capital, the providers of capital would meekly buy, at the price Morgan Stanley had set. But now Baldwin could see that because of the rise of the pension funds, mutual funds, and other institutional investors, the providers of capital were going to become more powerful, less passive. They were going to make demands, about pricing, timing, information, and even the behavior of corporation management, as a condition of committing their capital—in other words, the providers of capital were going to begin acting like textbook capitalists, as they hadn't for four decades. Other firms on Wall Street were already beginning to meet these demands. It was time for Morgan Stanley to start too.

3

TRANSACTION MAN

A brightly lit, windowless, carpeted function room in a resort hotel in Bermuda, done up in shades of white, beige, and gold that are meant to convey a kind of business-world elegance that would mitigate the resort setting. A couple hundred people with name tags around their necks (first names only), sitting in rows, facing a stage. In the back of the room, technicians manning a bank of consoles that control the sound system and the slide projector—appurtenances of the kind of seminar that people pay a serious price to attend. Onstage is a tall, thin, needle-nosed man with rimless glasses and curly gray-brown hair, wearing a wireless microphone that lets him pace back and forth while he speaks. He has a plain, flat midwestern voice. He says his name is Mike. He's happy—so happy that he needs to share the story of how he got that way.

Mike wants to talk about Wall Street. "That's where I lived for a long time," he says. "I was involved in reorganizing the financial industry. I didn't have a title, but nobody with a title could do it, so a bunch of us young guys did. I spent thirty years in finance." He pauses, dips his chin, looks across the audience, and then delivers the punch: "It's staggeringly bad! Banks: lying, cheating, stealing. The day is coming when people are going to jail. Close to no senior executive has been put in jail yet. That's a crime! I'm sickened by it."

The heart of the problem, Mike says, is lack of integrity; integrity is the most important thing in life. "The most wonderful things happen if you have integrity," he says. "I was incomplete as a human being. Was I successful? Sure I was successful. But I was incomplete." Now, as he hardly needs to say because it's so clear from looking at him, he is the contented, fulfilled, at-peace guy you see before you, and it's all because of integrity. He goes on: "Your life will keep improving as long as you keep putting integrity in your life. Who you are as a person is nothing more than your word. Nothing more."

Mike is Michael C. Jensen, one of the most influential economists of the late twentieth century. The seminar where he's speaking, which lasts for nine days, is called "Being a Leader and the Effective Exercise of Leadership: An Ontological/Phenomenological Model." The star attraction, and the reason the life coaches, executive trainers, and wellness consultants who make up most of the audience have enrolled in the course—many of them for the second or third time—is Werner Erhard, who back in the days when Jensen was involved with Wall Street was America's best-known self-help guru, capable of filling arenas with thousands of people who hoped that his Erhard Seminars Training—marketed in lowercase as est—would empower them and heal their wounds. Many twists and turns later, Erhard is still around, living in quasi-exile in the Cayman Islands and flying across the world offering seminars in Dubai, Abu Dhabi, Singapore, Cancún, and other far-flung locales. Jensen is his intellectual partner and, often, the opening act at the seminars; together they are the authors of a thousand-slide PowerPoint presentation that contains the vast, hard-won wisdom of both their lifetimes—a peculiar blend of philosophy, management theory, neurobiology, linguistics, psychology, and homespun homilies that they say has the power to transform anyone's life and work.

This is where Mike Jensen has ended up. Where he started was in a blue-collar, devoutly Catholic family in Minneapolis. His father was a linotype operator at the local daily newspaper and a loyal member of the oldest labor union in the United States, the International Typographical Union, founded in 1852. Jensen's father worked hard (in addition to his job at the newspaper, he drove a taxi), drank hard, and gambled hard, so the Jensens were always close to broke. The idea that there might be some other way of life for anybody in the family seemed fanciful. Mike

Jensen assumed that he would be a linotype operator too; his father's father had been a printer in a small country town in Minnesota, and his father had learned the same trade and done considerably better in a city in the years after the Second World War. Maybe, Jensen thought, if he went into the family trade, he might do just a little better too. He graduated from a vocational high school and made no plans to go to college. But one of his teachers, without telling him, had called a local college, Macalester, and recommended Jensen as a promising potential student. Over the summer, a Macalester recruiter called Jensen and asked him if he might be interested in coming there. Jensen had never heard of Macalester, so the recruiter had to do some explaining first, and then he had to make an argument about why going to college might be a good idea.

What are you interested in? the recruiter asked. Jensen thought for a minute. What was on his mind was whether there might be some way for him to make more money than his father made. A phrase popped into his head: the stock market. Do you teach that? Yes, we do, the recruiter said. It's called economics. So Jensen enrolled. He worked his way through Macalester in five years by joining the ITU and operating a linotype machine at the newspaper when he wasn't in class. When he was approaching graduation, the chairman of the Macalester economics department called the business school at the University of Chicago and arranged for him to get a fellowship there; he enrolled and switched after a year to a Ph.D. program in economics. So now he was in graduate school, taking classes by day, working the late shift in the *Chicago Tribune's* composing room at night.

Coming to the University of Chicago in 1962 was about as propitious for Jensen as going to work on Wall Street in the 1920s had been for Adolf Berle. Just as Berle had been able to observe firsthand the advent of the modern corporation, Jensen too was in on the start of something big. Chicago had become the intellectual home of the idea that markets, not the state, were the proper and most benign central institution of postwar society—and that the core ideas of the New Deal, which it seemed that everyone, even Republicans, had finally accepted, were wrong. Friedrich Hayek had moved to the university from the London School of Economics in 1950. A few years earlier, Milton Friedman, the conservative economist, had joined the Chicago economics department, and Friedman's brother-in-law, Aaron Director, had become a professor at the university's law school. Friedman and Director were both protégés of Hayek's, deeply influenced by him; Director had arranged for Hayek's appointment in Chicago. Friedman and Hayek were among the founders, in 1947, of the Mont Pelerin Society, which convened market-oriented intellectuals every summer in Switzerland.

Michael Jensen was conservative in an almost automatic way—in the sense that he deeply mistrusted the idea that government could improve social conditions—but political ideology wasn't his professional interest. What he was interested in was the stock market, and that was another Chicago specialty. In 1932 a newspaper heir named Alfred Cowles had founded an economic research institute in Colorado, and in 1939 he had relocated it to the University of Chicago. The institute was especially interested in funding statistical research into the way the economy, including the financial markets, behaved. In 1960, just before Jensen arrived, the university established the Center for Research in Security Prices, which kept data on stock prices going back to 1926. Even in the early 1960s, economics was still in the beginning stages of adopting advanced statistical techniques, which the profession had rarely used before the war. Gardiner Means, the economist Berle had recruited to do the supposedly technical calculations for *The Modern Corporation and Private Property*, was really just adding together numbers about the size and ownership of individual companies; there are no equations in the book. Now, at the University of Chicago, one of the ideas in the air was that, finally, it was going to become possible to study not just the economy as a whole but the financial markets in particular in a rigorous, disciplined, quantitative way.

In Adolf Berle's model of how the markets worked, millions of small individual purchasers of stocks and bonds simply held on to them as a form of savings, collecting dividends from the stocks and waiting for the bonds to mature. In Morgan Stanley's model, its partners, pretty much by instinct, set the prices of the stocks and bonds they issued, and the members of the syndicates the firm assembled gratefully bought the new issues up at whatever the price was. And all those bank trust department officers, local stockbrokers, pension and endowment administrators, and life insurance company asset managers who bought larger blocks of stocks and bonds were making their judgments about what to buy or sell based on their judgments about the prospects of the company that was issuing the stocks or bonds, along with how much they trusted the investment bankers selling the securities to them. To the extent that there was any real theory that a sophisticated investor could use, it was the one Benjamin Graham and David Dodd had used in their book *Security Analysis*, first published in the 1930s, which emphasized making detailed comparisons between individual companies' stock prices and the companies' actual financial condition, and then looking for bargains. (It wasn't until the 1962 edition of the book that Graham produced a simple one-line algebraic formula to express his technique.) The more advanced managers of stock funds—including Graham and Dodd's most famous protégé, Warren Buffett—used their method.

But what if everybody was wrong? What if one could invest even more successfully by ignoring specific information about how individual companies were managed and, instead, treating the markets as what they literally were: vast, constantly changing sets of transactions, which would yield their secrets only to complicated, purely mathematical analysis? The Cowles Commission for Research in Economics at Chicago was a center for this kind of thinking. The first breakthrough paper, published in 1952, was by a young Chicago Ph.D. student named Harry Markowitz, who had studied at the Cowles Commission. It demonstrated that the overall riskiness of a stock portfolio depended on how much the portfolio's stocks moved up and down in the markets in relation to one another: the more closely attuned to one another they were, the riskier the portfolio would be. One could simplify this into the idea that one should build a diversified portfolio, but truly applying Markowitz's model required an enormously complicated series of calculations based on equations he had devised; one had to figure out how related the movement of every stock in a portfolio was to the movement of every other stock. Peter Bernstein, in his book *Capital Ideas*, estimated that a portfolio of two thousand holdings would require more than two million separate calculations. Computers at the time were not powerful enough to do this quickly; most economists still used slide rules. So Markowitz's theory—which Bernstein calls "a landmark in the history of ideas"—was, for the moment, not used.

In the early 1960s William Sharpe, an admiring protégé of Markowitz's (Bernstein quotes him as saying, "Markowitz came along, and there was light"), figured out a way to simplify the application of Markowitz's model by measuring the movement of each stock in a portfolio against the movement of the stock market as a whole, rather than against every other stock in the portfolio. That cut the computing time for a portfolio of one hundred stocks from thirty-three minutes to thirty seconds and brought these ideas into much closer range of the real world of investing. Sharpe also invented a statistical formula for setting the price of a new stock or bond issue by comparing it with the expected movements of the market as a whole; this seemed to open up the possibility that an entire realm of Wall Street activity could change from informed guesswork— by people like the partners at Morgan Stanley—to pure science.

A few years earlier, two economists named Franco Modigliani and Merton Miller had published a paper arguing that the value of a company has nothing to do with the standard questions that professional investors had for years considered essential in deciding whether to buy a stock, such as how much debt the company is carrying and whether or not it pays dividends. In 1961, just before Jensen arrived, Miller moved to the University of Chicago, where one of his star graduate students was Eugene Fama. Fama developed, again through complicated statistical means, what he called the "efficient market hypothesis," which holds that well-functioning financial markets will set the price of a stock accurately, and therefore analysts who try to learn about individual companies in detail in order to decide whether their stocks are overpriced or underpriced are essentially wasting their time.

All these people—Hayek, Friedman, Markowitz, Sharpe, Modigliani, Miller, and Fama—wound up as Nobel laureates in economics. Back then, they were complete outsiders to the actual world of finance. The year that Mike Jensen came to Chicago, Thomas Kuhn's book *The Structure of Scientific Revolutions*, which introduced the idea of paradigm shifts, was published. Jensen wasn't widely read outside of economics, but Kuhn's book was a touchstone for him, something he quoted regularly for decades because he felt he had landed in the middle of a paradigm shift. Everything that everyone had always believed about this particular universe was wrong, and now, a small group of outsiders, widely considered eccentric or even crazy by other economists, let alone by people who worked on Wall Street, was demolishing the existing edifice of ideas and replacing it with a radically different one. This was a setup that made for a perfect fit with the cultural stance that prevailed in the University of Chicago economics department: we're outsiders, not wellborn or expensively educated, but we are more ruthlessly logical and, frankly, smarter than the self-satisfied grandees who run the world. With pure brainpower we can take down the structures they have built up to sustain their self-serving fantasy of where the public interest lies.

Jensen was almost theatrically plainspoken; he had the quality that very smart people sometimes have, of the world appearing to him to be not very complicated but very simple, a binary system cleanly divided between what was scientifically true and what was superstition. He spoke in a flat, burly midwestern accent and laid out his ideas—at least when he was talking about them to other people—in the least technical language he could manage. To Jensen, and to many of his Chicago colleagues, the world of finance had previously been in the hands of fancy-seeming people who believed in all sorts of precepts that they considered sophisticated, but were in fact nothing but unproven assumptions. Jensen had a habit of being extremely blunt, and his conversation was full of declarations that this or that widespread belief of respectable people was bullshit. He and his colleagues were, in their way, very much a part of the culture of the 1960s, though not noticed by the outside world in the way campus radicals or rock musicians were noticed. They may have been politically conservative, and they may have worn crew cuts and thick glasses, but they had just as much contempt for the settled culture of corporation-dominated America as the much better known social critics on the left, and just as much youthful conviction that taking it apart would make the world a better place. They simply wanted to use different means and to produce a different kind of society.

Jensen set to work with the new data from the Center for Research in Security Prices, aiming to test whether professional stock pickers who operated mutual funds produced better results than you'd get if you just captured the overall performance of the market. To do this required a good deal of complicated new statistical work. Jensen wanted to compare the actual performance of each of the 115 mutual funds he studied with the way a randomly selected portfolio would perform if it had holdings similar to those of the funds. Did the professionals produce a premium over the market's overall movement—something he named "alpha," a term that has become part of the basic vocabulary of the investing world? The answer, he found, was a resounding no. As Jensen drily noted, "The mutual fund industry . . . shows very little evidence of an ability to forecast security prices." There was an obvious application of Jensen's result, which would be for somebody to invent what we'd now call an index fund—a mutual fund based on replicating the overall performance of the market rather than quixotically attempting to find alpha by handpicking just the right stocks. That didn't happen immediately, owing to a lack of computing power. Still, Jensen's findings powerfully reinforced the theories of his Chicago colleagues. Once again, markets themselves, operating independently, were better at determining the proper prices of stocks and bonds than any supposed expert. And that meant that the customary operations of Wall Street firms were wrong and needed to change.

As a graduate student, Jensen shared an office with another young economist, Myron Scholes. In 1968 Scholes got a job at MIT; Jensen urged him to get in touch with Fischer Black, a mathematician living in Boston whom he had encountered a few years earlier at a meeting in Chicago. Soon Black and Scholes were working together, taking on the problem of how to price options, which are bets on the future movement of a stock. One could buy a share of a corporation's stock and watch its value rise and fall on the public stock market; that was what most people did. Or one could buy what was essentially a wager on the future value of the stock, predicting that it would rise or fall by at least a certain amount by a certain date. An option was cheaper than a stock, but also riskier, for if the stock didn't rise or fall by the amount you had bet it would, you would lose everything. Options were a small part of the financial markets, mainly for professionals, and were not openly traded on public exchanges.

Black and Scholes's idea was that options didn't have to be risky bets; instead, building on the work of the other young financial economists, they found a way to create a portfolio that would include a stock, an option on the stock, and other assets, and in the end produce an investment vehicle that would reduce risk, not increase it. The formulas Black and Scholes were developing could be used to create financial products called derivatives, which were not assets themselves, but synthetic creations derived from assets like stocks and bonds, or anything else for that matter, and then priced and traded. By purchasing derivatives, one could protect oneself against the potential losses that a straightforward portfolio of assets inescapably entailed. The Black-Scholes formulas could help determine the price of a derivative in a scientific way, and also the precise mix of assets and derivatives that would most reduce the risk in a portfolio. The cause they felt they were serving was reducing the beta, or volatility, of stock and bond holdings.

As complicated as the Black-Scholes formula was, the next and final major breakthrough in financial economics was even more complicated. It was invented by Robert C. Merton, a colleague of Scholes's at MIT. Merton adopted techniques developed by a Japanese mathematician named Kiyosi Itô (the only previous practical application of whose work was in plotting the trajectories of rockets) that allowed for "dynamic modeling" of the Black-Scholes formula, meaning that all the elements in a portfolio would be constantly recalculated and readjusted as conditions in the markets changed.

By this time, the early 1970s, the power of computers had increased so much that the work of Black, Scholes, and Merton (all of whom later won the Nobel Prize in economics for these discoveries) did not sit on a shelf for years, as had the work of the other pioneer financial economists. The Chicago Board of Trade created the Chicago Board Options Exchange, the world's first public marketplace for options, in 1973, and the new techniques were being used there almost immediately. The first index fund was founded in 1971. Wells Fargo Bank launched a short-lived mutual fund in 1974 that was based on a model devised by Black, Scholes, and Jensen. Within just a few years, the derivatives markets—options, futures, index funds, swaps, mortgage-backed securities; anything that could be assembled out of existing financial instruments and then priced, packaged, and traded—had gone from being insignificantly small to producing billions of dollars in activity every year, far more than the traditional stock and bond markets. Although the gentlemen in the syndicate department at Morgan Stanley and the insurrectionary young financial economists were, at that point, entirely unaware of one another's existence, their worlds would soon collide. And before too long, even quotidian Chicago Lawn, only five miles away from where the financial economists were making their recondite calculations, would feel the effects.

Michael Jensen, after he got his Ph.D. from the University of Chicago, became a professor at the University of Rochester's business school. The university had hired the dean of Chicago's business school to become its president; he had hired another Chicago-trained economist, William Meckling, to create a business school there as founding dean; and Meckling had hired a coterie of young Chicago economists such as Jensen to staff the school. Rochester was self-consciously a Chicago outpost, maybe even more Chicago than Chicago itself, by virtue of its being so new and owing to the special zeal possessed by missionaries sent off to work some distance from the mother church. Jensen founded an academic journal there called the *Journal of Financial Economics*, with himself, Eugene Fama, and Robert Merton as coeditors.

The world at large still thought of the corporation as the great, all-powerful father figure in the American economy, vast and impregnable, and of finance as a far more minor force. Adolf Berle routinely maintained that financial markets had become irrelevant because corporations no longer needed them—corporations were too rich. "Major corporations in most instances do not seek capital," he wrote in 1954. "They form it themselves . . . A corporation like General Electric or General Motors, which steadily builds its own capital, does not need to submit itself and its operations to the judgments of the financial markets." During the years when the financial economists were developing their formulas, Alfred Chandler, the premier historian of American business, was working on a landmark book, published in 1977, *The Visible Hand*, which placed itself in the line of descent from Berle and declared that "the visible hand of management replaced what Adam Smith referred to as the invisible hand of market forces."

■

What made the work of the financial economists so insurrectionary was that everybody but them seemed to believe that corporate managers were both economically puissant and socially wise. Much of the best-known financial activity during Michael Jensen's early career had to do with excitement over the rising stock prices of such young technology corporations of the day as IBM and Xerox, and with the creation of business conglomerates—groups of unrelated companies that had been assembled into a single corporation—such as ITT, Ling-Temco-Vought, and Gulf and Western. In all these cases, the idea was that the chief executives of the corporations were management geniuses who were practicing their profession so spectacularly well that they could be trusted to run just about anything successfully. This idea ran counter to the main thrust of financial economics, which was that markets are far better than people or institutions at figuring out what is and isn't economically valuable. The financial economists had laid waste to the traditional ways of thinking about the financial mechanisms associated with the almighty corporation—stocks and bonds—but what about the corporation itself? Shouldn't it be subject to the same kind of devastatingly rigorous and unsentimental analysis?

An early crack in the intellectual edifice around the corporation appeared way back in 1937, in the form of an article called "The Nature of the Firm," by Ronald Coase, a twenty-six-year-old British economist who joined the University of Chicago faculty not long after Michael Jensen had arrived there as a graduate student, and who later won the Nobel Prize. "Why is there any organization?" in business, Coase asked. Why not just let the unimpeded market, rather than corporate managers, decide where to build plants, when to launch products, and where to direct workers? Coase then answered his own question, proposing a new way to think about what functions a corporation should assume and manage through its own organization by calculating which alternative—performing a function internally or purchasing it from another firm—carried lower "transaction costs." At Alfred Sloan's General Motors, for example, it made economic sense to own and operate factories and an auto-lending division, but not dealerships or iron mines—going outside GM for the former had high transaction costs, but not going outside for the latter. The real importance of his article was in reviving the classic economic idea that in a market system, society, rather than resting on an unshakable foundation of major institutions, "becomes not an organization but an organism." Adolf Berle thought that the modern corporation had made Adam Smith's economic theories out of date; Coase was reviving them. By his way of thinking, big corporations run by managers would not necessarily dominate the modern world. Economic life should be fluid, not fixed.

Another important argument against the corporation came a quarter century later from a young law professor named Henry Manne, who had been a student of Aaron Director's at the University of Chicago and was briefly at Rochester during Jensen's early years there. In 1962 Manne published a long law review article dismissing most of the leading theories about the corporation. He called *The Modern Corporation and Private Property* "folklore," adding that Berle's more recent writings were no better: in endorsing the idea of corporate executives as statesmen who served a public purpose, Berle was running the risk of "losing the only objective standard available for judging quality among corporate managers," which was their economic performance. All attempts to consider the corporation as a social institution "represent disguised efforts to find an alternative to the price mechanism in economic matters." In a second article, Manne proposed a solution to the problems created by decades of muddy thinking about the corporation: the establishment of a "market for corporate control," in which a newly empowered breed of shareholders would, if management failed to perform well economically, arrange for the corporation to be acquired by a new owner who would better serve their interests.

Berle, invited to respond, reacted as if Manne were a visitor from a distant galaxy who knew nothing about how the country actually worked but had somehow gotten hold of an old classical economics textbook to read on the journey to planet Earth. Didn't Manne realize that the old, government-free American economic system had completely collapsed only three decades earlier? Didn't he see that shareholders, rather than being "investors," still had no power, or even much interest, in how corporations are managed? That corporations had become so rich that the ability of the capital markets to affect their behavior was minimal? That, therefore, Manne's idea of creating a takeover market "describes a totally imaginary picture"? Berle was completely untroubled by the idea of corporations serving a social purpose, which so bothered Manne. They had been bent to that purpose by government: "In fact, a large corporation is a variety of non-statist political institution." According to Berle, it was Manne who was purveying folklore in the guise of economic analysis.

In the meticulous records that Beatrice Berle kept of the Berles' innumerable dinner parties, one wouldn't have seen the names of many corporate executives. The ones Berle encountered, though, fit his model—or at least the nature of their contact with him would have made it appear that way. They worked at the most prestigious and established corporations, such as AT&T, IBM, General Motors, and DuPont. They were usually liberal Republicans (in those days there were liberal Republicans) who were actively involved in the civic life of the country by serving copiously on boards and commissions. Their corporations operated extensive, university-style research laboratories, had unionized labor forces, and offered their white-collar employees job security and generous pensions as recompense for their loyalty. Nothing about this picture communicated vulnerability.

■

The financial economists did not write for a popular audience, but Milton Friedman often did. In 1970 he published an article in *The New York Times Magazine*, "The Social Responsibility of Business Is to Increase Its Profits." Friedman was complaining about the most recent reappearance of the idea that corporations should do something to help solve the country's larger problems—by reducing pollution, restraining price increases, or giving jobs to the needy unemployed, for example. To Friedman this represented a step along the road to socialism. A corporate executive is merely "an employee of the owners of the business" whose job is "to make as much money as possible." For reasons that Berle gave in 1932 and had been continually restating since then, this did not accurately describe how most big corporations actually worked, but it was how Friedman seemed to think they worked. "The whole justification for permitting the corporate executive to be selected by the stockholders," Friedman wrote, "is that the executive is an agent serving the interests of his principal."

Friedman's article—indeed, all the attacks on the corporation, from the right, as not being sufficiently market-oriented—made a big impression on Mike Jensen. (He paid no attention to the arguments against the corporation from the left—for promoting conformity and not being attuned to progressive values—or to the old Marxist idea that corporations make their money through exploitation of workers and natural resources.) He liked Friedman's language about agents and principals, but he thought Friedman had not grasped the true nature of the problem. It wasn't that annoying liberals were pestering corporations to go into the business of reforming society; it was that corporations did not behave as pure market entities to begin with. For example, Friedman's assertion that the managers of corporations were chosen by stockholders, and then acted as their employees, was a kind of seminar-room fantasy.

The truth was that economists hadn't really studied corporations much in recent years, because it was so much more prestigious to study how markets worked (macroeconomics) than how organizations worked (microeconomics). It seemed as if the kind of rigorous economic thinking about markets that Jensen had been trained to do could now be applied to corporations, which, to Jensen's mind, were about as sloppily understood as finance had been before Jensen and his colleagues came along. And the result might be figuring out a way to get corporations to behave in the way Friedman said they should, rather than the way Berle had observed they did behave, which still held true. In consultation with his dean, William Meckling, Jensen set aside his work on financial markets and began working on a paper about business organizations.

Everybody, including Jensen, knew about Berle's theory of the separation of ownership and control, but Jensen and his colleagues didn't take Berle seriously, because he was not an economist and didn't use statistics. Most economists, on the other hand, believed that a corporation was an efficient, profit-maximizing entity that would keep growing as long as revenues exceeded costs, and then would stop growing. The more Jensen thought about this, the more his customary reaction to any aspect of the world to which he paid close attention kicked in: It was bullshit! Total crap! Made no sense! Zero! Decades' worth of economic thinking about corporations was based on a mistake. In fact, because corporations were so large, because their chief executives were managers rather than owners, because their boards were made up of cronies of the chief executive, because the shareholders were nowhere in sight, there was nobody in the picture who had an overpowering motive to focus on profits. Corporations were bureaucratic entities, not economic entities, and in that respect they were a black box: nobody really knew what went on inside them. But that could be changed.

In 1976 Jensen and Meckling produced a long, detailed, formula-filled paper called "Theory of the Firm" (the title is a tribute to Ronald Coase's article of forty years earlier) and submitted it to the leading economics journal that focused on organizations. The journal turned it down. (This was to Jensen's mind, especially later, a badge of honor and a sign that a paradigm shift was arriving; several crucial papers on financial economics had also been turned down by the leading finance journals.) Jensen's friends Eugene Fama and Robert Merton, hearing about this, decided to publish "Theory of the Firm" in the *Journal of Financial Economics*, which they had just started with Jensen. Today "Theory of the Firm," though much less accessibly written, stands as just as much of a landmark as Berle and Means's *The Modern Corporation and Private Property*. It is one of the most cited academic publications of all time. *The Modern Corporation and Private Property* prepared the ground for a great remaking of the corporation's relations with government in a way that wound up creating a corporation-dominated social order. "Theory of the Firm" prepared the ground for blowing up that social order.

"Theory of the Firm" began by noting Berle and Means's observation about the separation of ownership and control, but it defined the problem of the corporation completely differently. Berle and Means thought the corporation was too powerful; Jensen and Meckling thought the "agent," meaning the chief executive, was not sufficiently responsive to the "principal," meaning the shareholders. Instead of thinking about maximizing profits, the chief executive was likely to be thinking about such matters as "the physical appointments of the office, the attractiveness of the office staff, the level of employee discipline, the kind and amount of charitable contributions, personal relations ('friendship,' 'respect,' and so on) with employees, a larger than optimal computer to play with, or purchase of production inputs from friends"—that is, bullshit. That was because the chief executive usually wasn't a significant shareholder in his own corporation and had relatively little contact with shareholders.

The way to fix the corporation was not to regulate it in order to curb its untrammeled power, as Berle and his followers had believed, but to get rid of the "agency problem" by figuring out ways to make the chief executive behave more like a shareholder—to create a situation in which he personally bore the financial risks of his decisions. Jensen and Meckling were primarily concerned with identifying a problem— breaking open the black box—rather than with providing solutions, but they did mention a few possibilities. Significant shareholders could sit on corporate boards. Executives could be compensated more in stock and less in salary. Corporations could finance themselves more by taking on debt and less by issuing stock, because the need to make interest payments would put pressure on executives to find ways to make the corporation more profitable. Ideally, a corporation might even find a way to have a single, all-powerful owner rather than hundreds of thousands of powerless shareholders.

When ideas have influence, it's rarely just because of their singular force. Instead, there has to be a confluence between the ideas themselves, the spirit of the times, and the interests of powerful players who find the ideas congenial. For Adolf Berle, it was the Great Depression and the election of Franklin Roosevelt that gave *The Modern Corporation and Private Property* its impact. For Jensen, it made all the difference that "Theory of the Firm" was published in 1976, rather than, say, 1956, the apogee of the American industrial corporation. The signature corporation, General Motors, whose long-running success made it hard to argue that there was anything wrong with corporations economically, was beginning to lose ground to new competitors from Japan. The financial markets were becoming bigger, faster, and more powerful, partly because of the work of Jensen and his colleagues in financial economics. It was forty years after the Great Depression, and memories of government's essential role in ending it were fading; instead, with economic growth slowing and inflation rising, it was beginning to seem as if government could not manage the economy so well. Maybe the markets would do a better job.

Jensen himself, on fire with the ideas he had developed, began working in a more public, less technical, more opinionated vein. Within a few years, he had become the leading public advocate and justifier of a number of new techniques in the financial world that suddenly became pervasive: a large increase in mergers and acquisitions, including hostile ones; the development of the junk-bond market, whose high-risk, high-return instruments often financed these activities; enormous raises in the compensation of corporate chief executives, often in the form of stock options; the onset of leveraged buyouts and private equity as ways for financiers to take direct, usually temporary control of formerly publicly held companies. For a new coterie of raiders and financiers of a type Adolf Berle could hardly have imagined—Carl Icahn and Michael Milken, T. Boone Pickens and Irwin Jacobs—Jensen was the provider of the accompanying public philosophy, the scholar who could explain why their techniques were good for America.

Between 1981 and 1983 alone, there were more than two thousand corporate takeovers a year valued at more than $1 million, far more than the country had ever seen, enabled in part by Ronald Reagan's new administration in Washington signaling that it was going to interpret the antitrust laws more loosely. The market for corporate control had come roaring to life. During the 1980s as a whole, more than a quarter of the companies on the Fortune 500 list of the country's largest corporations were subject to takeover attempts. A third of the companies on the Fortune list in 1980 were no longer independent companies by 1990. There were thirty-five thousand of these transactions, worth $2.6 trillion, between 1976 and 1990. This amounted to a rapid and unexpected remaking of one of the foundation institutions of American society, and the public reaction was heavily negative. Hundreds of thousands of jobs at the country's traditional, supposedly unassailable corporations disappeared: AT&T, an extreme example, went from 850,000 employees to, at one point, less than 50,000. That meant the lifetime job security that had been an unstated part of the corporate social compact was gone, and so, before long, was the old system of company-paid pensions after retirement. Congress held hearings and proposed new regulations to limit the wave of takeovers. Traditional champions of the idea of the corporation as a social institution—many chief executives, and theoreticians, such as John Kenneth Galbraith and Peter Drucker—were horrified. Liberals who had always disliked the corporation now began focusing on greedy Wall Street financiers as villains, in a way they had not for half a century. Nobody was talking about the Organization Man anymore.

Jensen, on the other hand, saw the economic revolution taking place as entirely healthy, indeed necessary. As he saw it, during the quarter century after the Second World War, the self-satisfied chief executives of the largest American corporations had destroyed as much as a third of their companies' collective value—overexpanding for reasons of vanity, signing too-generous labor agreements in order to be regarded as statesmen, and otherwise ignoring the interests of their shareholders in the ways the system permitted them to do. Now, at last, the corporation's principal-agent problem could be solved. What was emerging from the great dismantling and rearranging of the corporation in the 1980s, Jensen felt, was a transition from the mass mispricing of corporations (because of the principal-agent problem, plus too much government regulation) to correct pricing by the market, via mergers, takeovers, and buyouts. At the end of the 1980s Jensen calculated that between 1977 and 1988, American corporations had increased in value by $500 billion as a result of the activation of the market for corporate control, and as a result, the United States had staved off what would have been an existential economic threat from Japan.

Of all the new financial techniques that emerged in the 1980s, the one Jensen liked best was the leveraged buyout, now usually called private equity. A buyout firm would acquire control or even total ownership of a public company, financing the transaction with borrowed money; reorient the company from whatever had been distracting it from pursuing purely economic ends; and then resell it, as a whole or broken up into parts, either to another company or to a new set of public shareholders. The total value of leveraged buyouts in the United States was $1.4 billion in 1979, and $77 billion in 1988. The leading early leveraged buyout firm (of many) was Kohlberg Kravis Roberts, headed by Henry Kravis; the leading supplier of the debt that financed the buyouts was Michael Milken of Drexel Burnham Lambert, who created a substantial market for high-risk bonds to fund ungentlemanly financial transactions. Jensen was a great admirer of both men.

On purely economic grounds, the argument against leveraged buyouts was that they piled too much debt onto the target companies. By Jensen's estimate, the debt at a typical bought-out company went from 20 percent to 90 percent of the company's total value; for all American corporations, debt increased by more than a trillion dollars in the 1980s. But Jensen saw this as healthy; it took away corporations' ability to horde large reserves of cash, which was another aspect of the principal-agent problem because it permitted chief executives to relax rather than being incessantly, almost desperately worried, as they should be, about making the company more profitable. He wrote: "Debt is . . . a mechanism to force managers to disgorge cash rather than spend it on empire-building projects with low or negative returns, bloated staffs, indulgent perquisites, and organizational inefficiencies." It "creates the crisis atmosphere managers require to slash unsound investment programs, shrink overhead, and dispose of assets that are more valuable outside the company."

Jensen worried that all the objections to the social and economic churn created by the market for corporate control would lead to another historic wave of restriction on financial activity, as had happened in the early days of the New Deal. He made himself into a passionate public opponent of such efforts. As far as he could tell, there had been no significant job losses. Corporate executives, even those dismissed with the very large payments known as "golden parachutes," were not being overpaid, and neither were people on Wall Street. All in all, he testified before a congressional committee in 1989, "it is difficult to find losers in these transactions." He went on: "The surprising thing to me is that there have been so few major mistakes or problems in a revolution in business practice as large as that occurring over the last decade."

In 1993 Jensen became the last of his cohort of former young insurrectionists to be elected president of the American Finance Association. In his presidential address, he announced that the United States was in the middle of a third industrial revolution. In the nineteenth century, he said, "the large costs associated with the obsolescence of human and physical capital generated substantial hardship, misunderstanding, and bitterness." Now this was happening again, and it was sure to become more severe in the coming years. Jensen reminded his audience that the average daily wage of an unskilled American worker was more than $100, compared with $2.89 in China and $1.51 in India; surely the advent of free trade and the end of communism would lead to wages averaging out worldwide, which would create massive unhappiness, and even possibly political violence, in the United States, as workers saw what they had gained during the years after the Treaty of Detroit taken away, never to return. (Jensen knew from personal experience that almost no one among his own extended family and friends from Minneapolis was succeeding in the new economy.) What to do? To Jensen the answer was clear: make the market for corporate control even more active, powerful, and all-encompassing; blow away the remaining aspects of the principal-agent problem—complacent chief executives, overgenerous union contracts, and passive boards of directors. Jensen believed so deeply in markets as right and just, and in the immorality of any arrangements that impeded them, that he didn't feel constrained to make the standard argument that they were better at creating general prosperity. They were just better. His greatest worry was that in response to all the moaning from politicians, liberal activists, and the press about the

1980s being the greed decade, Congress and the courts would make it impossible for the mergers and buyouts to continue at full bore.

But by that time it was becoming clear that the threats to the financial revolution that kept Jensen up at night had not materialized. Jensen's side had won. Wall Street continued to grow, and its balance of power with the corporation continued to move in its favor. The big pension funds, endowments, and other institutional investors, whose ownership share in corporations kept increasing, began to shed their historic passivity and invest in buyouts, takeovers, and mergers. Business schools and law schools began teaching ideas like those of Jensen, Henry Manne, and Eugene Fama. Their students reoriented their ambitions away from corporate management and toward careers in outside entities that broke corporations apart, such as buyout funds and consulting firms. Even Jensen conceded in one essay that the dominant and stable public corporation had been in its mid-twentieth-century heyday "a social invention of vast historical importance," but now that era may well have come to an end, at least for the older and more traditional firms.

In the mid-1980s Jensen left Rochester to become a professor at Harvard Business School. He moved in order to get, as he put it, close to the world, and being at America's most famous business school did enhance his prominence. At Rochester, Jensen and Meckling had turned their "Theory of the Firm" paper into a required course called Coordination, Control, and the Management of Organizations, known to students as CCMO. Harvard Business School, when Jensen arrived, was still corporation-oriented enough that the finance department rejected him as one of its members, but he was permitted to offer the CCMO course as an elective. By the mid-1990s it had become the most popular elective course in the history of the school, enrolling more than six hundred students, two-thirds of each year's class. That was a sign of the appeal of Jensen's ideas, at least to business students, and of the career opportunity his ideas seemed to represent. Another sign was that Jensen had gone from being an obscure financial economist to a celebrity business intellectual, constantly consulting and lecturing all over the world, always with total confidence in the rightness of his ideas. In 1984, for example, he had the nerve to come to an event commemorating the fiftieth anniversary of the publication of Benjamin Graham's *Security*

Analysis and debate Graham's most famous student, Warren Buffett, about whether it was possible for investors to make money by putting their money into specific companies they thought were well managed, as Buffett had made billions doing.

■

The world presented itself to Jensen in bright primary colors, with vivid distinctions between what was rigorous and right and intellectually honest and what was crap. Because it was so obvious to him, and because there wasn't much of a filter between what he thought and what he said, he went through life offending people. At the end of his first year at Rochester, in the late 1960s, the two leading finance professors there had called him in and said, as he remembered it, that they would not allow him to teach anything in finance classes that they did not understand— such as the revolutionary work of Markowitz, Miller, Modigliani, Sharpe, and Fama. Jensen blew up; shouted, That's your problem, not mine; and stormed out of the office where they were meeting. Fortunately for Jensen, his dean, William Meckling, protected him against such assaults and permitted him to teach the new financial economics. But Jensen and Meckling's relationship eventually came to a bitter end too. Because they were such close intellectual partners, Meckling had envisioned Jensen as his successor as dean. Aside from their both being interested in agency problems, another point of agreement between them was that Harvard Business School was, as Jensen put it, evil incarnate because it taught mainly by the case method, which was anecdotal rather than quantitative, and therefore intellectually second-rate. When Jensen left for Harvard, Meckling felt betrayed and broke off their friendship forever.

When a challenge to financial economics—in particular to the efficient market hypothesis—began to emerge, roughly speaking from the left, within the profession, it had two major components. One was the idea of information asymmetry: markets could not price everything perfectly if all participants did not have equal access to accurate information. The other was behavioral economics, which focused on the many ways the human mind was naturally prone to misperceive reality and how that would affect people's interactions with economic markets.

Both ideas, by positing that markets behaved imperfectly, were opening the door to a role for government in improving the way markets functioned, and this was a highly offensive idea to Jensen. The fathers of behavioral economics were two psychologists, Daniel Kahneman and Amos Tversky; their main link to economics was Richard Thaler, whose first job was as a junior faculty member at Rochester's business school. Naturally, Jensen and Thaler quarreled constantly. Thaler eventually left for the University of Chicago's business school, where he began to quarrel constantly with Eugene Fama.

Once, Jensen invited Tversky to a conference at Rochester, out of a combination of curiosity and eagerness to argue with him. The two of them, along with Thaler, went out to dinner one evening. According to Thaler, Jensen believed that he could "straighten out the confused psychologists." In a memoir he published years later, Thaler remembered the conversation this way:

> In the course of conversation, Amos asked Jensen to assess the decision-making capabilities of his wife. Mike was soon regaling us with stories of the ridiculous economic decisions she made, like buying an expensive car and then refusing to drive it because she was afraid it would be dented. Amos then asked Jensen about his students, and Mike rattled off silly mistakes they made, complaining about how slow they were to understand the most basic economics concepts. As more wine was consumed, Mike's stories got better.
>
> Then Amos went in for the kill. "Mike," he said, "you seem to think that virtually everyone you know is incapable of correctly making even the simplest of economic decisions, but then you assume that all the agents in your models are geniuses. What gives?"
>
> Jensen was unfazed. "Amos," he said, "you just don't understand."

In an earlier and unpublished version of his memoir, Thaler appended a kind of dream sequence to his account of the dinner, in which the long-dead John Maynard Keynes turns up at the restaurant in Rochester

to join the argument between Jensen and Tversky. But even the greatest economist of the twentieth century can't make a dent in Jensen's
certitude:

> Keynes: Professor Jensen, did you know that shares of ice com-
> panies were higher in summer months when sales are higher?
> Do you call that rational?

> Jensen: Well John, that might have been true in your day, but
> we have better data now, and if something like your story about
> the price of ice company shares rising in the summer were to
> happen, smart investors would jump in, make tons of money,
> and in so doing, they would keep prices rational.

> Keynes: Professor Jensen, do I look like I was born yesterday,
> or that these ideas are really new? Some people thought this
> way in the 1930s as well, but it was naïve then, and remains so
> now . . .

> Jensen: What bullshit! If prices diverge from intrinsic value,
> some investors will find it profitable to bet against the stupidity
> of the herd.

It wasn't only in his professional life that Jensen had trouble getting
along with people. He had a painful falling-out with his father, over his
telling the old man that he was never going to see a dime from the ty-
pographers' union pension he'd been faithfully paying into, as a rocklike
primary financial obligation, for decades. Jensen was being relentlessly
logical and candid as usual—he could see that his father's trade, operating a linotype machine, had become obsolete, and that pensions promising to pay out lifetime benefits were obsolete too—and it turned out he
was right. But if he hadn't felt the need to demonstrate that he had superior knowledge and had given precedence to being an empathetic son,
they might not have become permanently estranged. In just about any
social encounter, such as the receptions and dinners after lectures he
gave, Jensen wound up, as he liked to put it, acting like an asshole and
leaving people feeling insulted. A persistent rumor among economists is

that Jensen, unlike his closest colleagues (and his younger combatant, Richard Thaler), never won a Nobel Prize because the selection committee had invited him to participate in a panel discussion, as a kind of audition for his suitability for his profession's highest honor, and he had put on his usual arrogant performance.

By the end of the 1990s Jensen had been divorced twice. You can guess what it would have been like to be married to him from what Thaler quotes him saying to Tversky, or from this passage from an essay he wrote in the late 1970s:

> I consent to the wishes of my wife on occasion (for instance, by accompanying her to a movie or concert she wishes to attend) to make her happy and to maintain good relations—goodwill that I can draw upon the next time I unexpectedly bring home a colleague for dinner (or, worse yet, forget to come home for dinner). If I ignore her preferences too flagrantly, or she mine, the "exploited party" can retaliate in this game of life by voluntarily withholding future services or favors in many dimensions of the relationship.

Jensen has two daughters. One hadn't spoken to him for years, and the other was barely speaking to him. One day, the phone rang in his office at Harvard. It was his older daughter, Stephanie, the one who wasn't speaking to him at all. Hi, Dad, she said. I just want you to know that I love you. Jensen was floored. What had made that happen? Stephanie said she had just spent a weekend at a seminar called Landmark Forum, which was based on techniques invented by Werner Erhard, the founder of est. It was during the seminar that she realized that she loved him. Now she wanted him to take the seminar too. Jensen told her if that was what she wanted, he would do it.

Three weeks later, Jensen was sitting in a Landmark seminar, watching with mystified wonder as one participant after another would say, "I have a share," stand up at a microphone, and engage in a florid public therapy session with the seminar leader, in which the person would confess, weep, hug, laugh, and otherwise display the indicia of a profound personal transformation from something close to misery to something close to joy. Every so often the leader of the seminar would ask Jensen why he hadn't gotten up and spoken. Finally, toward the end of the weekend, he stood up and said he had a question. He went to the microphone. He began with a long recitation of his professional accomplishments as a renowned academic, just so everybody in the room would know whom they were dealing with: as he later put it, bray, bray, bray. Then he got to the question, which, in his glass-clear memory of the moment, was this: Most people think I'm an asshole. The road of my life is littered with debris. I don't understand why. The seminar leader thanked him and asked a question or two. Then she said, Do you think it could have something to do with arrogance? No, absolutely not, Jensen said.

Jensen went home impressed but confused by the seminar's evident large effect on the participants; he didn't think anything had happened to him. A few days later, he gave a long-scheduled, prestigious endowed lecture at the University of Virginia law school. It was the usual routine: the talk, then a dinner, then back to his hotel, then up early to fly home to Boston. On the plane he put down the tray table and prepared to work on his next assignment, as he always did when he was traveling, but something strange happened. He found that he couldn't work. He had a premonition that the plane was going to crash. He held the sides of the tray table and put his head down for a few minutes. He couldn't figure out what was going on. Then something occurred to him: unlike every other trip to give a lecture that he could remember, in Virginia he hadn't offended anybody. He hadn't been an asshole. So if, on the plane, he was going through some kind of small simulacrum of death and rebirth, it must have to do with his familiar self's having been mysteriously laid to rest without his even fully noticing it. And that must have been because of the Landmark seminar. Jensen decided he had to learn more about Landmark.

He immediately signed up for other seminars, and before long he had befriended one of Landmark's executives, Steve Zaffron, a deeply creased man with a kind, world-weary air who had been an aide to Werner Erhard for decades and functioned as Erhard's liaison to Landmark's clients in the business world. Erhard himself was hard to find in those days. His life had blown up in the early 1990s because of a tax investigation by the IRS and a story on *60 Minutes* in which one of his daughters went on camera and accused him of having sexually abused her and one of her sisters. Erhard officially relinquished control of his company and disappeared; his colleagues retired the name est, launched the name Landmark, and carried on their work. He lived in the Cayman Islands with his third wife, Gonneke Spits, another member in long standing of his professional entourage, and traveled around the world, but almost never to the United States.

Erhard had been born John Paul Rosenberg in Philadelphia, the son of a Jewish father and an Episcopalian mother, and raised at the lower edge of the middle class. His formal education ended when he finished high school; his girlfriend became pregnant, and under pressure from their parents, they married and he went to work as a car salesman. When he was in his early twenties and the father of four children, he abruptly left his family and moved west, first to St. Louis, then to Spokane, then to San Francisco, with another woman he had been seeing. (They married, had three children, and divorced.) During this time, he underwent the first of a number of self-reinventions; while leafing through a special issue of a magazine about West Germany, he decided to change his name—in emulation of Werner Heisenberg, the physicist, and Ludwig Erhard, the West German chancellor. He worked as a regional manager of door-to-door sales operations, first at a magazine company, then for a publisher of encyclopedias.

Along with all these moves went a spiritual quest that took Erhard through a wide sampling of American pop culture success and personal growth texts and programs: sales-oriented motivational material such as Napoleon Hill's *Think and Grow Rich* and Dale Carnegie's *How to Win Friends and Influence People*; New Age psychology like the work of Abraham Maslow and Carl Rogers; Eastern religions like Zen Buddhism and Subud; hypnosis; and cultlike seminar programs like Scientology and Mind Dynamics. In 1971 he left his career in sales and started est. Thin, intense, and voluble, with blue eyes, a booming voice, and a dominating manner, Erhard would lead his seminars for endless hours, not letting the participants eat, sleep, or go to the bathroom, leading them one by one through sessions at the microphone, where he would coax out painful childhood memories, goad, berate, and finally, magnanimously, redeem. He was the symbol of what Tom Wolfe, after attending an est seminar as a reporter, called the Me Decade—an individual psychological purveyor of the kind of breaking down of traditional social structures that Jensen and his colleagues were engaged in with corporations. At his peak Erhard attracted large audiences to the seminars, along with a coterie of show business celebrities who were willing to testify to his wondrous powers.

To the minds of Erhard's circle of close aides, his downfall had been the work of L. Ron Hubbard, the ruthless founder of Scientology, who considered est to be a threatening competitor and who, they believed, was the hidden force behind the devastating *60 Minutes* piece, whose core accusation Erhard's daughter later recanted. (One former aide to Hubbard says that shortly after watching Erhard appear on television in 1976, Hubbard wrote a memo to his staff laying out an elaborate long-running anti-est campaign that he called Operation Z.) Now Erhard was dispirited, ill, intellectually immobilized, and convinced that his life was in danger. For his part, Jensen was more and more fascinated and puzzled by the Landmark courses he had taken. The material he had encountered there seemed as powerful as the revolution in financial economics and his work on the principal-agent problem, but he didn't fully understand it, because it wasn't published, with equations and footnotes to explain how it worked. And it couldn't become as magically influential as Jensen's professional work as an economist had been, as it could be conveyed only in person by a handful of trained seminar leaders. It needed, Jensen thought, to be moved into universities. That was what had given the other work its power.

Jensen persuaded the dean of his old school at Rochester to let him develop and teach a Landmark-based leadership course. While they were working on it, Steve Zaffron told Jensen that Werner Erhard was now ready to meet him. Jensen and his partner, Sue Strober, flew to Japan, where Erhard had gone to meet with one of his friends from the world of Eastern religion, and they spent several hours together. Jensen left that encounter with the conviction that Erhard was the smartest person he had ever met—smarter than Robert Merton or Eugene Fama or Fischer Black, and possibly one of the greatest minds in history. That made it all the more vital that his work be brought before the public in a permanent form, the way history's other great thinkers' work had been.

Erhard, indirectly, had already done a lot for Jensen, but Jensen also had something valuable to offer Erhard. Erhard had an autodidact's exaggerated respect for academic certification, and he too believed himself to be a major intellectual, in a way that the world had not recognized.

For somebody who spent most of his time either alone or in the company of people who had been with him ever since they were all selling encyclopedias together, Jensen, a devotee who had a very large independent reputation, was a potentially crucial ally. A few years into the Rochester course, Erhard made a rare visit to the United States to teach there himself. And Jensen persuaded him that they should collaborate on a major work that would capture the principles Erhard had spent his life developing.

By this time, the first years of the twenty-first century, Jensen had retired from Harvard Business School. He had a well-paying part-time job with a consulting firm founded by one of his Harvard colleagues, but that left him plenty of time for the great project. He and Erhard would hole up together for lengthy sessions either at Jensen's vacation home in Vermont or at Erhard's house in the Cayman Islands. It didn't go well at first. Erhard had a master showman's lifelong commitment to concealing his trade secrets from his audience. As a participant in a course, you weren't supposed to understand what was happening to you—you were just supposed to be impressed that it *was* happening. That had been Jensen's own experience. "Understanding is the booby prize," Erhard would tell Jensen. Jensen would tell Erhard that his ideas were so powerful that they could change the world within just a few decades, as the ideas of Jensen's cohort of economists had, but that could happen only if he explained them. Both men are short-tempered; there was a lot of shouting. In the end, Jensen wore down Erhard's resistance, and they began trying to catalog Erhard's ideas systematically.

During this period, Jensen began to change his mind about Wall Street. All through the 1980s and 1990s he had been steadfast in insisting that much of what the public understood as financial greed and manipulation was actually a healthy and urgently necessary remaking of the American economy. Yet spectacular incidents that seemed to demonstrate deep flaws in the workings of the financial markets kept coming. There was the bursting of the Internet bubble in 2000, indicating that public markets actually might not be so good at pricing companies at their true value. There was the collapse of such companies as Enron, WorldCom, and Nortel, which had used fraudulent accounting to make themselves look far more successful than they were. There were the widespread complaints about even the best companies being under

relentless pressure to produce ever-increasing quarterly earnings statements, because that was all the markets paid attention to. At some point
during the endless procession of financial scandals that were at least notionally based on the application of his ideas, Jensen remembers saying
to himself, Holy shit, now it's doing more damage than good; anything
can be corrupted.

Not so publicly controversial but deeply distressing to Jensen were
a few incidents that made him lose faith in financial institutions he had
believed in. In the 1980s Robert Rubin, the future Treasury secretary,
had hired Jensen's friend Fischer Black at Goldman Sachs, hoping to
bring some of the magic of financial economics into the operations of a
Wall Street firm. Black told Jensen that although the partners at Goldman Sachs didn't understand his work, they were honorable people who
worried constantly about maintaining the firm's reputation. But then,
in 1999, Goldman Sachs turned itself from a private partnership into a
public company, which brought a big payday for its partners but made
it subject to Jensen's bête noire, the principal-agent problem, because
now the owners of the firm—the new public shareholders—were not the
people running it. Eventually even some of the private equity firms that
Jensen thought of as the perfect solution to the principal-agent problem,
such as KKR and Blackstone, went public too, so they were no longer
owner-managers either; they also started to make more and more of their
money by charging fees to investors instead of increasing the value of
their holdings. Didn't these people understand that they were supposed
to be engaged in a sacred cause, undoing the decades-old separation of
ownership and control that had nearly destroyed America? Was it actually for them, in the end, all about making as much money as possible
rather than enacting a principle? In a videotaped interview for a series
called *Pioneers of Finance*, Jensen applied what had previously been his
least favorite epithet to Stephen Schwarzman, the head of Blackstone—
"very greedy"—and predicted that his firm would fail.

In 2001 Jensen published an article meant to clarify his views on
what kind of value corporations should be trying to achieve. It wasn't
just a constantly rising stock price, it was "enlightened value maximization" of the firm as a whole, and that could include considering social
factors of the kind Jensen would previously have dismissed as silly or
even corrupting. In 2002 Jensen and a coauthor published an article

with the wildly uncharacteristic title "Just Say No to Wall Street," which treated the financial markets' preoccupation with quarterly earnings as a major impediment to good management. In 2004 he published an article arguing that, in effect, the principal-agent problem he had identified back in 1976 had now been turned on its head: rather than the great power shift from big corporations to the financial markets having solved the problem, the markets themselves had now become the main source of the principal-agent problem. By pressuring companies to keep raising their stock price, they were creating malign incentives for executives to misstate the condition of their companies and to make bad acquisitions that would look brilliant at first glance. Jensen compared this process to heroin addiction and said it had destroyed billions of dollars in economic value. "Once we as managers start lying, it's nearly impossible for us to stop," he wrote.

By now Jensen had turned against all his previously favorite solutions to the principal-agent problem—forming mergers, taking on a heavy load of debt, and tying executives' compensation to stock prices (which, he said, was "like throwing gasoline on a fire")—as being counterproductive. He had a new solution, which was to remake boards of directors so that they were composed of principals (that is, major shareholders) rather than agents (distinguished-seeming cronies of the chief executive). But the truth was, he had now departed in a profound way from the core idea that financial markets are a healthy force because they always set prices efficiently. Back in 1978, in the introduction to a special issue of the *Journal of Financial Economics* devoted to his friend Eugene Fama's efficient market hypothesis, Jensen wrote, "In the literature of finance, accounting, and the economics of uncertainty, the Efficient Market Hypothesis is accepted as a fact of life, and a scholar who purports to model behavior in a manner which violates it faces a difficult task of justification." For Jensen to abandon this view was heresy to the minds of his old friends in financial economics. Jensen had stood as a groomsman at Myron Scholes's wedding; now Scholes refused to speak to him. Solving the principal-agent problem had become a chimera: you'd eliminate what seemed to be its main cause, such as corporate managers who didn't have to pay attention to the markets, and a few years later the problem would reappear in a different form—Wall Street analysts preoccupied with quarterly earnings. Was there any way to create the perfect incentive structure that would make people behave as they should in perpetuity?

There was not a clear, obvious connection in Jensen's mind between his changing view of the financial markets and the dramatic remaking of his life that had begun when he took his first Landmark course and deepened when he met Werner Erhard. Still, they were going on at the same time, and the work he was doing with Erhard wound up being a synthesis of the two developments. The way Jensen's mind worked was that he would identify a vast area of human activity that, to him, was obviously tainted because it was based on automatic, lazy, and bad assumptions; then he would propose a single powerful new tool that would correct the problem. When he was a young economist, the problem was self-satisfied investment managers, and the solution was the new financial economics. Then the problem became corporations, and the solution was making their executives super-responsive to the financial markets. But frustratingly for Jensen, the world still needed fixing. So now he switched his focus again: reforming markets hadn't worked, reforming corporations hadn't worked, but maybe reforming people would work. That seemed to be the lesson of his own recent transformation.

Jensen began poking around in Landmark materials for ideas that he could weave into a new theory as all-encompassing as his previous ones. From Steve Zaffron he got the idea of emphasizing "integrity" as the fundamental business practice. By *integrity* he meant, as he later wrote, "a state or condition of being in whole, complete, unbroken, unimpaired, sound, perfect condition," the way an unmarred physical object would have integrity. For a person, integrity was an essential quality—who you were rather than a kind of behavior you could adopt. As an economist, Jensen was trained to be skeptical of anything "normative"—that is, any idea about the world based on how it should be rather than how it actually is. That was why, for example, organized religion, like the Catholicism of his youth, occupied a prominent place in Jensen's pantheon of bullshit: it was based on giving people rules to tell them how to behave. Integrity was about how to *be*, not what rules to follow. It was, as economists would put it, positive, not normative. And if integrity could be established as the inviolable grounding principle for business, there would be no more scandals, no more principal-agent problems, no more inefficient markets. On its face, integrity may not have sounded like

something a company could embrace in order to make more money, but
Jensen insisted that it was: it could provide "an unambiguous and actionable access to the opportunity for superior performance, no matter how
one defines performance."

■

A term that Jensen picked up from Erhard was "conversational domain."
That meant a language, or at least a set of terms, that generated a particular way of understanding the world among the people who used it.
Landmark, and est before it, used a whole library of specialized phrases
Erhard had invented: *rackets*, *walls of bricks*, *cause in the matter*, *on the
court*, *occurring*, *being a stand*, *getting complete*, *life sentences*, and many
more. Any paradigm shift, Jensen thought, had to create its own conversational domain. That was what financial economics had done; terms
like "shareholder value" and "free cash flow," which hadn't existed back
in Adolf Berle's heyday, led people trained to use them to think about
finance in a certain way. Now, if the world was to change again, a new
conversational domain for business and finance had to be invented, with
integrity as its centerpiece.

Jensen and Erhard began elaborately combing through all of Erhard's work over the decades and trying to turn it into a single, great
coherent system. Together they wrote version after version of an academic paper called "Putting Integrity into Finance: A Purely Positive
Approach," which was meant to be as world-changing as "Theory of the
Firm" had been thirty years earlier. At an even higher level of ambition,
they conceived the idea of a book called *A Positive Theory of the Normative Virtues*, a major philosophical text that would reveal and then correct
"the surprising source of many of humanity's difficulties and problems."
Like *The Key to All Mythologies*, the book Edward Casaubon was endlessly gestating in *Middlemarch*, Jensen and Erhard's book was taking a
long time; after more than ten years of work, all the public could read
of it was a brief introduction the authors had posted on an academic
website that Jensen had founded in the early days of the Internet. In
the meantime, though, they decided to launch a new seminar, longer
and more elaborate than any Erhard and his circle had ever staged, that
would cover essentially the same ground as the book. The curriculum for
the seminar was a PowerPoint presentation with more than a thousand

slides, which Jensen and Erhard tweaked constantly, which for the time being had to stand in the stead of their uncompleted masterpiece.

A term that Erhard hadn't been using, but that Jensen thought captured the essence of his work, was "ontology": the study of the nature of being. Ontology appealed to Jensen because it went along with his idea of integrity. It was about who you were, not what you had learned or what rules you had been taught to follow. A related philosophical term that Jensen liked was "phenomenology," the study of the nature of things as they appear to people. He and Jensen created a new nonprofit organization, the Erhard-Jensen Ontological/Phenomenological Initiative. Their new seminars were called "Being a Leader and the Effective Exercise of Leadership: An Ontological/Phenomenological Model."

Erhard, in his late seventies when "Being a Leader" began, no longer had the energy to run a seminar for hours on end, so there was always a coterie of several leaders, including Jensen. But Erhard was the star. He'd steal into the room unannounced, whippet-thin, silver-haired, often dramatically dressed in either all black or all white, and you'd hear a booming voice commenting on whatever slide was up on the projector. Whoever was presenting would retire, and Erhard would stroll up the center aisle and take the stage. He was alternately high-minded and earthy, menacing and supportive. One minute he'd be talking about Derrida and Wittgenstein, the biochemistry of the brain and Bayesian inference, and the next minute he'd be telling a dirty joke. When a participant came to the mike, Erhard would play him like a jazz musician improvising a solo. This is not psychology! he'd shout. This is ontology! Heidegger said, without phenomenology there can be no ontology. I hate these big words! (Here he'd cast a glance across the audience with a knowing smirk.) Life gets to be very fascinating when you're *out here*. Everything is interesting out here. Your outlook is a little bit shitty. Now give me a hug! I hate saying things that are nice, but I really do love you. (The final embrace would cue the curtain, so to speak, for the encounter.) Erhard is one of those people it's impossible not to watch, and he'd be expertly working the audience and the person at the mike at the same time, creating the exciting, elevated sense of danger that comes with ignoring customary social boundaries. By the end of the encounter he'd have glided the exchange downward into the safety of an inevitable moment of dissolved gratitude by the person at the microphone.

One can be forgiven for wondering how this amounted to a prescription for the systemic reform of the fallen financial world, but to Jensen's mind it all cohered. In the seminar, Jensen's contribution seemed to be wrestling Erhard's apparently random and nearly infinite pastiche of insights into a structured, systematized form: the four foundational factors, the two ontological constructs, the five design elements for creating a created future, the eleven factors contributing to the veil of invisibility, and so on, proceeding in some kind of logical order. Onstage, Jensen's main assignment was to be the lead presenter of the concept of integrity, which was the first and most important of the four foundational factors and the necessary precondition for becoming the kind of leader the seminar was supposed to turn you into. Integrity was based on "honoring your word," a principle that Jensen, typically, had divided into a scheme of six carefully adumbrated subcategories: Word One, Word Two, and so on. More important than the details was the idea that integrity was supposed to become a state of being, not a learned form of behavior—that was why the course was called "Being a Leader."

It didn't take much encouragement for Jensen to launch into a diatribe against Richard Thaler and the other behavioral economists, who, in his view, had taken the perfectly good insight that humans often behave irrationally and then tried to solve the problem by creating different and better incentives. A popular and influential book, *Nudge*, written by Thaler and a coauthor, summarized this approach. Jensen thought this was nothing more than an attempt to improve the world by manipulating or tricking people. With his principal-agent theory, he'd been through the business of trying to alter behavior by changing incentives. It didn't work. You had to change who people *were*—to get them into integrity—if you wanted to get anywhere. Otherwise they, and their organizations, would just keep screwing up again and again. Jensen liked to tell people that being out of integrity was like hitting yourself with an invisible hammer: it hurt like hell, but you had no idea why it was happening. You had to be able to see the hammer in order to stop hitting yourself, and getting into integrity as a state of being was the only way to do that.

When the financial system collapsed in the fall of 2008, a few years into his partnership with Erhard, Jensen was completely unsurprised: it was the inevitable result of the out-of-integrity behavior that had become ubiquitous on Wall Street. President Barack Obama's efforts to save the financial system didn't impress Jensen very much, because new safeguards and regulations couldn't solve the problem. Only integrity could. Jensen lived in absolute, serene confidence that the world would recognize this one day—that integrity would engender a benign revolution in human affairs. One reason Jensen insisted that integrity was "positive" rather than "normative" was that, to economists, *positive* meant testable, and *normative* meant squishy and vague. He was certain that soon people would prove, with rigorous, quantitative research, that companies adhering to his idea of integrity performed far better economically than companies that did not. That this had not happened yet did not affect his certitude.

Jensen and Sue Strober had bought a small complex of buildings, designed by a Japanese architect in a style meant to impart a sense of serenity, in Siesta Key, Florida, just south of Sarasota on the Gulf Coast. They planted lush, carefully tended tropical plants all over the property. When he wasn't traveling, Jensen spent his days in a small cottage a few steps away from the main house, working on the course materials and on the book he was writing with Erhard. Erhard would turn eighty in 2015, and his health wasn't great; Jensen was convinced, on the basis of genetic testing he'd had done, that his own mind would no longer be fully functional by the time he turned eighty, which would be in 2019. That gave the work a sense of deadline urgency. Jensen's work with Erhard was unpaid; in fact, he regularly made donations to the Erhard-Jensen Ontological/Phenomenological Initiative.

In 2012 Jensen posted an online version of the paper he and Erhard had written on integrity in finance. It was important to him that their work find an academic audience, because that was how it would live on after they were gone. His earlier articles on financial economics and principal-agent theory had been two of the great examples of academic work (far more abstruse and inaccessible than the work he was doing now) going from publication in journals, to being incorporated in courses for students, to becoming enormously influential in the world. Anytime he or Erhard had a chance to persuade a university to offer a version of their leadership course, they pursued it ardently. And Jensen submitted their paper to the *Journal of Financial Economics*, which he had cofounded and which had published "Theory of the Firm" after it was rejected elsewhere. The journal turned him down. That was disappointing, but not surprising. Financial economics had gone from being a paradigm shift that threatened the Establishment to being the Establishment itself, the foundational idea powering the immense expansion of Wall Street—so naturally it would be threatened by the next paradigm shift, the one Jensen and Erhard were promoting now.

Finally Jensen placed the integrity paper in another academic journal, which published it in the spring of 2017. By that time, through five posted versions over five years, it had acquired fewer than fifty academic citations. "Theory of the Firm" had more than sixty-six thousand.

Not long after the worst period of the financial crisis, Jensen got a call from someone at Morgan Stanley. The firm had decided to give him something called the Award for Excellence in Financial Economics, which came with a cash prize of $200,000, plus a special issue of the *Journal of Applied Corporate Finance*—a quasi-academic journal published by Morgan Stanley—in his honor. Jensen gave the prize money away to academic institutions that were willing to teach or do research on the new work he was doing with Erhard.

After the award ceremony in New York, there was a small dinner for the firm's top executives. At the dinner, though Jensen had given up being an asshole, he couldn't resist offering a short lecture on his ideas about integrity and the lack of it on Wall Street. As soon as he started, he could tell that the rest of the evening wasn't going to go well. Morgan Stanley was on the brink of bankruptcy, and the executives were obviously unaware of the turn Jensen's life had taken—they thought they were honoring finance's leading academic champion. In those days, Jensen was telling anyone who would listen that Wall Street had become a disgusting, stinking mess, that he was ashamed of its lack of integrity, that its troubles were its own fault, that the government shouldn't have bailed it out, that people should be put in jail. The deeper he got into it, the more stricken the faces of the people at the dinner. A couple of them actually got up and walked out before he finished. It didn't bother Jensen. He knew he was right. He was at peace. He flew home to Florida and went back to work.

4

THE TIME OF
TRANSACTIONS: RISING

Somewhere along the line, Robert Baldwin, when he was head of Morgan Stanley, started keeping in a desk drawer one of the old tombstone ads from the glory days of the syndicate department. The lead underwriter, whose name was at the top, was of course Morgan Stanley, and there were well over a hundred names of financial firms running in steadily decreasing type size down the page. Baldwin used the ad as a prop in arguing with anybody at the firm who thought he was moving too fast, pushing for too much change. He'd used a marker to cross out every firm on the ad that no longer existed as an independent entity, and by the late 1970s there were more cross-outs than names. The disappeared companies ranged from former titans like Kuhn, Loeb, a bulge-bracket firm that had been the chief rival to the original J. P. Morgan back in his heyday, to the regional firms that actually distributed most of Morgan Stanley's new stock and bond issues, such as G. H. Walker of St. Louis, whose founder was the namesake of the two Presidents Bush. That was the fate it was imperative for Morgan Stanley to avoid.

In 1973 Baldwin moved Morgan Stanley out of Wall Street, to midtown Manhattan—a mainly symbolic change (the business rationale was that it was supposed to bring the firm into closer contact with its clients) but one that older partners like Henry Morgan still found shocking. The firm also embraced a long-ago version of diversity hiring, which meant that among its entirely white and male senior workforce one began to encounter people who, for example, had mothers who hadn't made debuts, or who had attended a suburban public school before their Ivy League college, or who had ethnic-sounding names. These changes were secondary; what really mattered was Baldwin's piling on additional activities, things other financial firms did that were outside the tight frame of Morgan Stanley's focus on underwriting new stock and bond issues for corporations and selling them through the syndicate. The old Morgan Stanley operated on the assumption that the economically dominant, eternally stable corporation was the only kind of client it really needed. Baldwin saw that the big investing pools, the providers of capital, were rapidly becoming more powerful and that Morgan Stanley had to begin attending much more closely to their needs. If you truly believed that, it opened the way to destabilizing just about everything Morgan Stanley had traditionally done.

An early, spectacular example of one of Morgan Stanley's new activities was mergers and acquisitions. In the old days, when one of Morgan Stanley's corporate clients decided to acquire a smaller company, the firm—free of charge, just by way of keeping the relationship strong—would advise it on how to price and structure the transaction. Morgan Stanley made its money through its underwriting fees. Now, though, one of the firm's restless new hires, Robert Greenhill, a swaggering, flamboyant man who liked to be photographed wearing suspenders with dollar signs printed on them, got permission—enthusiastically from Baldwin, reluctantly from the other partners—to start a mergers and acquisitions department, which would charge a fee, much higher than the fee for underwriting, to advise clients who wanted to take over other companies.

In 1974 Greenhill persuaded the partnership to let him advise one of Morgan Stanley's long-standing clients, International Nickel, in a hostile takeover attempt against a company called Electric Storage Battery. Hostile takeovers—one company asking another company's shareholders to sell it a controlling interest without the approval of management—were something that top-of-the-bracket Wall Street firms just didn't do. These practices were unsavory and ungentlemanly, and, as is often the case with codes of conduct, there was an underlying economic rationale too.

A hostile takeover traduced Adolf Berle's idea of corporate shareholders as owners with no control; it was a very public demonstration that management (of the company being taken over, at least) wasn't really so powerful. In that way it undercut the rationale of Morgan Stanley's method of doing business, which assumed that executives of corporations, the people who hired Morgan Stanley, were powerful and that shareholders were supine. A typical takeover ended with the shareholders of the acquired company much richer and the chief executive out of a job.

International Nickel wound up acquiring Electronic Storage Battery at a highly inflated price, and from then on, Morgan Stanley, and most of the rest of Wall Street, was enthusiastically in the takeover business. Greenhill and his associates, along with the merger teams at the other leading firms, became business celebrities in a way that would previously have been very un–Morgan Stanley. They got to do this because they were generating more profits for the firm than any other department. Previously, the market for corporate control had been an arresting idea, promoted by intellectuals like Henry Manne and Michael Jensen. People like Greenhill and firms like Morgan Stanley gave the idea an institutional structure, a constituency of powerful champions who were active in the markets, and a big, demonstrated economic payoff for shareholders who bet right on these transactions. Berle once wrote, in another context, "A political force consists of a centrally attractive idea surrounded by an organizational apparatus." Now mergers and acquisitions had both, and so they became a powerful force in remaking much of American society.

Before the 1970s, the trading desk at Morgan Stanley was a glorified cubicle with a couple of guys who'd sell the occasional big block of stock as a favor for a client. In the way that everything on Wall Street was rank-ordered, with a heavy overlay of social class, trading was a lower activity than what Morgan Stanley did, the province of smaller and, to be frank about it, Jewish firms, in the same way that having clients who were in retailing or media, rather than industry, was lower, and also Jewish. If the prize client for a financial firm was one of the great industrial corporations, if these corporations were stable for eternity, and if their stocks and bonds were owned by people who only bought them and held on, what future was there in trading anyway?

But now Baldwin directed another of his protégés, Richard Fisher, to set up a full-dress sales and trading operation at Morgan Stanley. Fisher came from a middle-class background, by Morgan Stanley standards. He had recovered from a serious childhood case of polio that left him having to walk supported by two canes, and perhaps as a way of compensating he was preternaturally sunny and determined, great at making enthusiastic presentations to clients. Fisher and Bob Greenhill had been classmates at Harvard Business School and had always disliked each other, but from the firm's point of view they were both restlessly ambitious young partners trying to shove Morgan Stanley aggressively into lines of business the firm had once considered distasteful.

Having a sales and trading desk was another way of directing the firm's attention toward the providers of capital. When you thought of a typical buyer of stocks and bonds, if the person who came to mind was, say, a trust officer in a bank in St. Louis who had bought part of a new issue through G. H. Walker and Company and intended to hold on to it for a wealthy widow, well, that would suggest one way to behave toward the providers of capital: gently and reassuringly. But what if the typical buyer was the newly gigantic Fidelity Investments, running billions of dollars' worth of mutual funds that held the modest pooled wealth of middle-class Americans, or CalPERS, the likewise gigantic fund that held the pension contributions of employees of the state of California? These people were in and out of the markets every day (every hour— every minute!), buying and selling big blocks of securities. When they bought stocks, they did not intend to hold them and wait for the dividends to roll in, and when they bought bonds, they did not intend to wait until the maturity date and then redeem them.

If those were now the providers of capital and you wanted to do business with them, you had to get to know them every bit as well as Morgan Stanley bankers knew people like the treasurer of General Motors. You had to take them to a ball game and to dinner at a steak house—or, in the case of the head of a major desk at Fidelity, to a private golf game with Arnold Palmer or Jack Nicklaus. Aside from the social lubrication, the business relationship was different: the new providers of capital were more aggressive because they were more powerful. Rather than accepting the price Morgan Stanley had placed on a security, they might demand that it be priced lower. They also wanted Morgan Stanley to execute trades for them, at favorable prices, in securities the firm hadn't issued itself. To help with that, they wanted a lot of expert information about the companies that were issuing stocks and bonds—so Morgan Stanley hired a man named Barton Biggs to start a research department, with Baldwin, again, overruling the objections of the older partners. Morgan Stanley now had to know exactly who was buying blocks of which stocks and bonds, and who was selling them, in real time. So the firm had to have a roomful of people—traders, aggressive guys who yelled into the phone and thought in minutes, not years—who were right on top of the markets, all the time.

Selling securities through the syndicate system had happened slowly. Trading happened quickly. To buy or sell a block of stock for, say, a big pension fund, you didn't always have time to go out and find somebody to take the other side of the transaction. You had to buy the block yourself, using Morgan Stanley's own money at some agreed-upon momentary price, and then try to sell it later for a higher price. Syndication was practically risk-free; it hadn't required Morgan Stanley to maintain a substantial pool of capital to buy and sell securities, for the lesser firms in the syndicate had agreed to buy the stock before it even went on the market. Trading did require capital, and that put the whole way the firm was structured—as a private partnership with only a modest stock of capital put up by the partners—at risk: there wasn't enough partners' capital to enable high-level trading in the markets every day.

Next Baldwin created another new division, a kind of stockbrokerage aimed at very rich people, headed by an exemplar of the traditional Morgan Stanley sociology named Anson Beard (a direct descendant of James J. Hill of the Great Northern Railway, a client of J. P. Morgan's, and, through one connection or another, a phone call away from just about everybody in the old-line financial elite). Beard, the brother and look-alike of Peter Beard, the well-publicized photographer, adventurer, and man-about-town, had grown up as the son of a father who was socially impeccable but a lackadaisical stockbroker, whom he didn't respect. So he decided to have a career in his family's tradition, but in an untraditional way, seizing every opportunity to be aggressive in the mold of the unrestrained capitalists of the Gilded Age. He talked rapidly, joked, cajoled, prodded, trying to get the firm moving faster. His operation at Morgan Stanley required a sales force, which Morgan Stanley hadn't had, and more trading capacity and additional capital.

"Fixed income" is a Wall Street term that covers instruments that pay investors at a set rate—for example, a ten-year government bond that can be redeemed at the end of that time for the amount it cost, plus interest. The name connotes cautious, buy-and-hold investors, but as time went on, what it came to mean was almost completely different. Stocks are bought and sold on public exchanges, so their price at every moment is a matter of record. But if you own a bond and decide to sell it before its maturity date, you have to find someone to buy it. The price isn't public; it's set through a rapid private negotiation—as in, Do you want it at fifty-three dollars, or not? You've got five seconds. This kind of trading could go on continuously, every hour of every day.

Morgan Stanley set up a fixed-income department, headed by John Mack, an extroverted bond salesman from a small town in North Carolina. Mack was a protégé of Dick Fisher's—his department operated on the trading floor that Fisher had set up—and was another member of the restless, younger, nontraditional generation at Morgan Stanley. His family had originally come from Lebanon and had worked as shopkeepers; Mack himself was exuberantly theatrical and incautious, preoccupied with keeping large blocks of securities moving smartly on and off the floor. Because fixed-income trading did not take place on public exchanges, the Morgan Stanley traders knew more than their buyers or the sellers about prices. In fact, you had to be a trader, constantly in the market, to know what the prices were, as they were not listed. The firm's job was not to make sure both parties were getting a fair price; it was to match buyers (who thought the sellers were underpricing) with sellers (who thought the buyers were overpaying). Fixed-income was another division that required the firm to buy large quantities of financial instruments, at least temporarily, either with its own capital—or, increasingly, with borrowed money. When Morgan Stanley itself was the buyer or the seller, its job was to take advantage of the party on the other side of the transaction. If, as the traders liked to say, you could rip their face off, tear their eyes out, blow them up, or whatever cock-of-the-walk metaphor was in favor that day, that meant you were doing your job. Before long, fixed-income was producing far more trading volume than stocks, at Morgan Stanley and in the markets generally.

The older partners who objected to these new activities were, it's true, stolidly conservative, but they weren't wrong to worry about what was happening to the firm. The old Morgan Stanley was in the business of advising corporations, for a fee, about the stocks and bonds they wanted to issue. It could maintain a total focus on the client's interests. Every one of the departments the firm was now adding meant sacrificing a measure of its former purity. Mergers and acquisitions had an overwhelming incentive to push chief executives to make deals, whether or not the deals were in the company's best interest. The research department was supposed to offer objective analysis of companies that were Morgan Stanley's underwriting clients, which could either hurt the clients (if the research department's opinion was negative) or, more often, hurt whoever bought the company's securities (if the opinion was unrealistically rosy). And there was a fine line between Morgan Stanley's growing trading desk's owning securities temporarily, as a prelude to reselling them, and its maintaining a firm account and trading for its own profit in competition with its own clients. If a Morgan Stanley trader knew, for example, that somebody was trying to buy a block of securities at a certain price, he could locate the block, buy it for a little less, and keep it, knowing that it was worth more than he'd paid. In all these new activities, there was always some indistinction between acting on the client's behalf and acting on the firm's behalf. In Michael Jensen's terms, Morgan Stanley had gone from being an agent, working for its clients in exchange for fees, to being, much of the time, a principal whose interests were its own, not those of its clients. But if the price of maintaining purity was winding up as one of those crossed-out names on Bob Baldwin's tombstone ad, then it wasn't worth it.

Turning back was never really a possibility, but if any incident demonstrated that Morgan Stanley's former world was gone forever, it came one day in 1979, when three of Morgan Stanley's most senior partners went out to the headquarters of IBM in suburban Armonk, New York, to discuss a new bond issue that IBM was planning. By that time, the position of some of Morgan Stanley's old industrial clients had obviously deteriorated. One banker remembered being at a meeting with Roger Smith, the chairman of General Motors, and watching him pound the table and declare that GM was going to drive its Japanese competitors back into the ocean and that everybody GM did business with, including Morgan Stanley, would have to help by cutting their fees. But IBM was a technology firm. It still seemed to be invulnerable, so much so that it was the object of a long-running antitrust suit by the federal government. The Morgan Stanley bankers were expecting to have a familiar kind of meeting, in which they discussed the price of the bond issue and what kind of syndicate Morgan Stanley would assemble to distribute it.

Instead, they got the shocking news that IBM had been talking to Salomon Brothers about the bond issue, too, and had decided to make Salomon and Morgan Stanley comanagers, with Salomon in the top left position on the tombstone ad and Morgan Stanley in the top right. Salomon! A mere trading house, which ten years earlier would not have dared to call on a longtime Morgan Stanley client and would not have been welcomed by the client even if it had. But now Salomon was able to argue that it could manage the bond issue better than Morgan Stanley because it didn't need to assemble a syndicate. It was trading heavily in the markets all the time and knew exactly who was buying, who was selling, and at what price; and it was willing to buy large portions of new issues outright, risking its own capital, and then to decide what to hold and what to sell. That took any risk of delay off IBM's hands.

The three Morgan Stanley partners didn't respond to IBM immediately. Instead, they returned to Manhattan and called a meeting of the partnership to decide what to do. For more than forty years Morgan Stanley had never accepted anything but the lead manager's position in a new offering, and the partners decided that it wouldn't start now. They declined IBM's offer—and IBM simply went ahead with the issue, using Salomon as lead manager and Merrill Lynch (a mere retail brokerage firm, not even in the bulge bracket) as comanager, and Salomon and Merrill sold it successfully. From then on, the powerful mystique surrounding Morgan Stanley's underwriting business was severely damaged; any Morgan Stanley partner who might have hoped that underwriting could in the future continue to be the heart of the firm had to admit defeat. And there was no real remaining argument against continuing to charge ahead into newer, more complicated, riskier, more capital-intensive lines of business.

■

The financial system created at the outset of the New Deal was rather sleepy but quite stable. It depended on people putting their savings into banks and savings and loan companies, confident that their money would be safe because the government guaranteed deposits. The banks and savings and loans would lend out these deposits in their communities. Investment banks like Morgan Stanley would issue stocks and bonds, with the careful vetting of each issue by the Securities and Exchange Commission providing safety for the system and for individual investors. There was no financial crisis for fifty years, and this period was generally one of rising, and widely shared, prosperity in the United States.

When Wall Street began barreling forward into the power position in America, people who didn't like it often invoked a sudden rise in greed as the explanation, and people who did like it invoked the irresistible effects of larger economic and technological forces. Depending on where you stood, either the national character had deteriorated, or there was no excuse for standing in the way of progress. But greed had made it onto the list of the seven deadly sins back in the fourth century—why would an eternal trait abruptly become dominant? And other countries on which the same larger forces were operating confronted them in quite different ways, not by uniformly generating their own identical versions of Wall Street. Like the financial system created during the New Deal, the new financial system that began to replace it came into being because of a series of political decisions—decisions that changed the country profoundly, although the public hardly noticed them as they were being made.

During the 1970s the inflation rate rose dramatically, most obviously because of two sudden increases in oil prices, in 1973 and 1979. That led people to start putting their money into mutual funds, where its value might keep pace with inflation, instead of into banks, where the government had set interest rates on deposits at levels far below where inflation was now. So banks and savings and loan companies began lobbying the government to loosen the rules under which they operated. They wanted to be able to offer higher interest rates to depositors. That would cut into profits, so to compensate, they also wanted to use the money they collected in new, riskier ways. During the Depression it would have been insuperably difficult to push for these changes, because anti-bank sentiment was so strong. Now, because very few people were left who had memories of what it was like to lose everything in a bank failure, the country wasn't on alert about what banks were up to. The government made a lot of changes, and none of them generated much public attention or debate. They seemed to be the province of a welter of obscure federal agencies—the Federal Deposit Insurance Corporation, the Comptroller of the Currency, the Federal Savings and Loan Insurance Corporation, and so on—that adjudicated the technical disputes that bankers' lobbyists and representatives in Congress brought before them.

Politics had changed. The Republican Party was consistently opposed to government regulation, except when it worked to the advantage of interest groups associated with the party, so it was naturally friendly to deregulating finance. The Democrats were historically the party that wanted to regulate, but their focus was shifting. As early as 1964, Richard Hofstadter was writing that the period when American liberalism was centrally concerned with the economy had long since ended (he defined that period as the half century from 1890 to 1940). That, Hofstadter wrote, was because the regime of big corporations tamed by the central government was working so well: "The public is hardly unaware that the steepest rise in mass standards of living has occurred during the period in which the economy has been dominated by the big corporation." Therefore, "liberals do not often find themselves in a simple antagonistic confrontation with big business, as they did in the past." They were moving on to other concerns: the environment, civil rights, feminism.

Liberalism was not only no longer mainly about economics; the shrinking economic zone within liberalism was also changing its emphasis. Through most of American history, liberal economic language was offered up in defense of small, independent producers: farmers, local business operators, artisans, mechanics, and laborers, all of whom wanted protection from big economic interests. Back in 1832, when Andrew Jackson vetoed the charter of the Second Bank of the United States (a precursor to the Federal Reserve Board), he gave this justification: "When the laws undertake . . . to grant titles, gratuities, and exclusive privileges, to make the rich richer and the potent more powerful, the humble members of society—the farmers, mechanics, and laborers—who have neither the time nor the means of securing like favors to themselves, have a right to complain of the injustice of their Government." Decades later, during his three unsuccessful campaigns as the Democratic Party's presidential nominee, William Jennings Bryan often sounded this note. So did muckraking economic crusaders like Henry Demarest Lloyd and Ida Tarbell, the scourges of the Standard Oil trust. So did Woodrow Wilson, under the tutelage of Louis Brandeis, in his successful campaign for president in 1912. So, occasionally, did Franklin Roosevelt.

But after the Second World War, this kind of economic liberalism had almost disappeared from liberal thinking and national political rhetoric. The kinds of people first-rank liberal politicians and thinkers had previously championed now had to content themselves with lobbying, out of public view, to protect their interests. The national liberal conversation had become primarily concerned with the rights of consumers. National consumers' organizations date back to the 1930s, but they took off as a liberal force in the 1960s; the best-known consumer advocate was Ralph Nader, who became famous by attacking the most powerful corporation, General Motors, for not attending to the safety of its cars. Consumer-oriented liberalism wanted to offer people not just safety but also choice and low prices.

In 1975 the country's leading liberal politician, Senator Edward Kennedy of Massachusetts, held hearings meant to expose the unfairness of airline regulation. His chief assistant and guide in this project was a future Supreme Court justice, Stephen Breyer, a member of Kennedy's staff. Back in the 1940s, as one of his second-order assignments in government, Adolf Berle had helped create the airline regulation system, and the way it operated was consistent with his idea of how the economy ought to work. A well-established group of private airline companies was tightly regulated by a federal agency called the Civil Aeronautics Board: the CAB had to approve every route and every fare, and as a result, tickets were expensive, planes were half-full, and competition was light. To Berle, this was what social justice looked like; the system protected not just the airlines but also their employees. To Breyer and Kennedy it looked like a way of ripping off passengers in order to protect established interests.

Kennedy and Breyer envisioned a new world in which the airline industry would be operated for the benefit of the consumer: fares would drop, routes would proliferate, new companies would enter. Their hearings were not as sensationally attention-grabbing as the Pecora hearings about Wall Street back in the 1930s, but they did demonstrate how much liberal economic thinking had changed since those days. Kennedy assembled an ideologically diverse array of supporters of deregulation, including Nader and Milton Friedman; the main opponents were the airlines themselves and their labor unions. In 1978 the first Democratic president of the 1970s, Jimmy Carter, signed legislation abolishing the CAB entirely. Carter also deregulated trucking and railroads, and he signed the first of a series of major laws deregulating finance—giving banks, in the name of serving the consumer, the ability to pay much higher interest rates to their depositors.

In 1978 Robert Bork, a protégé of Aaron Director's at the University of Chicago Law School and a Republican law professor and government official, published *The Antitrust Paradox*, which argued that the only acceptable rationale for government regulation of the economy was consumer welfare. Therefore, Bork argued, the tradition of economic liberalism associated with Louis Brandeis was at best silly and at worst an indefensible form of welfare for undeserving small producers, at consumers' expense. And the opposing tradition of liberals like Berle, which proposed leaving big corporations intact but using government to make them behave properly, was just as bad because it overloaded corporations with social obligations in the mistaken belief that they were impervious to market forces. Berle's friend John Kenneth Galbraith, Bork wrote, was guilty of "sheer perversity" and "a willingness to state theory that will fit any facts" when he said such things.

Liberals hated Bork (among other things, he was the man who in 1973 had conducted the "Saturday Night Massacre" of Watergate investigators at the behest of President Richard Nixon) and understood him to be part of a large political apparatus that conservatives had created to wrest power from liberals. But his most influential ideas, the ones about economic regulation, were not part of the liberal critique. When Edward Kennedy spoke on the Senate floor in 1987 in opposition to Bork's nomination to the Supreme Court, he said that Bork's America would be "a land in which women would be forced into back-alley abortions, blacks would sit at segregated lunch counters, rogue police could break down citizens' doors in midnight raids, schoolchildren could not be taught about evolution, writers and artists would be censored at the whim of government." He didn't mention Bork's economic views.

This was the atmosphere in which banks began pushing hard to be deregulated—permitted to become far bigger and freer of constraints on their activities. The push came at a moment when nearly two hundred years of deep suspicion of concentrated economic power and forty years of heavy federal regulation of finance had lost all its force. There was not much to stand in the way. Even liberals had become significantly more suspicious of bureaucracy and regulation, the essential tools of Berle's generation, and much more trusting of markets, their ancient enemy. If the financial system could be reoriented so as to serve consumers first, to release the constraints on the markets, and to lessen the power of government agencies, that would not be alarming to liberals, and certainly not to conservatives. It seemed inarguably right. So dozens, hundreds, of changes in government policy cascaded through the financial system; only a handful of them got any public attention at all, and most went completely unnoticed except by the people directly involved. They seemed minor and technical, and in a general direction that was uncontroversial. Taken together, they profoundly changed not only finance but American society and the world—both economically and politically.

■

The leaders of Morgan Stanley, like most of their peers, were for deregulation in a general way, though some of the specific changes felt like setbacks because they chipped away at the privileged position the Glass-Steagall Act had given the firm back in 1934. What all the changes, as they emerged from Washington one by one, noticed by bankers but not by the public, had in common was that they were expressions of the mood of the time: they loosened restrictions, they trusted markets, they favored consumer interests over institutional interests. For Morgan Stanley in particular, each change pushed the firm in the direction of becoming bigger, more trading-oriented, hungrier for capital and profits, and more inclined to take risks.

In 1974 the Nixon administration abolished an obscure provision called the Interest Equalization Tax, which had been imposed by the Kennedy administration in 1963 and constrained American investment in foreign companies. That gave Morgan Stanley a big opportunity to become a global company, and it began opening offices all over the world. In 1975 the SEC abolished the long-standing system of high fixed com-

missions for stockbrokers. A liberal Democratic congressman from California, John Moss, had been the main crusader for this change—why
did stockbrokers need a federal welfare program? He held hearings and
then proposed legislation to abolish fixed commissions. Moss was acting
in the same spirit as Edward Kennedy when he campaigned against airline regulation: he wanted to generate more market competition in order
to lower prices to the consumer. Commissions dropped immediately, a
discount brokerage industry sprang up, and as a result, the economic
rationale of many of the firms in the bottom two-thirds of the syndicate system collapsed—which made the syndicate system itself much
shakier.

In 1974, after the collapse of the pension system of one of America's
venerable corporations, the Penn Central Railroad, Congress passed a
law regulating pensions, in order to make them safer. In 1979 the Department of Labor, which enforced the law, loosened a provision called
the "prudent man rule" so as to allow pension funds to be much less conservative in their investing. The rationale, once again, was protecting the
consumer (the retiree, in this case) against having a pension ravaged by
inflation. Prudent man rules were ubiquitous, not just in pensions but
also in university and foundation endowments, bank trust departments—
any institution that was supposed to manage a large pool of capital cau-
tiously, on others' behalf. Now the rules were relaxed, and that caused a
great flow of capital into mergers, leveraged buyouts, private equity, and
the other newly empowered, higher-risk forms of capitalism that were
breaking apart and reassembling the country's institutional structure.
As late as 1976, Peter Drucker was worrying that the growth of institutional investing might threaten capitalism's essential dynamism, as the
managers of pensions and mutual funds were so cautious that new businesses would not be able to get funded. Within ten years, anybody making
that kind of assertion would obviously have been kidding.

In 1980 the Internal Revenue Service established a little-noticed
regulation that created 401(k) plans, which today hold almost $5 trillion
in assets. This set off a wholesale shift from "defined benefit" pensions,
in which a company would guarantee a retiree a set monthly payment
forever, to "defined contribution" pensions, in which the money would
go into the markets under the employee's name and the retiree's pension would be a function of how well the retirement account was doing.

This wound up being an enormous boon to the providers of capital, especially the big mutual funds where most defined benefit pensions were invested. From Morgan Stanley's point of view, that meant more trading in order to get the mutual funds' ever-growing business. It also represented a large psychic shift in how Americans thought about their future: now more and more in the hands of the financial markets, less and less in the hands of the corporation. There was much less reason for employees to stay loyally at one corporation for their entire careers, and much less reason for corporations to have the same loyalty toward their employees. The corporation-dependent American version of the social welfare state was eroding.

In 1982 the SEC created a new regulation called Rule 415, which undid the nearly half-century-old requirement that it individually review every new securities offering. Instead, a corporation could file a "shelf registration," a general financial disclosure document that, if it satisfied the SEC, would allow the corporation to issue new stocks and bonds without getting specific approval for each one. The old system had given Morgan Stanley a substantial thumb on the scale because its corporation clients had no easy way of asking a number of firms to compete for their business; Morgan Stanley knew their finances well enough to file the registration documents with the SEC, and as soon as it did that, it was automatically the lead manager of the offering. But now a corporation could say to a group of investment banks: We want to create a stock or bond issue—who wants the business? How much do you want it? Enough to offer us a better price than your competitors? Enough to offer to buy the entire issue up front at that price, for your own account, so any delay or risk is removed from the corporation and put onto the bank? That year, Morgan Stanley itself bought an entire new issue of AT&T stock outright, for more than $100 million, in order to keep one of its most important corporate clients happy. It sold the stock within a day, through the equity trading desk, not a syndicate; in this new world, syndication was less possible, underwriting more risky and less assuredly profitable, and large-scale trading more necessary for Morgan Stanley.

The torrent rolled onward. In 1979 Jimmy Carter appointed Paul Volcker as chair of the Federal Reserve Board, and Volcker took severe action to reduce inflation. The result was three years of unusually high interest rates, which sent the country into a recession and also pumped more energy into the bond markets. When Ronald Reagan became president in 1981, his administration signaled that it would continue the move toward deregulation that Carter had launched, only more so. Reagan's Justice Department had a Robert Bork–like skepticism about antitrust enforcement, which further empowered the mergers and acquisitions departments at Morgan Stanley and the other Wall Street firms. Toward the end of the period of high interest rates, the savings and loan industry, which had lost its ability to attract deposits at its old modest interest rates, persuaded Congress to pass a major piece of financial deregulation, permitting it to acquire deposits in nontraditional ways, to offer adjustable-rate mortgages, and to make new and riskier kinds of investments—all while retaining federal insurance on their deposits. This meant the government would ultimately have to be responsible for all the new risk it was permitting the savings and loans to take on.

Adolf Berle's dream world of capitalism without capitalists had decisively ended within just a few years, without most of the world even noticing that a significant change had taken place or imagining that capital would now be looking for ways to take advantage of its new empowerment. But there were people who did understand. One of them was the most influential financier of the late twentieth century, Michael Milken of Drexel Burnham Lambert. That Milken—a guy in his thirties from a middle-class background, working out of Beverly Hills, California, for a formerly third-bracket investment firm—could be so important was a sign of how much and how quickly the financial world had changed. Milken saw that the bond markets were no longer the province of buy-and-hold trust officers and insurance companies; he created a market for high-risk, high-yield "junk bonds" that in the old days nobody would have wanted.

Selling junk bonds to the new breed of fixed-income traders on Wall Street generated much of the capital that fueled the mergers and acquisitions business in the 1980s, and of course the nature of the financing meant that successful acquirers of companies were heavily in debt. Milken also developed a client base for junk bonds in a group of western savings and loan companies that were looking for a source of capital that they could use to make risky but potentially highly profitable loans to commercial real estate developers. Often these savings and loan clients of Milken's would be both buyers and sellers of his junk bonds: he'd offer them junk-bond financing to pay for their own expansionist schemes, on the condition that they'd purchase other junk-bond issues of Drexel's. Other people would buy junk bonds issued by Milken on behalf of the savings and loans, and the savings and loans would buy junk bonds issued by Milken on behalf of companies that were clients of his, at artificially inflated prices. (It was this sort of arrangement that eventually landed Milken in jail and Drexel Burnham in bankruptcy.)

Whatever new was happening in finance, Morgan Stanley acted on it. It participated in mergers and acquisitions financed by Milken, including the biggest one of the 1980s, the takeover of RJR Nabisco by the buyout firm of Kohlberg Kravis Roberts, financed with Drexel Burnham junk bonds. In that deal, KKR paid Morgan Stanley's merger team an "advisory fee" of $25 million (Morgan Stanley had asked for $50 million), which people at the firm thought was less about providing advice and more about agreeing not to help KKR's competition in the battle for control of RJR Nabisco. When Morgan Stanley's venerable client General Motors caught merger fever and began acquiring technology companies, the firm was happy to help. When the head of the largest of these acquisitions, the cranky Texas billionaire Ross Perot, who had been paid in GM stock, became a pesky stockholder, GM bought his holdings in the company for more than $750 million. And when, a few years later, partly because of moves like this, GM began losing billions of dollars a year, Morgan Stanley was pleased to manage a new issue of more than $2 billion in new GM stock, which was one of the largest deals in its history.

The firm also created its own junk-bond department and its own leveraged buyout fund; it made a fee of $32 million on one buyout deal and $54 million on another. After another influential financier of the period, Lewis Ranieri of Salomon, figured out how to package large quantities of home mortgages into financial instruments and trade them—something made possible by the deregulation of the savings and loans, which not so long ago had made their money simply by collecting the monthly payments on the mortgages they had issued themselves—Morgan Stanley developed similar instruments of its own. When, in the late summer of 1982, Volcker's Federal Reserve, satisfied that inflation had been conquered, began lowering interest rates again, the stock market took off. Morgan Stanley developed an enhanced capacity to take people who had started new companies (such as Steve Jobs, of Apple Computer, and Donna Karan, the fashion designer—who insisted that her psychic approve the price of her company's stock) into the booming public markets. Issuing stock on their behalf was a service that paid much higher fees than traditional underwriting for established corporate clients.

Firms that didn't want to be left behind were also investing in the possibility that the new financial economics, which almost nobody on Wall Street understood substantively, might wind up becoming another way of making a lot of money. Goldman Sachs, by now Morgan Stanley's chief rival, had hired Fischer Black. Salomon hired Myron Scholes. Morgan Stanley didn't hire any future Nobel Prize winners, but it did begin to hire economics Ph.D.s from MIT and Chicago—for that matter, Ph.D.s in physics and mathematics—and to invest heavily in the additional computer capability that this kind of work required.

Derivatives—financial instruments derived from the price of something else, like stocks or bonds or commodities—had been around forever; they were essentially promises to buy or sell something in the future at a preestablished price, and therefore a way of betting that the price would rise or fall. The advent of financial economics and greatly increased computer power made it possible to create ever more complicated derivatives that depended on fast, complex, dynamically adjusted calculations of the values of groups of underlying securities or other instruments. Once you could do that, the traders on the floor could buy and sell the derivatives much more quickly and with fewer regulatory constraints than they could buy or sell old-fashioned stocks—so the marriage of financial economics and Wall Street was one more development enhancing the importance of trading at Morgan Stanley. In 1986 David Booth, a former protégé of Eugene Fama's at the University of Chicago who had gotten a job as a derivatives trader at Morgan Stanley, astonished the firm by making a $40 million profit on a single trade. By the late 1980s, derivatives trading accounted for half of the firm's profits.

In those days, traders still bought and sold over the phone, so the trading floor was loud. John Mack was a golf fanatic—he demonstrated his commitment to the advent of diversity at Morgan Stanley by offering free golf lessons to women and minority employees—and his troops on the floor would swing imaginary golf clubs between phone calls and light celebratory cigars after selling a big block at a good price. After one especially important trade, somebody gave Mack a smashed telephone headset, of the kind that an amped-up trader might create in the heat of a big trade, encased in Lucite as a parody of the old tombstone-ad souvenirs of corporate stock and bond issues. That was a handy symbol of what the firm had become.

Anson Beard, one of the senior partners who was pushing to make Morgan Stanley a global company, went to Tokyo and set up a derivatives business there. For $5 million, Morgan Stanley bought one of three seats that the Tokyo Stock Exchange had decided to offer to American companies. The Japanese corporate system was the opposite of what Adolf Berle described in *The Modern Corporation and Private Property*: stocks were narrowly controlled by corporations and their banks, so, compared with the United States, there was very little conventional buying and selling. This meant that the derivatives business, positioned to meet whatever pent-up demand for trading there was in Japan, grew rapidly. Morgan Stanley had invested in computer technology that enabled it to adjust prices after every trade instead of once a minute, and this helped it to become dominant in what was suddenly an enormous business—so much so that, in a traditionally xenophobic country, the head of the office in Japan had to commute to work wearing a bulletproof vest. Soon Morgan Stanley was making as much money abroad as it made in the United States. At the peak it had 60 percent of the $6 trillion Japanese derivatives market. Beard also talked the firm into establishing another new business line called prime brokerage, which executed trades for hedge funds, then a new kind of institution in the financial world— unregulated pools of capital that catered to rich clients and often invested heavily in the derivatives markets with borrowed money. At the partners' meeting where Beard proposed this, Bob Baldwin was skeptical; he had a hard time believing that hedge funds would ever amount to anything. Lewis Bernard, more presciently, said, Do you know how much risk you'll be taking on? He was aware that being in prime brokerage entailed Morgan Stanley's holding big positions temporarily, with its own capital. What if there was no immediate buyer? But in those days Morgan Stanley was being consistently rewarded for incaution.

There was always a contradiction at the heart of the derivatives business—not that many people noticed it at the time. The theory of financial economics was that it was using its highly technical calculations to reduce the risk and volatility of investing. In sales calls to clients, one could make the argument that pairing one derivative with another matched derivative in just the right way would protect you against either one's losing money. You could use derivatives to protect yourself against gyrations in interest rates, commodity prices, or currency valuations. But each derivative was itself an independent, tradable instrument, and the people buying and selling them on the floor had about the same relationship to them as a salesman at an auto dealership has to the engineering of the motor of the car he's selling. At one firm dinner during those wild years, a group of young men wrote a song by way of teasing Anson Beard, in which the person playing Beard expressed this sentiment about the office that created derivatives for Morgan Stanley: "I don't know what the hell goes on in there, but I know we make money on it!"

Because most of the new derivatives were designed to produce, out of their zillions of tiny calculations, incremental advantages, the way to make real money on them was a very old-fashioned one: buy them with borrowed money. (And many of the derivatives themselves were based on forms of borrowed money, like bonds, so the purchases were doubly indebted.) The leverage of borrowing turned small gains into large ones—if the trading strategy was successful. If not, it could produce large losses.

Back in the 1930s, the early federal regulators of the markets were well aware that investors buying stocks "on margin" (that is, with funds borrowed from their stockbrokers) could almost instantly send investors and firms into sudden failure if their bet went the wrong way, so they strictly regulated the practice. But they assumed that bonds were not going to be actively traded, and they didn't envision the new derivatives markets at all. So there was no limit on buying with borrowed money in those markets, and no capacity at the Securities and Exchange Commission for monitoring the risk that the investment banking firms it regulated were taking on. All over Wall Street, including at Morgan Stanley, traders were using more and more of their firms' own capital—and, increasingly, borrowing against their firms' capital, otherwise known as "using the balance sheet"—to invest in markets they didn't fully understand. Lewis Bernard remembers once visiting the trading floor at the French-headquartered firm Phibro and being amazed to see a person sitting next to each trader at his desk, like a shadow. Who were those people? he asked. They were there to watch the traders and make sure they didn't make a costly mistake. Morgan Stanley didn't have anyone like that.

In 1985, on the occasion of its fiftieth anniversary, Morgan Stanley took out a full-page ad in *The Wall Street Journal*, reviewing its history and traditions and ending with a promise always to remain a private partnership. From the outside, Morgan Stanley still looked very Morgan Stanley. Bob Baldwin had retired, and his replacement as head of the firm was Parker Gilbert—in full, Seymour Parker Gilbert III—whose father, who had died young, had been a partner of J. P. Morgan's; whose stepfather was Harold Stanley; and whose godfather was Henry Morgan. Everything about this impression was misleading. Dick Fisher had pushed hard to become Baldwin's successor, but Baldwin was never fully comfortable with him, so he chose Gilbert as a kind of transitional figure. When it came time for Gilbert to retire, in the early 1990s, he had trouble making up his mind about who his successor should be. He told the two leading contenders, Fisher and Bob Greenhill, the head of the mergers and acquisitions department, to work it out between themselves. They offered to run the firm as a team. That was a disaster: the two had always been rivals, and Greenhill, who had become an enthusiastic licensed pilot, was rarely in the office. Soon he had left, and so had Lewis Bernard. That left the firm in the hands of Fisher and his protégé, John Mack—both peppy guys from the sales and trading business. That was the future of the firm.

Just a year after announcing that it would always be a private partnership, Morgan Stanley reversed itself and decided to sell shares in itself to the public. That seemed to be one more move made in service of avoiding being left behind, and it changed the firm more, perhaps, than any of the many changes that preceded it. Up to that point, if you were a partner at Morgan Stanley, you made a lot of money, but not the kind of fortune that the most visibly successful people in finance were making in the 1980s. Bob Baldwin's salary when he retired in 1984 was $800,000—a small fraction of what people like Milken and Henry Kravis had accumulated. His share of the firm was worth close to $10 million, which he'd get in five equal annual payments after he retired at sixty-five. Because partners' capital was tied up in the firm, they were reluctant to risk the firm's money or to add too many new partners too quickly, lest the value of their ownership share in the firm decrease.

And the old ethic that employment at a Wall Street firm was a lifelong relationship was eroding, just as the idea that firms should not compete with one another for underwriting business had eroded. Stars in the newer and more profitable lines of business—merger and buyout specialists, traders, analysts, quants who designed derivatives—were being recruited by other firms or leaving to start their own small firms. Morgan Stanley wasn't set up to be able to match what they were being offered elsewhere.

And every one of the firm's new activities, it seemed, had one thing in common: an ever-larger pool of firm capital was a prerequisite. As much as partners' capital had increased—by a factor of fifty since Baldwin became head of Morgan Stanley—it was never enough. Traders needed capital to build inventory that they could sell at just the right time. The firm wanted to trade on its own account. Underwriting deals required more and more capital; John Mack remembers going to Seoul once to pitch Morgan Stanley as the underwriter for privatization of the South Korean telephone company, and being told that he could have the business if he promised to buy the entire offering, for a billion dollars, on the spot. Capital bought information about who was buying and selling and at what price, along with the ability to respond instantaneously to activity in markets that were never closed. Capital was power. Banks and mutual funds could be active in the markets with funds they'd taken in from depositors and investors. Morgan Stanley didn't have those options.

The firm's initial public offering, in the spring of 1986, was a big success: Morgan Stanley's new stock sold out instantly for more than $200 million and quickly began rising higher than the opening price. Within a day, Baldwin and the other most senior people in the firm had made more than $50 million each, and this was real money, not highly constrained partners' capital. From then on, Morgan Stanley was active in the markets with, in Louis Brandeis's phrase, other people's money, not the partners' own money. The firm had far less incentive to be cautious about taking on risk.

The big payoff for star performers was not the partners' capital, which they wouldn't see until they were seventy; it was the annual bonuses they'd get just after the end of the year. The sense of shared enterprise—and of forced primary attention to the long-term health of the firm—was severely diminished. The competition for talent became more and more intense, and bonuses ate up more and more of Morgan Stanley's annual profits—eventually, more than 80 percent. The places that were poaching from Morgan Stanley, such as buyout firms and technically oriented investing companies, had essentially no connection with the ongoing welfare of the companies they were investing in, because they had to return their investors' funds after a few years. That ethos was seeping into Morgan Stanley too. A former Morgan Stanley junior trader named Frank Partnoy reported in a tell-all memoir that on bonus day one year, one of the traders gave out T-shirts making fun of the earnest credo J. P. Morgan, Jr., had scribbled down the night before his testimony to the Pecora committee in the 1930s: the shirts read FIRST CLASS BUSINESS IN A SECOND CLASS WAY. An investment banker who worked at Morgan Stanley in the 1990s, Jonathan Knee, wrote a memoir in which he reported that bankers there and elsewhere on Wall Street had developed an acronym they used in deciding to go ahead with anything that might be short-term profitable but long-term dangerous: IBGYBG—meaning that by the time any bad consequences become evident, "I'll be gone and you'll be gone."

■

In the 1980s it was becoming clear that the steady upward economic progress of the American middle class—which began with the New Deal and continued for almost half a century—was ending. Economic inequality began to increase; the idea had disappeared that, as a kind of truism, children would do better than their parents; the rewards of economic growth were going disproportionately to the people at the top.

These developments coincided with the great shift from an institution-based to a transaction-based society, which was making itself felt not just at Morgan Stanley but practically everywhere in the country. Just as politics had created the economic order that was passing, politics—by undoing many of the rules and arrangements the New Deal had created—was now assisting at the birth of the new order that was beginning. And soon politics would have to respond to the dislocations and discontents that the new order was generating.

The financial system, now roaring to life, had been essentially crisis-free for decades: low risk, low return. The failure of significant financial institutions, something that had been a constant in American history before the New Deal, was almost unheard-of. In the late 1980s that began to change. On October 19, 1987, financial markets around the world plunged more in one day than they ever had before, even during the crash of 1929, at least partly because large institutional investors had adopted some of the techniques of financial economics, such as automated, computerized trading that proceeded almost instantly in response to complex calculations about the direction of the markets, without any human participation in the decisions to buy or sell. During the same period, more than a thousand savings and loans—a third of the total number in the country—failed, substantially because the deregulation of a few years earlier had permitted them to make highly risky investments that had gone sour. Because the savings and loans had managed to keep their federal deposit insurance through deregulation, their failure became the government's problem, and it wound up costing taxpayers well over $100 billion.

Back in 1984, a former aide to Ronald Reagan named Edwin Gray, who was the head of the federal agency that regulated savings and loans, had begun warning publicly that deregulation had gone too far and was introducing too much risk into the system. This got him treated as an unreliable, misguided, disloyal eccentric, especially by members of his own party. Alan Greenspan, then a paid consultant to one of the most aggressive savings and loans, who was soon appointed chairman of the Federal Reserve Board, the most powerful job in financial regulation, wrote Gray a long, admonishing letter, pointing out that many savings and loans were posting record profits. (Of the seventeen savings and loans Greenspan mentioned by name in his letter, fifteen were out of business four years later.) Gray resigned in 1987, just before savings and loans started failing en masse, and he was replaced by a savings and loan lobbyist.

One of the few members of Congress who was consistently and loudly skeptical of financial deregulation was James Leach, a moderate Republican from Cedar Rapids, Iowa. Leach was the grandson of a small-town banker who had also served as state banking commissioner, and whose bank later failed. He was adept at playing the part of the fair-haired, blue-eyed, plainspoken midwestern rube, and he had a generous measure of the old middle-of-the-country rural suspicion of big banks

on the coasts—their power and their tendency to take risks that could
wind up hurting people like farmers and smallholders. Leach also was
neither as conservative nor as unsophisticated as he appeared; he had
a rare command of the actual workings of all those agencies that over-
saw aspects of the financial system. He often argued with the economic
policy makers from New York and Washington, calling them "coastal pro-
vincials," meaning that they were no less parochial in their view of the
world than he was—and maybe even more parochial. And he considered that most of his fellow members of Congress who were involved in
financial issues had been, as he put it, "bought, lock, stock, and barrel"
by campaign contributions from banks. Leach himself refused to accept
out-of-state money or contributions above $500. Unlike many of his col-
leagues, he sounded warnings all through the 1980s about the dangers
of deregulating the savings and loans.

In 1992 Bill Clinton recaptured the White House for the Democratic Party, which had been out of power in the executive branch for all
but one of the previous six presidential terms. He did this substantially
by persuading voters that he understood the economic troubles of the
middle class and knew how to fix them—in contrast to the Republicans,
who were capable only of cheering the onward rush of the markets. He
promised to cut taxes for the middle class and to pass an immediate
economic stimulus program. When he accepted the Democratic nomination, he said he was doing so "in the name of the hardworking Americans
who make up our forgotten middle class."

A few weeks after the election, Alan Greenspan, by now in his second term as chairman of the Federal Reserve, came to see Clinton at
the Arkansas governor's mansion. Greenspan gave Clinton a detailed
argument for a quite different economic program than the one Clinton had run on: instead of a middle-class tax cut and a stimulus program, Clinton should focus on reducing the federal deficit that Reagan's
large tax cuts had created. That would bring down long-term interest
rates, which in turn, by making borrowing easier for ordinary people,
would stimulate the economy far more effectively than any new spending program could. Clinton took Greenspan's suggestions very seriously,
even though they were incongruent with the rhetoric of his campaign.
Like a lot of successful politicians, he thought of himself as someone
who could not be easily categorized, who could bring together people

who weren't accustomed to voting for the same party. He was a child of struggling small-town Arkansas, and he had an instinctive connection to people like himself, but he was no populist. He listened to people from the financial world and wanted their respect.

Rather than manage these tensions behind an impenetrable facade, Clinton put them on full display, at least to his staff. He appointed the farthest to the left of his economic advisers, Robert Reich, as head of his economic transition team, but he also created a new National Economic Council, modeled on the National Security Council, in the White House and put Robert Rubin, the cohead of Goldman Sachs and a major Democratic fund-raiser, in charge of it. When he felt he was being pushed too far in a Wall Street direction, Clinton would blow up, as if the people urging him on had no idea who he really was. Bob Woodward, in his book *The Agenda*, quotes Clinton as saying in one early meeting, "Roosevelt was trying to help people. Here we help the bond market, and we hurt the people who voted us in." But he wound up adopting the policy Greenspan had urged on him. The major economic legislation of his first year in office was a deficit reduction bill, which won the support of liberals by increasing taxes on upper-income people and preserving government benefits for the less well-off. Soon he was being brought daily bulletins on the fluctuating price of thirty-year bonds—instruments Clinton and his political aides had hardly heard of not so long ago—because that had become the test of whether his economic program was going to be successful. He twice reappointed Greenspan, a Republican whose basic inclinations were libertarian, to the chairmanship of the Federal Reserve, which made Greenspan the most powerful financial policy maker and regulator during the entirety of Clinton's presidency.

In his first year in office, over the opposition of most members of his own party, Clinton helped to push through the congressional passage of the North American Free Trade Agreement, which permitted the loosening of trade restrictions past the point that, not so many years earlier, even a corporation-oriented liberal like Adolf Berle would have thought conceivable. The next year, Clinton continued the ongoing undoing of the New Deal's constraints on finance by enthusiastically signing a bill legalizing interstate banking, ending one of the country's historic proscriptions on concentrations of financial power. In 1995 the World

Trade Organization, meant to push the globalization of trade further forward, opened, with the United States as a founding member. (The key member of the WTO, China, joined in 2001, not long after Clinton had signed a bill establishing it as a full trading partner of the United States.) Another Clinton campaign promise, crafted by Reich, was that salaries of more than a million dollars a year should not be deductible as business expenses by the companies that were paying them. As soon as there was a Clinton administration, the rest of the economic team quashed this idea, replacing it with a requirement that very high pay be linked to the performance of the business—which encouraged businesses to pay their executives and star performers even more, but in the form of bonuses and stock options rather than salaries.

Robert Rubin encouraged people in the administration never to talk about rich people at all, as it would encourage resentment and spook the markets. "People who have done well" was better. After Reich, as secretary of labor, made a speech calling for an end to "corporate welfare"—undeserved subsidies for big companies—the White House chief of staff, Leon Panetta, called him in and told him that Rubin had threatened to resign unless he stopped using that term. A few weeks later, Reich used the term "corporate responsibility"—innocuous not so long before—in another speech, and Rubin summoned him to the Treasury for an in-person chastisement. In 1996, after Clinton was reelected, Rubin, by now secretary of the Treasury, stayed on, and Reich resigned. "It was becoming difficult for him," Clinton wrote in his memoir; "he disagreed with my economic and budget policies."

The second term of the Clinton administration began in an atmosphere of overwhelming conviction that the president's unorthodox (for a Democrat) economic program was working splendidly. The unemployment rate was falling. The stock market was rising. Clinton had no politically potent opposition within his own party, and the lines of attack his Republican enemies had chosen had nothing to do with economic policy. Although the Republicans controlled the House of Representatives and the Senate, the 1996 presidential election hadn't been close; Clinton seemed to have discerned the outlines of a political coalition that might prove to be as durable as Reagan's coalition in the 1980s.

Inside the small world of people who made economic policy, the conviction was even stronger. Most of the Clinton administration's officials had grown up around liberal intellectual dissatisfaction with the mature New Deal order: its soggy slowness and automatic resistance to change, its tendency to focus on the claims of politically empowered "incumbents" over the needs of society's forgotten members and of consumers, its vulnerability to the capture of regulatory agencies by interest groups. Traditional liberalism, incapable of discipline about taxes and government spending, seemed to be the party responsible for inflation and slow growth. Communism had failed. Its main competitor, American capitalism, was producing miraculous innovations like the personal computer and the Internet. These officials had come of age at a time when many of the smartest students at the elite universities they had attended, people they respected as peers, had chosen careers that entailed participating in the financial revolution and otherwise rearranging the major institutions of American society. Freeing markets from constraint looked like the royal road to bringing a better life to people who needed and deserved one, all over the world. It was the best way for government to fulfill its most basic mission.

Clinton economic officials were, mostly, late-twentieth-century liberals in the Hamiltonian, rather than Jeffersonian, tradition. Like their forebears from eighty or ninety years earlier, they thought that traditional conservatives failed to understand how complex modern society was—how much, in order to function properly, it required a strong central government staffed by technicians. They also saw themselves as having the sort of powerful social conscience, the commitment to helping people in need, that most conservatives lacked. The person who first introduced Clinton to Robert Rubin was another Goldman Sachs executive, Ken Brody, who had become a Clinton fund-raiser because, as Clinton noted approvingly in his memoir, "he had gotten close enough to the national Republicans to see that they had a head but no heart." Rubin himself was heavily involved in charity work aimed at helping poor people, and he was proud to include in Clinton's economic plan, along with deficit reduction, deregulation, and the easing of trade restrictions, a big tax credit for low-income people. The Republicans would not have done that.

Just as Walter Lippmann and Herbert Croly saw William Jennings Bryan as a mere nostalgist, not someone who had ideas that deserved to be taken seriously, Clinton's economic officials were impatient with politicians who struck them as provincial or resistant to the inevitability of change. This was a category that included many liberal Democratic members of Congress and also some of the people working in the financial regulatory agencies. For Progressive Era liberals, applying an intelligent, reasoned critique to unimpeded markets was a central project, maybe *the* central project. For their successors in the 1990s, the project was almost the opposite: overcoming the by then ingrained liberal resistance to markets and instead embracing them as a tool to be used in service of liberal causes, such as making working people more prosperous. They wanted to use markets to help people rather than to create countervailing institutional power to markets. As Bob Woodward put it, "Two or three decades ago, a great ideological chasm in economics had divided Republicans from Democrats, but now on many issues a consensus was emerging. No longer could Alan Greenspan be so easily distinguished from Bill Clinton."

Clinton himself was far less personally involved in economic policy during his second term than he had been at the outset of his presidency. Presidents necessarily ignore most of what goes on in their administrations, focusing on crises and disagreements that only they can settle. With Robert Reich gone, Clinton's economic advisers agreed on most questions. The economic crises that absorbed most of their attention involved foreign debt—in Latin America, East Asia, and Russia—and it appeared that they were handling them adeptly. The overall lesson of these crises seemed to be not that American financial institutions had to be constrained from reckless lending abroad, but that governments around the world had to be brought more firmly under the discipline of an American-dominated global financial system.

In addition to healthy financial markets, another by-product of Clinton's economic policies was a substantial weakening of Wall Street's historic blood bond with the Republican Party. More and more people in finance began contributing to the increasing number of finance-friendly Democrats. Bill and Hillary Clinton themselves were moving their home base—first psychologically, later physically—to New York, the financial capital. Their daughter and son-in-law later made their careers in the new transaction-oriented parts of the financial world, she for a few years, he permanently. High on the list of more pressing matters that Clinton had to worry about was the impeachment drama that took up much of the last three years of his presidency. In a sense this was collateral damage from financial deregulation, since it had all begun with an investigation of a typically risky real estate investment, called Whitewater, made by an Arkansas savings and loan that went out of business, but Clinton of course didn't register it that way. Continuing deregulation of finance had an implicit green light from him to proceed, but very little of his attention.

During the first year of Clinton's second term, his Office of Management and Budget issued a report on the costs and benefits of government regulation. A couple of junior staff members at the Council of Economic Advisers got hold of an early draft of the report and reported to their boss, in an incredulous memo, that it "concludes that the benefits of 'economic regulation' are essentially zero." They went on:

> The OMB report estimates that the cost of banking regulation is roughly $5 billion a year. Although the costs imposed by the Federal Reserve Board, the Securities and Exchange Commission, and the Federal Deposit Insurance Corporation are not measured, all three agencies are mentioned among the list of regulators who place burdens on the economy. No attempt is made in the report or in the studies it cites to estimate the benefits of regulation of financial markets.

Weren't the people at OMB aware, the memo went on, of the influential work of the young economist Ben Bernanke—future chair of the Federal Reserve—"that argues that the collapse of the (unregulated) banking industry was a central cause of the Great Depression"?

The OMB report was far closer to the prevailing mood inside the Clinton administration than were the doubts of the Council of Economic Advisers staff members. The administration had a "Working Group on Financial Markets," whose energies were devoted mainly to planning the further deregulation of the financial system. At the top of its list of targets was the Glass-Steagall Act, the landmark 1934 law that had put the collapsed American banking system back on its feet and established a basic system of rules that functioned successfully for decades. Like the savings and loans in the early 1980s, the biggest banks were now arguing that the old restrictions placed on their activities—no

underwriting of stock and bond issues, no advising mergers and acquisitions, no risky investing—did not make sense any longer, because the
financial world had changed so much. They wanted to have the limits
removed, but, like the savings and loans, they wanted to keep their federal deposit insurance and also their access to short-term loans from the
Federal Reserve at special low rates. Although almost nobody seemed
to notice it at the time, because the idea of modernizing the financial
system seemed so powerfully right, this meant that the government, in
permitting banks to take on more risk, would be taking on more responsibility if anything went wrong.

Even before Clinton's second term began, the administration was
working up legislation that would eliminate most of Glass-Steagall's old
restrictions. In March 1997 Gene Sperling, who had succeeded Rubin as head of the National Economic Council, wrote Clinton a memo
summarizing the consensus among his advisers. "The old statutory restrictions remain on the books—imposing needless regulatory and management costs, and impeding competition, innovation, and consumer
choice," Sperling wrote. "Allowing financial firms of all types to affili-
ate holds promise that consumers will benefit as fair competition—less
hindered by regulatory restrictions—will drive firms to achieve and pass
savings on to consumers." Sperling assured Clinton that "increased affil-
iation will increase intra-firm diversification, which will almost certainly
reduce the risk of institutional failure."

Bank-friendly members of Congress had been proposing similar legislation for years, and bank-friendly regulators, at Treasury and the Fed
and in state governments, had been granting exemptions and approving
mergers that, taken together, amounted to a substantial erosion of Glass-
Steagall. To the minds of most people in the Clinton administration, the
only reason Congress hadn't passed one big bill to bring banking regulation up to date was opposition from not quite cutting-edge businesses
to whom Glass-Steagall provided safe harbor (stockbrokers, insurance
companies, and so on) and from old-fashioned liberals who were still
sentimentally attached to the idea that banks, especially big banks, were
up to no good. Sperling's memo went on:

> The decision whether to proceed with this legislation is one
> of weighing the very real—though hard to quantify—benefits

to the economy and consumers from rationalizing a financial services regulatory system that was established sixty years ago, under totally different economic conditions, against the concern that traditional Democratic allies are likely to express—strongly— that the legislation will lead to increased economic concentration and less credit, capital, and financial access to underserved consumers and communities.

As Sperling was presenting it, on the merits that wouldn't be a very difficult decision to make; as he put it, "All your economic advisors believe financial modernization reform is long overdue, that it is good government, good for the American economy and good for the American consumer."

■

The chairs of the banking committees in the Senate and the House were Phil Gramm and James Leach. Gramm was a Democrat turned conservative Republican from Texas, a former economics professor who liked to present himself as having a mystical bond with ordinary rural and small-town people (especially a character he liked to talk about in speeches—a printer in Mexia, Texas, whom he called Little Dickie Flatt), but he was close to the big New York banks and went to work for one of them after he left politics. Other than deregulation, Gramm's cause was eliminating or at least severely weakening the Community Reinvestment Act, which required banks to lend money in distressed neighborhoods. He had a special dislike of Jesse Jackson, the Chicago activist-politician whose organizations got some of their funding from Chicago banks, and he dreamed of a bill that would cut off bank funds that went to Jackson and people like him. This gave the Clinton administration an opportunity to go into moral battle against Gramm: their variety of defending liberal principles would be to protect the Community Reinvestment Act rather than traditional bank regulation. The administration let it be known that Gramm-style provisions were absolutely unacceptable.

Leach had earned the dislike of the Clinton White House by holding lengthy hearings on the Whitewater affair, which he regarded as a way to reexamine the savings and loan scandal via Bill and Hillary Clinton's investment in a busted financial institution. He was also skeptical

about the rapidly growing derivatives markets. During the first year of
the Clinton administration he had the Banking Committee's staff produce a nine-hundred-page report on the dangers derivatives posed to the
stability of the financial system—which the administration ignored—
and proposed legislation to create a new board to supervise derivatives,
which went nowhere.

Leach's main worry about a sweeping revision of Glass-Steagall
was that, in the hands of Rubin and Greenspan and their friends in
finance, it might permit combinations of banks and commercial businesses, so that Chase could buy Ford (or, as he thought more likely,
Microsoft could buy Chase), creating a small group of behemoths that
would control the economic life of the country. He imagined, for example, a combination that owned both a bank and McDonald's and
wouldn't extend credit to anybody else who wanted to open a fast-food
restaurant. Leach asked the General Accounting Office, a federal agency
set up to do objective research, to look into this, and its chief economist
responded with a long letter full of warnings: these business-financial
combinations could "affect the safety and soundness of the financial
system" and lead to "increased concentration of economic power." Leach
repeated these warnings every chance he got. "To Wall Street, con-
glomeration is a way of life," he said in one public statement. "To Main
Street, it is the jeopardization of livelihoods." Within Clinton's Working
Group on Financial Markets, this kind of concern was entirely absent—
the worry instead was that the financial system was not concentrated
enough, which made it too slow and inefficient, so that overseas competitors might threaten its primacy. Leach didn't get much more respect
than Phil Gramm. But he had enough power to be able to function as a
block against at least this one kind of deregulation.

Through the mid-1990s the grand revision of Glass-Steagall stood in
a suspended state because the administration wasn't willing to approve
any version of the law that Congress was willing to pass. The person
who got it unstuck was Alan Greenspan. In 1998 Sanford Weill—a financier who, through many mergers and acquisitions over the years, had
built a small brokerage house into a big financial services company with
many subdivisions—arranged for a merger between his company and
one of the country's biggest banks, Citicorp. It was the largest merger in
history, and the resulting combination was the largest financial company

in the world, with more than one hundred million customers. In the past it had been possible to ignore deals that nibbled away at the edges of Glass-Steagall, but this was an enormous, obvious, flagrant violation, as the company Weill had put together owned a bank, an investment bank, and an insurance company—all activities that Glass-Steagall had separated. Because the Federal Reserve regulated the biggest banks, the deal went there for approval. Greenspan granted Weill a waiver from the law, with a two-year duration. That meant the merger could proceed, and it essentially forced the Clinton administration and Congress to pass the bill they had been unable to agree on. One couldn't very well break up Citigroup two years after it had been massively reconstituted. As the financial world realized that a new law was now inevitable, it poured a great wave of cash into the political system—nearly $400 million in lobbying expenses and campaign contributions in 1998 and 1999—to try to achieve a favorable outcome.

Weill and John Reed, the head of Citicorp, came to Washington to argue their case before Rubin, but he hardly needed persuading. One Treasury aide remembers listening to Rubin joust teasingly with another Treasury official who had previously worked at Bank of America over who would emerge as dominant in the post-Glass-Steagall era: the investment banks, like Goldman Sachs and Morgan Stanley, or the commercial banks. Rubin thought the investment banks would win—they were more nimble and had smarter people. (Rubin belonged to the same generation of leadership at Goldman Sachs as Dick Fisher at Morgan Stanley—the first generation to rise from the trading floor to top management; being part of the astonishing success of that business obscured the advantage the commercial banks had in being insured and regulated by the federal government.) There was no question that the starting gun was about to sound on a race to expand, and to Rubin, this was properly understood as the unleashing of healthy business competition, entailing no risk. During the negotiations on what became the Financial Services Modernization Act of 1999, one of Gene Sperling's aides sent him a handwritten note reporting on a concession the administration was willing to make, which couldn't be announced because it was a couple of notches closer to what the banks wanted than its official negotiating position. "Please eat this paper after you have read this," she wrote. The job at hand was to pass the bill (which, to Leach's lasting embarrassment, carried his name as a cosponsor—the price of getting the barrier between banking and commerce he'd insisted on). Everybody believed that it was not what it would have ordinarily seemed to be—a major change in policy; it was a technical catch-up whose merits all knowledgeable people agreed on.

Bill Clinton signed the bill in a fifth-floor conference room in the Executive Office Building next to the White House, without the maximal flourishes available to a president signing landmark legislation. In his remarks he made it clear that to his mind, this was one more aspect of the spectacularly successful reinvention of economic liberalism his administration had engineered. The markets were booming. The economy was growing. Inflation was low. The federal budget deficit had become a surplus. An antiquated, industrial-age system was being replaced by a modern, information-age one, designed to serve consumers rather than bankers. "This is a very good day for the United States," Clinton said.

With the end of the Glass-Steagall restrictions, along with interstate banking, the globalization of trade and finance, and the management of foreign debt crises, the Clinton administration completed what it had set out to do in finance. There was one more major struggle, though, which the administration's senior economic advisers had not anticipated and which was especially surprising because it took the form of an attack from within.

Derivatives, by now the most rapidly growing part of the financial system, were still mainly unregulated. To the extent that anybody was keeping an eye on them, it was a small, obscure agency called the Commodity Futures Trading Commission, which had been created in 1974, just after the Chicago Board of Trade opened the first public options market—a development that the work of the financial economists a few miles away in the University of Chicago economics department had made possible. Because the Chicago Board of Trade's roots were in the trading of agricultural futures, the Commodity Futures Trading Commission's congressional oversight came not from the banking committees in the House and Senate, but from the agriculture committees. Among the members of the Clinton economic team, the reputation of the commission was as the textbook example of regulatory capture—a small, ineffectual agency that did the bidding of the Chicago Board of Trade, which was able to have its way by contributing generously to the campaigns of members of the agriculture committees, who otherwise usually didn't have access to wealthy political donors. During most of Clinton's second term, the head of the commission was Brooksley Born, a veteran Washington lawyer who moved in a different circle from the senior members of the Clinton economic team, with their deep ties to finance in New York.

Within a few weeks of taking office, Born made it known that she believed the derivatives markets—not just corn and cattle futures at the Chicago Board of Trade, but all the proliferating options, futures, and swaps that financial economists were creating, which were becoming a leading source of income for trading desks on Wall Street—should be regulated by the federal government. The volume of unregulated derivatives trading, mainly by a handful of large financial institutions that set them up as private trades between two parties, had grown to the point that it was a $28-trillion-a-year market, far larger than the public, exchange-based futures markets that the commission regulated. The last Republican chair of the Commodity Futures Trading Commission, Wendy Gramm—Senator Phil Gramm's wife and, like him, a conservative economist—had issued a ruling just before leaving office that the big banks interpreted as a permanent exemption from regulation for most derivatives. That set off a period of rapid growth in the markets. In 1994 there were three well-publicized scandals involving unregulated derivatives: the bankruptcy of Orange County, California, because of a loss of $1.5 billion on derivatives that Merrill Lynch had sold it; and losses in the tens of millions by two private companies, Procter & Gamble and Gibson Greetings, on derivatives that Bankers Trust had sold them. And a few years later, Enron, whose board Wendy Gramm had joined just after leaving the Commodity Futures Trading Commission, collapsed because of fraudulent accounting practices, many of them associated with derivatives trading approved by Gramm.

On New Year's Eve 1996, Brooksley Born wrote an official letter to Richard Lugar, the chairman of the Senate Committee on Agriculture, informing him that she and Rubin's Treasury Department disagreed about derivatives regulation; a month later, Rubin wrote Lugar to say that Treasury believed that, for example, foreign exchange markets, where traders could speculate on fluctuations in national currencies, "should be entirely exempt" from regulation by Born's commission because "the public is well served by deep and liquid foreign exchange markets." Born and the rest of the administration quickly settled into a low-grade hostile standoff. In April 1997 a Treasury aide, in a memo previewing the next meeting of the Working Group on Financial Markets, wrote, "Brooksley Born will do about a 10 minute presentation laying out her position, after which she will probably get taken apart more or less politely by everyone else in the room." During this period, Alan Greenspan invited Born to a get-acquainted lunch in his private dining room at the Federal Reserve. As she remembers it, he said, Well, Brooksley, I guess you and I will never agree about fraud. Why is that? she asked him. Because, Greenspan said, you think there should be *laws* against it. She did a double take. Greenspan explained: if a trader engages in fraud, the company will fire him. Problem solved.

To the other members of the Working Group, there were several possible interpretations of Born's behavior, none of which entailed taking her concerns seriously. The most charitable one was that she and her patrons at the Chicago Board of Trade saw an opportunity to enhance their power—at the commission and on the trading floor—by putting more of the derivatives markets under their control. A less charitable one was that she, like most people who were not economists or financial professionals, simply did not understand derivatives transactions, which were mainly complicated, technical private financial arrangements made between sophisticated parties in order to reduce their risk. Or else, least charitable of all, she was simply a crank who didn't realize that the New Deal era had ended.

In the spring of 1998 Born turned what had been an ongoing series of skirmishes into an all-out war. Having heard that the Securities and Exchange Commission, chaired by Arthur Levitt, a veteran Wall Street figure who had once been a partner of Sanford Weill's, was preparing to propose that the SEC regulate the derivatives market itself at a low level of supervision, she produced a document called a "concept release," proposing that the Commodity Futures Trading Commission be given large new regulatory powers over at least those derivatives that could be considered futures contracts. Most of the Clinton economic team felt that Born had tricked them by producing her proposal without forewarning. As one Treasury aide's notes put it, "Basically, Brooksley Born is 'thumbing her nose at the working group.' No heads up that this was coming."

Just before an April meeting of the Working Group, Born got a call from someone at Treasury warning her that Rubin and his deputy,

Lawrence Summers, were very upset about her proposal and that Rubin was going to bring it up at the meeting even though it wasn't on the agenda. The notes that a Treasury aide kept at the meeting engender a vivid sense of Born being ganged up on by the rest of the working group:

Greenspan: *Economics* should inform these definitions.

Rubin: Financial community "petrified" . . . that swaps are futures . . . Raises uncertainty over trillions of dollars of transactions . . . Treasury will put out statement that CFTC has no jurisdiction if CFTC goes forward . . . Massive concern.

Levitt: *Better ways* to air issue.

Summers: Given that, rightly or wrongly, Treasury, Fed, SEC, and industry view concept release as being disastrous for market, is there not a better way to proceed?

Born: Rubin is asking CFTC not to uphold the law.

Greenspan: Worry . . . that OTC [over-the-counter, meaning not traded on public exchanges] derivatives market could flee to London (or Europe) if this isn't handled well. That would be a *failure* on CFTC's part . . . Can't "put cork back in bottle." Once we begin process, has possibility of serious uncertainty. There are contradictions in the CEA [the 1974 law that created Born's commission]—but that shouldn't induce us to do things that will undercut the system that we are beholden to serve.

After the meeting, Summers called Born and told her that if she moved forward with the concept release, she would be precipitating the worst financial crisis since the end of the Second World War. His argument was that because the new world of derivatives trading was made up of private contractual arrangements between the two parties to each trade, the introduction of a new third party, the federal government, would remove the "legal certainty" underlying each contract and so would make it impossible for the markets to function. Born tried to set up a private meeting with Rubin, but he would not return her phone calls. As an internal White House memo put it, "The many forces arrayed against the CFTC (Treasury, Fed, SEC, and most of the futures industry) regard the CFTC's concept release as at best a mere exercise in turf protection and at worst a destructive exercise in regulatory over-reaching." Within a few weeks, Born made a copy of the concept release public; Rubin, Greenspan, and Levitt instantly issued a joint statement expressing "grave concern about this action and its possible consequences."

Every administration has internal disputes, but it's unusual for such disputes to become as public and as bitter as this one—especially because a regulatory agency like the Commodity Futures Trading Commission is supposed to be independent of presidential control. In June the administration sent its senior economic officials to Capitol Hill to oppose Born in hearings before the House and Senate Agriculture Committees, and it proposed legislation to deny her commission the ability to regulate derivatives. As Summers testified in the Senate, "The joint legislative proposal of the Treasury, Fed, and SEC is a grave step (in that it aims to restrict the independence of the CFTC, even if in a small and temporary way) and it is not taken lightly. However, this gravity reflects the magnitude of the danger posed to the OTC market by the CFTC's concept release." Congress wound up passing a temporary ban on the commission's assuming any new regulatory powers in the derivatives markets, and Born's opponents in the administration secured the public support of three of the five members of the Commodity Futures Trading Commission. Forbidden to act by Congress, preemptively outvoted by her own colleagues, Born was checkmated. She resigned in the spring of 1999.

In September 1998, just a few weeks after Congress had temporarily banned any further regulation of derivatives, there was another big failure in the financial markets, one that could almost have been scripted by Born as a way to prove her contention that derivatives were actually much riskier than most people realized. Long-Term Capital Management—an investment fund founded by a former star trader at Salomon—which was proud to be an advanced user of technical derivatives trading techniques (Robert Merton and Myron Scholes were among its founders), went out of business.

Long-Term Capital was a hedge fund, a member of a category of new, unregulated financial institutions that was growing rapidly in the 1990s. The name implies a fund that was carefully balancing one investing bet against another to reduce the overall risk to which it was exposing its investors. But for Long-Term Capital, like most hedge funds, no matter how much it claimed to be using new, foolproof technical portfolio management techniques, its investing strategy was based on some eternal verities. If you purchase a financial instrument and its value goes up, you can make money. If you purchase the same instrument with borrowed money and its value goes up, you can make a lot more money. And if you place a bet on the future directional movement of the instrument by buying a derivative, and you're right, you can make a lot more money than if you owned the instrument itself. And what happens if you're wrong is similarly magnified in all these instances. Long-Term Capital was investing massively in the derivatives markets with money it had borrowed from banks, especially investment banks; it was investing almost thirty times the amount of capital it had from investors. When a few of Long-Term Capital's investments went spectacularly wrong, it was ruined because it couldn't pay back what it owed the banks; and worse, the banks themselves were at risk of being ruined too if they couldn't recover the large sums they had lent to the firm.

As that became clear, Treasury and the Fed began to hold emergency meetings. What people in Washington hadn't realized was that a single hedge fund with assets of a few billion dollars had the potential to bring down the entire financial system. The notes of one Treasury conference call have one of its top officials saying, "The firm can't survive because of liquidity problems—the firm was very successful in getting a huge book on such little capital . . . Could it cause a broker-dealer [meaning an investment bank] to fail? . . . Are some hedge funds too big to fail?" After last-minute attempts to save the firm were unsuccessful, the Fed decided it had to organize a rescue: it would extend credit to a group of big banks that would enable them in turn to buy low-priced ownership stakes in Long-Term Capital Management. This worked in the sense that, although it didn't save Long-Term Capital Management, it did save the banks that were its major lenders. Hedge funds were unregulated because they were supposed to represent private investment arrangements between wealthy, sophisticated parties who were prepared to absorb whatever losses they suffered; what this episode showed was that government and taxpayers may have had no power to monitor hedge funds, but they could wind up with the responsibility for covering their losses.

Especially because it came at a time when the question of the government's regulating the derivatives markets was in play, the fall of Long-Term Capital Management got people's attention in Washington. James Leach held hearings, and a group of liberal Democratic members of Congress commissioned an investigation by the General Accounting Office. The Treasury announced that the Working Group on Financial Markets would be producing its own report; it declined to send someone to testify at Leach's hearings, for fear that the hearings might provide support for Brooksley Born's position. Within the Working Group, the most naturally cautious person aside from Born was the group's only other female member, Janet Yellen, the economist and future Fed chair who was then head of the Council of Economic Advisers. (Perhaps it's only a coincidence, but there are references in Yellen's office files to the Treasury's sometimes neglecting to invite her to Working Group meetings.) As the Treasury was working on its report about Long-Term Capital Management, Yellen's deputy, Doug Elmendorf, was working with her to try to figure out where she stood on derivatives regulation. Because it tracks so closely with what actually happened ten years later, one memo from Elmendorf to Yellen, from December 1998, is eerily prescient about the possibility for disaster that the new financial system had created. Elmendorf wrote:

> One specific effect of asymmetric information [meaning that in over-the-counter derivatives markets, no party to a transaction knew the underlying economic condition of the other parties] is to increase the risk of a general financial panic ("systemic risk"). Because market participants cannot judge the financial health of institutions they deal with, bad news about one institution has a contagion effect on other institutions, reducing their access to capital as well. The doctrine of "too big to fail" is based on this point . . . Financial innovation has worsened this problem. Institutions have many new avenues for taking risk that are difficult for even sophisticated market participants to fully understand, and the interrelationships are even more complex . . . In

the case of banks, the existence of deposit insurance coupled with access to the payments system [operated by the Federal Reserve] creates moral hazard with a clear incentive for excessive risk-taking. This is, after all, the rationale for regulating and supervising banks. In the case of other financial intermediaries there may be implicit but not explicit guarantees because many are too big to fail—a recognition that the failure of such entities also creates a systemic risk.

A couple of weeks later, Elmendorf wrote Yellen to say that he was going to tell one of Rubin's deputies that her view was that "on balance, more regulation could, and probably should, occur." But in the spring of 1999, when the Working Group on Financial Markets issued its report on the collapse of Long-Term Capital Management, it called only for what Rubin, in a memo to Clinton describing the report, described as "indirect regulation"—mostly requirements that hedge funds disclose more information to their lenders. The report did not, Rubin went on, recommend "direct regulation" of hedge funds and derivatives dealers, or government supervision of the general financial condition of investment banks. By contrast, the GAO's report on Long-Term Capital Management, published a few months later, took a harder line. It said that the Working Group had not proposed enough regulation, especially of investment banks, and that more was needed to ensure the safety of the financial system.

Less than a month after the release of the Working Group's report, Rubin resigned as Treasury secretary. Not long afterward, he took up a senior position at Citigroup, his friend Sanford Weill's firm, whose rise to the status of financial superpower he had helped from his government position. Summers succeeded Rubin as Treasury secretary, and it fell to him to complete the work on derivatives that Brooksley Born's attack had made necessary. Summers was an academic economist, the scion of an economics royal family—the Nobel Prize winners Kenneth Arrow and Paul Samuelson were both his uncles. The inventors of modern derivatives were the kind of people for whom he had the greatest respect. "Larry thought I was overly concerned with the risks of derivatives," Rubin, who had run the trading floor at Goldman Sachs and thought of himself as an expert on prudent assessment of risk, wrote in his memoir. "Larry thought I just wanted to keep markets the way they were when I'd learned the arbitrage business in the 1960s—his point about 'playing tennis with wooden racquets' again." In the limited time remaining in the Clinton administration, Summers pushed hard to get a bill passed that would make it impossible for the worries Brooksley Born and others maintained about derivatives ever to find expression in government policy. The Working Group on Financial Markets issued another report, recommending not only that the unregulated derivatives markets remain that way, but that the government be legally prohibited from regulating over-the-counter derivatives.

The Commodity Futures Modernization Act of 2000, which was based on this recommendation, was one of the Clinton administration's last pieces of legislation. Bill Clinton signed it on December 21, 2000, just a month before leaving office, and there is no evidence that it had much of his attention. (Clinton has since said that it was a mistake.) As the bill was moving through Congress, a few liberal Democrats warned that derivatives were too risky, but the bill's most consequential opponent was Phil Gramm, whose concern was that it did not go far enough in ensuring that over-the-counter derivatives could never be regulated. The final version of the bill, which passed overwhelmingly in both houses of Congress, was significantly more deregulatory than where even the Treasury had been during its fight with Born two years earlier: it prohibited both the Commodity Futures Trading Commission and the Securities and Exchange Commission from regulating most derivatives, and it preempted all state laws that might presume to regulate them. By that time the over-the-counter derivatives market had grown to $95 trillion, and it grew much more rapidly after the bill had passed. This meant that an investment bank like Morgan Stanley, which wasn't officially protected by the federal government, was more and more performing without a net. Being in the derivatives markets meant committing ever-larger large amounts of capital to instantaneous, increasingly complicated, nonpublic, unregulated transactions. But how could you not?

■

Whenever a Republican administration succeeds a Democratic one, it assumes that one of its tasks is to decrease the excessive level of regulation that its liberal predecessor imposed. So when George W. Bush became president, there was no sense among the members of his economic team that the Clinton administration had overdone it on financial deregulation. Alan Greenspan, reappointed by Clinton for a second time toward the end of his term, was at the height of his prestige, held in awe by most of Washington and Wall Street for his ability to keep the economy humming through a series of deft manipulations of interest rates. It's difficult to find a contemporary account of Greenspan that even mentions his libertarian views on financial regulation, let alone questions them. Believing that the economy was overheating in the late 1990s, Greenspan raised rates; then, after the dot-com bust in 2000 and the September 11 terrorist attacks in 2001, he lowered them, nine times in a row, to keep the economy from going into a recession. He publicly endorsed Bush's initial economic program, as he had Clinton's, even though it had the opposite effect of raising the deficit through heavy tax cuts; in 2002 Bush reappointed Greenspan to yet another term as Fed chair.

When interest rates go down and it's cheaper to borrow, the price of assets that people buy with borrowed money rises. The total value of residential housing in the United States doubled between 2000 and 2007, from $11 trillion to $22 trillion. That was partly because of Greenspan's repeated cuts in interest rates, and partly because mortgage lending standards had become dramatically more lax than they had been even a few years earlier. During the decades after the Second World War, homeownership expanded greatly, mainly through the means of thirty-year mortgages made by savings and loans at fixed interest rates. The homeowner would make identical monthly payments to the lender until the loan was retired. Now, after more than two decades of financial deregulation, local savings and loans were disappearing, and most new mortgages were made at low initial rates that rose steeply after two years.

The new growth in homeownership was among people with less money, many of whom didn't fully understand how quickly their monthly payments were going to rise. Their mortgages, called subprime, had a total value of $35 billion in 1994 and $625 billion in 2005. They often originated with local mortgage brokers who approved loans quickly and immediately resold them up the financial chain; often these new mortgages wound up inside mortgage-backed securities or other new financial products devised by Wall Street—including derivatives that entailed betting on the directional movement of the mortgage-backed securities, which were derivatives themselves. So it was the financial markets—rather than traditional bankers who made loans to people they knew—that were providing credit to new homeowners. The markets were flush with capital, and the proliferating new hedge funds and private equity funds needed to produce higher-than-average returns for their investors. With too much capital chasing too few genuine investment opportunities, mortgage-backed securities began to look far more attractive than they should have.

Before deregulation, the federal government regularly inspected the institutions that made mortgage loans, to make sure they were operating prudently. After deregulation, much of the mortgage system moved outside the government's purview. In theory, private ratings agencies were supposed to check on the quality of the mortgages that were bundled and sold as derivatives, but in practice, the agencies, which were paid by the Wall Street firms they were supposed to be judging objectively, had notoriously easy standards. A-rated mortgage packages often turned out to be just as risky as B-rated packages. Another marcher in the skimpy parade of financial Cassandras who had been appearing occasionally during the decades of deregulation was Edward Gramlich, an economist who was one of the governors of the Federal Reserve Board and so in an ideal position to give Greenspan his argument about the risks in the mortgage market in person. But he got nowhere. (Gramlich published a book expressing his worries in 2007, just before he died.) Greenspan's core convictions were that deregulation was healthy, that derivatives were technical devices that sophisticated financial players used to reduce risk, and that financial firms could be trusted not to be imprudent, because they had a natural incentive to survive and prosper. The Fed had the legal authority to regulate mortgage lending, but Greenspan declined to exercise it.

In the 1990s the big commercial banks had pushed hard for the end of the Glass-Steagall restrictions because they wanted to be able to participate in the new markets where the investment banks were making so much money. Now that they had succeeded, they had special advantages over the investment banks. The commercial banks could use their customers' federally insured deposits as capital to trade in the markets—but the investment banks couldn't take deposits. To keep up with the newly empowered commercial banks, they stepped up their borrowing: that was where they got enough capital to keep playing at the highest levels in the derivatives markets. Unregulated over-the-counter derivatives were growing, to a value of $672 trillion by 2008, but there was no system for monitoring how much institutional risk the investment banks were taking on. Treasury and the Fed were legally required to keep tabs on the safety of the commercial banks; the investment banks' regulatory agency, the Securities and Exchange Commission, was not set up to do that.

In 2002 the European Union, concerned that financial institutions, in order to participate in the derivatives markets, were borrowing too heavily, announced that it was going to impose new, tougher standards for how much capital a firm had to keep in reserve in order to participate in European financial markets—unless it could prove that it was being regulated just as strictly by its own national government. It was unthinkable for investment banks like Morgan Stanley and Goldman Sachs to leave the European market, so instead they made an arrangement with the Securities and Exchange Commission in which they would voluntarily submit to SEC regulation of their capital reserves, using supposedly advanced technical measures the banks themselves had devised. The SEC took on this mission with a small, untrained staff. It was inclined to be trusting anyway. Between 2000 and 2007, Morgan Stanley, for example, increased its debt-to-capital ratio by 67 percent, to forty dollars borrowed for every dollar in reserve.

The country hadn't had a referendum on it, exactly, but it had decided, through a long series of specific changes that rested on a general change in the atmosphere, to drop the central premises that had been established during the Great Depression. The financial system no longer required close supervision. Markets deserved an automatic trust, government and other big institutions an automatic suspicion. Thus unencumbered, the United States and the world could zoom forward into a modern, prosperous future.

5

THE TIME OF
TRANSACTIONS: FALLING

E verything that was happening in the American economy made itself felt locally in Chicago Lawn, and none of it was for the good. The market for corporate control that Michael Jensen had promoted so enthusiastically affected all the major private employers in the neighborhood, always in the same way: fewer jobs. The American Can Company factory on Western Avenue shut down following a series of acquisitions of the company, first by a Wall Street investor named Nelson Peltz, then by a French conglomerate. So did the Kool-Aid plant on South Rockwell Street, also after a series of mergers and acquisitions involving its parent company, Kraft. So did the factory on South Kedzie Avenue that made Rheem water heaters, after the company was acquired first by an American company and then, a few years later, by a Japanese company that moved its production from Chicago to Mexico. So did the largest store in the neighborhood, a Sears branch on Western, after a merger followed by a takeover by a private equity investor. Most of the name-brand auto dealerships that had lined Western Avenue were gone, replaced by used-car lots and scruffy repair and spare parts shops.

Nabisco, whose towering factory on South Kedzie was a neighborhood landmark and the largest private employer in Chicago Lawn, went through one merger in 1981 and another in 1985, soon followed by its takeover by Kohlberg Kravis Roberts, the private equity firm. Then came a long series of spin-offs and other transactions, each producing bountiful fees for investment bankers, executives, investment funds, and private equity firms, and then another merger in 2000 and another spin-off in 2011. After that the Nabisco plant was the Mondelez plant, operating only one production line, which the company planned to move to Mexico. During the 2016 presidential campaign, both major party nominees, Hillary Clinton and Donald Trump, made stops at the plant, promising to keep the remaining jobs in Chicago; after that the company kept producing cookies there at a modest level.

Talman Savings, the rock on which rested Chicago Lawn's status as a stable residential working-class neighborhood for first-time homeowners, was a casualty of the savings and loan crisis. It went through a forced merger with two other savings and loan companies. Then one of the big downtown Chicago banks bought the resulting combination, and finally one of the largest banks in the country, Bank of America, bought the Chicago bank. Beginning in the mid-1990s, mortgage loans for residents of Chicago Lawn came not from savings and loans or even from banks, but from dozens of unregulated storefront mortgage brokers who appeared in the neighborhood. People started calling Pulaski Avenue, at the western edge of Chicago Lawn, Mortgage Row, because for fifteen or twenty blocks it was lined with the new offices of mortgage brokers— more than ninety of them at the peak. These companies' job was to originate home mortgages and home equity loans and then sell them as quickly as possible to other financial companies; many Chicago Lawn home mortgages wound up being bundled inside the mortgage-backed securities on which Wall Street firms were making a lot of money by assembling and selling them to investors.

In the spirit of the age and from a distance, this could be made to look like a change for the better. The new system was making homeownership, with its miraculously positive social effects, possible for a new group of Americans who previously hadn't been able to afford it. Wall Street and deregulation had created highly technical new instruments that seemed to reduce the risk of holding mortgages, taking them out of local institutions and putting them into either packaged financial instruments, priced to account for risk, or into the hands of a new breed of national subprime lenders, such as Countrywide and New Century, that were expanding rapidly by acquiring mortgages in Chicago Lawn and other neighborhoods like it.

The traditional means of making mortgages available to working-class families was through the help of such federal government institutions as the Federal Housing Administration, which was created during the New Deal. It insured mortgages, but only after carefully reviewing a borrower's financial situation. Now, as in other parts of the economy, the market rather than the government was going to take on this function, without the burden of politics and heavy regulation. The simple economic incentive to survive and prosper would take the place of the old, outmoded bureaucratic structures. For decades the government had monitored both home buyers and mortgage lenders to make sure they were making prudent decisions, but now that seemed unnecessary. During the 1990s, Chicago Lawn was going from half white and one-quarter black to half black and one-quarter white (the rest of the neighborhood was mainly Latino and Arab American). The rapid changes in its ethnic composition went along with the rapid changes in the mortgage market. The new kinds of mortgages were meant for new kinds of homeowners—that is, black and brown ones. Chicago Lawn was always a neighborhood for financially unsophisticated first-time homeowners. Back when they were white, the old regime of government regulation was in place. Now the new, nonwhite home buyers were being thrown into a different, deregulated world.

Socially, the traditional holy trinity of Chicago Lawn had been corporate America, the Chicago Democratic Party political machine, and the Catholic Church. The first of these was disappearing as a presence in Chicago Lawn. The second had been embodied in the neighborhood by two especially powerful Irish American politicians, both sons of fathers who had been lower-level lifelong functionaries in the machine: Edward Burke, the longest-serving Chicago alderman, and Michael Madigan, speaker of the Illinois House, the longest-serving state legislative leader in the country. But as the neighborhood became less white, they arranged to have their districts redrawn to include less of it. That left the church, which was itself struggling; nearly all of Chicago Lawn's old white residents were active Catholics, and very few of its new black residents were.

In 1988 a group of Catholic parishes formed an organization called the Southwest Catholic Cluster Project, which was aimed at saving themselves by shoring up Chicago Lawn as it went through the kind of sudden economic and racial changes that put the whole life of a neighborhood in peril. In 1996 the project reorganized and renamed itself the Southwest Organizing Project so that it could include non-Catholic groups. Its headquarters sits on a corner in Chicago Lawn in close proximity to the other pillars of the new social structure of the neighborhood: the local office of Neighborhood Housing Services of Chicago, the Greater Southwest Development Corporation, and the Inner-City Muslim Action Network, all built around organizing. So now, if you were looking for the neighborhood's leaders, you'd find people who weren't traditional religious officials, politicians, bankers, or businessmen. They were, instead, people like Mike Reardon, an infinitely patient ex-priest who had mastered the intricacies of the mortgage market; Rami Nashashibi, a young, streetwise sociologist turned Muslim activist; Father Tony Pizzo, a short, solid, crew-cut spark plug of a man who had spent his whole career shoring up Catholic parishes in distressed neighborhoods on the South Side and who now ran St. Rita's in the heart of Chicago Lawn; and Jeff Bartow, a tall, shy man, married to a Guatemalan refugee, who had spent decades organizing in Latino neighborhoods around Chicago. It fell to them, and their fragile new organizations, to save Chicago Lawn, for in the new American political economy, nobody else seemed to have that responsibility—or even to realize that there were places all over the country where the official narrative about the success of the new order felt like science fiction.

No less than government officials in Washington, community organizers in Chicago held in their minds a set of beliefs about how the world works, and these guided the way they planned their activities and responded to events. But they operated a lot closer to the ground, so the cycle between the appearance of counterevidence and revision of their beliefs had to go a lot faster. It was ingrained in the community organizers that their mission was to fight to expand credit to minority home buyers; the movement that led to the passage of the Community Reinvestment Act had Chicago roots. In the mid-1990s the organizers in Chicago Lawn began to hear alarming stories about the companies along Mortgage Row: how they promised low monthly payments to people who were thinking of buying houses in the neighborhood, not mentioning that the payments were going to rise steeply in two years; how they blanketed the neighborhood with leaflets meant to persuade retired people whose houses were deteriorating to get second mortgages to repair them, even though the borrowers had no prospect of earning enough money to make the payments. The most notorious of the mortgage brokers, Tamayo Financial Services, targeted Latinos, many of whom were not citizens, didn't speak English, and couldn't produce any documentation of their income, because they worked in construction or home service for cash—but no problem, they'd still get loans they didn't understand and couldn't afford. The organizers in Chicago Lawn had to rethink their assumptions; now the problem was too much credit, not too little. What made that obvious was that not long after the advent of Mortgage Row—to be precise, as soon as the first wave of higher third-year mortgage payments kicked in—house foreclosures began spreading across the neighborhood.

The brokers were making loans to people who spoke only Spanish, even though all the documents they were signing were in English. Or they'd make "no stated income" loans, based on no information at all about the borrower's finances. Or they'd simply invent an income for borrowers who didn't have one. Or, if a home buyer didn't have the money to make a down payment, they'd issue a second loan to cover that. Or they'd make multiple home equity loans on the same house in the space of a few months, even though the homeowner's finances hadn't changed. Once, a woman who was legally blind came into the office of the Southwest Organizing Project and showed the people there a loan she'd been issued, with a monthly payment that was triple her total income. She couldn't make even a single payment. The brokers didn't care—they made their money on the total stated value of the loans they originated, not on how the loans performed, and if they could renegotiate an existing loan at a higher rate, they would get a bonus. (One of the brokers on Mortgage Row drove a car with license plates that read WECLOSEM.) And when a loan didn't perform, whoever owned the loan, which was never the mortgage broker, would foreclose.

In theory, the value of a house in Chicago Lawn was appreciating rapidly, from well below $100,000 in the 1990s to well above $200,000 ten years later. But this didn't reflect any real improvement in the incomes of the people in the neighborhood. It was mostly notional, to justify more lending. By 2007 the average mortgage loan amount in Chicago Lawn was for 120 percent of the value of the house. So, although people could borrow more, they couldn't afford to pay more. When there was a foreclosure, they didn't have a lot of options. They couldn't sell their house at the supposedly high price listed on their loan documents; it wasn't worth that much. They couldn't afford to move to the suburbs. So, often, they simply disappeared, sometimes in the middle of the night, and after that the house stood empty. Abandoned houses were a disaster for a neighborhood like Chicago Lawn, which was trying to hang on as a decent place to live. The houses would deteriorate. Thieves would come and take away anything of value, like copper pipes and hot-water heaters. Street gangs would take over the houses and use them as headquarters for drug dealing. That would generate more crime on the street. And once a block had several abandoned houses, it became nearly impossible to persuade anybody to move there. The houses were separated from each other only by narrow alleys, so your neighbor's problems were going to be your problems. And more empty houses in the neighborhood meant fewer students in the schools and fewer customers in the stores.

The organizers in the neighborhood moved on every front they could think of. They set up counseling programs in the schools to help parents and children understand how to prevent the neighborhood's rising level of economic and social chaos from ruining their lives. They lobbied banks to try to get them to ease the terms of people's loans instead of foreclosing. They boarded up empty houses. They looked for ways to help people open stores and restaurants. They helped people from Mexico, who had crossed the border illegally, with their immigration problems. A man named Rafi Peterson, a child of Chicago's housing projects who had served a twelve-year prison sentence for murder and had converted to Islam, walked the streets in the afternoons and evenings, talking to teenage boys about the perils of a life of crime. As foreclosures steadily rose to the top of the neighborhood's list of woes, the organizers' most sustained attention, increasingly, went to the political system. What they were struggling against was a set of conditions that had been made by faraway government officials—not one that had sprung up naturally. The best way to respond, beyond helping people one by one, was to try to persuade government officials who were closer at hand to remake those conditions.

Chicago Lawn organizers started spending a lot of time in Springfield, the Illinois state capital. In 2000 the state legislature passed a bill calling for a new set of regulations to limit the worst practices of the mortgage brokers. The governor, Rod Blagojevich, signed the bill in Chicago Lawn, with the state senator Barack Obama, whose district during his first term included part of the neighborhood, sitting nearby on the dais. In 2003 the legislature passed another law tightening home loan standards. By 2005 Michael Madigan, the House speaker, was hearing a lot of complaints about foreclosures from his precinct captains; he asked the Chicago Lawn organizers to set up a public meeting about it. The meeting took place at a Catholic girls' high school, with more than a thousand people there; the organizers put slides on a screen naming the "dirty dozen" worst subprime lenders. Countrywide was at the top of the list. Not long afterward, Countrywide's general counsel called and said he'd like to fly in from California to meet with the organizers. That meeting was at the residence of the Sisters of St. Casimir, an order of elderly Lithuanian nuns. It began with a prayer and ended with an argument about whether it was a good idea to make everyone a homeowner.

By this time Michael Madigan was fully engaged. On the last night of the 2005 session of the Illinois legislature, using his political wiles to their fullest extent, he managed to pass another law, which required home buyers in Chicago Lawn, and a few other parts of the South Side where the foreclosure rate was especially high, to have a counseling session with a third party before they could take out a mortgage—and required the mortgage brokers to pay for it. As that law went into effect in the first months of 2006, the lenders, who had fought its passage and lost, kept on fighting. They lined up black mortgage brokers and ministers who went to meetings and said that the law was nothing but the latest attempt to deny black people the privilege of homeownership. After a few months, Blagojevich announced that he was simply going to stop enforcing the law. Subprime lending surged back to life, but not for very long. In 2007 the subprime mortgage market began its spectacular collapse. By 2008, Mortgage Row had disappeared.

That hardly solved Chicago Lawn's problems. As the full force of the financial crisis made itself felt, Chicago Lawn had to weather a new wave of foreclosures, by far the largest yet, plus a severe recession. Six hundred houses in the neighborhood stood vacant; Chicago Lawn was one of the most severely affected neighborhoods in the country. Tony Pizzo was hearing constant entreaties from his parishioners about the abandoned houses. Couldn't he do something?

Pizzo had grown up in Chicago. The fate God handed him, after he was ordained, was to have a career managing the decline and fall of the white urban working-class Catholic world that had seemed eternal when he was growing up. First he was posted to Detroit, then to Kenosha, Wisconsin, a factory town just north of the Illinois state line. Chrysler had a plant in his parish, with a bar across the street. When he got there, the company's chief executive, Lee Iacocca, was investing in new production; the bar had a sign in the window that said LEE IACOCCA FOR PRESIDENT. Within a year, that sign came down and a new one went up: LEE IACOCCA LIED TO US. The parish withered, and Pizzo was transferred to Chicago. Soon he figured out that if the church was going to have a future on the Southwest Side, where he was assigned to one declining parish or another starting in 1991, it had to learn to attract Latinos. By the time he got to St. Rita's in Chicago Lawn, in 2006, he had spent two summers in Mexico City learning Spanish, and he had developed a whole set of techniques for reorienting a white-ethnic parish to immigrants from Latin America. He closed St. Rita's school, after its student body had declined from more than a thousand to fewer than three hundred, and rented it out to the Chicago Board of Education. That helped with cash flow. He started offering services for undocumented immigrants. After he'd presided over the funerals of a few teenage boys, he got to know the leadership of the Latin Kings gang and persuaded them to help him start an after-school sports program. He worked with the police. He started neighborhood safety patrols. He wasn't just going to let things go, and he wasn't afraid to piss people off.

Before he got to Chicago Lawn, Pizzo didn't know much about housing. Right across the street from St. Rita's was an abandoned home, whose deterioration, in full daily view of churchgoers and schoolchildren, Pizzo had been observing. One day somebody found a weeping teenage girl in the house; she'd been raped there. Pizzo decided that was enough. He called Mike Reardon, who ran the Neighborhood Housing

Services office a short distance away, and asked him who owned the
house. Father, Reardon said, it's Deutsche Bank. Well, Pizzo said, let's
go to their office and show them pictures of the house. If they see the
pictures, they'll do something. Father, Reardon said, that won't work.
Why the hell not? Pizzo asked. Because, Reardon said, their office is in
Germany. That's where the decisions are made. This is not real, Pizzo
said. This is nuts. This isn't happening anymore. He got the police to
come and board up the house, and then the Inner-City Muslim Network
went to court and got an order that enabled it to buy the place, fix it up,
and turn it into the headquarters for one of its programs. But the larger
lesson was obvious: it was time to go back into politics, at a higher level
than before, to try to get some relief.

Richard Durbin, Democratic U.S. senator from Illinois, had always had a soft spot in his heart for Chicago Lawn; his mother was
Lithuanian, and when he was a kid, the neighborhood had been the
Lithuanian capital of Chicago. In 2007, before most of the rest of the
country realized there was a crisis, Durbin had sponsored a law that
would have saved millions of homeowners from foreclosure by lowering
their interest rates; a fierce lobbying campaign by the mortgage industry helped defeat it. After the crisis became obvious, a delegation from
Chicago Lawn got an appointment with Durbin in his Chicago office,
which, in the late fall of 2008, he shared with the Obama presidential
transition team. Durbin's visitors showed him a map they had made,
which displayed in especially dramatic form—an engulfing swarm of red
dots, one for every house affected—the full extent of foreclosures across
the less well-off sections of the South Side. (After a couple more years
and several rounds of updates of the map, there were so many more red
dots that they bled together into a single great red mass.) That worked:
Durbin picked up the phone while his visitors were still there and made
an appointment for them with Bill Daley, the son and brother of Chicago mayors, a crucial supporter of Presidents Clinton and Obama, and
a Chicago-based executive of J.P. Morgan Chase, one of the major holders of foreclosed mortgages in Chicago Lawn. That meeting took place a
couple of weeks later. Daley, surrounded by aides, was cordial but a little
distant. He looked at the map filled with red dots and heard the visitors'
account of Chicago Lawn. He said he was going to have to get back to
them. He ended by being candid. First, he said, if you think things are

bad now, you have no idea how much worse it's going to get in 2009. Second, the only real way to solve the problem would be for the federal government to take over all the foreclosed mortgages.

That is exactly what the federal government did for the big financial institutions and their bad debt, but for working-class homeowners, it didn't happen. (Daley did get Chase to establish a temporary office in Chicago Lawn to negotiate individually with homeowners who couldn't pay their mortgages.) The Chicago Lawn organizers concluded that the insider approach wasn't going to work for them; next time they'd be openly confrontational. Their target would be Bank of America, which had made the mistake of seeing the impending collapse of the subprime mortgage market as an investing opportunity. It had acquired what remained of Talman Savings' old mortgage portfolio in 2007 and had bought Countrywide in the early months of 2008, just before the worst of the financial crisis. That made Bank of America the largest holder of foreclosed mortgages in Chicago Lawn. In May 2009 a couple hundred people from the neighborhood, led by Tony Pizzo, showed up unannounced at the Bank of America branch at Fifty-Fifth and Kedzie—a modest structure that stood where Talman Savings' grand headquarters had been—and demanded that Barbara Desoer, the president of Bank of America Home Loans, come to Chicago to meet with them. What they got instead not long afterward was a promise that Andrew Plepler, the Bank of America executive who was in charge of "social responsibility," would fly out from the bank's headquarters in Charlotte, North Carolina, and hold a public meeting in Chicago Lawn. The organizers had hundreds of yard signs printed that said, in English and Spanish, BANK OF AMERICA HAS FAILED OUR NEIGHBORHOOD THROUGH FORECLOSURE. They debated whether to put them up along Plepler's route from Midway Airport to Chicago Lawn, but decided against it—to give the guy a chance.

The meeting was at St. Rita's church in July. It lasted for more than two hours. The organizers' strategy was to present themselves as calm, rational, and professional, not as people who had more emotions than ideas. They presented a carefully worked out proposal for Bank of America to rescind all its foreclosures and, instead, modify the loans so that the homeowners' monthly payments would be set at 30 percent of their income and continue until the loans were paid off. That way, in the long run, the bank would lose less money. But the bank wouldn't agree—it was afraid of being sued by investors who'd bought packages of loans on the promise that they would never drop below a certain stated value. Instead, the bank would provide the organizers with a list of the owners of its delinquent properties in Chicago Lawn, almost all of whom were dodging Bank of America's letters and phone calls, so that the organizers could go see them in person and try to work out some solution, owner by owner. The Southwest Organizing Project wound up creating a team of fifty people who knocked on the door of every holder of a soured Bank of America mortgage in Chicago Lawn and, in many cases, found some way for the family to stay put.

The Obama administration, in its first few weeks, had created a new federal program that was supposed to help millions of people who were in financial trouble to modify their mortgages and stay in their homes. Mike Reardon assigned Katie Van Tiem, a young counselor on his staff, to research the program in detail. She concluded that it wasn't working and couldn't work. By Van Tiem's estimate, only 1 percent of the people the program was supposed to help had actually gone through a success- ful loan modification. She wrote a memo detailing what she called the six tragic flaws of the program—for example, for lenders who held bad mortgages, participation was voluntary, not mandatory. There was an- other trip to Washington in the spring of 2010. Senator Durbin had Van Tiem testify before a Senate subcommittee, and he also arranged a meeting between the Chicago Lawn organizers and the Obama admin- istration official in charge of the loan modification program, an assistant secretary of the Treasury named Michael Barr. Like Daley, Barr was sympathetic, candid, and not very helpful. I can't get any traction on this, he said. Nobody's talking about it. And the banks can't take the hit.

There wasn't going to be a grand solution to Chicago Lawn's fore- closure problem. Instead, whatever happened was going to have to happen in the neighborhood, lender by lender, block by block, house by house. All the residents, organizers, shopkeepers, priests, nuns, and ex-offenders who had been fighting to save Chicago Lawn for a quarter century or more fortified themselves to fight again. The signs about fail- ing the neighborhood that hadn't gone up when Andrew Plepler came to town did go up a year later, all over Chicago Lawn, except now there were hundreds more of them and they included the names of Citibank, Chase, Wells Fargo, and Deutsche Bank as well as Bank of America. That generated more meetings with people at the banks. In the end, through persistence and ingenuity, patching together arrangements with banks, foundations, government agencies, real estate developers, and individual homeowners, the organizers wound up negotiating six hundred loan modifications in Chicago Lawn. More than a hundred empty houses were rehabilitated. It was like fighting a flood: the waters of social and economic chaos would be made to recede in one place by getting the houses occupied; then they would rise in another because shady investors from outside Chicago Lawn would buy up houses in bulk at their now radically reduced prices and try to resell them quickly for more than they were worth to people who couldn't afford them. There were months when things looked better and months when things looked worse.

With the factories in Chicago Lawn reduced or departed, by far the largest remaining employer in the neighborhood, with eleven hundred jobs, was Holy Cross Hospital, another Catholic institution, founded in 1928. It sat in a small cluster of buildings controlled by the aging and dwindling group of nuns in the Sisters of St. Casimir order who had stubbornly stayed on in the neighborhood. There was the hospital; Maria High School for girls, which back in the 1950s and 1960s had had more than a thousand students; and the Mother House, where the nuns, now mostly in their eighties, lived. Holy Cross had been in economic trouble for years. Its administrators and the nuns had allied themselves with the Southwest Organizing Project and lobbied Michael Madigan, successfully, for extra state funding. When the financial crisis hit, Holy Cross was back in existential peril, and if it went down, it might take Chicago Lawn down with it. The nuns donated $1.8 million from their own retirement fund to Holy Cross just so that it could make payroll for a few weeks. Another urgent round of lobbying produced millions of dollars in emergency funding from the state, and using the breathing room these funds provided, the nuns sold the high school to the city, which turned it into a charter school, and the hospital to the Sinai Health System, a Jewish nonprofit organization that agreed to let Holy Cross remain a Catholic institution (that last arrangement had to go all the way to the

Vatican for approval). Those moves, along with the passage of the federal law known as Obamacare, which enabled a lot of the hospital's patients to pay for their medical care, made the hospital look safe, at least for a while.

The only large new building in Chicago Lawn was the headquarters of the Chicago Police Department's 8th District, which took up most of a block on Sixty-Third Street. By 2010 the neighborhood was about half black and half Latino; both groups regarded the 8th District with suspicion, if not fear, and the feeling was mutual. The district had only ever had white commanders. One of them once told Jeff Bartow, the director of the Southwest Organizing Project, that he regarded his officers as an occupying force in Chicago Lawn. Organizers in the neighborhood maintained somewhat dutiful official relations with the 8th District, but they did not rely entirely on the police to keep crime under control. For that there were volunteer patrols, block clubs, and school programs. In Chicago, especially in neighborhoods, and especially working-class neighborhoods, everything is about personal connections. People who had been around for a while often had specific officers whom they knew and trusted. Tony Pizzo had a nephew on the force. Over the years, some of the 8th District's commanders had been better than others. What you wanted was to have an officer's personal cell phone number, and that's what you'd call when you needed help—not, God knows, the 8th District switchboard.

People in Chicago Lawn had two ideas about what caused crime in the neighborhood. First, back in the 1990s, police and prosecutors had gone to great lengths to put the heads of Chicago's big street gangs in prison—and now everyone believed that in the days before that happened, the police, or community leaders, or politicians could call these people in and tell them to cool it, and they would. Today there are lots of little gangs that fight for control of single blocks; ignore the old, informal prohibitions on violence against children, women, and the elderly; and can't be negotiated with. One can't spend much time in Chicago Lawn without hearing a story about somebody or other having visited the surviving legendary gang leaders from the old days—Larry Hoover of the Disciples and Jeff Fort of the El Rukns—in the Colorado super-max prison where they are both inmates, and returning with the news that even they are distressed about the gang violence in Chicago now. The second idea is that when the Chicago Housing Authority tore down the notorious Robert Taylor Homes, the world's largest public housing project, beginning in the mid-1990s, many of the former residents who were gang members got rental housing vouchers and moved to Chicago Lawn, where they took up their old bad habits. Most people in Chicago Lawn would rather have a homeowner struggling to keep up with mortgage payments for a neighbor than someone renting from a financially secure landlord who lives far away and, with a guaranteed income from housing vouchers, doesn't have any incentive to maintain the property.

Officially, crime rates in Chicago Lawn were lower than they had been in the nineties, but personal experience and vivid anecdotes count for more than statistics when it comes to feeling safe. And feeling safe counts for more than rational economic calculation when it comes to making decisions about whether to buy a house or open a store. One afternoon in 2014, just a block from the office of the Southwest Organizing Project, a college freshman named Kevin Baker was getting off a city bus with his cousin when another teenage boy from Chicago Lawn accosted them and asked for their cell phones. They handed the phones over. The boy asked Baker if he was in a gang. Baker said no. Then the boy pulled a gun and killed him with one shot to the body and one to the head.

Baker's murder hardly attracted notice outside the neighborhood, but then there were violent incidents on the South Side that got the whole country's attention and inescapably lodged themselves in the consciousness of Chicago Lawn. In 2014 seventeen-year-old Laquan McDonald was killed by Jason Van Dyke, an 8th District police officer who shot him sixteen times at close range on Pulaski Avenue, just outside Chicago Lawn. The incident reinforced people's ambient fear of the police. If you knew the neighborhood and you saw a group of teenage boys on the corner posturing and being loud, you could talk to them; you'd even know which of them was the most likely to listen. If you saw a Latino man walking down the street, you'd know that he had a job and went to church. But many police officers would see the same people and see only somebody to arrest or shoot or deport. The more fathers the police sent to prison or back to Mexico, the more sons joined gangs.

In 2015, a couple of neighborhoods away on the South Side, nine-year-old Tyshawn Lee was taken from a playground swing into an alley one afternoon and murdered, evidently as an act of revenge against his father, who a few months later sought his own revenge by shooting three people connected to his son's killers. In Chicago Lawn, every notorious incident like this was an impetus to leave, for those people who could; what those who couldn't leave wanted was to feel assured that the police were committed to preventing violence even if it wasn't horrible enough to make headlines. Instead, a lot of people in Chicago Lawn had the impression that if black people were killing black people, the police didn't care. A persistent neighborhood legend had somebody finding a crumpled, half-completed police report on the ground the morning after a shooting, because the officer who answered the call had decided it wasn't worth filing.

Chicago Lawn was holding on. If you wanted to be optimistic, you'd look at the diminishing number of empty houses; the four- and six-unit apartment buildings on some of the neighborhood's street corners that developers were rehabilitating; the half dozen or so large, thriving Mexican restaurants that had opened. The long decades of jarring, almost instantaneous neighborhood ethnic transitions in Chicago seemed to have ended, generally and in Chicago Lawn in particular. Almost all the whites and Arab Americans had left, but Chicago Lawn had evidently stabilized as a mixed black-Latino neighborhood, more black to the east, more Latino to the west, not strictly segregated anywhere. In the summer of 2016 Rami Nashashibi organized a large, celebratory parade on the fiftieth anniversary of Martin Luther King's disastrous march in Chicago Lawn to protest housing segregation—on the same route, ending in the same place, Marquette Park, but with the unveiling of a grand stone monument to King rather than a white riot. That was meant to signal that the neighborhood was profoundly different now, stable and optimistic.

But if you wanted to be pessimistic, you'd look at the persistently empty storefronts up and down Sixty-Third Street or the gang symbols spray-painted on walls. You'd notice the houses that were still boarded up and the clusters of boys demonstrating their dominance of many of the street corners. You'd notice the endless flat gray skies that seemed to be the rule on the South Side of Chicago, not the blue skies that seemed to be the exception. The South Side has never had much tolerance for the grand, abstract perspective. Whether the neighborhood would make it was something the local elders talked about candidly all the time. Maybe it would, maybe it wouldn't. Every day mattered.

■

Earl Johnson grew up in the Robert Taylor Homes, the child of a Mississippi-born single mother who worked as a nursing assistant. When he graduated from high school, in 1991, he persuaded his mother to move the family out of the projects to someplace quieter and less violent. Earl found a rental apartment in Hyde Park, a much better neighborhood not far away, but after a year their landlord raised their rent from $900 to $1,000 a month. For that much money, Earl told his mother, they could buy a house. So he called a Realtor and began looking all over the South Side for a place they could afford (which knocked out Hyde Park) and where they could feel safe (which knocked out Englewood). In 1992 they bought a run-down brick bungalow at 6352 South Rockwell Street, with the standard undersized porch, front lawn, and backyard, in the heart of Chicago Lawn. The Johnsons were the third black family on the block—everybody else was white. Earl got a job in the concessions department at an arena near O'Hare Airport.

Like a lot of the pioneering black families in Chicago Lawn, the Johnsons got a cool reception from their neighbors. As time passed, the white people who stayed on the block got used to their being there. Earl kept an eye on his white neighbor's house; as the man got older and started drinking more, Earl would help him up the stairs when he came home and get him settled inside. But most of the white people on the block were leaving, and their replacements were a mixed bag—some fine; others, to Earl's mind, the kind of people he'd thought he was leaving behind when he persuaded his family to move out of the Robert Taylor Homes. One day a carful of gang members drove down the block looking for members of a rival gang. They found them standing near Earl's house and started shooting. Earl's mother was sitting on the porch. One of the bullets went in her direction, missed her by not much, and hit the wall of the porch a few feet above her head. The bullet hole was still there ten years later.

After that, Earl decided he'd better start acting like a homeowner with something to protect. He started going to community meetings. At one, held at the 8th District headquarters, he got up and gave a little speech: crime was rising in the neighborhood, and the police didn't seem to be doing anything about it. Gang members from Robert Taylor were now in Chicago Lawn. Didn't the police care? Afterward, an officer pulled Earl aside, out of everyone else's hearing, and said, Well, Mr. Johnson, you kind of hit the nail on the head. I know, because I just transferred over here from that district, and I'm seeing a lot of familiar faces.

Earl got involved with the Southwest Organizing Project and Neighborhood Housing Services. He went to a lot more meetings. Sometimes he hung out on the street corners with Rafi Peterson, talking to teenage boys about the choices they were making. Earl is a tall, open, informal man whose laid-back manner can make it easy to miss how energetic and determined he is. He didn't intend to let the neighborhood go down. The parts of the struggle to save Chicago Lawn that were about Chicago as a city—or Washington, D.C., or the global economy—were outside his reach, but by making good unskilled jobs scarcer and housing more speculative, they added a few extra degrees of difficulty to what was always tough in Chicago, even in good times: managing a racial transition. For Earl, what was at hand for him to work on were the closely intertwined issues of housing and crime. He made himself into the unofficial mayor of the 6300 block of South Rockwell. He'd greet new neighbors and try to disperse knots of teenage boys. When he saw that somebody's garage door had been pried open, he'd close it. More than once he came home from work and found boys sitting on his porch, as if they owned it. Do you pay rent here? he'd ask them. Do you pay taxes? This is my neighborhood. This is my house. It's not yours. And they'd leave.

Earl kept in close touch with the police. There were times when the 8th District had a commander who struck him as caring about the neighborhood, and there were other times when it didn't. Once, when crime on the block was ticking upward, he was able to persuade officers he knew and trusted to station a squad car on his corner for days. Another time, he arranged to have a plainclothes officer sit with him, day after day, on his porch, so that he could point out the rhythms of the block—when people were stashing drugs or weapons, who was okay and who wasn't. (Earl called this "covert operations.") That helped. But then there were times when it seemed as if the attitude of some police

officers was, Who cares about another dead nigger? Or when the police seemed incapable, or not motivated enough to be capable, of distin-
guishing troublemakers from ordinary black people who lived in fear of
crime—presuming that if you were black, you were a criminal. And at
those times, Earl would let the police know how he felt.

On one cold winter night Earl was sitting in his car, parked in front
of his house, with the engine running in order to warm it up. A police car pulled up next to him, and the officers asked him what he was
doing there. They made him get out of the car so they could search it.
Earl said it was his car, his home address was on the registration, and
they shouldn't be harassing him like this. The officers pushed him. He
pushed back. He shouted at them. They shouted at him. Within a few
minutes, the whole block was full of police summoned by the officers
who had approached Earl, as well as residents who had come outside to
see what was going on. It was one of those incidents that tap into the
deep store of mutual fear and hostility that had built up through years
of encounters like this one, which is why the temperature of the block
spiked so quickly. Before it all died down, the police had beaten up
Earl's brother.

Earl went to work full-time for Neighborhood Housing Services,
doing maintenance at its neighborhood offices around Chicago. That got
him even more involved in the struggle to save Chicago Lawn, and for
a while he was feeling optimistic. The abandoned houses on his block
were being boarded up, rehabilitated, and filled one by one. During the
heyday of the mortgage brokers, Earl himself took out a home equity
loan—his house always needed repairs that he couldn't afford—and he
couldn't keep up the payments when the interest rate zoomed upward.
Mike Reardon and Katie Van Tiem helped him modify the loan and
keep his house, as they had helped other homeowners on the block who
had gotten in trouble with the mortgage brokers.

But then came the 2008 financial crisis, a fresh, severe blow to the
block. There were more foreclosures, more abandoned houses, and another spike in crime. For Earl, it was like tumbling back to the bottom of a
steep, hard-won hill and beginning the climb all over again. He couldn't
help thinking that the world didn't care whether black people lost their
homes, just as it didn't care whether black people robbed and killed
other black people—but he cared. He kept working the block, going

door-to-door to meet new neighbors, keeping an eye out for the early warning signs of crime, introducing people who needed loan modification to Neighborhood Housing Services, and trying to find sympathetic police officers who would come to the block when there was a need for them and, when they did, do more than beat people up indiscriminately.

Earl's sister died in 2014. The extended family gathered for a memorial service, and afterward everyone went back to Earl's house on South Rockwell. Earl's father had come up from Memphis. Earl was getting ready to drive him to the Greyhound bus station to go home. He was sitting in his tiny backyard, talking to friends and family, when an aggressive, loud teenage boy walked in and started insulting Earl. Who the fuck are you? Earl said. This is my house. I don't want you on my property. He grabbed the boy by the arm and took him to the front of the house. The boy, who wasn't cowed in the least, raised his shirt to show Earl that he had a gun tucked into his waistband. In that situation, what do you do next? Earl took the boy by both arms and shoved him up against the tall black metal fence he had put up in front of the house as a deterrent to crime. The situation was nowhere near under control, and Earl had to keep the boy pinned to the fence while he figured out what to do about the gun. But then one of the boy's friends came up, plucked out the gun, and shot Earl in the back. Both boys ran away while Earl lay on the ground in front of his house, gasping for breath and spitting up blood.

The next thing Earl knew, he was lying in a hospital bed, a police detective standing over him. The detective told him that he'd gotten a call from the 8th District commander: this isn't an ordinary crime victim, and this isn't an ordinary case. This one has to be solved. So the police and Earl, severely weakened and with the bullet still somewhere inside him, worked together. Earl knew the two boys only by their street names, Tuwon and Shoe, but he used his network of contacts in the neighborhood to find out the real name and the home address of the boy he had seen. The police went to his house, but he had run away. They put out an all-points bulletin and eventually found him, brought him in to 8th District headquarters, got Earl to come down and identify him, and extracted the name of the boy who had fired the shot: Jonathan Johnson. He had already been in prison. Now he was on parole, so the police arranged for his parole officer to call him in for a routine check-in, and when he came, they were waiting to arrest him.

The state's attorney asked Earl whether he was ready to do what it would take to put Jonathan Johnson back in jail. Earl said, Look, he did this before he did it to me. I survived. He'd do it again. Would that person survive? So he went to a series of court dates and testified, and the boy got a twenty-year prison sentence. The next Sunday, Earl went to church and asked the pastor to forgive him.

Two years later, Earl went back into the hospital and had surgery to remove the bullet. By that time you'd see one of the two boys, not the one who'd fired the gun, walking around the neighborhood. He had supposedly reformed, but he was just one person. The crime hadn't stopped. Once, Earl heard shots in the middle of the night and rushed outside to find that one of his neighbors had been wounded by a stray bullet during a battle between two small gangs. Another time, one block down South Rockwell from Earl's house, there were two murders within twenty-four hours, again in connection with a fight between gangs. The block itself looked a lot better than it had a few years earlier; there weren't many empty houses left. Earl had had a lot to do with that, but after nearly a quarter century on the block, he was weary. Between the gangs and the police, he just didn't feel confident that he and his family were safe. There was a lot he could do, but he couldn't stop a bullet fired by somebody who didn't care about what happened to him.

Earl decided to look for another place to live and work; as he liked to say, some chapters tend to come to an end. He found a new five-bedroom house in Lowell, Indiana, a farm town fifty miles south of Chicago that was just starting to acquire modest suburban development. The real estate agent asked him how he, a city boy, thought he'd like encountering wildlife in his new home. If the wildlife can't shoot me, I'm fine, Earl said. He found a new job at a Ford factory at the far southern edge of the Chicago suburbs, with good pay and benefits, where the company built, among other things, police cruisers. The factory was twenty miles from his new house and just a few minutes away from Park Forest, the setting of *The Organization Man.*

■

At Morgan Stanley, through most of the 1990s, the team of Dick Fisher and his protégé and chosen successor, John Mack—the former leaders of the sales and trading operation—was firmly in charge of the company.

Parker Gilbert, the Morgan banking scion who had supervised Morgan Stanley's becoming a public company, had retired, and so had the other leading partners of his generation, such as Anson Beard and Lewis Bernard. The firm's going public had made them quite rich. They all had several homes—Gilbert had acquired a historic plantation in South Carolina—and philanthropies and investments and art collections to attend to.

Morgan Stanley kept widening its reach all over the world, and trading kept growing as a portion of the firm's activities. More and more lines of business involved technical, quantitative computer-driven financial transactions, running twenty-four hours a day, designed by people with advanced academic training whom the firm had hired. Dick Fisher, and John Mack after him, liked to say that three forces were driving the new financial world: deregulation, globalization, and technology. Morgan Stanley pursued enthusiastically anything that seemed attuned to those forces. The firm started a quantitative trading division run by a team of mathematicians. It invented new kinds of derivatives. It became a force in Silicon Valley, where its star analyst, Mary Meeker, wrote optimistic reports about the future of technology and also made Morgan Stanley the leading manager of the initial public offerings of companies like Netscape and Google.

In 1993 Morgan Stanley's investment bankers advised Dean Witter, a big retail stockbroker that was especially strong in the Midwest, when it spun itself off from Sears, the venerable chain of stores, and became a separate company. It was a typical move in the new age of the American corporation: Sears had first decided, as the old Glass-Steagall restrictions were beginning to break down, to remake itself into a "financial supermarket" and had acquired Dean Witter and a number of other companies to help it do that. The mastermind of the strategy at Sears was Philip Purcell, a former management consultant who hadn't come up through the ranks of the retail business. When it looked as if Sears' new strategy wasn't working, Purcell arranged for Dean Witter to become a separate company, with himself as the chief executive.

By that time, John Mack was preparing to succeed Dick Fisher as chief executive of Morgan Stanley. Mack loved growth, and he loved making deals. All the senior executives at the firm were worried about what would happen when Glass-Steagall was completely gone, for the commercial banks would then be able to compete with them in the ever more important trading side of the business, using deposits rather than borrowing the money as Morgan Stanley had to do, and also compete for merger and acquisition clients. Knowing from Morgan Stanley's involvement in Dean Witter's departure from Sears that it was a financially solid company, Mack and Fisher began working on what would become by far the most dramatic expansion at a single stroke in Morgan Stanley's history: a merger with Dean Witter, which would give it access to millions of retail brokerage accounts that could be used as firm capital.

In February 1997 Fisher, Mack, and Philip Purcell announced the merger, creating the world's largest securities firm. This represented Morgan Stanley's having gone in twenty-five years from a few hundred employees to more than fifty thousand—growth that was a mirror image of the shrinkage of most of its leading corporate clients during the same period. Fisher would take the honorific title of executive chairman for a few years before he retired, Purcell would be chief executive, and Mack would be president. Purcell, tall, dour, and analytical, was a very different kind of person from Mack, but officially, they were going to lead the merged firm in tandem. In his eagerness to make the deal, Mack had failed to pay enough attention to one point Purcell had negotiated: the chief executive officer, but not the president, could be removed only by a 75 percent vote of the board of directors. This meant that Purcell was really the one in charge, and his relationship with Mack soon turned sour—over, among other things, what Mack regarded as Purcell's excessive caution about taking risks in the firm's trading businesses, which meant profits were lower than Mack thought they should be. Four years after the merger was announced, Mack resigned.

Morgan Stanley's retired senior partners, many of them stationed in close proximity to one another in a suite of offices—nicknamed Jurassic Park—that the firm maintained for former executives, did a brisk trade in horror stories about Philip Purcell. It wasn't just that he had pushed out Mack and many other old hands, or that he lacked charm, or that he didn't seem to understand the firm's grand traditions; it was also that he was costing them money. Morgan Stanley's stock was underperforming. In 2005 eight retired senior Morgan Stanley executives, organized by Parker Gilbert, launched a public campaign to force Purcell out. This included such highly uncharacteristic (for Morgan Stanley) techniques as taking out full-page ads in *The Wall Street Journal* and appearing on television. Gilbert and his allies were, in a sense, underdogs, as they were not major shareholders or directors, but they still had their golden contacts in the world of capital, plus the inarguable logic, in an age of financial-market dominance, that for shareholders there was more money to be made if they got their way. Within a few months Purcell had resigned, taking with him a $113 million exit payment, and not long after that, John Mack returned to Morgan Stanley as chief executive officer.

At the meeting marking his return in triumph, Mack announced to a large group of Morgan Stanley employees that he intended to restore the firm's "swagger," and to do that, he was going to "use the balance sheet"—meaning, borrow more aggressively in order to trade more aggressively. Mack was a natural leader, adored by the people who worked for him, and not inclined to think very carefully before charging forward. One former Morgan Stanley executive compared him to General George Patton: he's the guy you want to use to take the hill, but not the guy you want to decide which hill to take (that would have been Lewis Bernard). Another executive, who worked with complex financial instruments, recalled that Mack kept his office door open and would warmly welcome anyone who wandered in, usually offering a piece of candy. But once you got a few sentences into presenting a problem to him, he'd cut you off and ask, Do we buy it, or do we sell it? Mack's first year as head of the firm—a year in which he increased Morgan Stanley's leverage ratio to 40 to 1, which was evidently okay with the new office at the Securities and Exchange Commission charged with monitoring investment banks' risk—was financially spectacular, its best ever. Revenues, profits, and the stock price all rose significantly, and Mack himself earned $40 million on the basis of the firm's performance. Patricia Beard, in her detailed and sympathetic account of the battle to remove Philip Purcell, wrote, "A key driver of the improved financial performance was increased risk-taking."

When the financial markets were running red-hot, as they were in 2005 and 2006, what worried executives like Mack was not so much that the economy would turn sour, but that the company might fall behind in the relentless daily competition for business. Morgan Stanley was paying out well over half of its operating profits in the form of annual bonuses to high-performing employees; if it didn't, they might leave for Goldman Sachs (which had converted itself from a partnership to a public company in 1998) or a hedge fund or a private equity firm. Clients, too, were demanding ever more favorable terms from Morgan Stanley, lest they take their business to a competitor. Mack remembers calling Timothy Geithner, the president of the New York branch of the Federal Reserve, during this period and complaining that one of the big private equity firms had wanted Morgan Stanley to lend it more money to finance one of its deals than the firm thought prudent. Morgan Stanley balked, and the private equity firm quickly got the terms it wanted from a commercial bank, which was spreading its wings now that Glass-Steagall was gone. It's out of control, Mack told Geithner. I can't hold on to my people in this environment. That's funny, Geithner said, I just got a call from the bank that took your place on that deal—they had the same complaint.

That was how things felt if you were inside the intense competition among banks. One level up was another competition, between nations, over who would be home to the increasingly global, mobile, Internet-resident financial industry. As much as the American banks were fighting with one another for deals and talent, they were united in arguing that any attempt by the government to impose restraints on them would force them simply to transfer most of their activities somewhere else, such as the newly finance-friendly London, or maybe Hong Kong. Henry Paulson, the former head of Goldman Sachs who became Treasury secretary in 2006, issued a report warning against regulation for this reason, and so did New York City's mayor, Michael Bloomberg (himself a former trader on the fixed-income floor at Salomon Brothers), and New York's senior senator, Chuck Schumer. At that moment, warnings about risk in the financial system were extremely rare, but when they emerged, the threat of going overseas could quash them. So the party went on.

One of the few things Philip Purcell and John Mack had in common was that they both adored Zoe Cruz, the firm's highest-ranking woman and another star from the trading side of Morgan Stanley. Mack made it clear that Cruz, who had the title of president, was the person he had in mind to become his successor as chief executive. She was directly in charge of the part of Morgan Stanley that was responsible for managing risk on the trading desk. In late 2007 Morgan Stanley reported a $9.2 billion loss on a single trade—what Michael Lewis, in *The Big Short*, called "the single greatest proprietary trading loss in Wall Street history." Derivatives may have been designed by mathematicians, physicists, and economists, but they were bought and sold by people like Howie Hubler, a blustery former college football player who was Morgan Stanley's number one trader at the time: his team generated a billion dollars in profits in 2006. Hubler made a very big bet that the subprime mortgage market was about to turn sour, buying a derivative that would make a great deal of money if a bundle of B-rated mortgages did not perform. This was the right idea, but because it was officially a short position, which meant it had to be paid for with borrowed money, Cruz's division had to pay the interest on the loan until it sold the position. That imperiled the division's profits.

To solve that problem, Hubler made the opposite bet—taking a long position—on a derivative based on a bundle of A-rated mortgages. The money to buy that was interest-free firm capital. Hubler's idea was that the money he could make from selling off pieces of the long position would cover the interest payments on the short position until it could be sold, producing a big payday. Cruz approved all this, and she didn't feel the need to get Mack's approval, even though there was more than $13 billion of the firm's money at risk in the long position. Of course, it turned out that A-rated subprime mortgages weren't any better than B-rated subprime mortgages—hence the $9.2 billion loss. Hubler, Cruz, and Mack (when it fell to him to defend the trade after the loss became public) evidently all believed that pairing the two positions, short on B-rated and long on A-rated, was a classic risk-reducing hedge, right out of the University of Chicago portfolio management playbook. That demonstrates how little they understood the instruments that they'd been betting so much of the firm's money on.

By the time Mack announced the big loss on Hubler's trade, it had become clear that the kinds of subprime lenders whose names often appeared on home mortgages in Chicago Lawn, such as Countrywide and New Century, were going down. The ordinary people who took out unaffordable subprime mortgages were hardly powerful, but collectively, when they stopped making payments, they triggered a great cascading economic disaster. Unpaid mortgage payments and unsellable houses meant that the subprime lenders couldn't stay in business. Packaged, traded financial assets based on subprime mortgages, if the mortgages themselves went bad, had the potential to take down the investment banks too. The investment banks had the potential to take down the whole financial system. The financial system had the potential to take down the economy, throwing millions of people all over the world out of work for year after painful year—often the same people who'd been the victims of high-pressure mortgage brokers in the first place.

In March 2008 Bear Stearns, one of the big investment banks, collapsed because of its exposure to subprime mortgages. The Federal Reserve arranged for J.P. Morgan Chase to take it over at a bargain price. And six months after that, another big investment bank, Lehman Brothers, went bankrupt for the same reason. Suddenly it looked as if the entire investment banking business was about to dematerialize. This was a direct result of deregulation. The end of Glass-Steagall had brought the investment banks direct competition from commercial banks and pushed them to take more risks; the SEC had failed in its new mission of guarding their stability; and the ban on regulation of derivatives had permitted them to take on enormous debt in order to trade in volatile new instruments they didn't fully understand. Morgan Stanley was next in line. For one terrifying week in September 2008 it appeared to be doomed to go out of business.

Monday, September 15, 2008, was the day the failure of Lehman Brothers became public. Morgan Stanley had $178 billion in readily available capital that morning. Among the many derivatives in the markets was one that insured against drops in the price of Morgan Stanley's stock: the less confidence there was about Morgan Stanley's stock price, the more this derivative would cost. Its price doubled that Monday. Hedge funds that were customers of Morgan Stanley's prime brokerage division withdrew $10 billion from the firm. On Tuesday, John Mack decided to try to restore confidence by releasing Morgan Stanley's strong third-quarter earnings statement one day early—but this backfired because the markets interpreted the change in timing, correctly, as a sign of incipient panic. Morgan Stanley's stock price fell by 28 percent that day, another 42 percent the next, and another 46 percent the next. On Wednesday, hedge funds withdrew another $35 billion. Mack, for whom the role of the leader-in-battle came naturally, periodically walked the floor of the prime brokerage division, shouting, "Control your clients! Control your clients!"

The reason Morgan Stanley was so vulnerable was that it lived inside a system—that it had helped to create—in which everybody was heavily in debt, money was instantaneously mobile, and confidence was fragile. Industrial companies, with lots of physical assets, decline gradually; financial companies, which have only office space and employees, can die instantaneously. Most hedge funds were making their money by placing large bets with borrowed funds. (A government report in the late 1990s showed that D. E. Shaw, one of the most quantitative and academic of the hedge funds, where Lawrence Summers worked part-time in the years leading up to the financial crisis, was leveraged at a ratio of 70 to 1.) If one of the investment banks that was clearing their trades failed, they would fail too—that was why they were withdrawing capital from Morgan Stanley. Morgan Stanley itself was borrowing heavily through an enormous and obscure sector of the financial system called the repurchase market, in which it would sell securities, usually government bonds, and agree to buy them back within a day or two as a way of getting cash to lend to its clients and to trade in the markets. Its two biggest counterparties in this market, J.P. Morgan Chase and Mellon banks, got nervous and asked for billions of dollars in extra collateral to protect them against their overnight loans not being paid back. By the end of that week in September, hedge fund withdrawals from Morgan Stanley were up to $86 billion and repurchase market withdrawals were up to $31 billion; by the end of the month, the firm's capital reserves were down to $55 billion.

None of this was merely Morgan Stanley's problem; the government's highest economic officials, terrified that the firm's failure would lead to a complete collapse of the financial system and then the economy as a whole, were in constant contact with John Mack. The government's idea was that a larger and more stable bank should take over Morgan Stanley quickly, and through the week, officials lined up a succession of possible partners: J.P. Morgan Chase, Citicorp, Wachovia (which was itself failing), Goldman Sachs, a big Chinese investment fund. Mack, for his part, with the help of New York's two senators, Schumer and Hillary Clinton, lobbied the government to call a temporary halt to short selling of financial company stocks; short sellers were swarming all over Morgan Stanley that week, trying to drive its stock ever lower so they could make more money. Despite the obvious irony in Mack's request—most of the short sellers were Morgan Stanley clients, and the firm itself regularly shorted stocks for its own account—the Securities and Exchange Commission did impose a ban on Wednesday, September 17.

That was not enough to stop the panic. Over the weekend—at a point where Ben Bernanke, the chairman of the Federal Reserve; Henry Paulson; and Timothy Geithner were calling Mack in concert to demand that he sell Morgan Stanley to J.P. Morgan Chase before the markets opened on Monday morning (which would have reunited the original House of Morgan that Glass-Steagall had sundered back in 1934)—he finally found a rescuer in Mitsubishi, the giant Japanese financial and manufacturing company. It agreed to pay $9 billion for a 21 percent ownership stake in Morgan Stanley. The news of that arrangement persuaded the government to allow Morgan Stanley to stay in business as an independent company. In return, both Morgan Stanley and Goldman Sachs agreed that weekend to reconstitute themselves legally as commercial banks rather than investment banks, which meant that from then on, they would be regulated by the muscular Fed rather than the timorous Securities and Exchange Commission. That, along with the Mitsubishi arrangement, was enough to stanch the panic of the previous week.

One year later, Mack announced his retirement as chief executive of Morgan Stanley. What became clear only several years after that, following a Supreme Court ruling that mandated the release of previously secret documents, was just how extensive the Fed's role in saving Morgan Stanley had been, even after Mitsubishi's investment. The Fed extended trillions of dollars in emergency low-interest loans to financial institutions to keep them alive during the crisis—even firms outside the United States; Morgan Stanley got the most of any firm in the world, $107 billion. Having been created as a result of rules imposed by the federal government in the aftermath of one financial crisis, it was saved by the federal government in the aftermath of another. In the reregulation of the financial system that followed the financial crisis, Morgan Stanley was designated a "systemically important financial institution," meaning that the government was essentially guaranteeing that it would stay in business and in return was going to subject it to much stricter controls. This was where the course Bob Baldwin had set the firm on four decades earlier—to survive, expand—had wound up. Today, government employees are permanently stationed on Morgan Stanley's trading floor to keep an eye on things.

Some time after the financial crisis, Robert Reich ran into his old combatant from the Clinton administration, Robert Rubin, at an event and asked him whether he'd changed his mind about financial regulation. Rubin said no. The financial crisis, he told Reich, had been a "perfect storm," a never-to-be-repeated combination of highly unlikely events occurring simultaneously. Financial progress must proceed. Over the years, some bankers, economists, and government officials have expressed regrets. Sanford Weill said that the end of Glass-Steagall, for which he had been the leading advocate and lobbyist, had been a mistake. Bill Clinton and Arthur Levitt, Clinton's head of the Securities and Exchange Commission, both said that the Commodity Futures Modernization Act of 2000 had been a mistake. Alan Greenspan said he'd been wrong to assume that financial firms could be counted on to protect themselves from excessive risk.

Yet among people who had their hands on the levers of finance, such views were probably atypical. Rubin and Summers remained stout defenders of their roles in financial deregulation. Just after Obama took office, Brooksley Born was invited to a small White House dinner to discuss how to respond to the financial crisis; there she encountered Summers, who told her, by way of making peace, that there was one minor feature of the Commodity Futures Modernization Act that he now regretted—she'd been right and he'd been wrong. But what she took from the conversation was that to Summers's mind, in every other instance he'd been right and she'd been wrong. Robert Merton, the Nobel Prize–winning financial economist who'd invented the key techniques that made the derivatives markets possible, was outraged by what he considered grandstanding after the crisis by Paul Volcker (who said there hadn't been a useful financial innovation since the automatic teller machine) and Warren Buffett (who called derivatives "financial weapons of mass destruction"); Merton went around the world giving presentations about how "an explosion of extraordinary financial innovation" had rescued the world from the "major financial and economic crisis" of the 1970s. When the Financial Crisis Inquiry Commission finished its forensic work, it sent to the Obama Justice Department a list of nineteen financial executives, including Rubin, who the commission thought might be investigated for breaking the law. Nobody on the list wound up being charged with anything; and of course most of the actions that led to the financial crisis were legal, having been legalized during the decades of deregulation.

In the spring of 2010 Carl Levin, a veteran Democratic senator from Michigan, summoned Lloyd Blankfein of Goldman Sachs to testify before a subcommittee Levin chaired. He focused on a derivative Goldman had created before the crisis, at the request of a client, that entailed betting that subprime mortgages would crash. The client, and Goldman on its own account, bought the derivative and made money, and Goldman sold the other side of the trade to other customers, who lost money, without telling them how it was betting. The exchange between Levin and Blankfein made for an unusually pure illustration of the complete difference in perspective between Wall Street and the nonfinancial world in the twenty-first century: Levin couldn't believe that a company would sell a product it didn't believe in ("I wouldn't trust you!" he said), and Blankfein couldn't believe that anybody could seriously object to Goldman's making a market in a security. The people who bought the side of the trade that turned out to be disastrous, he said, "wanted a security that gave them exposure to the housing market, and that's what they got."

It would be far too facile to say that after the financial crisis, Levin's perspective won. Public opinion notched back in the direction of approving of financial regulation, but the great shift in economic power from corporations to finance, and from institutions to transactions, had not been reversed. A handful of large financial companies, including Morgan Stanley, now controlled a higher share of the country's capital than ever before: more than half of all bank assets were in the hands of the top half dozen firms. The pools of investment capital that were the banks' major customers kept growing, too, and they looked to the markets to provide high returns, not social stability. University endowments, union and state employee pension funds, and foundations—bedrock institutions of American liberalism—lived by the logic of investing too. Transactions and finance were no longer identifiably liberal or conservative, Democrat or Republican.

The country's best-off and most influential people increasingly had made their money by investing in markets over the short to medium term, and they tended to think about society as a whole in investment-influenced terms: How could existing arrangements be moved around, broken apart, made more fluid and efficient and less bureaucratic, to produce a better result quickly? People who hadn't figured out how to make themselves part of this new world fell further and further behind, and if they weren't organized to get specific help from government as the big financial firms had done, they often turned to political populism as their best hope of a remedy.

■

Morgan Stanley's lifesaving deal with Mitsubishi closed on Columbus Day, October 13, 2008. That same day, a delegation of executives from General Motors, once Morgan Stanley's most prestigious client, came to see Henry Paulson at the Treasury. They told Paulson that the company was at the brink of failure and asked him for $10 billion in emergency government loans.

General Motors had been in a long, slow decline for decades, but its most immediate threat came from the financial crisis. The auto business, no less than the residential real estate business, lives on debt. Just about everybody buys cars with borrowed money. When you're at an auto dealer and the salesman asks you to wait a minute while he talks to his manager, he's probably going on a computer terminal in the back office and sending your deal out for instantaneous bidding on a global debt market; what he finds out within a minute or two will determine what kind of monthly payments he offers you. Just as there are subprime mortgages, there are subprime auto loans, with higher interest rates, and they had been a booming business during the period before the financial crisis. Also, GM and other auto companies manage their payments to hundreds of thousands of parts suppliers by borrowing money in the overnight markets—often from money market funds, which are not covered by federal deposit insurance. The same week that Morgan Stanley almost failed, one of the biggest money market funds, the Prime Reserve Fund, announced that it would no longer let depositors withdraw their money at full value. That led to a wave of panicked withdrawals from money market funds, which dried up the overnight lending system, which meant that GM couldn't pay its suppliers, which meant that they were in danger of failing too.

An old auto business maxim has it that you can sleep in your car, but you can't drive your house to work—meaning that most people, in a real pinch, will stop making house payments before they'll stop making car payments. That may have been comforting, but in the fall of 2008 it no longer held true. More and more car loans were delinquent, and that, along with the almost incredible daily accretion of alarming economic news, destroyed the confidence of the auto lending market. Credit for car loans dried up, and that meant cars weren't selling. GM had sold a controlling interest in its auto lending division, GMAC, to a big private equity firm called Cerberus, whose name (taken from the mythological guardian of the gates of hell) communicates how unlikely it was to be tolerant about a few months' worth of absence of credit.

At the beginning of October, Congress had passed an emergency bill authorizing the government to lend hundreds of billions of dollars to banks to get them through the crisis. GM was asking Paulson for some of this money, but he said no: the money was for banks, not corporations. Having struck out with the Bush administration, the chief executives of the three major auto companies came to Washington not long after the election of Barack Obama to ask Congress for $25 billion in emergency loans. They didn't get anywhere, partly because they had made the disastrous public relations error of flying to Washington in their companies' private planes. In December the auto company chief executives returned to Washington, this time driving there from Detroit in fuel-efficient cars, but they still could not get Congress to approve the loans. Finally, just a month before leaving office, with two of the three companies, GM and Chrysler, about to fail, George W. Bush reversed Paulson's decision and agreed to make some of the emergency loan money for banks available to auto companies—though, as Paulson noted in his memoir, "we crafted terms that would put the automakers on a path to reorganization through bankruptcy proceedings and would make it difficult for President Obama to avoid that outcome."

Obama could, conceivably, have continued lending GM and Chrysler money, which was what they wanted; at the other extreme, he could have let them go out of business. Instead, on March 30, 2009, Obama went on television to announce that the government was going to force

GM and Chrysler into bankruptcy. Chrysler wound up being sold to Fiat, the Italian auto company; GM wound up being temporarily owned by the government and then made into a reconstituted public company. The advantage of bankruptcy was that it functioned as a kind of economic and legal trump card: all existing arrangements, with shareholders, bondholders, unions, suppliers, and dealers, lost their force and were open to unilateral revision.

The person in charge of that was Steven Rattner, a finance guy and a major Democratic fund-raiser who had spent the early years of his career at Morgan Stanley and now ran a private equity firm. In the Obama administration, the people who were in the room deciding the fate of General Motors were all economists, financiers, and consultants, not people who had worked in the auto industry or even in corporations; they exemplified the shift in how the country deployed its talent. (Rattner's immediate superior was Lawrence Summers, now back in government as head of the National Economic Council.) Most of them had come of age in the 1970s, so they had grown up thinking of GM not as the world's greatest large organization, but as the leading symbol of a certain kind of American failure: it was too big, too slow, too encumbered by the Treaty of Detroit, and unable to respond adeptly to the sudden rise of oil prices and the subsequent successful invasion of the American market by Japanese companies like Toyota, Nissan, and Honda. "Solving the auto crisis, I understood," Rattner later wrote, "would not be a management assignment like running a corporation; it would be a combination of restructuring exercise (cleaning up the mess) and private equity task (investing new capital)."

Rattner, who served as the person in charge of restructuring the auto industry for only six months, acted quickly, with a great deal of self-confidence and without the supplicating auto companies having much ability to push back. He fired GM's chief executive, Rick Wagoner, who struck him as second-rate, and replaced him with a retired executive from another industry. The one person on Rattner's team who, to Rattner's mind, was understood as speaking on behalf of a particular constituency was his deputy, Ron Bloom, another finance guy but one who had worked for the United Steelworkers and had a deep emotional commitment to organized labor. Although the Democratic coalition that had brought Obama to office was quite different from what it had been in the twentieth century (Obama had gotten far more in campaign contributions from Wall Street than his Republican opponent, John McCain), the Democrats were still the party of labor, as diminished as labor was, and this was especially important in states like Pennsylvania, Ohio, and Michigan, all of which Obama had carried. In the restructuring, autoworkers' jobs and wages were protected, and the funds to pay for retired autoworkers' health benefits got an atypically merciful treatment.

Automobile dealers, on the other hand, were a constituency that didn't tug on the heartstrings of anybody on Rattner's Team Auto. Rattner quickly absorbed the idea that GM's and Chrysler's large and deeply rooted dealer networks were a significant drag on the companies' finances, even though the companies didn't own them; that the Japanese companies' much smaller, suburb-centered networks represented the right model; and that many dealers were alive more because of the political protection they had been able to get from state legislatures (which bankruptcy instantly undid) than because of their economic performance. Team Auto pushed GM and Chrysler to use bankruptcy to accelerate, from gradually to instantly, the plans they already had to reduce their dealer networks. The idea was that they would be relieved of the expense of overproducing cars, and of dealer relations, for all those superfluous provincial stores. In May 2009 GM notified eleven hundred dealers that they were going to be out of business, and Chrysler sent the same news to nearly eight hundred of its dealers.

Nick D'Andrea, operating a single Buick dealership that was one of the businesses trying to hang on in Chicago Lawn, got one of these letters. Alan Spitzer, a big third-generation dealer who operated seventeen dealerships in four states out of a headquarters in the town of Elyria, Ohio, got ten of them, seven from Chrysler and three from GM. For them, and for most of the hundreds of other dealers in the same situation, it was as if a great fissure in the solid surface of the earth had suddenly opened and they had fallen in. Only six months earlier, the auto companies had enlisted the dealers' trade association as a vigorous supporting player in their campaign to persuade Congress to give them emergency loans. Now these dealers were cut off, with no forewarning and a company-imposed deadline giving them a few weeks to liquidate their businesses. The dealers, especially one-store dealers like Nick D'Andrea, had a complicated relationship with the auto companies:

bone-deep loyalty to "The General" and faith in its permanence, combined with resentment of the dependency embedded in the arrangement. The company could force you to spend a lot of money renovating your store. It could change the terms of the GMAC loans that were the lifeblood of your business. It could redraw the map of your sales territory. It could allocate too few hot-selling cars to your store or, as dealers liked to say, jam too many slow-selling ones up your butt. But these were all aspects of the basic trade-off inherent in an institutional relationship: the frustrations were the price you paid for stability and mutual abiding loyalty. Now, with the arrival of one FedEx delivery, that was gone.

Many of the terminated dealers knew one another from years of conventions and sales conferences; instantly, the wires lit up with outraged complaints, rumors, and ideas about how to fight back. How had GM and Chrysler come up with their lists of whom to terminate? Was it the people who hadn't played company politics, or whose stores were near the stores of other dealers who had, and who wanted them out of the way? Why did the National Automobile Dealers Association seem to be so slow off the mark in fighting the terminations—had some of the big national dealership chains actually welcomed the idea of using bankruptcy and restructuring to get rid of a lot of smaller family dealerships that were competing with them? What everybody agreed about was that it was inconceivable that the automotively virginal members of Rattner's Team Auto (who'd spent just one day during the course of their work on a pro forma group visit to Detroit) actually knew what they were doing—and that whatever fighting back the dealers did had to happen immediately.

One evening Alan Spitzer was watching television and saw Greta Van Susteren, a host on Fox News, standing in front of a dealership interviewing a friend of his, Jack Fitzgerald, a veteran dealer from Maryland who'd gotten Chrysler terminations. Spitzer thought, This is an omen. God is telling me what to do. He picked up the phone and called Fitzgerald. Here's what we have to do, he said. The bankruptcy overrides all the state laws that protected us from termination without any warning or appeal mechanism—so let's override the bankruptcy by getting a federal law. Let's go to Congress.

Fitzgerald put Spitzer in touch with Tamara Darvish, a fiery young woman whose father had fled the Iranian revolution, become a medical doctor, and then decided that he'd really rather sell cars. The Darvishes operated another chain of dealerships in Maryland, some of which had been terminated. Together the three of them started an organization called the Committee to Restore Dealer Rights, hired a Washington lobbyist, and got to work. Most auto dealers were active political contributors, and they started complaining to whomever in government they could get to—a city councilman, a mayor, a governor, a member of Congress. Spitzer, by virtue of running such a big operation and of being the relatively rare dealer who was a Democrat, was especially well-connected. At a fund-raiser for his representative in Congress, Betty Sutton, Spitzer talked to anyone who would listen about the injustice of the dealer terminations. As he was leaving, Sutton's chief of staff pulled him aside and asked whether he'd like to meet Steny Hoyer, the House majority leader, who was coming to Ohio the following week to speak at another fund-raiser in Akron. Tell you what, Spitzer said. If you can get me a private meeting, I'll come, and I'll bring twenty other dealers with me.

A week later, Spitzer and a delegation of dealers were waiting in a conference room at a Hilton hotel outside of Akron. The time of the meeting came and went. Everyone was nervous—would they be forgotten again? But then a line of cars arrived, bearing Hoyer and his entourage. Hoyer represented Jack Fitzgerald and Tamara Darvish in Congress, so he'd already heard about the dealer terminations; now he stayed with the group Spitzer had assembled for a full hour, through their elaborate scripted presentation, until well past the time the fund-raiser was scheduled to begin. The next day, Fitzgerald called Spitzer and said, Boy, you really got him fired up. (In the 2010 election cycle, Spitzer held a fund-raiser for Betty Sutton at his house, with Hoyer as the guest speaker.) In early June there were hearings in both the Senate and the House of Representatives about the dealer terminations, where the members listened sympathetically as a few dealers told their stories and then berated the auto company executives whom they had summoned to testify. Alan Spitzer testified at the House hearing. His wife, Pat, was on her way from Ohio to Washington; she walked into a bar at the Cleveland airport and announced, I'll buy everyone here a drink if you'll switch the television from the game to CSPAN. That was how she, and everyone else in the bar, was able to watch her husband testify. He was a familiar figure in Cleveland because of decades of local Spitzer dealership television ads, in which members of the Spitzer family had often appeared. Pretty soon everyone in the bar, watching him, was cheering as if the game were still on.

Tamara Darvish, meanwhile, had assembled a national network of terminated auto dealers who were angry and who wanted the country to hear their stories: Jeff Duvall from Clayton, Georgia; Colleen McDonald from Livonia, Michigan; Frank Blankenbeckler from Waxahatchie, Texas; Patrick Painter from Nephi, Utah; and dozens of others. Darvish had the idea of organizing a mass rally of terminated dealers on the steps of the Capitol, with as many members of Congress visibly participating and as much television coverage as possible. She had a badge made up for every dealer who came, with the number of jobs that person's termination would cost; the total job loss, for all the dealers at the rally, was 169,632. The noise Darvish was making had attracted the attention of Nick D'Andrea's stepdaughter, Elaine Vorberg, a lawyer in Chicago who was representing him free of charge. She got in touch with Darvish and became part of her network of the aggrieved. She and Nick flew to Washington for the rally, which was held on July 14, 2009. Just beforehand, they joined a group of terminated dealers from Illinois for a meeting with an aide to Senator Dick Durbin, the same person who'd received the entreaties of the organizers from Chicago Lawn about mortgage foreclosure. He became another public supporter of the dealers.

Steven Rattner was amazed, and annoyed, at the ability of the Committee to Restore Dealer Rights to attract the sympathetic attention of leading members of Congress, no matter where they were from or what party they belonged to. The dealers' anger, he later wrote, "simmered all summer, erupting periodically like a geyser fed by a vast underground reservoir of superheated water. Hapless members of Team Auto would be summoned to Capitol Hill at such times to get browbeaten by legislators or their staffs." One of the politicians who took up the dealers' cause rose to the top of the list of Rattner's objects of irritation—the "tall, jowly, gravel-voiced" Steny Hoyer: "I was mystified that the House majority leader chose to devote so much time to this. The nation was plagued by economic and financial crises; why would the second most important member of the House after Speaker Pelosi think that two car dealerships merited his personal attention?"

On the day before the dealers' big rally in Washington, it was announced that Rattner would be resigning from the Obama administration. His private equity fund was under investigation by the New York State attorney general, which made his ongoing presence potentially politically damaging to the administration, and anyway he felt that his work was mainly done; he had just finished building a house on Martha's Vineyard and was looking forward to spending the month of August there. The dealers took Rattner's announcement as another sign from God: Keep fighting, it's working. On the way to the rally, Nick D'Andrea and Elaine Vorberg were listening to the news on their car radio, and a snatch of Aretha Franklin singing "Respect" came on. Maybe she's going to be the new car czar, Nick said—at least she's from Detroit.

In December, when Congress passed its big annual spending bill, it contained a provision giving every terminated dealer the right to challenge the auto companies' decision in an arbitration process. That was the closest thing to a climactic victory for the terminated dealers, though lawsuits they'd filed to challenge the terminations went on for years afterward. Some of them wound up having their dealerships restored. Some of them got settlements and retired. Some went bankrupt, losing their houses as well as their dealerships. A couple even committed suicide. What just about all of them agreed on was that America looks like a very different country when you're on the receiving end of a sudden and severe manifestation of the new economic order that had emerged over the past generation and that the only—the essential—available remedy is politics.

Nick D'Andrea, like most of the terminated dealers, knew perfectly well that he didn't have a dealership that looked great on paper. Chicago Lawn wasn't what it used to be, and neither were his sales. Once, the burglar alarm at D'Andrea Buick had gone off in the middle of the night, and he rushed down to see what was going on. At two in the morning the corner of Seventy-First and Western was alive, as you'd expect it to be at nine in the morning, and not just because the alarm had gone off. That was when a lot of people in the neighborhood, especially young men, were out doing whatever it was that they did. Nick's wife, Amy, who had grown up in Chicago Lawn and who worked as a substitute teacher farther down on the South Side, was nervous about going there now, even during the daytime. But Nick's attitude was, Let me decide whether or not to stay in business. I'm the one who's here. I'm the one who owns the store, who bought the cars from GM. I'm the one who has figured out how to stay profitable, despite everything.

But because of the substantial debt GM had forced him to take on in 2008, when it insisted that he begin selling Pontiacs as well as Buicks—just a matter of months before it shut down the Pontiac division—Nick was in an impossible position. He'd had to mortgage his house to GMAC to buy the Pontiacs that were now impossible to sell. One of the lessons he'd tell people that he'd learned was, Never trust a guy in a suit and tie again. Once Elaine had gotten him a settlement, he was out. He laid off all his employees a few days after the rally in Washington. He kept in touch with a lot of them and tried to help them get new jobs. One guy sold clothes out of his car for a while and finally got a job as a hotel doorman. Another had a hard time finding work because he was so fat, and he ended up having to move out of Chicago to find a dealership that would hire him. But most of them eventually found something, some-where, at another auto dealership. D'Andrea Buick's building was torn down, and the site was a vacant lot for a few years. Now it's a Wendy's.

Alan Spitzer wound up getting four of his terminated Chrysler deal-erships back and one of the GM dealerships. In May 2009 he had writ-ten a long letter to President Obama laying out in detail his argument about the injustice of the auto dealer terminations. He never got an an-swer. In the fall of 2010 Obama came to Ohio to speak at a fund-raiser for Ted Strickland, Ohio's governor, who was running for reelection. Spitzer wrote a check big enough to get him the privilege of coming to the event and having a moment with Barack and Michelle Obama in a receiving line: a handshake, a photograph, a quick word. He handed Obama another copy of his letter and used his allotted few seconds to complain about the terminations. "We wanted to be sure the remaining dealers were profitable," Obama said. Spitzer was ready with his reply: "The marketplace, Mr. President. The marketplace should be the judge of who lives and who dies!" Ever the salesman, he was convinced that he had turned Obama around. "I sensed in his tone of voice that he knew I was right," Spitzer later wrote. "At any rate, he was very gracious, said he was sorry, and understood my point of view."

When Obama ran for reelection in 2012, he once again carried Ohio, Michigan, and Pennsylvania. Joe Biden, his vice president, used to go out on the campaign trail and tell people, especially in that part of the country, that they had to know only two things about the Obama administration: it had found and killed Osama bin Laden, and it had saved the auto industry. Obama's campaign also made great use of the fact that his opponent, Mitt Romney, had written an article in *The New York Times* under the headline LET DETROIT GO BANKRUPT. Romney made for a perfect representative of the American economy's transition: the son of an automobile company chief executive, he had spent his career in private equity, taking apart and reassembling the kinds of companies his father's generation had spent building up. Obama's campaign frequently reminded voters of this too.

One could say that Obama, having hired his own private equity guy to restructure the auto industry quickly and ruthlessly, was trying to have it both ways. But he played the politics of the auto bankruptcies well, if the test of that was what would help him be reelected in 2012. What people, especially in the Upper Midwest, remembered was that General Motors and Chrysler, which could have disappeared, still existed. Their workers hadn't been made to suffer the worst consequences of the bankruptcy. What had happened to the dealers went down as an instance of excess during a time of such extreme economic chaos that it didn't attract broad public notice. The inspector general of the government's post-crisis Troubled Asset Relief Program produced an unsympathetic report about the dealer terminations, saying they were "all based on a theory and without sufficient consideration of the decisions' broader economic impact" and "may not have been necessary." ("The report was ludicrous," Rattner wrote.) The new chief executive of GM whom Rattner had installed reinstated hundreds of the terminated dealers, with a gruff quasi-apology.

Alan Spitzer, within a few years, had brought his daughter Alison into the business so that she could become the fourth-generation Spitzer in charge of the family's dealerships. Unlike Nick D'Andrea, he'd come out of the experience feeling confident; he thought he'd seen democracy beat back a bad decision. A few years later, by now in his late sixties, he invested in one hundred empty spaces for the section of the cemetery in Elyria, Ohio, where members of the Spitzer family were buried. That was how sure he was that they'd always be able to figure out how to stick around.

6

NETWORK MAN

If, in the years that followed the financial crisis, you went back to the old question of how the economy should be organized so as to engender a good society, you would find almost nobody who still believed in Adolf Berle's idea of a carefully managed equipoise between big corporations and the federal government. By then very few people had even heard of Berle, and after decades of ever-rising mistrust of the major institutions, it seemed almost fanciful that for a decade or two after the Second World War, people had put so much faith in them. The crisis also devastated whatever faith there had been in a transaction-based society of the kind Michael Jensen and his colleagues had promoted as an alternative to an institution-based one. Jensen himself had lost faith in his old ideas, or at least in the way they had been enacted.

So what was left? Was there another organizing principle, beyond institutions and transactions? If you went looking for one, you might well wind up in Silicon Valley, the narrow band of territory that ran along the western edge of the San Francisco Bay and was home to suddenly enormous companies such as Apple, Google, and Facebook. Silicon Valley was primarily a business site, but—just as the people who built the great industrial corporations of the early twentieth century also had a social vision in which they themselves occupied a central position—the leaders of Silicon Valley considered themselves to be far more than merely economically successful. They also knew how the world should work in the new century.

The official founding date of Silicon Valley was 1939, when two young engineers, William Hewlett and David Packard, founded Hewlett-Packard, an electronic instrument company, in a garage not far from the campus of their alma mater, Stanford University. The Valley in its recognizable present form really dates from 1968, when a group of eight engineers left Fairchild Semiconductor to start Intel, which became the leading manufacturer of silicon chips. It's worth recalling how little the founding of new companies was part of the prevailing narrative of how business worked in the middle decades of the twentieth century. It was an article of faith for Adolf Berle and his intellectual allies that only large corporations could create successful new technology-based products; their size, their large capital reserves, the passivity of their shareholders, and the security they offered their employees made it possible for them to maintain research divisions that smaller businesses could never afford. AT&T, IBM, and General Motors all had celebrated research labs where technologists worked with a great deal of independence and freedom. The founders of Intel had begun their careers as protégés of William Shockley, the inventor of the transistor. Shockley had developed his crucial inventions at AT&T's Bell Labs, and when his crew of young engineers got sick of working for him, they joined an established East Coast military contractor, Fairchild, which was closely allied with IBM. That was in 1957. It took more than a decade for them to take the terrifying step of starting their own company.

The rise of Silicon Valley required not just a loosening of the psychological bonds that tied people to corporations but also the nearby presence of Stanford, whose engineering school was an essential training ground, supplier of talent, and conductor of the basic research new companies could build on. This shift required a new form of capitalism too. Company founders had a hard time getting loans from banks; they had no collateral, and the odds were that they were likely to fail. The money to start Intel came from Arthur Rock, an expatriate investment banker from the East Coast who had started a venture capital fund in San Francisco that invested in technology companies. Rock and his investors weren't lenders but rather owners: in return for taking on the risk that conventional bankers would not, they were able to demand half ownership of the new companies they funded, plus a role in management. For years, Rock was chairman of the board of Intel, and it was the work of Intel and other companies in developing ever smaller and more powerful silicon chips that made the personal computer possible. Arthur Rock's venture firm was also the crucial early funder—and Rock was chairman of the board—of the pioneer personal computer company Apple, founded in 1976.

Big pools of capital, such as insurance and pension funds and university and foundation endowments, impressed by the spectacular returns produced by Silicon Valley's successes and newly freed from the investing constraints that the old prudent man rule had imposed on them, began pouring money into venture capital. By the twenty-first century, Silicon Valley venture capital was a small industry with an unofficial headquarters, Sand Hill Road, a strip of low-rise office parks across the street from the Stanford campus, where dozens of firms entertained thousands of pitches from people who wanted to start technology companies. Arthur Rock, by now retired, looked at the venture capital industry with bewilderment. Rock worked in San Francisco's financial district, the traditional West Coast outpost of American finance; he came to work every day in a suit and tie, and often had lunch at his club. On Sand Hill Road, the style was ferociously casual, as if there were a competition for who could come across as the most low-key or the most culturally opposite to the old Organization Man. Wearing a suit and tie would be disqualifying. Lunch was usually granola from the office kitchen. Dogs padded down the hallways. Performance bicycles hung from hooks on the walls. People talked about their lives in terms of "chapters," not careers. And nobody seemed to want to invest in anything physical anymore, like chips or computers, only in software—instruction sets. Nobody's idea seemed to require conventional plants and equipment; or distribution systems, supply chains, or physical products. Everything happened on the Internet.

The ideal that Sand Hill Road devoted itself to pursuing was a company that would turn out to be like Facebook, which had, only a few years after its founding, a total value on the stock market of more than $400 billion, with fewer than twenty-five thousand employees. General Motors by now was worth only $50 billion, and even in its reduced and post-glorious state, it still had more than two hundred thousand employees. And Facebook had thought it wise to acquire even newer potential rivals, for prices like $1 billion for Instagram, when it had thirteen employees, and $19 billion for WhatsApp, when it had fifty-five employees, when both were years away from being profitable or even from producing significant revenues. Successes like these were exceedingly rare. One study of Silicon Valley start-ups found that almost three-quarters of company founders who got funding from venture capital firms—and these were the lucky ones, representing a small minority of those who pitched to the venture firms—wound up making nothing. The common wisdom in Silicon Valley had it that one start-up a year, of perhaps thirty thousand, would wind up being as valuable as all the others combined, and that the ten most successful would account for more than 95 percent of the value of all of them.

Silicon Valley has created an amazingly effective mechanism for drawing talent and money into a game that almost all the players will lose, and for generating a handful of companies that make useful products, grow very large very quickly, and make their founders astonishingly rich—obviously not the basis of a successful social system. One of the Valley's core principles is that the old Treaty of Detroit, if it still applied, would make success impossible: Silicon Valley is a zone of no pensions, no unions, and no de facto guarantees of lifetime job security. Even so, its view of itself is as a place with a comprehensive and workable idea of how the world could function far better than it does now and for the benefit of everybody. It is an unofficial requirement of its leading figures that they be able to put forth a grand, all-encompassing program, just as the early industrial tycoons did, only with different touchpoints: innovation, mass empowerment, cultural tolerance, and the overturning of existing arrangements, instead of Christianity, order, obedience, and social Darwinism.

Reid Hoffman's association with Silicon Valley began at birth: Stanford Hospital, in 1967. He was the firstborn and only child of young parents who thought of themselves as part of the sixties generation—maybe not radicals, but people who intended to spend their lives building a new kind of world, who took their son to events like anti–Vietnam War rallies and Grateful Dead concerts. His father, Bill Hoffman, was the grandson of a Los Angeles newspaperman named W. D. Hoffman, who wrote a series of pulp Westerns with such titles as *Gun Gospel* and *Law of the Lash*. His mother, Deanna Ruth Rutter, grew up in Silicon Valley before people called it that. They met in connection with a beauty pageant at Foothill College in Sunnyvale, married, and separated a year or two after Reid was born, when they were still in their early twenties. Both went on to become lawyers, and both married and divorced again. Reid grew up shuttling between the homes of his parents (who moved around a good deal) and his grandparents. For a while he lived in Alaska with his mother, who had gone to work for an oil company; then with her parents in Sunnyvale; then with his father, who had remarried, in Marin County; then in Berkeley after his father had divorced and entered a new relationship. Reid was brainy, awkward, self-reliant, overweight, and lonely. During the years when his parents were trying to figure out their own lives, he had to get accustomed to a degree of instability that most middle-class children are spared.

Bill Hoffman, the parent with whom Reid lived for most of his childhood, wound up working for a prominent corporate law firm, but he stayed fixed in Reid's mind as the Berkeley-dwelling firebrand who had represented Black Panthers and spent time as a legal foot soldier in the waning days of the federal government's War on Poverty. Reid liked to think of himself, too, as a crusader on behalf of the outsider and the underdog, but he found quite a different channel for those impulses than his father had. At the age of eight or nine, he became a devoted player of fantasy board games, especially Dungeons & Dragons. One of his classmates at Martin Luther King Jr. Middle School told him that a game company called Chaosium had an office in Emeryville, a town right next to Berkeley, and that it occasionally invited groups of boys to come in and test its products. That was about as exciting a piece of news as Hoffman could have received. Soon he got himself into one of the product-testing groups, but he wasn't content to leave the connection at that. Chaosium had published a set of role-playing scripts, called a scenario pack, for Dungeons & Dragons; Hoffman went through it in enough detail to find a number of errors. He outlined them in a detailed memo, which he took to the Chaosium office and presented to Steve Perrin, a legendary game developer who was working there at the time. Perrin was impressed enough to give Hoffman more scenario packs to review. Hoffman also began writing reviews, for modest fees, for *Different Worlds*, a gaming magazine that Chaosium published.

Gaming and the adjacent realms of science fiction and fantasy—in comic books, movies, and fiction—have never left the center of Hoffman's consciousness. His next early move, however, was in a different, though just as escape-oriented, direction. From another classmate he learned about a small, progressive boarding school called Putney, in deep-rural Vermont, where students studied big ideas and also tended farm animals. It was about as far from what he was used to as he could imagine, short of being able to enter the world of one of his fantasy games. He applied and was admitted, and then he persuaded his highly skeptical parents to send him. When he arrived, though, he found himself being bullied by other boys, including his friend from Berkeley, in a manner right out of one of his favorite books, *Lord of the Flies*. He asked himself how he'd handle the situation if it were happening in a game rather than in real life—meaning, try to will yourself into a state of emotional imperviousness and respond rationally. The answer was, change his tormentors' calculation of incentives. So he threatened to break all their possessions unless they left him alone, and they did.

The miseries of Hoffman's early life ended when he enrolled as an undergraduate at Stanford, in 1989. He became one of the first students in a new major called Symbolic Systems, a combination of philosophy, linguistics, psychology, and computer science. He met his future wife, Michelle Yee, whom he won over, at least as he remembers it, in a typically Hoffman way by outsmarting a much more conventionally handsome rival for her affections. He also made a group of lifelong friends, such as Peter Thiel, a German-born libertarian, later to become famous as a Silicon Valley investor who liked to make provocatively candid pronouncements that were designed to offend people. (Hoffman and Thiel ran successfully for the Stanford student senate as a kind of balanced ticket, with Hoffman as the left-winger and Thiel as the right-winger.) Hoffman was a tireless organizer of student activities and an outstanding student. When he was a senior, he won a Marshall Scholarship to study at Oxford. He went there intending to become an academic philosopher or maybe a public intellectual. What changed his mind, the more he thought about it, was that the limited reach of such people bothered him. An important paper by a philosopher might have an audience of a few dozen people, all of them professional colleagues with the same specialty. When Hoffman talked to people about what he wanted to achieve, he used words like *scale* and *impact*—and he meant in the millions, the same order of magnitude that gamers and science fiction heroes had in their notional worlds.

Hoffman returned from Oxford with the idea of finding work in Silicon Valley and, maybe, starting a company one day. He wasn't a computer scientist per se; he thought of himself as someone who understood how technology could successfully align itself with human nature so as to become especially influential. Through a connection of his mother's, he found a job at Apple. During that early time back in California, Hoffman and Thiel spent a weekend at Hoffman's grandparents' house in Mendocino County, talking about what they were going to do with their lives. Hoffman told Thiel, with great enthusiasm, about a science fiction novel he'd just read, *Snow Crash*, by Neal Stephenson, which takes place in a twenty-first-century California where government has collapsed and people create avatars and try to find a new way to live through a technology-based virtual society called the Metaverse. This was before the term "Internet" was in general circulation, though the technology for it existed. The possibility that got Hoffman excited was something Internet-enabled but more specific: creating an online society, with rules as elaborately defined as those of a game, where large numbers of strangers in different locations could meet and engage in some mutually agreed-upon activity. It's irresistible to wonder whether the appeal of that idea was especially powerful for Hoffman because he had grown up without the usual providers of a sense of belonging—family, community, ethnicity, or religion. In any event, this idea, online networks, became the master theme of Hoffman's professional life—and eventually of his ideas about politics and society too. What big institutions were for Adolf Berle, what unimpeded transactions were for Michael Jensen, networks were for Hoffman. They could be the foundation on which everything rested.

The job at Apple was with a short-lived online service called eWorld. Hoffman's next job was at WorldsAway, a "virtual chat" community owned by Fujitsu, where users interacted through fictionalized graphic representations of themselves. In 1997 Hoffman started his own company, SocialNet, which created a way for people to connect with each other for various purposes, mainly dating, using pseudonyms. After a few years, he sold SocialNet to a company called Spark Networks, which now owns the religious dating sites Jdate and Christian Mingle. Then he became the chief operating officer of PayPal, the money transferring service, where Peter Thiel was the founder and chief executive officer. Hoffman had always believed that online communities should be organized around some fundamental human need, such as love or money—he liked to say that you have to tap into at least one of the seven deadly sins. Now he was switching from lust to greed, also correcting an initial mistaken hypothesis he had absorbed from the gaming world, that people would not want to join online communities under their real names.

PayPal became enduringly important in the lore of Silicon Valley because it launched several important careers—not just Hoffman's and Thiel's, but also that of Elon Musk, founder of Tesla and SpaceX—and helped establish a set of guiding principles for the Internet generation of technology companies. One of these principles was extreme adaptability. PayPal began as a security system for PalmPilot, a short-lived handheld device, and evolved into a system for processing transactions on eBay, the world's first successful online marketplace. Another principle was that speed and aggressiveness, at a level beyond what the rest of the world thinks of as normal, are essential to success. (Silicon Valley's favorite motto is, "It is better to beg for forgiveness than to ask for permission.") As Hoffman later wrote, "At PayPal, we broke the rules, but we did so because we were working toward a better set of rules for everyone." In the expected order of things, big financial institutions would have established themselves as dominant in the online payments business. That a group of young men whom Peter Thiel liked to describe as having Asperger's syndrome got out ahead of Visa, Wells Fargo, and other competitors—not to mention an internal division eBay had launched to offer its customers the same service that PayPal offered— was testament to their willingness to operate outside the constraints that governments impose on banks and to their unconventional conviction that building up a big user base was more important than making money, at least in the short run. In its early days PayPal paid people five and then ten dollars for getting someone else to join the service, which produced losses in the tens of millions a year. Hoffman's personal pre-occupation with scale turned out, at least for Internet businesses, to be an economic strategy as well.

Compared with the rest of the PayPal team, Hoffman had, as he put it, "a massively better idea of where another person was coming from and how to bridge the gap." He took on the role of ambassador to the outside world—the person who could figure out the minimum degree of conventional negotiation that would be necessary if the company was going to survive. He had in mind, as a model to avoid, Napster, the early file-sharing music program that became the first Internet company to go public, which had chosen simply to ignore copyright laws and wound up going out of business after only two years. Hoffman found a way, for example, to operate in Japan, a tightly constrained market, by persuading an influential friend there to arrange for PayPal to be registered in the country as a web browser rather than a bank. He used the antitrust suit that the federal government was then pursuing against Microsoft as an opportunity to convince eBay that if it simply shut down its customers' access to PayPal and forced them to use its own payment system, it might well be sued too. And he was willing to be practical rather than defiantly stick with a course on principle. In October 2001 the passage of the Patriot Act in response to the September 11 attacks on New York and Washington severely damaged PayPal's second line of business—handling cash transactions for gamblers. Hoffman, seeing that this represented an existential peril to the company, helped arrange for a quick sale of PayPal to eBay, its former archenemy.

The sale left Hoffman moderately rich and unemployed, a common, even enviable, situation in Silicon Valley. He had to decide what to do next. He continued to believe that creating a very big online community represented the brightest future for an Internet business; it was just a question of what the community's guiding principle would be. In 2003 he and a friend of his named Mark Pincus, who was especially interested in creating online video games that millions of users could construct and play together, bought the patent for a program called Six Degrees, which was designed to create social networks online. Pincus went on to start a gaming company called Zynga; Hoffman's next start-up was LinkedIn, a social network meant to enable people's business

careers and also to embody what was becoming Hoffman's idea about
how economic life should be organized.

The term "six degrees" comes from a paper by the psychologist Stanley Milgram, published in 1969, reporting on an experiment that showed
how easy it was to create a set of connections from just about any person in the world to any other person in six steps or fewer. Academics
had been studying social networks at least since the 1930s, when the
psychologist Jacob Moreno devised a way of graphing people's connections to one another. Hoffman keeps such a graph framed on his office
wall, showing his own especially large and dense web of connections. But
Silicon Valley doesn't have the same kind of direct connection to these
theories as it does to the academic work in computer science that made
all of the Valley's businesses possible.

Along with Milgram's paper, the academic work about social networks that people in the Valley mention most often is a 1973 paper by
the sociologist Mark Granovetter, called "The Strength of Weak Ties,"
which shows how consequential nonobvious, non-immediate linkages
can be in people's lives. The paradoxical title means that one can often
make more useful connections through people one doesn't know well—
that is, through weak ties—than through people one knows intimately
based on shared membership in an enclosed, tight-knit community.
Strong ties provide limited access; weak ties open up new possibilities.
The applicability of this theory to online networks is obvious. Granovetter is a member of the Stanford faculty, but as far as he knows, he has
never met anyone in the online social network business, even though
most of its leading companies are within a few miles of the Stanford
campus. Once, he got a call from Peter Thiel, inviting him to come to
a dinner for a group of important people from technology businesses,
with the assignment that he would present a "brilliant idea" to the group
in no more than ten minutes. Granovetter declined. Network theory
as practiced by Silicon Valley companies in those early days was like
laissez-faire economics as practiced by the early industrialists: it was less
the application of an academic concept and more the enactment of an
instinct about how to make a lot of money.

The allure of social networks in Silicon Valley was how astonishingly advantageous they could be as a business premise. The potential of

the Internet as a communications medium was hard to miss, but many people who wanted to exploit it commercially, especially people from outside the Valley, understood it as a version of broadcasting—a way for producers to make almost infinitely large quantities of information available to consumers anywhere in the world where there was an on-line connection, instantaneously and at no cost. People like Hoffman, Thiel, and Pincus—and Mark Zuckerberg of Facebook, whom all three met and invested in soon after his arrival in Silicon Valley as a teen-age Harvard undergraduate—saw that the Internet would become a bi-directional medium that was more about creating connections among individual users than between a single purveyor and a mass of users. That was because technology had evolved away from enabling end us-ers to communicate with massive central computers, and toward en-abling small, stand-alone computers to communicate with each other. The apt analogy was to the telephone, not to radio or television. An Internet business could become successful merely by creating an online space—what Hoffman calls a "social operating system"—that enabled one-to-one human contact en masse. It didn't have to create whatever it was that people were coming to it to get: information, secondhand goods, lodging, potential romantic partners, whatever. The customers of the business provided that material for free. The economic rents would go to the owner of the network—"much as levies were imposed in the bygone Republic of Venice," as Hoffman put it—not to whoever had created the content the network carried.

In traditional economic theory, what was supposed to protect a suc-cessful business from competition was the prohibitive cost of building factories, buying raw material, and so on. Internet network businesses didn't have those things. Their protection was the size of the network itself. More users meant more available material on the network—why would anybody want to join the number two network, especially if that meant abandoning their own elaborately built-up online presence on the number one network? A broadcast-era business maxim, called Sarnoff's law after the founder of NBC, was that the value of a network var-ies arithmetically with the size of its audience. Silicon Valley's updated twenty-first-century version was Metcalfe's law (named after Bob Met-calfe, the inventor of Ethernet technology, which permits direct, non-centralized communication between computer workstations), which has it that the value of a network varies exponentially with its number of users. (As a young engineer helping to design an early automatic teller machine for Chase Manhattan Bank, Bob Metcalfe was given a brief audience with the bank's chairman, David Rockefeller, who had on his desk a five-foot-wide custom-built Rolodex containing more than a hundred thousand cards. So that's how the world works, Metcalfe remembers thinking: networks. They're just not technologically enabled yet.) Networks were a winner-take-all game; one of Peter Thiel's bad-boy pronouncements was that in network-era Silicon Valley, the only way to make money was to become a monopoly. Hoffman liked to explain the economics of online networks by quoting the bullying sales manager in the movie *Glengarry Glen Ross*: "First prize is a Cadillac Eldorado. Second prize is a set of steak knives. Third prize is you're fired. Get the picture?" In order for any online network, including LinkedIn, to succeed, scale—Reid Hoffman's long-running obsession—was essential.

LinkedIn incorporated in 2003. Hoffman believed that people would want to conduct different parts of their lives in different online communities. LinkedIn would be the dwelling for your professional identity, while you kept up with friends and family on Facebook and elsewhere. A second and more fundamental assumption was that LinkedIn would fill a social and economic vacancy that had been left when the old Organization Man world had blown apart. In the fat middle decades of the twentieth century, the corporation as employer had functioned as the psychic center of white-collar life: people expected to stay with the same company for their entire careers, or at least for many years, so their economic future depended on managing their relationship with that one institution. Now, just as computing power had been distributed and personalized, so had careers. Corporations were no longer so loyal to their employees, at least if the measure of that was de facto job security and pensions, and employees weren't so loyal to their employers either. Strong ties mattered less, weak ties mattered more—and weak ties were what the Internet was good at. Hoffman's dream was that the entire white-collar population of the world would join LinkedIn, making LinkedIn the new psychic center of the white-collar world, the replacement for the corporation.

At least in Silicon Valley, and Hoffman assumed elsewhere, everyone was always on the market. (In 2014 Hoffman and two of his protégés published a book, *The Alliance*, which argued for what they obviously thought of as a daring proposition, that employees and employers agree on four years—yes, that long!—as the ideal job tenure.) The steward of your career wasn't the company where you worked, it was you. You would maintain a detailed, constantly updated personal profile on LinkedIn that told the world what you'd done, what you were good at, and whom you knew. That would be the way you found your next job or, if you were hiring somebody, your next employee (LinkedIn had a higher-priced service that gave employers access to its users' information). Hoffman liked to say that your LinkedIn page is an autobiography, not a biography; another of his books is called *The Start-Up of You*. One of LinkedIn's first moves was to ban résumés, because they would make it seem too conventional, too impersonal, insufficiently visionary about the future of work. Hoffman, in his ceaseless proselytizing for LinkedIn, presented it not as an online version of the want ads in a newspaper—that is, a database matching employees and employers—but as a true social network where each user created and managed a personal list of hundreds or even thousands of contacts with other members of LinkedIn. Your network, not any one employer, would hold the key to your future. And users, not LinkedIn's own employees, would work ceaselessly to produce the company's product for free.

In the early years, LinkedIn didn't make any money, but that didn't matter. Only scale mattered. Hoffman believed that LinkedIn had to have a minimum of five hundred thousand members to succeed. It reached a million on its 477th day in business. Because people were meant to experience LinkedIn as a network, one of the rules was that it would recruit members through invitation by other members, not direct solicitation by the company. To make this go faster, LinkedIn would ask new members for access to their email contacts list; this explains why, in the early years, people would be bombarded by emails that disingenuously claimed that some distant acquaintance had personally asked that they join LinkedIn. (In the mature and more restrained version of LinkedIn, the site suggests people you should invite to join your network.) One of Hoffman's maxims is "Business is the systematic playing of games"; he and his associates were constantly, obsessively coming up with new ways to make LinkedIn more like a game that would make you feel like a winner if you had an elaborate profile and a lot of contacts. At first

LinkedIn banned photographs, to distinguish itself from Facebook and dating sites. Then it reversed itself and permitted them. At first profiles were private. Then they became partly public, so that if you typed someone's name into a Google search, that person's LinkedIn profile would be one of the top results. LinkedIn began publishing the number of a member's connections, so that people would compete to add to their total (and therefore to LinkedIn's user base); then it decided to cap the number it would publish at five hundred so people wouldn't feel embarrassed by their own networks' inadequacy compared with those of LinkedIn's "supernodes." It recruited dozens of "Influencers" (Bill Gates, Deepak Chopra, Arianna Huffington, Richard Branson, and of course Hoffman himself) to post nuggets of career and business advice on the network. Anything for scale.

Five years on, LinkedIn had thirty-two million members—but Facebook had a hundred million. What if Facebook decided to start a business-oriented offshoot? LinkedIn kept pushing. To the distress of its public relations department, which didn't appreciate the association with the Third Reich, Hoffman likes to use the term "blitzscaling" to describe his preferred way of doing business. That was the ethos at LinkedIn. Hoffman hired a chief executive officer named Jeff Weiner, a man so obsessed with the company that a system check by LinkedIn's engineers revealed that he was logged off of the site for only thirty minutes a day, between 3:30 and 4:00 in the morning. LinkedIn began aggressively expanding abroad, especially in China, the world's biggest market, which Hoffman visited several times a year.

Hoffman and Weiner began talking about their ambition to make LinkedIn the Economic Graph, meaning the central place where all three billion people in the world who work, including blue-collar workers and students, would manage their careers. As is typical in Silicon Valley, Hoffman's vision was soaring, utopian, and self-interested. Like everyone in his social-network-founding generation, he had deeply absorbed the old critique of the postwar America of large, stodgy, stable institutions and a large government imposing a regime of paternalism on corporations. The new world he wanted to help create would be unconstrained, creative, empowering the individual. It wouldn't require all the old structures for apportioning prosperity and opportunity: corporations, unions, government agencies, universities—though it would require

LinkedIn. Many millions of people would be liberated, enabled to flour-ish as entrepreneurs, or at least self-fashioners, rather than employees. An unstructured—in fact, forcibly *de*structured—economic and political order would be a better order.

In 2011, shortly after breaking through the hundred-million-member barrier (today it has more than five hundred million members), Linked-In offered the public the opportunity to buy its stock on the New York Stock Exchange. By the end of the first day of trading, the share price had doubled, and Reid Hoffman, at forty-four, was officially a billionaire.

■

Things had been moving in this direction for some time, but LinkedIn's initial public offering firmly established Hoffman as Silicon Valley's un-official mayor, or Godfather, or chief theoretician: "His Reidness," as some of his old friends began calling him. He was below the very top level of wealth and public renown that such people as Larry Page and Sergey Brin of Google or Mark Zuckerberg of Facebook occupied, but for the role he wanted to play, that was an advantage. Hoffman could still drive his own car and meet people in restaurants and coffee shops (though he'd begun making reservations under an assumed name), so he was able to circulate constantly in the community. He was not an engi-neer interested only in technical issues, and he was far more diplomatic than, say, Peter Thiel, and so was unusually likely to be sought out by people from the outside world who wanted entrée to Silicon Valley. Ever since the sale of PayPal, Hoffman had been actively investing in start-ups, usually as the "angel investor"—the first person to write a check and therefore the investor likely to get the highest return if the company succeeded. It was through this part of his life that he had met Zucker-berg. Just before LinkedIn went public, Hoffman joined Greylock, one of the top-tier venture capital firms on Sand Hill Road, as a partner. He began spending part of every week at Greylock and part at LinkedIn, where he worked in an office next to Jeff Weiner's. This put him more formally in the position he'd been in informally for years, with as much access to deal flow, the lifeblood of Silicon Valley, as anybody. As he casually remarked to a visitor once, "If there's anything in the Valley, I'm going to know about it."

Greylock played host to an endless procession of people who wanted funding for start-ups, almost all of them young men in jeans and T-shirts. At least in the middle of the second decade of the twenty-first century, most of their businesses had cute one-word names (Meerkat, Sprig) and bright, simple logos, and they involved creating a network that people would reach through their mobile devices and use to buy a service that had previously been obtainable only through more conventional means. It was too late to emulate Google or Facebook, but maybe not too late to emulate Uber or Airbnb (where Hoffman was an early investor), if you could find a different realm—office space, meal delivery, pet care, trucking—where you could connect bargain-hunting customers with owners who had slack capacity. Hoffman and his partners would watch the company founders' "deck"—its ten-minute slide presentation—and then pepper the supplicants with questions: Who else is in this space? How fast can you scale up? Do you need access to legal services, technical expertise, lobbyists? How much ownership, for how little money, could Greylock get in return for taking on the risk of investing and possibly losing everything if the company failed?

A favorite word in these sessions was *disruption*: the idea that the central opportunity for a new business, at least if it was an online network, lay in taking down a more traditional and inefficient existing set of institutions. Already the online networks had successfully disrupted such businesses as newspaper publishing, taxis, bookstores, and hotels. Truly grand ambition meant thinking about other sectors that could be replaced. How about colleges and universities through online courses? Banks and national treasuries through cryptocurrencies? One of Hoffman's partners, Simon Rothman, who had founded the car sales division of eBay, dreamed, patiently but constantly, of disrupting the auto industry by giving buyers a way to order custom-built cars online and have them home-delivered. Perhaps the day was coming when even Amazon or Google would have become complacent enough to be disrupted.

Hoffman's round of activities radiated outward from his regular time at LinkedIn and Greylock. He spent a good deal of time receiving petitions, in the manner of a district official in a Chekhov story, from friends whose careers were stalled, kids whose start-up idea wasn't yet at a level where it could be presented to Greylock, heads of nonprofit organizations who wanted him to join their boards, or visitors from abroad who wanted advice about how to start their own country's version of Silicon

Valley. In those meetings, Hoffman, usually dressed in a black T-shirt, black shorts, black sneakers, and white socks (think of the equipment manager for a Pearl Jam reunion tour), would listen attentively to what his visitor had to say, nod, occasionally mumble Yep yep yep, and then, at the first pause, ask, How can I be helpful?

Most days, including on weekends, he would also meet someone for breakfast at a coffee shop and someone else, usually a person who was more of a peer, for dinner at a restaurant. Those meals would usually begin with Hoffman pulling a small notebook out of his pocket and reading an agenda of topics he'd written beforehand in a tiny, indecipherable scrawl: the course on blitzscaling he was teaching at Stanford; the latest video games; politics; wealth management; whether artificial intelligence was more promising than augmented reality, or vice versa. Then he'd ask for the other person's list, and they'd start the conversation. Moonfaced, with small, animated features, thick glasses, and an unruly tousle of brown hair, he would become more excited and pay less attention to his food as he talked, roughly in proportion to the grandiosity and world-changing aspects of the idea he and his companion were discussing.

Beyond his immediate territory, Hoffman often attended elite gatherings where people could talk about big ideas outside of the daily press of business. These included the World Economic Forum, in Davos, Switzerland; two annual conferences, one in Sun Valley and one in Tucson, put on by Allen & Company, an investment firm; Bilderberg, the venerable international-relations conference in Europe; dialog, in Utah, which Peter Thiel cohosts every other year; an annual get-together in Montana hosted by Eric Schmidt, the former chief executive of Google; TED, an annual conference whose initials stand for Technology, Entertainment, and Design; and FOO, which stands for Friends of O'Reilly, staged by Tim O'Reilly, a technology guru and publisher based in San Francisco. In the aggregate, these conferences comprised an enclosed environment where well-known people from a range of fields could discuss the great issues of the day in a strictly delimited form that privileged a combination of confidence and simplicity. TED Talks were limited to eighteen minutes; sometimes at a FOO the participants would be asked to introduce themselves using only three words.

One could explain all this activity by saying that people are motivated to do what is in their interest to do. The business of Hoffman's Silicon Valley was necessarily anti-provincial and dependent on the occasional dramatic breakthrough that pays for everything else, so it made sense to circulate as widely—and to traffic in ideas as rapidly and on as high a conceptual plane—as possible. But Hoffman was hardly forcing himself to enjoy this sort of thing. He loved being the Ubernode, the relentlessly networking personification of the theory behind LinkedIn. The closest thing he had to an extended-family vacation was The Weekend to Be Named Later, a highly scripted annual conference for 150 people and their families, held between Christmas and New Year's at a Southern California resort, which he and a friend had founded, where the participants took part in panel discussions all day and played games in the evenings. Hoffman also enjoyed spending time with people from Hollywood—especially directors and producers of fantasy-related material, like J. J. Abrams (*Star Trek, Star Wars*) and Joss Whedon (*The Avengers*)—and he served as a kind of informal consultant to Mike Judge, the creator of the satirical HBO show *Silicon Valley*, to help make sure all the jokes landed. He had an uncanny, even jarring ability to move seamlessly between the purely notional realm of gaming and science fiction and the intensely practical one of investing in and managing business applications of new technologies.

One evening in 2015 Hoffman was having dinner with one of his frequent companions, Mark Pincus, and after getting a few preliminaries out of the way (such as recaps of Hoffman's recent meetings with the secretary-general of the United Nations and the Duke of York, and a new book he'd read called *Superintelligence*), Pincus, an enthusiastic, boyish-looking middle-aged man, brought up an idea he was especially excited about. "In this election, we'd want a million people to raise one billion dollars to run Mike Bloomberg"—the former mayor of New York—"for president. Through Kickstarter. Say the minimum is five hundred million. I think he'd be the best. It'd be pretty cool. That would change politics forever." He leaned closer to Hoffman. "Why couldn't that happen? A million people buying the presidency. Look at Star Citizen." That's an online multiplayer simulation game about the governance of the United Empire of Earth in the thirtieth century. "It's a game that runs for two years, they have a hundred million users a year, two to three hundred thousand a day. People are passionate about the game, and the guy who does it is a star. If you can do that, why can't people buy the presidency? A million people give a thousand dollars each. I believe there's a million people who'd like to give a 'fuck you' to both political parties."

"I think Bloomberg had his people look at it," Hoffman said.

"He's not seventy percent sure he'd win," Pincus said. "If he thought he'd win, he'd run. If he knew this would work, he'd do it. The media attention would be so massive! I think he's, like, shy. Maybe a little risk-averse."

"To some extent, that's what happened with Obama," Hoffman said.

This kind of conversation was more than just two old friends having fun. In 2012, newly flush with the proceeds of LinkedIn's public stock offering, Hoffman became one of the country's major political donors. He gave a million dollars to Priorities USA, a Democratic Party political action committee whose main project at that moment was getting Barack Obama reelected as president. Pincus gave a million dollars too. That brought both of them into Obama's circle, perhaps not as intimately as Adolf Berle had been in Franklin Roosevelt's, but not casually either. What radio had been for Roosevelt, a new mass medium that offered unprecedented possibilities for a politician who wanted to connect with the public, the new online networks—which by now had far bigger audiences than newspapers, radio, or television—were for Obama.

The White House hired a former LinkedIn executive, DJ Patil, as its first chief data scientist. LinkedIn provided proprietary data about the employment market to the White House, to be used in the annual "Economic Report of the President." When the website associated with Obama's health-care reform legislation had an unsuccessful debut, Hoffman was part of a group of Silicon Valley executives that organized a rescue operation. Pincus had been granted a forty-five-minute private audience with Obama in the Oval Office, where he gave the president a PowerPoint presentation on "the product-management approach to government," and he also spoke to Obama on the phone occasionally. Hoffman regularly attended meetings and dinners at the White House, including a small gathering in 2015 to discuss Obama's postpresidential future, and he organized a meeting in Silicon Valley to advise the people who were setting up Obama's foundation on how to harness the power of social networks. On Obama's regular visits to Silicon Valley, Hoffman was usually on the list of people who saw him.

Silicon Valley was also, by now, an important Democratic Party business interest group. Obama was friendly to a number of the Valley's political causes, such as permitting generous allotments of H-1B visas, under which technology firms can hire engineers from abroad; net neutrality, which forbade Internet service providers from charging higher prices to heavy users of video, music, and gaming services; and a new law, opposed by Obama's own financial regulators, that permitted online sales of stock in technology start-ups. The Obama administration gave a $465 million loan to Tesla, the electric car company founded by Hoffman's friend Elon Musk. When the White House gave a state dinner for Xi Jinping, the president of China and therefore the person who controlled access to the most important growth market for LinkedIn, Reid Hoffman (in a tuxedo!) and Michelle Yee were among the guests. On Hoffman's office wall were framed photographs, impossible for any visitor to miss, of himself with Obama, Bloomberg, and Bill Clinton. Once, at a private meeting for big donors from the entertainment industry, one of the guests asked Obama why he had sided with Silicon Valley over Hollywood during a fierce regulatory battle over copyright law in 2011 and 2012: Hollywood, the makers of content, was for stricter protections, and Silicon Valley, whose business was to distribute as much material as it could for free, was against them. Silicon Valley won. (In this instance, and others, one of Silicon Valley's lobbying techniques was to mobilize its vast user base in support of its political goals.) It's simple, Obama told his Hollywood supporters: they do a lot more to help me than you guys do.

Hoffman was anything but a cynic—rather, he was the reverse, someone who sincerely believed that everything he did would improve life, not just for him but for millions, even billions, of other people. Although, like most of the new technology billionaires, he was publicly committed to philanthropy (it was distinctive to Hoffman that he said his inspiration and guide in this was Spider-Man comic books and movies), he didn't see that there was a bright distinction between philanthropy and business. It was deep in the culture of Silicon Valley that business was the way to improve the world, and that both government and philanthropy would succeed to the extent that they structured themselves so as to resemble business—online network businesses in particular—as much as possible. Most of Hoffman's giving was to "social entrepreneurs" whose idea was that they could bring the benefits of network-enabled entrepreneurial capitalism to people in needy faraway places such as Bangladesh and sub-Saharan Africa, and most of his investing was in network-enabled start-ups that were trying to bring better services to consumers. He had also come to believe that American democracy, especially the two-party system, was broken, and that remaking it as a technology start-up was the way to fix it.

In theory, Edmund Burke's idea that people should "love the little platoon we belong to in society" did not conflict with the principles of social networks—after all, one can have a small network—but in practice, Hoffman was powerfully drawn only to new projects with the potential for, in his words, "massive, outsize, discontinuous impact," for "helping humanity at scale." Partly for that reason, he and his wife had decided not to have children: a family was too small a project compared to the time it would take from working on larger ones. Although neither Reid Hoffman nor Michelle Yee was conventionally religious—Hoffman liked to call himself a "mystical atheist" or a "techno-utopian"—they were both drawn to Buddhist meditation practice, and there was a strong element of home-brew religion in the way that Hoffman saw the world. He liked coherent belief systems, with instructive, heroic myths and legends, and moral principles enforced through rules. As a freshman at Stanford, he had encountered—and posted on his dorm room door where his future wife could see it—this famous quote from Hillel, the ancient Jewish sage: "If I am not for myself, who will be for me? If I am not for others, what am I? And if not now, when?" More recently, he had commissioned a design firm to devise a personal system of twenty-eight symbols that look like the petroglyphs at ancient Native American sites in the West—one for each essential virtue and one for Hoffman's initials.

Another of Hoffman's favorite dinner companions was James Manyika, an elegant, Zimbabwe-born, Oxford-educated engineer who was the McKinsey consulting firm's man in Silicon Valley. Manyika was better versed in philosophy than most of Hoffman's friends, so he was a particularly good partner for discussing the various eschatological scenarios that were popular in Silicon Valley. (One of Hoffman's friends called him an "epiphany addict.") There was seasteading—rebuilding cities on floating islands constructed in the ocean, where there would be none of the government regulations that constrain human possibility. Or transferring large populations to Mars or some other location in outer space. Or the "simulation hypothesis": the idea that what we experience as human life is merely a game devised by computers, which we are playing under their rules. Or "the singularity," in which the technology of artificial intelligence would advance to the point that humans, with all their insufficiencies, could be entirely replaced by smarter and more moral machines. That was a central topic at one of Hoffman's dinners with Manyika.

"We are the model of an intelligent being," Hoffman said in his customary tone of insistent, slightly amused curiosity. "But any form of AI is actually a different species. It's not copies of human beings. You're really seriously jumping into the deep end. How do we create ethical AI? We have to address this in a more spiritual way. How is the ethical algorithm developed? What are the ethical outcomes of life systems? Could you imagine a system that decided it would be better to eliminate human beings? You could make an argument. We"—humans—"are screwing up the climate, we're killing off other species."

The two of them were in a private room at a sushi restaurant in Silicon Valley, free to let the conversation ascend as high as they wanted. Hoffman's arms rose above his head, as if pulled upward by invisible wires. He went on: "Is what we should create an ethical system, or a system that doesn't contravene humans?" As one who likes to think outside conventional bounds, Hoffman wasn't willing to dismiss automatically the idea of a posthuman world. "There will be some people who think whatever's right is to let the next step in evolution play out. That's a scary thought."

Manyika's role with Hoffman was similar to Hoffman's role with Mark Pincus: the calmer head who gave measured response to his friend's unrestrained speculations. "There's a nonzero chance that AI will be smarter than humans," he said.

That only spurred Hoffman to take his thought a step further. "Isn't that one hundred percent? Isn't it just a time coefficient? . . . Nobody knowledgeable thinks it's zero. Everybody knows it's ten to a hundred years."

What all these grand musings had in common was an impatience with the current forms of society, or at least an inclination to see them as only temporary, and a powerful optimism that the new world that most people in Silicon Valley thought was aborning would be far better than the present one because it would reverse the currently unfair power equation between older established institutions and the great mass of powerless people. Mark Pincus, in an essay he posted online in the early days of online networks, called for "a revolution of the ants." He decided to get involved in politics after he arrived one morning at his neighborhood park in San Francisco with his beloved dog, Zynga, the namesake of his gaming company, and found that a group of people had successfully petitioned to have the park changed into a soccer field for their children, with no dogs allowed. This, to someone with Pincus's level of certainty, showed that politics was corrupt, incapable of serving the public interest. Having such a strong conviction that one was right justified a kind of buccaneering behavior, not just in one's own business but also in public life.

Hoffman loved the book *Nonzero*, by Robert Wright, published in 1999, because it posited a political world without fundamental trade-offs, where policies could be found that would benefit everybody rather than helping some people at the expense of others. He'd flown Wright to Silicon Valley a couple of times for personal consultations. His favorite board game was Settlers of Catan, a German-originated simulation of civilization building: as in Hoffman's business life, playing the game entailed a lot of tactical shows of cooperation, but in the end one player won and the others lost. Hoffman had a custom version of the game made up, called Startups of Silicon Valley (with products instead of settlements, disrupters instead of robbers, talent instead of wheat), which he sent to his friends as a gift. He also had it in mind to write a book on friendship. He thought that conflict, rather than being fundamental to society, could become a relic of the pretechnological past, and that there was no reason to fear power when it was in the right hands. In the book on blitzscaling that he wrote after teaching his course on the subject at Stanford, he brought up Louis Brandeis's suspicion of bigness, but only to dismiss it as a relic of the early twentieth century. "We disagree with this position on the harmfulness of scale in today's world," he wrote. "We believe that while big can sometimes be bad, big can also be great."

As the increase in inequality that had begun in the last decades of the twentieth century continued apace, Hoffman and his friends in Silicon Valley spent a lot of time discussing what to do about it. It was in the nature of the Valley's culture to assume that such a large global problem could be solved through technology, innovation, and entrepreneurship. In 2015 a number of prominent people in technology, along with five Nobel Prize–winning economists, signed a statement called "Open Letter on the Digital Economy," which struck a much more pessimistic note than you'd ordinarily hear in the Valley: "The majority of US households have seen little if any income growth for over 20 years, the percentage of national income that's paid out in wages has declined sharply in the US since 2000, and the American middle class, which is one of our country's great creations, is being hollowed out." The letter called for instituting an ambitious program of new research and changes in government and business policies, and for using the digital revolution as "an opportunity to re-invent the corporation and our business systems." That was not far from being a restatement of Adolf Berle's attitude almost a century earlier, when he had begun thinking seriously about the corporation as a social institution. Since then the corporation had been forced to become more attentive to society, and then freed from such obligations. Now the cycle might be starting again.

Hoffman, on the advice of his senior staff at LinkedIn, declined an invitation to sign the letter—it wasn't necessarily good for business to offer governments all over the world what they might take as an invitation to regulate technology firms more heavily. Anyway, although he liked to associate himself with liberal causes, it didn't really represent his own ideas about how to solve economic problems. Another cause that was becoming popular with Silicon Valley's left wing, including some of Hoffman's partners at Greylock, was a government-provided universal basic income, to provide for the needs of people who had been left behind by technological advances, but Hoffman was not comfortable with that either. He liked to quote a statistic he had picked up from a United Nations report: the global economy will have to create six hundred million jobs over the next twenty years in order to keep most of the population decently fed and housed. Hoffman believed that existing businesses could supply only ten to twenty million of these jobs—the rest could have to come from start-ups. So countries everywhere would have to reorient themselves to become more encouraging to entrepreneurship, especially through online networks. That would be the solution to the problem of rising inequality.

LinkedIn's official idea of the economic future was that conventional long-term full-time employment would become less and less common, but that would be okay. People would start their own ventures, or move rapidly from job to job, or piece together "portfolio lives" stitched out of pieces of part-time employment they had found through such online networks as Uber and TaskRabbit. Hoffman's Greylock partner Simon Rothman had coined a term for such people: "uncollared workers." It was clear that the portion of the workforce whose lives were built this way was growing, but it was too early to tell whether such arrangements would continue to increase until they became the dominant form of work. Would most people who no longer had conventional salaried jobs feel liberated or terrified? LinkedIn had commissioned a study, by a hand-picked economist, that used its trove of private data about the careers of its members. It implied, unsurprisingly, that the Economic Graph the company had been promoting was the key to growth: whether or not it was a direct case of cause and effect, cities with denser networks of LinkedIn connections produced more new jobs than cities with sparser networks. The perpetually exuberant intellectual culture of Silicon Valley had rediscovered Ronald Coase's old essay "The Nature of the Firm"; the current read of it was that the Internet had reduced transaction costs so radically that conventional business organizations were becoming unnecessary (which of course meant that conventional benefits and pensions would be unnecessary too). Even the most complex projects could be executed by loose, temporary assemblages of talent. Important innovations would come from small new companies, not big old ones. The old-fashioned managerial capitalism that had dominated the twentieth century was dead. "The Internet is nothing less than an extinction-level event for the traditional firm," one technology guru proclaimed in 2015.

That was the theory. In practice, there were five dominant technology companies: Apple, Google (now called Alphabet for corporate purposes), Amazon, Microsoft, and Facebook. All were less than half a century old, all but Apple had living founders, and most of the time they were the five most valuable companies in the United States. One could see the connection between their astonishingly rapid success and Silicon Valley's confidence in entrepreneurship and innovation. (One of Hoffman's friends ended a conversation by exclaiming, "We are living in Florence in the Renaissance!") But, by now, all of them were fairly conventional large corporations. They had built close ties to the political system. They had lavish corporate headquarters; LinkedIn had built two, a campus in Silicon Valley and an office tower in San Francisco. The network-based companies, including LinkedIn, made most of their money selling accumulated data about their members to other big corporations. They had longtime employees, who got constant, conventional personnel evaluations and whose most obvious difference from the old Organization Man was that they would not dare to leave work at five o'clock. Google did a survey of its employees' email habits and found that two-thirds of them are essentially never off of the company's email system except for brief breaks for meals and longer ones to sleep.

These companies were structured so as to re-create Adolf Berle's idea of the separation of ownership and control—and to repeal, at least for themselves, the shareholder revolution of the late twentieth century. Companies like Google and Facebook had created two classes of stock, one for the founders that had more voting power, another for ordinary investors who were willing to accept enforced passivity as the price of the high returns they were hoping for. Reid Hoffman had set up this kind of system when LinkedIn went public: he controlled 58 percent of the voting stock. In the venture capital world, ownership and control still went together. The firms on Sand Hill Road usually demanded a high level of power at the companies they invested in, including the ability to fire the founders. But that was in the early stage of a company's life; increasingly, the few start-ups that succeeded would wind up being sold to one of the Big Five and taken out of the reach of control by shareholders. The leading corporations in Silicon Valley weren't so different from the corporations a reader would have encountered in the pages of *The Modern Corporation and Private Property*. They were very big (and getting bigger), very powerful, relatively immune to interference from either investors or government regulators, and also free of most of the economic obligations to employees that had been imposed on the Industrial Age corporations as they got older. As a locus of economic power, Silicon Valley, jarringly new as it was, had followed an old, familiar pattern.

Although Hoffman had protected LinkedIn from control by its investors, by taking the company public he had sacrificed his protection from Wall Street's preoccupation with quarterly earnings statements. In February 2016, the day after LinkedIn released a fourth-quarter report for 2015 that showed its profits and membership growing more slowly than it had predicted, its stock price dropped by sixty points, or 44 percent of its value, in just a few hours. Hoffman didn't know exactly what had happened; he assumed that a couple of big institutional investors had decided to dump their entire holdings in LinkedIn in response to the fourth-quarter report. More than $10 billion in the company's value had dematerialized in one trading day. Hoffman was far too much the committed game player to find the role of principled loser attractive, and he was aware that, with more than three hundred million members at that moment, LinkedIn was still at the lower edge of the scale an online network company needed to achieve lasting success. For some time he had been quietly exploring the idea of selling the company. That disastrous day on the New York Stock Exchange provided a strong final shove in that direction. In June 2016 LinkedIn announced that it was going to be bought by Microsoft—the most business-oriented of the Big Five and the one most lacking an online network—for $26.2 billion. Hoffman himself made more than $2.5 billion in the sale. A few months afterward, he joined Microsoft's board of directors.

■

The year of the sale of LinkedIn to Microsoft was also the year of another presidential election. Hoffman didn't feel nearly as enthusiastic about any candidate as he had about Obama, but by now he was accustomed to being involved in presidential politics. His favorite among the Republican candidates was Jeb Bush. The only Democrat he considered seriously was Hillary Clinton. He had private meetings with both of them, Clinton several times, and wound up giving to Clinton, though at a far lower level than he had given to Obama. (He gave more than a million dollars to Obama's postpresidential foundation.) He saw Obama as a modernizer and Clinton as a traditionalist. In one of their conversations he asked her why she was so supportive of teachers' unions; it was an article of faith in Silicon Valley that the unionized public schools attended by the vast majority of American children had failed and that unions were substantially the cause. They're my constituency, she said, and I support them, the same way you would support an entrepreneur. That wasn't the answer Hoffman was looking for, because he didn't think politics should be about constituencies.

Hoffman's grand passion of the campaign year, equivalent to his enthusiasm for Obama in 2012, was his dislike of Donald Trump, who could hardly have repelled Hoffman more if he had been an avatar designed specifically for that purpose. As Hoffman put it, "More or less all the things Donald stands for, I abhor." Trump's flamboyantly nostalgic slogan, "Make America Great Again," conjured up the opposite of Hoffman's futuristic vision of the good; Trump's constant militant invocations of the dream of an authority-worshipping, unapologetically white America dominating its rivals stood in total contrast to Silicon Valley's idea of a unified, multicultural global market that was good for everyone. Trump often took a poke at technology companies specifically; and the blustery, grandiose way he dressed, spoke, and carried himself grated on Hoffman's sensibilities. Most of Silicon Valley agreed wholeheartedly with Hoffman, with the predictable exception of Peter Thiel, who gave a prime-time nationally televised endorsement of Trump at the Republican National Convention.

Hoffman made a $250,000 contribution to an anti-Trump political action committee. He produced a custom-made anti-Trump version of one of his favorite games, Cards Against Humanity, called Trumped-Up Cards: The World's Biggest Deck, and sent copies to his friends. He rearranged his schedule so that he could devote almost all of the forty-five days leading up to the election to anti-Trump activities. Hoping he could use game logic to throw Trump off, he publicly offered to donate $5 million to a veterans' group if Trump would release his tax returns—reasoning that Trump might have a hard time saying no, not only because he had positioned himself as a champion of veterans but also because Trump had made a nearly identical offer to Obama, about Obama's student records, during the 2012 campaign. When Trump didn't respond, Hoffman came up with the idea of appearing on Fox News with Trump and saying, I'm prepared to raise my donation to the veterans to $50 million if you'll match me, and I've brought my checkbook. Let's both write identical checks, right now, on the air. The beauty of this scenario was that it would force Trump to make it clear not only that he was less committed to veterans than the bespectacled liberal from Silicon Valley, but also that he wasn't as rich. But it never materialized. Hoffman thought seriously about relocating to someplace far away—perhaps New Zealand—if Trump won.

Like most liberals, Hoffman believed that Hillary Clinton would beat Trump. He was involved before the election in planning for the technology aspects of her presidential transition and administration. On election night, after it became clear that Trump was going to win, Hoffman went home, and he and his wife watched an old episode of *The West Wing*, the 1990s television show about a heroic liberal president. Afterward, instead of leaving the country, he became one of the top Democratic donors nationally in 2017, making dozens of contributions to campaigns all over the country. In partnership with Mark Pincus, he founded a "virtual political party" called Win the Future (the acronym was an intentional, unmissable joke about the election result), which aimed to create a massive online network that would disrupt the political system, with results its founders were sure would be benign. In 2018 Hoffman and a group of former Obama administration officials made plans to create a comprehensive database of information about the country's liberal voters that would compete with, or replace, the Democratic Party's own state and national databases and so help to disempower the party as the keeper of American liberalism. It was a further blow to Hoffman's relationship with the Democratic Party when it came out that another political organization he cofounded, called Investing in US, had contributed to a Russian-style campaign on Facebook that deliberately disseminated misleading information to help elect a Democrat from Alabama named Doug Jones to the U.S. Senate.

At one of Hoffman's meetings with Obama, the president had warned him that the middle of the country was feeling disenfranchised. The 2016 campaign provided a demonstration: the main surprise was that in both parties, the most populist candidate—Trump in the Republicans' case, Bernie Sanders in the Democrats'—did far better than anyone had expected by tapping into that feeling in very different ways. Even before the campaign, there were warning signs about the lack of general enthusiasm for the economic future that seemed to be emerging. One of Hoffman's Silicon Valley friends, Mike Maples, Jr., who runs a venture capital fund and is, like Peter Thiel, one of the Valley's rare Republican conservatives, went to Dallas to talk with Glenn Beck, the right-wing talk-show host, whom he admires. He gave Beck the pitch about the coming miracle of the network economy, but Beck wasn't buying. What do you say to a guy like me? Beck said to Maples. How do you answer the argument that there are forty million people in red states who are going to be displaced? And that was a reaction from the right, the side that is supposed to be reflexively pro-market.

The support for candidates like Trump and Sanders mystified Hoffman. To his mind, people like himself and Mark Pincus were the real populists; they understood the power of markets and technology to bring a better life to most people. His faith in networks as the new social model remained unimpaired. Although he was now very rich, politically powerful, on intimate terms with the top officials of some of the world's most valuable corporations, and an official of one of them himself, he still saw his life as being about dismantling structures that impeded the dreams of ordinary, disempowered people—for their benefit, not the benefit of people like him. Why didn't the rest of the world see it that way?

AFTERWORD: AN ATTEMPT
TO USE A TOOL

In spite of the bankruptcy of past systems of belief, it is hard to surrender our faith in system and in some wholesale belief. We continually reason as if the difficulty were in the particular system that has failed and as if we were on the point of now finally hitting upon one that is true as all the others were false. The real trouble is with the attitude of dependence upon any of them . . . Wholesale creeds and all-inclusive ideals are impotent in the face of actual situations; for doing always means the doing of something in particular.

—John Dewey

This book has examined a succession of grand conceptions of how to organize the economy to produce a good society. That is a topic that was new as the twentieth century began. Americans were just beginning to understand that trusts, corporations, and other large economic units could vie with government and match it in size and power, and in effect on people's lives. What should be done about that?

Adolf Berle was at the younger end of a generation of Progressives who had wrested the great political question of the day away from populists and socialists on the left and uncritical celebrators of business on the right, and made it the province of liberal government officials. Berle wanted to keep economic power concentrated so that it could be better managed by the state. And he wanted the power of the state to be concentrated, too, in Washington.

By the middle of the twentieth century, Berle believed that his solution to the economic problem had been enacted successfully. The corporation, ever larger and more dominant, seemed to be accepting its role as the social bedrock of the country, the provider of job security and pensions and health care—perhaps because that was the right thing to do, perhaps as a small price to pay for its economic dominance and security. The most established corporations, at least, seemed to have given up fighting against all forms of unionization and government regulation, and government seemed to have accepted the corporation's size and power. Liberal intellectuals may have fretted about the ethic of conformity that they felt corporations imposed on the culture, but their discontent was more a complaint about the social order than a threat to it. The United States looked like a country of big, powerful institutions that had more or less made peace with one another. Prosperity was increasing and inequality was falling. People like Berle simply didn't see what we'd now consider the obvious shortcomings of American society at the time, such as the legal rank ordering of the races.

The most consequential attack on that system, when it came, was from an unexpected quarter: the long-quiescent financial world. Empowered by the advent of large, mobile pools of capital and freed by government from its old constraints, Wall Street established dominion over the corporation. The ideas of Michael Jensen and his allies about transferring control of the corporation to shareholders provided both overall justification and specific techniques for doing this. The result was that the corporation maintained its economic purpose but ceased to function as the heart of a social order. The markets wouldn't permit that. And thanks in large part to the work of Jensen's generation of financial economists, capital became much more fluid and tradable, and financial power more centralized, globalized, and mobile. All that changed the basic orientation of the country, away from institutions and toward transactions.

By that time, liberalism, the traditional countervailing force against the excesses of capitalism, had substantially changed its direction. Louis Brandeis–style economic liberalism, with its emphasis on breaking up large concentrations and attending to the interests of medium-size businesses as well as consumers, had pretty much disappeared. Clash of the Titans liberalism, in the preferred form it took for Berle—direct control of the operations of the corporation by the state—had also disappeared, at least as an ideal that excited reformers. Instead, a market-oriented form of economic liberalism had become the dominant strain. It would have the national government continue to manage the economy, but invisibly, by manipulating interest rates, tax rates, and the overall level of government spending. Elite liberals had become far more kindly disposed toward markets and suspicious of economic regulation.

So there was very little liberal opposition to the long-running deregulation of the financial system and other sectors of the economy during the last quarter of the twentieth century, which proceeded apace through both Democratic and Republican administrations. Once again, as in the early days of industrial capitalism, big winners were spectacularly rewarded, economic power was concentrated, inequality and risk rose, and local institutions weakened. And this time, the old picture of a country that could offer a better life to each succeeding generation seemed not to apply any longer. This has generated enormous alienation and anger that has made itself felt in politics and elsewhere.

Today the Transaction Man mentality, which is neither liberal nor conservative, is as deeply rooted as the Organization Man mentality was when William Whyte conferred a name on it. When a challenge presents itself—how to educate our children, how to fight poverty, how to change politics, how to improve the tone of a polarized society—any proposed solution that can be characterized as relying on bureaucracies, organizations, government agencies, or established interest groups is doomed to lose the argument. Only innovation, disruption, destructuring, and individualizing can possibly work. In the manner of someone who thinks the cure for a hangover is another drink, the country keeps reacting to troubles produced by the deterioration of its institutional life by embracing further deterioration. In polls, faith in the core institutions of American life—government, business, religion, public schools, news organizations, the legal system—has been falling for decades. In response, we persist in thinking about solutions that would continue to weaken these institutions, to the point that it would become nearly impossible for them to regain our trust. We want politics and government to be taken away from career professionals, charter schools to replace traditional public schools, higher education to take place online at home, journalism to be turned over to citizens, religion to become informal and deritualized. It's no accident that the major institution that has been best at maintaining its position of respect, the military, is also the one least susceptible to changes like this.

The dreams of Reid Hoffman's generation in Silicon Valley of a network-based society, if they came true, would mean, for most people, fewer conventional jobs, less economic security, less privacy, and a faster pace of change. It's a dream that has quickly lost its broad appeal; the country has pivoted from awestruck admiration of the big new Internet network companies to resentment and suspicion, as it has become clear that the social and economic benefits of the new system belong mostly to the companies themselves and not the users of their products. It's hard to imagine that a society with a handful of enormous companies and an ever-larger mass of the casually employed would generate a higher level of political and social contentment.

Despite their differences, the three big ideas we've seen for organizing the economy—institutions, transactions, and networks—have a common thread. They share a kind of conceptual grandeur, a conviction that if we aim at producing a good society by adopting one all-encompassing principle, the result will be positive for everybody. It's only necessary that the game be constructed so as to guarantee that somebody's notion of the good guys—a government-corporate partnership, or the financial markets, or online networks—will always win.

But if we go back to the beginning of our story, when the country was first coming to terms with the presence of big business and all its effects, we can find another potential master concept for a good society—one that is forgotten today and is quite different from the others because it envisions a messy, contentious system that can't be subordinated to one conception of the common good. It refuses to designate good guys and bad guys. It distributes, rather than concentrates, economic and political power. It honors a process in which nobody, good or bad, ever gains control. It's called pluralism, and it deserves a revival.

■

In 1893, on a Dutch ocean liner called the *Maasdam*, two young Americans, both the sons of rich businessmen from small towns in the Midwest, struck up what turned out to be a lifelong friendship. Both of them were budding intellectuals who were planning to enroll as students at the University of Berlin. One, Hutchins Hapgood, was what people in Germany would call a *Luftmensch*—interested in literature and art, but partly as a pretext for escaping the social strictures of his background. The other, Arthur Bentley, was much more serious. Many years later, Hapgood recalled their first encounter this way:

> A few days after the departure of the ship, I met on deck a strangely vivid young man, Arthur F. Bentley. He was passionately determined to solve the mystery of society . . . I knew I was going on a romantic quest. I had been set free, and many-colored adventures lay before my mind's eye. But Bentley was realistically passionate, with a serious purpose of learning everything known about sociology, and with a determination to add to that knowledge and solve the puzzle of human society.

Bentley, then in his early twenties, did indeed become a serious student in Berlin, with teachers who were among the most important social theorists of the day. He returned to the United States, got a Ph.D. from Johns Hopkins, and moved to Chicago. "Bentley's passionate desire to discover the sociological ultimate revealed an infinite mental turmoil," Hutchins Hapgood wrote. "He was an unhappy restless soul, bitterly critical of himself and his ability to reach the heights." This quality may help explain why a trial academic appointment Bentley took up at the University of Chicago, offering a seminar to five students, was an instant disaster. As one of his colleagues wrote, "Owing to the ambitiousness and difficulty of the subjects proposed by Bentley for study by the group, they and Bentley quietly agreed to discontinue their meetings after only five sessions." Cast out of what would have seemed to be his natural environment, Bentley went into journalism as a reporter and an editorial writer for a Chicago daily newspaper that has long since gone out of business. This work gave him a constant intimate exposure to politics as it was really practiced in a big, rough, machine-run city. At a time when most educated American liberals believed that both business and politics had become shockingly corrupt and needed to be brought under the control of civilized people like themselves, Bentley's experiences were leading him in a different direction.

In his off-hours, Bentley worked on a long, strange, mesmerizing manuscript that aimed to unite what he was seeing of politics as actually practiced with the social theories he had imbibed in Berlin and at Johns Hopkins. The result was a book called *The Process of Government: A Study of Social Pressures*, which was published to almost no notice in 1908. In the meantime, Hutchins Hapgood had married a pioneering feminist writer named Neith Boyce and embarked on a life in Europe and the United States as one of those people who seem to know everyone worth knowing—Gertrude Stein, Lincoln Steffens, Eugene O'Neill, Bertrand Russell—and as an advocate of open marriage. He practiced this far more ardently than his wife did, until, perhaps partly out of jealousy, she had an affair with Bentley, who was also married. Years later, Hapgood published an anonymous (and widely banned) free-love memoir, called *The Story of a Lover*. There he reported that his wife had confessed to him that "she had met a man who moved her in a strong, primitive way," a man who "had a root-like, sensual charm for her," perhaps because, in contrast to Hapgood, "he was lonely and unsocial and graceless, remote and bad, excitingly, refreshingly bad."

That was Bentley. Hapgood reacted badly. As men often do, he maintained that his many affairs were merely "adventures," and that he had taken care not to fall in love as his wife had done. During one of their conversations about her relationship with Bentley, Hapgood confessed, "I took her by the throat! . . . It happened without consciousness! At that moment I understood murder." The Hapgoods moved from Italy to Indianapolis, where Neith Boyce had a nervous breakdown. Bentley returned to his newspaper job in Chicago and had a breakdown of his own. In 1911 he and his wife moved to the rural hamlet of Paoli, Indiana, where he operated an apple orchard. Years later, he sent Neith Boyce a basket from his farm as a gift. He wrote, maybe having more than just apples in mind, "To grow apples requires a slight madness—an adoration of the fruit, a desire to make gifts of it, an inability to comprehend that a gift of apples is not the highest mark of favor that can be shown."

Bentley remained in Paoli for more than forty-five years, until his death in 1957. Photographs of him show a bald man in a suit and tie, with rheumy eyes and a droopy mustache, looking more like the small-town banker's son he was than a German-educated intellectual, a Chicago newspaperman, or a wandering bohemian. Over the years, he traveled, drank, worried about his dwindling inherited means, produced a series of increasingly abstruse books (sample title: *Linguistic Analysis of Mathematics*), and corresponded voluminously with the likes of Albert Einstein, Thomas Mann, and, especially, John Dewey, the pragmatist philosopher; a published collection of the Bentley-Dewey letters runs to more than seven hundred pages. His reputation grew steadily as time passed, mainly because of *The Process of Government*, which by the time Bentley died was considered the most important study of politics and society ever produced by an American—required reading for anybody studying those fields seriously. Today it is out of print and hardly remembered.

■

Hutchins Hapgood reported in his memoir that Bentley made "demands on himself with great intensity, and worked very hard, but on the whole unhappily." The cause of the unhappiness was "his passionate disappointment in not being able to solve the mystery of sociology." Hapgood may of course have harbored an animus against Bentley that led him to paint Bentley's career in dark hues (though they remained friends); also, he confessed that Bentley's books "to me are incomprehensible because of the progressively almost mathematical quality of his thought." It's hard to believe that if he had actually read *The Process of Government*, he would have continued to insist that Bentley never believed he had solved the mystery. One couldn't have been much more repetitively insistent than Bentley that he had in fact solved it. The solution was interest groups.

The Process of Government begins with a peculiar declaration, printed all by itself on a page: "This Book Is an Attempt to Fashion a Tool." Although Bentley was a lifelong enthusiastic supporter of liberal causes, and occasionally was active in political campaigns, he meant for *The Process of Government* to serve as an ideologically neutral guidebook that, if properly understood and faithfully used, would explain all of politics and government, everywhere in the world and at every time in history. The key principle was straightforward: humans inevitably form themselves into groups, groups inevitably take action, and the actions they take are usually aimed at influencing government. Therefore, if you want to understand politics, you must study the activities of groups—and, no less important, you must never claim that anything else can explain the way a political question turned out. As Bentley put it, "All phenomena of government are phenomena of groups pressing one another, forming one another, and pushing out new groups and group representatives (the organs or agencies of government) to mediate the adjustments."

Bentley devoted long, cranky stretches of *The Process of Government* to explaining why the leading social theorists of the day—some still remembered (Herbert Spencer, Francis Galton, Karl Marx), others long forgotten (Rudolf von Jhering, Albert Venn Dicey)—were misguided because they paid too much attention to other factors and too little to groups. Bentley had no use for such broad concepts as class, race, leadership, or the public, because they did not pertain to self-consciously organized group activity. Only groups mattered. Groups could just as easily form around social or moral causes (Bentley called those "liberty and equality groups") as narrow economic interests. States and cities were "locality groups," the legal system was a collection of "law groups," income categories were "wealth groups," devoted followers of a popular politician were "personality groups"; interest groups lay at the functioning heart of monarchies and dictatorships as well as of democracies. "When the groups are adequately stated, everything is stated," he wrote. "When I say everything, I mean everything."

No person, Bentley believed, could be understood simply as a member of one group, because people are attracted to various groups, and their level of engagement with each one varies over time. It was equally useless to try to understand an entire society in terms of one monolithic set of interests being pitted against another (the left versus the right, for example), or of a contest between special interests and the public interest. The interplay of interests was too constant and complicated for that. A more useful distinction was between, in Bentley's terminology, "organization groups" and "talk groups." The former, which had made themselves into real institutions, were far more significant than the latter, which were merely what we would now call virtual, and which got more attention than they deserved because they involved the work of the press and intellectuals—people who were engaged in, as Bentley dismissively put it, "that particular form of activity which consists in the moving of the larynx or the pushing of a pencil." Organizations, in Bentley's conception of politics, have a kind of earned importance that the opinions of fortunately situated people do not.

Because Bentley's theory accorded respect to the activities and aspirations of all groups, on a number of specific points he seems prophetic. Unlike most progressive intellectuals, he was witheringly dismissive about eugenics and other race theories that denied political legitimacy to entire populations. He was attentive to the rights of women. He was skeptical about where the brewing revolutionary spirit in Russia might lead, with its idea that the supposed leaders of one class could be entrusted to look out for the good of all without the benefit of democracy. He had no use for the notion that the world could be divided into civilized nations and barbaric ones and that the former should establish dominion over the latter. Writing on the verge of half a century of world war, economic catastrophe, dictatorships, and all-encompassing ideologies, Bentley was refreshing in his insistence on the legitimacy of particular concerns and small-stakes political struggle.

Still, it's worth pausing for a moment to note how massively counterintuitive Bentley's ideas seem today. Most people, or at least people who belong to talk groups, believe that there is a discernible public interest, the pursuit of which should determine political outcomes, and that it would be great if there were a way to eliminate interest groups from politics so that the path to the public interest would be clearer. It takes a real effort to shake loose this conviction—to absorb the possibility that what you deeply believe is right for everyone actually might not be. Bentley, with typical sarcasm, dismissed the idea of an "assumed pure public spirit which is supposed to guide legislators, or which ought to guide them, and which enables them to pass judgment in Jovian calm on that which is best 'for the whole people.'" That was ridiculous, because "there is nothing which is best literally for the whole people."

Although Bentley crankily insisted that he was merely describing the way politics worked, not advocating for anything, he obviously saw merit in pluralism. He was suspicious of educated reformers who felt themselves devoid of self-interest, merely advocates on behalf of moral principles or of people in need—asking what made them so sure that they were right, that their views should be empowered? That they were not merely serving their own interests, whether they realized it or not? And he respected people who did the hard work of forcing the political system to attend to their needs. When Bentley was writing, among the practitioners of pluralism he surely had in mind were the functionaries of the Democratic Party machine in Chicago, who, though condemned by educated and well-off reformers as exemplifying political corruption, were able to get their poor, illiterate, immigrant constituents' immediate needs met. The pluralists in this book have been people like the residents of the economically devastated neighborhood of Chicago Lawn and the auto dealers who were terminated during the bankruptcy of General Motors. Left out of some larger calculation that made sense to people far away, they turned themselves into interest groups and got a measure of redress from government. On the other hand, none of the three major thinkers in this book was a pluralist.

Adolf Berle was in his precocious early teens when *The Process of Government* was published. As a young man, he was instinctively drawn to the dominant strain of Progressive thought, in which centralized political power is put into the hands of benign, trained, disinterested experts who can be counted on to do what is right for the people. Bentley was a Progressive entirely at odds with this kind of Progressivism. He didn't have any use for the kinds of reform schemes that usually captivated the Progressive mind, since they entailed removing bosses, political machines, interest groups, lobbying, and bargaining from politics. To Bentley these were not serpents in the Eden of American democracy; they *were* politics. And the mature version of Berle's views, in which government regulatory agencies act as benign supervisory partners to a handful of economically and socially dominant corporations, has nothing in common with Bentley-style pluralism. It's too static, too organized, too inclined to reduce political participation to a limited number of big players.

One of Bentley's projects in the years after he moved to Indiana was writing a book about the role of business in politics and of politics in the economy. The book, called *Makers Users and Masters*, was never finished, partly because Bentley was unable to interest a publisher in it. A protégé of his got hold of the manuscript and arranged to have it published after Bentley's death. It shows that Bentley was just as concerned as other Progressives about the power of big business. In *Makers Users and Masters* (which, curiously, was dedicated "To Walt Whitman, the Livest American"), Bentley offered up a horrified review of the high, and still rising, levels of inequality of income and wealth in the United States—at about the same level today as they were back then, after a long period of decreasing inequality in between—and asserted that the country now had an "industrial government" along with a traditional political government. Corporations, rather than being just one element in the continual jostling for influence over government, had grown to the point where they had become, collectively, an alternative system—a competitor with government, and not a benign one. "Our political government is democratic: our industrial government is autocratic," Bentley wrote. Now there were two choices: either business could force government to join it in autocracy, or government could force business to join it in democracy.

Although Bentley was not specific about what this would entail, one can adduce from his own political activities that he supported government's regulating industry, strengthening unions, and otherwise exerting political power over economic institutions to force them to respond to others' needs. Bentley's sympathies were clearly more with Woodrow Wilson's New Freedom, with its mistrust of concentrations of economic and political power, than with Theodore Roosevelt's New Nationalism, which envisioned a large central government taming, but not breaking up, the trusts. He quoted Louis Brandeis repeatedly and admiringly, and his title proposed an economy that balances the interests of the corporations (Masters) with those of smaller businesses (Makers) and consumers (Users). It was typical of Bentley to prefer, as an ideal, multiple organized interests sharing power rather than a strong central government pursuing what it imagined to be the interest of the people as a whole.

Bentley had the good fortune to be able to watch, from his farm in Indiana, as his ideas went from obscure and cranky to broadly accepted, indeed applauded. In *The Process of Government*, he remarked almost in passing that interest-group politics was remarkable "for the trifling proportion of physical violence involved considering the ardent nature of the struggles." After the politics of the twentieth century had engendered the violent deaths of many millions of people and the rise of totalitarianism in Nazi Germany, the Soviet Union, and elsewhere, this point had a great deal more force than it did back in 1908. By the 1950s pluralists were important or even dominant in the leading universities. One of them, David Truman, at Columbia, wrote a book whose title, *The Governmental Process*, was meant to show that it was explicitly an homage to Bentley. Many politicians, whose work makes them instinctive pluralists, embraced the nub of Bentley's theory, probably without knowing it was Bentley's.

During the heyday of pluralism in the 1950s, many of its proponents slid from what might be considered the true faith—a stern insistence on unlovely managed conflict among interest groups as the mark of a healthy society—into a Panglossian satisfaction with how well American society was functioning. To say that all the major interest groups are working together satisfactorily in a successful, happy country where all the big arguments have been settled is really faux pluralism—pluralism without strife. Adolf Berle had this attitude. So did many other prominent thinkers. In their blindness to the dissatisfaction of the many Americans who hadn't been cut in on the bargain, and in their failure to appreciate that spirited conflict should be a constant in a healthy democracy, such people sowed the seeds of the destruction of their ideas. That came quickly in the 1960s. Within just a few years of its apotheosis, interest-group pluralism had become deeply unrespectable, and Arthur Bentley's journey back to obscurity was well under way—unfairly to him.

■

When pluralism began to lose its appeal to liberals, the major argument against it was that only the powerful were able to organize themselves into effective interest groups—so, in a pluralist regime, those whom liberalism was supposed to help would always lose out. Well-financed interests would always get what they wanted because they, and only they, could afford to mount the kind of expensive lobbying campaigns required to get the attention of government. As one early, stinging critique put it, "The flaw in the pluralist heaven is that the heavenly chorus sings with a strong upper-class accent." Another influential critique blamed "interest-group liberalism" for America's failure to address its environmental and racial crises. Another argued that interest groups, with their petty but passionately held concerns, have an insuperable built-in advantage over efforts to attend to the larger welfare of a society. Surely there must be a better way of conducting politics, one that puts the real needs of the country first and pushes aside the system-clogging, money-wasting, self-interested claims of interest groups.

It makes sense, doesn't it? But if you look back through history at the kinds of problems interest groups supposedly can't solve, you will see that if progress took place, interest groups were usually involved. Interest groups, if they want to win, have to make arguments that will appeal more broadly and form coalitions; still, such efforts begin with well-organized people focused on their own cause. Abolitionists helped end slavery, suffragists got women the vote, labor unions won better conditions for workers, the civil rights movement took down the Jim Crow system, environmental groups engendered antipollution policies. Conversely, a long parade of supposedly modernizing, interest-neutral, morally superior elite ideas have failed to attract a broad political constituency, or their proponents didn't see that they were ignoring a crucial element of society. After the Civil War, liberal elites who thought of themselves as clean-government reformers turned passionately against the idea that the federal government should enforce the constitutionally guaranteed civil and voting rights of African Americans in the South. At the end of the twentieth century, the architects of globalization, no less reform-minded, believed that they were universalizing prosperity. These policies, and many others just as well-intended, have generated spirited revisions and rebellions that took their authors by surprise. Organizing and advocating for the interests of one's group is the only effective way to get protection against the inevitable lacunae in somebody else's big idea.

Embracing pluralism has to begin with a kind of radical humility. It's human nature, especially for people who think of themselves as educated, sophisticated, and public-spirited, to believe that what you want the world to look like is a broad, objectively determined meliorist plan that will help everyone. As James Madison, back in 1787, wrote in "Federalist Number 10":

> It is in vain to say that enlightened statesmen will be able to adjust these clashing interests, and render them all subservient

to the public good. Enlightened statesmen will not always be at the helm. Nor, in many cases, can such an adjustment be made at all without taking into view indirect and remote considerations, which will rarely prevail over the immediate interest which one party may find in disregarding the rights of another or the good of the whole.

The truth is that everyone's perceptions are limited. To understand that about yourself, and to accord a measure of respect to the perspectives of people who fail to see the merits of your plan, doesn't come automatically.

Pluralism requires accepting a degree of messiness, squabbling, pettiness, and bargaining in the governing of a society: these things are a feature, not a bug. People have a strong and often demonstrated tendency to try to settle their differences through violence. Pluralism means to redirect this tendency into managed, nonviolent conflict. It imagines a system of groups endlessly in vigorous contention. No one group should be able to establish its dominion over the others, either out of selfishness or in the conviction that it represents some inarguably right outcome.* There is no such thing as a commonsense solution to a major problem, one that is good for everyone. Nonpartisanship should not be a hallowed quality of good politics. For the mostly economic issues in this book, pluralism often means that groups organize and then use politics to win special treatment for themselves. That's legitimate too. When it works—as when, for example, employees of technology companies

---

*Even Herbert Croly, Arthur Bentley's exact contemporary and the purveyor of a completely opposite political vision, was by the end of his life beginning to question his original faith in government by disinterested experts. Fifteen years after the publication of *The Promise of American Life*, he wrote,

> The social engineer tended to become in practice a revised edition of the traditional law-giver who knew what was possible and good for other people and who proposed to mold them according to his ideas . . . These experts do not know enough and should not pretend to know enough to justify them in the assumption of a responsibility so grave and yet so vicarious. Even though they acted in the name of a state whose decisions were supported to be made righteous by popular consent, the consent would in the case of the great majority of the ordered individuals be fictitious. It would not be born of their active and intelligent participation.

unionize, or domestic industries try to protect themselves from unimpeded free trade—it should be understood as making a market system
fairer, not ruining it. It's legitimate to impede the perfect functioning of
markets in order to protect people from severe disruptions and to try to
spread prosperity more evenly.

Pluralism treats democratic processes, not particular outcomes, as
moral absolutes. The right to vote, the right to organize, and the right
to speak need constant, vigilant protection. The never-ending attempts
of interests with money to give themselves more than their fair share
of power should be resolutely resisted. Pluralist societies are meant to
reward interest groups that learn to be good at politics. They should help
to correct, not help to enhance, the imbalances that economic market
systems inevitably create. The removal of black Americans' short-lived
right to vote in the late-nineteenth-century South was intolerable, from
a pluralist point of view—but the right-wing Tea Party movement of the
second decade of the twenty-first century was not, because it was based
on civil organizing. Current complaints about interest-group liberalism
often attribute excessive power to "identity politics," meaning groups
representing the very people whom anti-pluralists half a century ago saw
as having been shut out of an interest-group-dominated political system.
In a pluralist system, the way to fight unacceptable views is to outorga-
nize the people promoting them.

Pluralism mistrusts concentrations of power, economic or political, even if they seem to serve good causes or promote efficiency. The
American political system is built on distributing power among different levels and branches of government in order to guard against what
Madison called "the superior force of an interested and overbearing
majority." The economic system, since the Industrial Revolution, has
periodically generated extreme concentrations of power and wealth. Imbalances in economic power always turn into imbalances in political
power, unless the political system forcibly corrects them. Concentrations of power always wind up harming people, no matter how benign
the holders of power believe themselves to be. We are now seeing, after
decades of quiet, the beginnings of a revival of Brandeis-style opposition
to bigness, directed especially against the giant technology companies.
When it has been effective, such opposition has usually depended not
just on broad public sentiment but also on the passionate engagement

of self-interested parties, often other businesses being choked to death by the giants. That's honorable and legitimate, and in the coming years we may see the same energies directed at other concentrated industries. Even people who aren't able to advocate for themselves—such as the members of future generations whose lives will be harmed by climate change—have a demonstrated ability to attract effective interest-group advocacy. It's impossible to change things without interest groups.

■

What all the major thinkers in this book had in common was an intolerance for organizing the country, in particular the economy, around a never-ending political struggle among non-gigantic interest groups. This meant that in each case, they upheld a pure and alluring idea that was supposed to transcend the inherent contention and untidiness of life in a democracy. Adolf Berle wanted to put the corporation under government's dominion. He had in mind a two-player game that would begin in conflict but mature into tranquility. Michael Jensen dreamed of a society built around the discipline imposed by markets. The corporation-based American welfare state that Berle helped create was a casualty of the rise of transactions as our governing economic principle. A transaction-based society is anti-pluralist by definition because it lets decisions rest entirely with markets that move instantaneously, and it disempowers groups that aim to attain their goals through political means. Reid Hoffman's idea of a technologically enabled, network-based society has brought with it a pluralist-sounding rhetoric about distributing power, giving voice to the voiceless, and enabling political organizing. This stands in contrast to the new economic and political world that the Internet-based networks have created thus far, which looks awfully similar to the world made by the railroads and oil companies and electric utilities in their early days of bigness. Pluralism requires institutions that will enact and maintain democratic ideals. A network society promotes a form of pluralism that is virtual and institution-free. That is impossible.

Our notional turn away from institutions doesn't mean that institutions no longer exist. People are social; they naturally form themselves into groups. The more established groups become institutions, and the less established try to influence institutions; and institutions constantly struggle for advantage against one another. To remove institutions from the tableau of how society is supposed to work is, inevitably, merely to allow the powerful institutions to become more powerful and the more vulnerable ones to weaken. This has happened in almost every area of American life. Deregulation produced the greatest concentration of financial power in American history, in six big companies. The advent of the supposedly power-distributing Internet produced the five big companies that now dominate technology. Understanding institutions as necessary is the only real protection against a few institutions becoming too powerful.

The great project of organizing economic life so as to give most people a sense of security, belonging, and hope is still an urgent one. The economy we have now is not doing a good job of generating social trust, political calm, or widely shared prosperity. Instead, it has produced a series of terrifying economic shocks that have given rise to equally terrifying political upheavals fueled by voters who feel so ignored and angry that they are willing to blow up the system just to see what happens. The solution to this problem surely will not entail returning to some fondly remembered arrangement from the past. History moves in only one direction, forward. But the tool that Arthur Bentley attempted to fashion, with its insistence on understanding the world in terms of a ceaseless but often productive contention between groups, where the best outcomes are complicated and inclusive bargains, provides useful guidance. Using it properly entails understanding that most people, even people who think of themselves as cosmopolitan, even in the age of globalization and the Internet, live parochial lives. They are neither atomized individuals nor part of a great undifferentiated mass of the public. What's in front of them are the groups they belong to and the institutions they can see and touch: the schools that educate their children, their local governments, the places where they pray, their trade associations, their ethnic organizations, their political movements. Those are their means of protecting themselves, of improving their condition, of addressing their needs as they define them. Reaching people, doing right by people, building the next good society means using these institutions. Not transactions. Not big ideas.

NOTES

PROLOGUE

4 *On May 15, 2009, FedEx dropped off*: Nick D'Andrea's story comes from author's interviews with Nick D'Andrea, Amy D'Andrea, and Elaine Vorberg.

11 *One of the marchers at Marquette Park*: Ann Collier Neal's story comes from author's interviews with Neal.

16 *"They are the ones of our middle class"*: William H. Whyte, *The Organization Man*, University of Pennsylvania Press, 2002, 3.

16 *"This is the new suburbia"*: Whyte, *Organization Man*, 10.

16 *"inner-directed"*: David Riesman, *The Lonely Crowd: A Study of the Changing American Character*, Yale University Press, 1961, 8. This is only the first of many passages in the book using the terms "inner-directed" and "other-directed."

17 *"He has plunged"*: Whyte, *Organization Man*, 287.

17 *"He must fight"*: Whyte, *Organization Man*, 404.

18 *"Men, wherever they are observed"*: David B. Truman, *The Governmental Process: Political Interests and Public Opinion* (second edition), Institute of Governmental Studies, 1993, 505.

18 *"countervailing power"*: John Kenneth Galbraith, *American Capitalism: The Concept of Countervailing Power*, Houghton Mifflin, 1956, 111. As the subtitle indicates, the idea of countervailing power appears throughout the book.

1. INSTITUTION MAN

24 *"All who recall the condition"*: John Marshall Harlan, decision in *Standard Oil Company of New Jersey v. United States*, 221 U.S. 1 (1911).

24 *It was into this situation*: An excellent biography of Berle is Jordan A. Schwartz, *Liberal: Adolf A. Berle and the Vision of an American Era*, Free Press, 1987. Berle also documented his own life extensively, through books, articles, diaries, and interviews. His papers are at the Franklin D. Roosevelt Presidential Library and Museum in Hyde Park, New York. See below for specific attributions of direct quotations from Berle. After Berle's death, Beatrice Berle assembled a selection of his papers for publication as a book, which makes for a useful transportable source of primary materials about Berle. It is *Navigating the Rapids 1918–1971: From the Papers of Adolf A. Berle*, Harcourt, Brace, and Jovanovich, 1973.

25 *"to instruct a small number of superior children"*: Adolf Berle Papers, FDR Library, Box 2, folder labeled "Personal Correspondence (1917–1919) Berle family." The quotation is from a pamphlet advertising The Berle Home School.

26 *"a palatial palace"*: Adolf Berle, diary entry for December 7, 1918. Berle Papers, FDR Library, Box 1, folder labeled "Diary Entries, Nov-Dec 1918."

26 *"hosts of minor retainers"*: Adolf Berle, diary entry for December 8, 1918. Berle Papers, FDR Library, Box 1, folder labeled "Diary Entries, Nov-Dec 1918."

26 *"a naughty show"*: Adolf Berle, diary entry for December 15, 1918. Berle Papers, FDR Library, Box 1, folder labeled "Diary Entries, Nov-Dec 1918."

27 *"start the whole game of competitive armaments"*: Adolf Berle, letter to his father, February 17, 1919. Berle, *Navigating the Rapids*, 11.

27 *"I have come to the conclusion"*: Adolf Berle, letter to his father, May 6, 1919. Berle Papers, FDR Library, Box 2, folder labeled "Personal Correspondence 1917–1919."

27 *"The quiet intoxication"*: Adolf Berle, letter to his father, May 25, 1919, 2. Berle Papers, FDR Library, Box 2, folder labeled "Personal Correspondence 1917–1919."

27 *"abortion of compromise and hate"*: A. A. Berle, Jr., "The Betrayal at Paris," *The Nation*, Volume 109, Number 2823 (August 9, 1919), 171.

27 *"For the ghastly fact is"*: Berle's daughter Beatrice, at the time his last surviving child, invited the author to her house in Washington, D.C., to read several boxes of private family papers. This quotation is from a diary entry for November 22, 1922. Berle Private Papers, Box 1, file 5. Beatrice Berle Meyerson has donated these papers to the FDR Library, so they will likely be filed under a different heading there.

28 *"the isolated establishment"*: Charles and Mary Beard, *The Rise of American Civilization*, Part II, Macmillan, 1930, 176.

29 *"In essence, this monster"*: Quotation from Liang Qichao, "The Power and Threat of America" (1903), in R. David Arkush and Leo O. Lee, editors, *Land Without Ghosts: Chinese Impressions of America from the Mid-Nineteenth Century to the Present*, University of California Press, 1989, 88.

29 *European socialism*: See, for example, Berle's unpublished, undated essay, "The Next American Revolution," Berle Papers, FDR Library, Box 2.

30 *"The net result of the industrial expansion"*: Herbert Croly, *The Promise of American Life*, Cosimo Classics, 2005, 116.

30 *"plutocracy"*: Walter Weyl, *The New Democracy: An Essay on Certain Political and Economic Tendencies in the United States*, Macmillan, 1912, 29 (and many other places in the book).

30 *"the true Don Quixote"*: Walter Lippmann, *Drift and Mastery*, Mitchell Kennerley, 1914, 130.

31 *"the day of the rule of the captain of industry"*: William Allen White, *The Old Order Changeth*, Macmillan, 1910, 244.

31 *"does not fear commercial power"*: This is from a memorandum called "Suggestions for Letter of Governor Wilson on Trusts," September 30, 1912. Melvin J. Urofsky and David W. Levy, editors, *Letters of Louis Brandeis: Volume II, 1907–1912: People's Attorney*, State University of New York Press, 1971, 688.

32 *"the little man"*: Woodrow Wilson, *The New Freedom*, Gray Rabbit Publications, 2011, 76.

32 *"In a score of cities and hundreds of towns"*: Richard Hofstadter, *The Age of Reform*, Vintage, 1955, 137. Hofstadter's reference to Berle is on page 162.

33 *Adolf Berle's wife, Beatrice Bishop*: An excellent general source on Beatrice Berle is her autobiography, Beatrice Bishop Berle, *A Life in Two Worlds: An Autobiography*, Walker and Company, 1983.

34 *"I must never invite a Jew"*: Beatrice Berle, diary entry for November 19, 1924. Berle Private Papers, Box 1, file labeled "1910s."

34 *"I would like you to remove your goods and chattels"*: Beatrice Berle, *Life in Two Worlds*, 96.

34 *"Erect, an irrepressible little wave"*: Berle, *Life in Two Worlds*, 63.

35 *"we walked around the lake"*: Berle, *Life in Two Worlds*, 110.

35 *"through the exploring and the marriage"*: Berle, *Life in Two Worlds*, 124.

36 *"so that she wouldn't miss any of his sudsy wisdom"*: John McCarten, "Atlas with Ideas," *The New Yorker*, January 16 and January 23, 1943. Part I, 23.

36 *"He has one of the few creative minds"*: Beatrice Berle, diary entry for October 7, 1938, Berle Private Papers, Box 1, file labeled "BBB Diaries 1971–79," 2. This seems to have been typed for possible inclusion in Beatrice Berle's memoir.

36 *"a social prophet"*: Beatrice Berle, diary entry of September 12, 1934, 3. Berle Private Papers, Box 1, folder labeled "1929–36 BBB diary."

37 *"The huge corporation"*: Adolf A. Berle, Jr., and Gardiner C. Means, *The Modern Corporation and Private Property*, Commerce Clearing House, 1932, 44.

37 *"The economic power"*: Berle and Means, *Modern Corporation and Private Property*, 46.

38 *"prestidigitation, double shuffling"*: William Z. Ripley, *Main Street and Wall Street*, Little Brown and Company, 1927, 303.

38 *"Perhaps . . . the individual"*: Berle and Means, *Modern Corporation and Private Property*, 24.

39 *"It involves a concentration of power"*: Berle and Means, *Modern Corporation and Private Property*, 352.

39 *"The dissolution of the atom of property"*: Berle and Means, *Modern Corporation and Private Property*, 8.

39 *"The recognition that industry"*: Berle and Means, *Modern Corporation and Private Property*, 124.

40 *"the community"*: Berle and Means, *Modern Corporation and Private Property*, 356.

40 *It was called, simply*: The book is Adolf A. Berle, *Power*, Harcourt, Brace & World, 1969.

41 *"they are guardians of all the interests"*: E. Merrick Dodd, Jr., "For Whom Are Corporate Managers Trustees?," *Harvard Law Review*, Volume 45, Number 7 (May 1932), 1157.

42 *"This is a problem of government"*: Berle, letter to Stephen G. Williams, April 14, 1929. Berle Papers, FDR Library, General Correspondence 1928–1940, folder labeled "Wi."

42 *"The industrial 'control'"*: Adolf Berle, "For Whom Corporate Managers Are Trustees: A Note," *Harvard Law Review*, Volume 45, Number 7 (May 1932), 1367.

42 *"discovered that they had harbored"*: Adolf A. Berle, "Modern Functions of the Corporate System," *Columbia Law Review*, Volume 62, Number 3 (March 1962), 434.

42 *"Rereading your collected essays"*: Berle, letter to Louis D. Brandeis, February 18, 1932. Berle Papers, FDR Library, General Correspondence 1928–1940, folder labeled "Br-Bu."

43 *"for the first time, the United States has come within hailing distance"*: Adolf A. Berle and Louis Faulkner, "The Nature of the Difficulty," May 1932, Berle Papers, FDR Library, Box 18, 29. The same document is reprinted in Berle, *Navigating the Rapids*, 45.

44 *"the then revolutionary conception"*: "The Reminiscences of Adolf A. Berle Jr.," Oral History Research Office, Columbia University, 1974, 173.

44 *"It was one of those rare Spring days"*: Beatrice Berle, diary entry for October 7, 1938, 3. (This is a long entry that has a memoirlike aspect, covering several years.) Berle Private Papers, Box 1, folder labeled "1929–1936 BBB diary."

44 *"I took my memorandum"*: "Reminiscences of Adolf A. Berle Jr.," 169.

45 *"A. has been in great & constant demand"*: Beatrice Berle, diary entry for September 12, 1934. Berle Private Papers, Box 1, folder labeled "1929–36 BBB diary."

45 *"For an intellectual"*: "Reminiscences of Adolf A. Berle Jr.," 186.

45 *"quite definitely become the protagonist"*: Berle, Memorandum to Governor Franklin D. Roosevelt, August 16, 1932, 1. Berle Papers, FDR Library, Box 15, file labeled "Memoranda from Campaign."

46 *"Fundamental issue today"*: Berle, telegram to FDR, September 19, 1932. Berle Papers, FDR Library, Box 15, file labeled "Moley, Raymond."

46 *"a group of financial Titans"*: Roosevelt's Commonwealth Club address is easy to find online; the FDR Library's online version is here: http://www.fdrlibrary.marist .edu/_resources/images/msf/msf00534.

48 *"Brandeis dreams"*: Adolf Berle, letter to George W. Anderson, November 14, 1932. Berle Papers, FDR Library, General Correspondence 1928–1940, folder labeled "Ami-Au."

48 *"These measures"*: Adolf Berle, letter to Hermann Habicht, December 7, 1932, 2. Berle Private Papers, Box 1, file labeled "Letters BBB & AAB 1926–38."

48 *"As for it being a good show"*: Undated memorandum by Beatrice Berle, Berle Private Papers, Box 1, file labeled "BBB Diary 1929–36," 1.

49 *"I never saw a more disorderly meeting"*: Interview with Adolf Berle, June 18, 1969, Oral History Research Office, Columbia University, 28.

49 *"pulling out from the government now"*: Undated memorandum by Beatrice Berle, Berle Private Papers, Box 1, file labeled "BBB Diary 1929–36," 1.

49 *"Before the Brain Trust days"*: Beatrice Berle, diary entry for October 7, 1938, 4. Berle Private Papers, Box 1, folder labeled "1929–1936 BBB diary."

50 *"govern and change the course of history"*: Beatrice Berle, diary entry for October 7, 1938, 6. Berle Private Papers, Box 1, folder labeled "1929–1936 BBB diary."

50 *"He is a man of unlimited ambition"*: Beatrice Berle, diary entry for October 7, 1938, 7. Berle Private Papers, Box 1, folder labeled "1929–1936 BBB diary."

50 *"Suddenly you find yourself connected"*: Interview with Adolf Berle, June 18, 1969, Oral History Research Office, Columbia University, 13.

51 *"masterless money"*: Adolf Berle, untitled, undated, undelivered speech draft for Franklin Roosevelt, 16. Berle Papers, FDR Library, Box 17.

51 *He had hoped, for example*: See Adolf Berle, Memorandum to the Committee on Stock Exchange Regulation, October 24, 1933, Berle Papers, FDR Library, Box 22.

51 *"Dear Caesar"*: Adolf Berle, letter to Franklin Roosevelt, April 23, 1934. Berle Papers, FDR Library, Box 10, file labeled "Roosevelt, Franklin D."

52 *"As to our friend of the highest court"*: Franklin Roosevelt, letter to Adolf Berle, April 30, 1934. Berle Papers, FDR Library, Box 10, file labeled "Roosevelt, Franklin D."

53 *Decades later, a historian discovered*: See Bruce Allen Murphy, *The Brandeis/Frankfurter Connection: The Secret Political Activities of Two Supreme Court Justices*, Oxford University Press, 1982.

53 *"I wish I could agree"*: Berle, letter to Charles D. Williams, September 5, 1935. Berle Papers, General Correspondence 1928–1940, folder labeled "Wi-Wr."

54 *Berle's old writing partner*: There is an exchange of letters between Keynes and Means from 1939, and also a memorandum by Means describing his visit to Keynes, in the Gardiner Means Papers at the FDR Library, Box 117.

55 *"looking like an old hag"*: Undated memorandum by Beatrice Berle, Berle Private Papers, Box 1, file labeled "BBB Diary 1929–36," 3.

56 *"Berle is always more literary"*: Joseph Alsop and Robert Kintner, *American White Paper*, Simon and Schuster, 1940, 66.

56 *"It is a big job"*: McCarten, "Atlas with Ideas," Part II, *The New Yorker*, January 23, 1943, 33.

57 *"There is not one iota of doubt"*: Joseph P. Lash, editor, *From the Diaries of Felix Frankfurter*, W. W. Norton, 168.

58 *"If there is a lower class"*: Author's interview with Beatrice Berle.

59 *a small group of powerful men*: Berle's memorandum about the conference, dated December 23, 1937, is in the Berle Papers, FDR Library, Box 9.

59 *"I do not think we are going to get rid of big units"*: Adolf Berle, letter to Congressman Emanuel Celler, June 26, 1950. Berle Papers, FDR Library, Box 105. This box also contains a long memorandum Berle wrote to the House Judiciary Committee opposing antitrust measures, which anticipates the arguments made by Robert Bork more than two decades later.

60 *"Its aggregate economic achievement"*: Adolf A. Berle, *The Twentieth Century Capitalist Revolution*, Harcourt, Brace, and Company, 1954, 10.

60 *"a mixed system"*: Berle, *Twentieth Century Capitalist Revolution*, 109.

60 *"would be the first to deal with the facts"*: Adolf A. Berle, *Power Without Property*, Harcourt, Brace, and Company, 1959, 13.

61 *"meant risking unemployed workers"*: Berle, *Twentieth Century Capitalist Revolution*, 129.

61 *"conscience-carrier of twentieth-century American society"*: Berle, *Twentieth Century Capitalist Revolution*, 182.

61 *"The capital is there"*: Berle, *Twentieth Century Capitalist Revolution*, 39.

61 *"Stockholders do not hold the center"*: Berle, *Twentieth Century Capitalist Revolution*, 169.

62 *"Bigness is"*: David Lilienthal, *Big Business: A New Era*, Harper and Brothers, 1953, 6.

63 *"to the naked eye"*: John Kenneth Galbraith, *American Capitalism: The Concept of Countervailing Power*, Houghton Mifflin, 1956, 79.

63 *"the provision of state assistance"*: Galbraith, *American Capitalism*, 128.

64 *"I find it very difficult"*: Adolf Berle, Lecture in the Graduate School of Journalism, November 4, 1960, Oral History Research Office, Columbia University, 27.

65 *"You are the cog and the beltline"*: C. Wright Mills, *White Collar: The American Middle Classes*, Oxford University Press, 2002, 80.

65 *"corporate rubbery obstruction"*: Norman Mailer, *An American Dream*, Dial Press, 1965, 127.

65 *"can be thought of as a single vast"*: Charles Reich, *The Greening of America*, Random House, 1970, 79.

67 *Probably the most important economics publication*: Arrow-Debreu paper: Kenneth J. Arrow and Gerard Debreu, "Existence of an Equilibrium for a Competitive Economy," *Econometrica*, Volume 22, Number 3 (July 1954), 265–90.

68 *"Adolf and I sat down together"*: Beatrice Berle, *Life in Two Worlds*, 237.

69 *"Innovation at the hands"*: Edward S. Mason, editor, *The Corporation in Modern Society*, Harvard University Press, 1959, 2.

2. THE TIME OF INSTITUTIONS

70 *In the summer of 1940*: The story of Peter Drucker and Karl Polanyi comes from Peter Drucker, *Adventures of a Bystander: Memoirs*, HarperCollins, 1991, 123–40.

71 *Burnham devoted several pages to summarizing*: James Burnham, *The Managerial Revolution*, Penguin Books, 1962, 87–93.

71 *"At the heart of the Industrial Revolution"*: Karl Polanyi, *The Great Transformation: The Political and Economic Origins of Our Time*, Beacon Press, 2001, 35.

71 *Adolf Berle thought so highly*: Adolf Berle, Lecture in the Graduate School of Journalism, November 4, 1960, Oral History Research Office, Columbia University, 7.

72 *"centralized bureaucratic despotism"*: Peter Drucker, *The Future of Industrial Man*, New American Library, 1965, 203.

72 *Drucker was surprised to get a call*: Drucker's account of his engagement with General Motors is in Drucker, *Adventures of a Bystander*, 256–93.

72 *"The large industrial unit"*: Peter Drucker, *The Concept of the Corporation*, New American Library, 1964, 18.

72 *"sets the pattern and determines the behavior"*: Drucker, *Concept of the Corporation*, 21.

73 *"Only now have we realized"*: Drucker, *Concept of the Corporation*, 123.

74 *"Mr. Durant was a great man"*: Alfred P. Sloan, Jr., *My Years with General Motors*, Currency Doubleday, 1990, 4.

74 *"the reported approach"*: Drucker, *Concept of the Corporation*, 108.

75 *"to develop citizenship and community"*: Drucker, *Adventures of a Bystander*, 272.

75 *"We were largely unprepared"*: Sloan, *My Years with General Motors*, 405.

76 *"Is America to continue"*: "The Responsibility of Management," a collection of statements by General Motors executives, 13. United Auto Workers papers, Wayne State University, UAW Research Department, Box 87, folder labeled "GMC, Policy Statements, 1936–46."

77 *"On a farm, when a man was young"*: Charles Wilson, "Where Are We Going From Here?," talk delivered to the American Bottlers of Carbonated Beverages, Detroit, Michigan, November 15, 1949, 3. United Auto Workers papers, Wayne State University, UAW Research Department, Box 87, file labeled "GMC, Industrial Relations, 1949–50."

77 *"I grudgingly yield"*: Drucker, *Adventures of a Bystander*, 274.

77 *Reuther, in the same spirit*: "1950 Contract Negotiations, April 6, 1950," memorandum in the United Auto Workers papers, Wayne State University, UAW President's Office: Walter P. Reuther Records, Box 102, folder labeled "UAW, Contract Negotiations, 1950."

78 *"General Motors may become"*: Daniel Bell, "The Treaty of Detroit," *Fortune*, July 1950, 53.

78 *"to work out an American solution"*: Charles Wilson, "Five Years of Industrial Peace," speech at the National Press Club, Washington, D.C., June 8, 1950, 13. Charles E. Wilson Collection, Anderson University, file labeled "Addresses 1950."

78 *Daniel Bell, a few years later*: The book is Daniel Bell, *The End of Ideology: On the Exhaustion of Political Ideas in the Fifties*, Harvard University Press, 1960.

79 *"for thirty years has devoted itself"*: Adolf Berle, Foreword to Edward S. Mason, editor, *The Corporation in Modern Society*, Harvard University Press, 1959, xiii.

79 *"The impact of many corporations"*: Berle, *Twentieth Century Capitalist Revolution*, 27.

79 *"We must approach this group of people"*: Berle, *Twentieth Century Capitalist Revolution*, 77.

79 *Auto dealerships were mainly family businesses*: General information about auto dealers comes from author's interviews with Len Bellavia, Tamara Darvish, Patrick Painter, Alan Spitzer, Jeff Duvall, Colleen McDonald, Mike Bellavia, Richard Faulkner, Frank Blankenbeckler, Elaine Vorberg, and Nick D'Andrea.

82 *Spitzer family*: Author's interviews with Alan Spitzer, Pat Spitzer, and Alison Spitzer. Also see Alan Spitzer, *Grand Theft Auto: How Citizens Fought for the American Dream*, New Year Publishing, 2011.

82 Ten Step Sales Procedure: Alan Spitzer gave a copy of the film to the author.

83 *On the South Side of Chicago*: General background and history on Chicago Lawn comes from author's interviews with Jeff Bartow, Rafi Peterson, Betty Guttierez, Sister Immacula Wendt, Sister Margaret Zalot, David McDowell, Dennis Ryan,

Mike Reardon, Rami Nashashibi, James Caprano, Earl Johnson, Nick Burnick, Ghian Foreman, Tony Pizzo, Paul Marshalonus, Kathy Headley, Ann Neal, Nick D'Andrea, Amy D'Andrea, Dennis Hart, Earl Johnson, Pat Butler, Carolina Rivera, Philip Ashton, Rhodel Castillo, and Chris Brown. Useful books on Chicago Lawn include Maria Kefalis, *Working-Class Heroes: Protecting Home, Community, and Nation in a Chicago Neighborhood*, University of California Press, 1943; Kathleen J. Headley and Tracy J. Krol, *Legendary Locals of Chicago Lawn and West Lawn*, Legendary Locals, 2015; and Richard White, *Remembering Ahanagran: A History of Stories*, University of Washington Press, 1998.

86 *"Friday night in Talman"*: Alan Ehrenhalt, *The Lost City: The Forgotten Virtues of Community in America*, Basic Books 1995, 104.

87 *Dennis Hart was born*: Hart's story comes from author's interviews with Dennis Hart.

89 *Morgan Stanley was the love child*: General background and history on Morgan Stanley comes from author's interviews with Deborah McLean, Jonathan Knee, William Kneisel, John Mack, Lewis Bernard, Robert Scott, Thomas Saunders, Anson Beard, John Zacamy, Amy Lane, Richard Bookstaber, and Vikram Pandit. Useful books on Morgan Stanley include Ron Chernow, *The House of Morgan: An American Banking Dynasty and the Rise of Modern Finance*, Grove Press, 2010; Patricia Beard, *Blue Blood and Mutiny: The Fight for the Soul of Morgan Stanley*, HarperCollins, 2007; and Anson M. Beard, Jr., *A Life in Full Sail*, TidePool Press, 2012. In 1977 William Kneisel wrote a twenty-eight-page internal history of the firm, called "Morgan Stanley & Co. Incorporated: A Brief History." He gave the author a copy.

90 *"If I may be permitted to speak of the firm"*: Chernow, *House of Morgan*, 364.

93 *"the myth of domination"*: Harold Medina, opinion in the case of *United States v. Morgan et al.*, 118 F. Supp. 621, District Court, Southern District of New York, 1953, 214.

93 *"absolute integrity"*: Harold Medina, opinion in *United States v. Morgan*, 238.

94 *"if the business is satisfactorily done"*: Medina (quoting from Harold Stanley's testimony), opinion in *United States v. Morgan*, 244.

94 *"I am told that Morgan Stanley"*: Medina, opinion in *United States v. Morgan*, 254.

95 *"A dry raconteur"*: Patricia Beard, *Blue Blood and Mutiny*, 200.

96 *"planning system"*: John Kenneth Galbraith, *Economics and the Public Purpose*, Houghton Mifflin, 1973, 44. This is the first appearance of a phrase Galbraith uses throughout the book.

97 *"all the Marxist church fathers"*: Peter Drucker, *The Unseen Revolution: How Pension Fund Socialism Came to America*, William Heinemann, 1976, 4.

98 *"a bigger shift in ownership"*: Drucker, *Unseen Revolution*, 34.

98 *"the pension funds are not 'owners'"*: Drucker, *Unseen Revolution*, 82.

98 *"a society in which the performance"*: Drucker, *Unseen Revolution*, 114.

99 *"RHBB wants to see you immediately!"*: Author's interview with Lewis Bernard.

3. TRANSACTION MAN

100 *A brightly lit, windowless, carpeted function room*: Michael Jensen's story comes from author's interviews with Jensen.

100 *"That's where I lived for a long time"*: The author attended one of Werner Erhard and Michael Jensen's nine-day "Being a Leader" seminars in Bermuda in November 2014. All quotations from the seminar are from firsthand observation.

102 *Coming to the University of Chicago*: This account of the birth of financial economics comes from author's interviews with Michael Jensen, Eugene Fama, Richard Thaler, and Robert C. Merton. An excellent history of these developments is Peter L. Bernstein, *Capital Ideas: The Improbable Rise of Modern Wall Street*, John Wiley & Sons, 2005, and its sequel, *Capital Ideas Evolving*, John Wiley & Sons, 2007.

104 *"a landmark in the history of ideas"*: Bernstein, *Capital Ideas*, 41.

104 *"Markowitz came along"*: Bernstein, *Capital Ideas Evolving*, xii.

107 *"The mutual fund industry"*: Michael C. Jensen, "The Performance of Mutual Funds in the Period 1945–1964," *Journal of Finance*, Volume 23, Issue 2 (May 1968), 414.

109 *"Major corporations in most instances"*: Adolf Berle, *The Twentieth Century Capitalist Revolution*, Harcourt, Brace and Company, 1954, 40.

109 *"the visible hand of management"*: Alfred D. Chandler, *The Visible Hand: The Managerial Revolution in American Business*, Belknap Press, 1977, 1.

110 *"Why is there any organization?"*: Ronald H. Coase, "The Nature of the Firm," *Economica*, Volume 4, Number 16 (November 1937), 388.

111 *"folklore"*: Henry Manne, "The 'Higher Criticism' of the Modern Corporation," *Columbia Law Review*, Volume 62, Number 3 (March 1962), 407.

111 *"losing the only objective standard"*: Manne, "'Higher Criticism,'" 415.

111 *"represent disguised efforts"*: Manne, "'Higher Criticism,'" 431.

111 *"market for corporate control"*: Henry Manne, "Mergers and the Market for Corporate Control," *Journal of Political Economy*, Volume 73, Number 2 (April 1965), 110.

111 *"describes a totally imaginary"*: Adolf A. Berle, "Modern Functions of the Corporate System," *Columbia Law Review*, Volume 62, Number 3 (March 1962), 438.

111 *"In fact, a large corporation"*: Berle, "Modern Functions of the Corporate System," 445.

112 *"an employee of the owners"*: Milton Friedman, "The Social Responsibility of Business Is to Increase Its Profits," *New York Times Magazine*, September 13, 1970.

113 *"Theory of the Firm"*: Michael C. Jensen and William H. Meckling, "Theory of the Firm: Managerial Behavior, Agency Costs and Ownership Structure," *Journal of Financial Economics*, Volume 3, Number 4 (October 1976), 305.

114 *"the physical appointments"*: Jensen and Meckling, "Theory of the Firm," 11 (this refers to the page number in a freestanding PDF version of the article, which can be found on the database Jensen founded, SSRN).

116 *Between 1981 and 1983 alone*: A useful summary of all this activity can be found in Gerald F. Davis, *Managed by the Markets: How Finance Reshaped America*, Oxford University Press, 2009.

117 *Jensen calculated*: Michael C. Jensen, "Eclipse of the Public Corporation," *Harvard Business Review*, September–October 1989, 6 (for this and other Jensen

articles, the page numbers are for the PDF versions of the articles posted on the SSRN site).

117 *"Debt is"*: Jensen, "Eclipse of the Public Corporation," 11.

118 *"it is difficult to find losers"*: Jensen's testimony was published as Michael C. Jensen, "Active Investors, LBOs, and the Privatization of Bankruptcy," *Journal of Applied Corporate Finance*, Volume 2, Number 1 (Spring 1989). The quotation is on p. 11.

118 *"the large costs associated with the obsolescence"*: Michael C. Jensen, "The Modern Industrial Revolution, Exit, and the Failure of Internal Control Systems," *Journal of Finance*, Volume 48, Number 3 (July 1993), 2.

119 *"a social invention of vast historical importance"*: Jensen, "Eclipse of the Public Corporation," 5.

121 *"In the course of conversation"*: Richard Thaler, *Misbehaving: The Making of Behavioral Economics*, W. W. Norton, 2015, 51.

122 *"Keynes: Professor Jensen"*: This is a passage from the original manuscript of Richard Thaler, *Misbehaving*, which Thaler gave to the author. It does not appear in the book.

123 *"I consent to the wishes of my wife"*: Michael C. Jensen, "Toward a Theory of the Press," in Karl Brunner, editor, *Economics and Social Institutions*, Martinus Nijhoff Publishing Company, 1979, 11.

126 *One former aide to Hubbard*: Author's interview with Nancy Many.

128 *"very greedy"*: Ralph Walking, *Pioneers in Finance* (a series of video interviews), interview with Michael C. Jensen, December 20, 2011. Available on the SSRN site.

128 *"enlightened value maximization"*: Michael C. Jensen, "Value Maximization, Stakeholder Theory, and the Corporate Objective Function," Tuck Business School Working Paper 01-09, October 2001, 1.

129 *"Just Say No to Wall Street"*: Joseph C. Fuller and Michael C. Jensen, "Just Say No to Wall Street: Putting a Stop to the Earnings Game," *Journal of Applied Corporate Finance*, Volume 14, Number 4 (Winter 2002), 41.

129 *"Once we as managers start lying"*: Michael C. Jensen, "Agency Costs of Overvalued Equity," *Financial Management*, Volume 34, Number 1 (Spring 2005), 3.

129 *"like throwing gasoline on a fire"*: Jensen, "Agency Costs of Overvalued Equity," 7.

129 *"In the literature of finance"*: Michael C. Jensen, "Some Anomalous Evidence Regarding Market Efficiency," *Journal of Financial Economics*, Volume 6, Numbers 2–3 (1978), 3.

130 *"a state or condition of being"*: Werner Erhard, Michael C. Jensen, and Steve Jensen, "Integrity: A Positive Model That Incorporates the Normative Phenomena of Morality, Ethics, and Legality," Harvard Business School NOM Unit Working Paper 10-061, 3.

131 *"an unambiguous and actionable access"*: Erhard, Jensen, and Jensen, "Integrity: A Positive Model," 3.

131 *"Putting Integrity into Finance"*: Werner C. Erhard and Michael Jensen, "Putting Integrity into Finance: A Purely Positive Approach," *Capitalism and Society*, Volume 12 (2017).

131 *"the surprising source of many"*: Werner Erhard, Michael C. Jensen, and Steve Zaffron, "Course Materials for: 'Being a Leader and the Effective Exercise of Leadership: An Ontological/Phenomenological Model,'" available on SSRN.

4. THE TIME OF TRANSACTIONS: RISING

136 *Somewhere along the line*: See above for a list of the interviews from which the story of Morgan Stanley is drawn.

138 *"A political force"*: Adolf Berle, *Natural Selection of Political Forces*, University Press of Kansas, 1968, 22.

142 *if any incident demonstrated*: Author's interview with Thomas Saunders, who was at the meeting.

142 *One banker remembered*: Author's interview with John Zacamy.

145 *"The public is hardly unaware"*: Richard Hofstadter, *The Paranoid Style in American Politics and Other Essays*, Vintage Books 1965, 212.

145 *"When the laws undertake"*: Andrew Jackson's veto message of the Second Bank of the United States, July 10, 1832. http://avalon.law.yale.edu/19th_century/ajveto01.asp.

146 *In 1975 the country's leading liberal politician*: Stephen Breyer gives a full account of airline deregulation in *Regulation and Its Reform*, Harvard University Press, 1982.

147 *"sheer perversity"*: Robert Bork, *The Antitrust Paradox: A Policy at War with Itself*, The Free Press, 1978, 185.

147 *"a land in which women"*: Edward M. Kennedy, speech opposing the nomination of Robert Bork to the Supreme Court of the United States, July 1, 1987. *Congressional Record*, Senate, July 1, 1987, 18518.

151 *Milken also developed a client base*: The 269-page brief by the celebrated trial lawyer David Boies in the case of *FDIC v. Milken et al.* (1991), in the Southern District of New York, lays out these arrangements in detail.

153 *smashed telephone headset*: Frank Partnoy, *Fiasco: The Inside Story of a Wall Street Trader*, Penguin Books, 1997, 14.

154 *Do you know how much risk you'll be taking on?*: Author's interview with Anson Beard.

155 *"I don't know what the hell"*: Author's interview with Anson Beard.

158 *FIRST CLASS BUSINESS IN A SECOND CLASS WAY*: Partnoy, *Fiasco*, 202.

158 *IBGYBG*: Jonathan Knee, *The Accidental Investment Banker: Inside the Decade That Transformed Wall Street*, Oxford University Press, 2006, xvii.

159 *more than a thousand savings and loans*: An excellent overall account is Stephen Pizzo, Mary Fricker, and Paul Muolo, *Inside Job: The Looting of America's Savings and Loans*, McGraw-Hill, 1989. Alan Greenspan's letter to Edwin Gray is described on p. 266.

159 *One of the few members of Congress*: James Leach's story comes from author's interviews with Leach. Leach also gave the author an unpublished, undated thirty-five-page manuscript called "The Lure of Leveraging: Wall Street, Congress, and The Invisible Government," which was useful in producing this account.

161 *"Roosevelt was trying to help people"*: Bob Woodward, *The Agenda: Inside the Clinton White House*, Simon and Schuster, 1994, 81.

162 *"People who have done well"*: Woodward, *Agenda*, 240.

162 *After Reich, as secretary of labor, made a speech*: Author's interview with Robert Reich. See also Robert B. Reich, *Locked in the Cabinet*, Knopf, 1997, 210, 296.

162 *"It was becoming difficult for him"*: Bill Clinton, *My Life*, Knopf, 1994, 738.

162 *The second term of the Clinton administration*: Information about the views of the Clinton economic team come from author's interviews with Laura Tyson, Robert Reich, W. Bowman Cutter, Ellen Seidman, Paul Dimond, Lawrence Summers, James Leach, and Brooksley Born. Also useful is Brooksley Born, "Deregulation: A Major Cause of the Financial Crisis," *Harvard Law and Policy Review*, Volume 5, Number 2 (Summer 2011), 231–43. An excellent broad overview of the shift that Clinton-era economic policy represented from the Democratic Party's post–Second World War stance is Frank Levy and Peter Temin, "Inequality and Institutions in 20th Century America," NBER Working Paper 13106, May 2007.

163 *"he had gotten close enough"*: Clinton, *My Life*, 377.

164 *"Two or three decades ago"*: Woodward, *Agenda*, 59.

165 *"concludes that the benefits"*: Chris Carroll and Aaron Edlin, memo to Jeffrey Frankel, August 29, 1997. William Clinton Presidential Library, 2105-0223-F, Box 1, Folder 2. At this writing, the Clinton Library does not maintain a traditional filing system for presidential records; instead, it releases records in response to Freedom of Information Act requests and then files them under the request numbers. That explains the notation used here.

166 *"The old statutory restrictions"*: Gene Sperling, memo to President Clinton, March 1997. Clinton Library, 2010-0384-F—Financial Services Modernization Act & Community Reinvestment Act.

168 *he had the Banking Committee's staff produce a nine-hundred-page report*: "Safety and Soundness: Issues Related to Bank Derivative Activities, Hearing Before the Committee on Banking, Finance, and Urban Affairs," House of Representatives, 103rd Congress, first session, Government Printing Office, 1994.

168 *"affect the safety and soundness"*: James L. Bothwell, letter to James Leach, March 17, 1997, 1. Clinton Library, 2010-0384-F, Box 1, Folder 14.

168 *"To Wall Street"*: James A. Leach, Statement Before the House Banking and Financial Services Committee's Subcommittee on Capital Markets, Securities, and Government-Sponsored Enterprises, March 1, 1997, 3. Clinton Library, 2010-0384-F, Box 2, Folder 8.

169 *One Treasury aide remembers*: Author's interview with Paul Dimond.

169 *"Please eat this paper"*: Handwritten note from Sarah Wardell to Sally Katzen and Gene Sperling, March 22, 1998. Clinton Presidential Records, National Economic Council, Sally Katzen. OA/Box Number: 17444.

170 *"This is a very good day for the United States"*: CSPAN's video recording can be found here: https://www.c-span.org/video/?153587-1/financial-services-bill-signing.

171 *Brooksley Born wrote an official letter*: Brooksley Born, letter to Richard Lugar, December 31, 1996. Clinton Library, 2010-0673-F, Box 1, Folder 6.

171 *a month later, Rubin wrote Lugar*: Robert Rubin, draft letter to Richard Lugar, January 29, 1997. Clinton Library, 2010-0673-F, Box 1, Folder 6.

172 *"Brooksley Born will do"*: Ellen S. Seidman, memorandum to Gene Sperling and Kathy Waldman, February 14, 1997. Clinton Library, 2015-0223-F, Box 1, Folder 1.

172 *During this period, Alan Greenspan invited*: Author's interview with Brooksley Born.

172 *"Basically, Brooksley Born"*: Jason Seligman, handwritten notes labeled "Discus-

sion of Roger Anderson (Treasury) re CFTC concept release," August 5, 1998. Clinton Library, 2010-0673-F, Box 3, Folder 5.

173 *The notes that a Treasury aide kept*: Jason Seligman, handwritten notes labeled "financial markets working group principals' meeting," April 21, 1998. Clinton Library, 2010-0673-F—President's Working Group on Financial Markets, Box 3, Folder 3.

174 *"The many forces arrayed"*: Derek A. Chapin, memorandum to Michael Deich, June 2, 1998, 2. Clinton Library, 2010-0673-F—President's Working Group on Financial Markets, Box 5, Folder 1.

174 *"grave concern"*: Robert Rubin, Alan Greenspan, and Arthur Levitt, draft letter to House Speaker Newt Gingrich, undated (June 1998). Clinton Library, 2010-0673-F, Box 3, Folder 5.

174 *"The joint legislative proposal"*: John Quiero, memorandum for Sarah Rosen, July 31, 1998, "Re: Senate Agriculture Committee Hearing on H.R. 4062, 30 July 1998." Clinton Library, 2010-0673-F, Box 3, Folder 5.

175 *"The firm can't survive"*: Handwritten notes labeled "Gary Gensler conference call 9/23/98." Clinton Library, 2010-0673-F, Box 3, Folder 5.

176 *Perhaps it's only a coincidence*: See, for example, William B. English, email message to Ellen Seidman, April 29, 1997. Clinton Library, 2010-0384-F, Box 4, Folder 1; and Jeremy Rudd, memorandum to Janet Yellen, November 10, 1997, Clinton Library, 2010-0673-F, Box 3, File 3.

176 *"One specific effect"*: Doug Elmendorf, memorandum titled "Questions and Answers," December 7, 1998. Clinton Library, 2010-0673-F—President's Working Group on Financial Markets, Box 4, Folder 1.

177 *"on balance, more regulation"*: Doug Elmendorf, memorandum to Janet Yellen, December 21, 1998, 1. Clinton Library, 2010-0673-F, Box 1, File 2.

177 *"indirect regulation"*: Robert Rubin, memorandum to the president, April 22, 1999. Clinton Library, 2010-0673-F—President's Working Group on Financial Markets.

177 *GAO's report on Long-Term Capital Management*: General Accounting Office, "Long-Term Capital Management: Regulators Need to Focus Greater Attention on Systemic Risk," October 1999.

177 *"Larry thought I was overly concerned"*: Robert Rubin with Jacob Weisberg, *In an Uncertain World: Choices from Wall Street to Washington*, Random House, 2004, 288.

180 *Another marcher in the skimpy parade*: See Edward Gramlich, *Subprime Mortgages: America's Latest Boom and Bust*, Urban Institute Press, 2007.

5. THE TIME OF TRANSACTIONS: FALLING

182 *Everything that was happening in the American economy*: See above for a list of the author's interviews about Chicago Lawn. A useful study of the foreclosure crisis in Chicago Lawn is Philip Ashton and Susanne Schnell, "'Stuck' Neighborhoods: Concentrated Subprime Lending & the Challenges of Neighborhood Recovery," unpublished manuscript, 2010.

189 *Pizzo had grown up in Chicago*: Tony Pizzo's story comes from author's interview with Pizzo.

192 *By Van Tiem's estimate*: Katherine Van Tiem, "Home Affordable Modification Program (HAMP) Critique: Response from a Hemorrhaging Neighborhood," Southwest Organizing Project, January 2010.

197 *Earl Johnson grew up in the Robert Taylor Homes*: Earl Johnson's story comes from author's interviews with Johnson.

201 *At Morgan Stanley, through most of the 1990s*: See above for a list of the author's interviews about Morgan Stanley.

204 *"use the balance sheet"*: Author's interview with Anson Beard.

204 *One former Morgan Stanley executive*: Author's interview with Anson Beard.

204 *Do we buy it, or do we sell it?*: Author's interview with Richard Bookstaber.

204 *"A key driver"*: Patricia Beard, *Blue Blood and Mutiny*, 335.

205 *Mack remembers calling Timothy Geithner*: Author's interview with John Mack.

206 *"the single greatest proprietary trading loss"*: Michael Lewis, *The Big Short: Inside the Doomsday Machine*, W. W. Norton, 215.

207 *Morgan Stanley had $178 billion in readily available capital*: Books with useful material about Morgan Stanley during the financial crisis include Henry M. Paulson, Jr., *On the Brink: Inside the Race to Stop the Collapse of the Global Financial System*, Business Plus, 2010; Andrew Ross Sorkin: *Too Big to Fail: The Inside Story of How Wall Street and Washington Fought to Save the Financial System—and Themselves*, Penguin, 2010; and *The Financial Crisis Inquiry Report: Final Report of the National Commission on the Causes of the Financial and Economic Crisis in the United States*, Public Affairs, 2011.

208 *"Control your clients!"*: Author's interview with Anson Beard.

208 *A government report*: Doug Elmendorf, memorandum to Janet Yellen, December 21, 1998, 2.

209 *Morgan Stanley got the most*: Bradley Keoun, "Morgan Stanley at Brink of Collapse Got $107 Billion from Fed," *Bloomberg News*, August 22, 2011.

210 *"perfect storm"*: Author's interview with Robert Reich.

210 *Just after Obama took office*: Author's interview with Brooksley Born.

210 *"an explosion of extraordinary financial innovation"*: Robert C. Merton, "On the Role of Financial Innovation and Derivative Markets in Financial Globalization and Capital Markets," slide presentation prepared for International Capital Markets Conference, Bangkok, Thailand, November 30, 2015.

211 *"I wouldn't trust you!"*: Lloyd Blankfein, testimony before the Senate Government Affairs Subcommittee on Government Relations, April 27, 2010. A video record of the exchange can be found on CSPAN's website.

212 *a delegation of executives from General Motors*: Sources on the General Motors bankruptcy are author's interviews with Steven Rattner and Ron Bloom; also, Steven Rattner, *Overhaul: An Insider's Account of the Obama Administration's Emergency Rescue of the Auto Industry*, Mariner Books, 2011; Paul Ingrassia, *Crash Course: The American Automobile Industry's Road to Bankruptcy and Bailout—and Beyond*, Random House, 2011; and Bill Vlasic, *Once Upon a Car: The Fall and Resurrection of America's Big Three Automakers—GM, Ford, and Chrysler*, William Morrow, 2011.

213 *"we crafted terms"*: Henry M. Paulson, Jr., *On the Brink: Inside the Race to Stop the Collapse of the Global Financial System*, Business Plus, 2010, 428.

214 *"Solving the auto crisis"*: Rattner, *Overhaul*, 11.

216 *Many of the terminated dealers*: See above for a list of author's interviews with auto dealers.

216 *One evening Alan Spitzer*: Alan Spitzer's story comes from author's interviews with Alan Spitzer, Pat Spitzer, and Alison Spitzer.

216 *Tamara Darvish, a fiery young woman*: Tamara Darvish's story comes from author's interview with Darvish; Tamara Darvish and Lillie Guyer, *Outraged: How Detroit and the Wall Street Car Czars Killed the American Dream*, iUniverse, 2011.

218 *The noise Darvish was making*: Nick D'Andrea's story comes from author's interviews with Nick D'Andrea, Amy D'Andrea, and Elaine Vorberg.

218 *"simmered all summer"*: Rattner, *Overhaul*, 264.

218 *"tall, jowly"*: Rattner, *Overhaul*, 264.

220 *"We wanted to be sure"*: Author's interview with Alan Spitzer.

221 *LET DETROIT GO BANKRUPT*: Mitt Romney, "Let Detroit Go Bankrupt," *The New York Times*, November 8, 2008.

221 *"all based on a theory"*: Office of the Special Inspector General for the Troubled Asset Relief Program, "Factors Affecting the Decisions of General Motors and Chrysler to Reduce Their Dealership Networks," July 19, 2010, 31.

221 *"The report was ludicrous"*: Rattner, *Overhaul*, 302.

6. NETWORK MAN

222 *you might well wind up in Silicon Valley*: General background and history about Silicon Valley comes from author's interviews with Arthur Rock, Hal Varian, Laszlo Bock, AnnaLee Saxenian, Bob Metcalfe, Ben Rosen, Reid Hoffman, Thomas Perkins, John Doerr, John Lilly, David Sze, David Hahn, Michael Mandel, Joe Kraus, Josh Kopelman, Nancy Lublin, Joi Ito, Peter Thiel, Simon Rothman, George Arison, David Sanford, Mark Pincus, Jeff Weiner, Premal Shah, James Manyika, Evan Williams, Allen Blue, Ann Miurako, John Etchemendy, Mike Maples, Roy Bahat, Terry Winograd, Ian McCarthy, Jen Pahlka, Tim O'Reilly, Linda Rottenberg, Ben Casnocha, and Dan Portillo.

224 *Arthur Rock, by now retired*: Author's interviews with Arthur Rock.

225 *One study of Silicon Valley start-ups*: Susan E. Woodward and Robert E. Hall, "Benchmarking the Returns to Venture," NBER Working Paper Number w10202 (January 2004).

225 *Reid Hoffman's association with Silicon Valley*: Reid Hoffman's story comes from author's interviews with Hoffman.

229 *"At PayPal, we broke the rules"*: Reid Hoffman, *Blitzscaling*, Currency, 2018, 180.

230 *"a massively better idea"*: Author's interview with Reid Hoffman.

230 *Six Degrees*: Jeffrey Travers and Stanley Milgram, "An Experimental Study of the Small World Problem," *Sociometry*, Volume 32, Number 4 (December 1969), 425–43.

231 *Academics had been studying social networks*: See Jacob Moreno, *Who Shall Survive? Foundations of Sociometry, Group Psychotherapy and Sociodrama*, Beacon, 1953.

231 *"The Strength of Weak Ties"*: Mark S. Granovetter, "The Strength of Weak Ties," *American Journal of Sociology*, Volume 78, Number 6 (May 1973), 1360–80.

232 *"much as levies were imposed"*: Hoffman, *Blitzscaling*, 84.

233 *As a young engineer*: Author's interview with Bob Metcalfe.

233 *"First prize is a Cadillac Eldorado"*: Hoffman, *Blitzscaling*, 11.

233 *In 2014 Hoffman and two of his protégés*: See Reid Hoffman, Ben Casnocha, and Chris Yeh, *The Alliance: Managing Talent in the Networked Age*, Harvard Business Review Press, 2014.

234 The Start-Up of You: Reid Hoffman and Ben Casnocha, *The Start-Up of You: Adapt to the Future, Invest in Yourself, and Transform Your Career*, Crown Business, 2012.

234 *"Business is the systematic playing of games"*: Author's interview with Reid Hoffman.

236 *"If there's anything in the Valley, I'm going to know about it"*: Author's interview with Reid Hoffman.

236 *Greylock played host*: The author attended all the meetings described here.

239 *Hoffman was having dinner with one of his frequent companions*: The author was present at Hoffman's conversation with Mark Pincus.

240 *"the product-management approach to government"*: Author's interview with Reid Hoffman.

241 *at a private meeting for big donors*: Author's interview with a source who was there.

242 *"massive, outsize, discontinuous impact"*: Author's interview with Reid Hoffman.

242 *Another of Hoffman's favorite dinner companions*: The author was present at Hoffman's conversation with James Manyika.

244 *"a revolution of the ants"*: Mark Pincus, *Revolution of the Ants*, Mark Pincus blog, July 30, 2004.

244 Nonzero: Robert Wright, *Nonzero*, Pantheon, 1999.

244 *"We disagree with this position"*: Hoffman, *Blitzscaling*, 280.

245 *"Open Letter on the Digital Economy"*: http://openletteronthedigitaleconomy.org.

246 *"uncollared workers"*: Simon Rothman, "The Rise of the Uncollared Worker and the Future of the Middle Class," *Medium*, July 7, 2015.

246 *LinkedIn had commissioned a study*: Michael Mandel, "Connections as a Tool for Growth: Evidence from the LinkedIn Economic Graph," *South Mountain Economics*, November 2014.

246 *"The Internet is nothing less than an extinction-level event"*: Esko Kilpi, "The Future of Firms. Is There an App for That?," *Medium*, February 16, 2015.

247 *"We are living in Florence"*: Author's interview with Linda Rottenberg.

248 *In one of their conversations*: Author's interview with Reid Hoffman.

249 *"More or less all the things"*: Author's interview with Reid Hoffman.

251 *One of Hoffman's Silicon Valley friends*: Author's interview with Mike Maples.

AFTERWORD: AN ATTEMPT TO USE A TOOL

252 *"In spite of the bankruptcy"*: John Dewey, *Individualism Old and New*, Prometheus Books, 1999, 79.

256 *"A few days after the departure"*: Hutchins Hapgood, *A Victorian in the Modern World*, Harcourt, Brace and Company, 1939, 84.

256 *"Bentley's passionate desire"*: Hapgood, *Victorian in the Modern World*, 99.

256 *"Owing to the ambitiousness"*: Hapgood, *Victorian in the Modern* World, 112.

257 *a pioneering feminist writer named Neith Boyce*: See Carol DeBoer-Langworthy, *The Modern World of Neith Boyce: Autobiography and Diaries*, University of New Mexico Press, 2003.

257 *"she had met a man"*: Hutchins Hapgood, *The Story of a Lover*, Trieste Publishing, 2017, 123.

257 *"I took her by the throat!"*: Hapgood, *Story of a Lover*, 132.

257 *"To grow apples requires"*: Arthur Bentley, letter to Neith Boyce, September 10, 1925. Hapgood Family Papers, Yale University, Box 1, Folder 14, "Bentley, Arthur F. 1894–1932."

259 *"All phenomena of government"*: Arthur F. Bentley, *The Process of Government: A Study of Social Pressures*, Belknap Press, 1967, 269.

259 *"When the groups are adequately stated"*: Bentley, *Process of Government*, 208.

260 *"that particular form of activity"*: Bentley, *Process of Government*, 181.

260 *"assumed pure public spirit"*: Bentley, *Process of Government*, 370.

262 *"Our political government"*: Arthur F. Bentley, *Makers Users and Masters: In Defense of Income and of Property and of Their Enjoyment by All of the People*, Syracuse University Press, 1969, 38.

262 *"for the trifling proportion"*: Bentley, *Process of Government*, 453.

263 *"The flaw in the pluralist heaven"*: E. E. Schattschneider, *The Semisovereign People: A Realist's View of Democracy in America*, Holt, Rinehart, and Winston, 1960, 35.

263 *"interest-group liberalism"*: Theodore Lowi, *The End of Liberalism*, W. W. Norton, 1969.

264 *petty but passionately held concerns*: Mancur Olson, *The Logic of Collective Action: Public Goods and the Theory of Groups*, Harvard University Press, 1965. Also see Olson's *The Rise and Decline of Nations: Economic Growth, Stagflation, and Social Rigidities*, Yale University Press, 1982.

264 *"It is in vain to say that enlightened statesmen"*: James Madison, "Federalist Number 10," *The Debate on the Constitution*, Volume 1, Library of America, 1993, 393.

265 *"The social engineer tended to become"*: Herbert Croly, introduction to Eduard C. Lindeman, *Social Discovery: An Approach to the Study of Functional Groups*, Republic Publishing Company, 1936, xii.

266 *"the superior force"*: Madison, "Federalist Number 10," 390.

ACKNOWLEDGMENTS

This book began when a letter arrived from John Hennessey, then the president of Stanford University, inviting me to give the Tanner Lectures there. The timing was fortuitous: just in advance of my first-ever year off from any regular job. I spent that year at New York University's Institute for Public Knowledge, thanks to the generosity of its director, Eric Klinenberg. I had been thinking about the past generation's worth of dramatic changes in the American economy, culminating in the 2008 financial crisis, and about how those changes seemed also to have turned politics upside down. Having time to read and think—with the lectures providing a focus and a deadline—launched the process of turning a broad curiosity into an argument and a story.

At Stanford, the Center for Ethics in Society presents the Tanner Lectures. At the center, Debra Satz and Rob Reich were especially helpful in aiding me with framing the topic. (It seems providential, by the way, that the man who endowed the lectures, Obert Tanner, made his fortune purveying souvenirs and mementos of mid-twentieth-century corporate life.) They also arranged for four people to come to the lectures and offer critiques: Paul Pierson and Theda Skocpol, political scientists; Brook Manville, business consultant; and Joshua Ferris, novelist. All four are gifted teachers whose comments were essential to the progress of the book. Once I had settled on corporations, finance, and Washington as the nexus I wanted to explore, my editors at *The New Yorker*, David Remnick, Dorothy Wickenden, and Henry Finder, were generous in allowing me to take on a series of assignments that enabled me to home in more closely on the subject. At Columbia Journalism School, the high command—Steve Coll, Bill Grueskin, and Sheila Coronel—helped arrange my teaching life so that I could take two full years off to work on this book; Coll, Jelani Cobb, and Tali Woodward temporarily took over the courses I usually teach.

Reporters depend on the generosity of their subjects. This book would have been impossible without the cooperation of the many people I interviewed. A few of them stand out for their willingness to spend a lot of time with me even though they don't appear as major characters in the book. They are Jeff Bartow, the director of the Southwest Organizing Project, in Chicago; Anson Beard, formerly of Morgan Stanley, in Palm Springs, Florida; Jeff Duvall, of the Duvall Automotive Group, in Clayton, Georgia; William Kneisel, formerly of Morgan Stanley, in New York City; and former congressman James Leach, in Cedar Rapids, Iowa. Of the three people profiled at length in this book, the two who are living, Michael Jensen and Reid Hoffman, were copiously cooperative with this project; the third, Adolf Berle, died in 1971, but his last surviving child, Beatrice Berle Meyerson, let me spend a day at her house in Washington, reading and copying family papers that were not yet in the public Berle papers at the Franklin Roosevelt Presidential Library. I owe thanks to the staff of the Roosevelt Library, as well as the staffs of the other manuscript collections whose resources I used: the William J. Clinton Library in Little Rock, Arkansas; the Walter P. Reuther Library at Wayne State University in Detroit; the Tamiment Library and Robert F. Wagner Labor Archives at New York University; the Columbia Center for Oral History in New York; and the Anderson University and Church of God Archives at Anderson University in Indiana.

A few of the many people I consulted about the book were particularly generous with their advice, either along the way or in response to an early draft of the manuscript that I had given them: George Akerlof, Roy Bahat, Richard Bookstaber, Jeffrey Frank, Rakesh Khurana, Frank Levy, and Elisabeth Sifton. My agent, Amanda Urban, and her husband, Ken Auletta, suggested that I make Reid Hoffman one of the profile subjects in the book and introduced me to him. My editor at Farrar, Straus and Giroux, Alexander Star, did a superb job of helping me sharpen and clarify my arguments and tell the book's stories more engagingly. At home, my wife, Judith Shulevitz, was—well, the standard words, such as *encouraging* and *supportive*, don't really cover it. Better to say that she expected me to make a large and sometimes daunting topic into something urgent and immediate. If I've done that, it's because Judith thought I could.

INDEX

abolitionists, 264
Abrams, J. J., 239
Absentee Ownership (Veblen), 37–38
Addams, Jane, 25
advertising, 62–63, 68
African Americans, *see* black Americans
Agenda, The (Woodward), 161, 164
Airbnb, 237
airline regulation, 56, 61, 146–47
Allen & Company, 238
Alliance, The (Hoffman), 234
alpha, as economic term, 106–107
Alphabet, 246; *see also* Google
Alsop, Joseph, 56
Aluminum Co. of America, 38
Amazon, 237, 246–48
American Can Company, 182
American Capitalism (Galbraith), 18, 62, 63
American Dream, An (Mailer), 65
American Finance Association, 118
American Nazi Party, 11, 88
American Telephone and Telegraph,
    see AT&T
angel investors, 236; *see also* venture capital
Antitrust Paradox, The (Bork), 147
antitrust suits, *see* trustbusting
Apple Computer, 222, 228, 246–48; funding
    of, 152, 224
Arab Americans, 184

Arnold, Thurman, 53
Arrow, Kenneth, 67, 177
artificial intelligence, 243
AT&T, 38, 61, 91, 99, 111, 150; job cuts at,
    116; research at, 223
auto dealers, 4–10, 79–83, 182, 215–21;
    associations of, 9–10, 81, 215, 216, 217,
    261; franchise agreements of, 5, 80, 216;
    online, 237; *see also* General Motors
automatic teller machines, 210, 233
Automobile Dealer Economic Rights
    Restoration Act, 10

Baker, Kevin, 195
Baldwin, Robert Hayes Burns, 98–99,
    154; changes made by, 136–40, 210;
    compensation of, 156, 157
Bankers Trust, 171
banking, 40; in auto industry, 5, 9, 80, 89;
    during Depression, 48–49; deregulation of,
    see deregulation; local, 85–86; regulation
    of, 43, 44, 49, 50, 61, 86, 89–90; *see also*
    investment banking; Morgan Stanley;
    savings and loans
Bank of America, 169, 183, 191–92, 193
bankruptcy, 214
bank trust departments, 96, 103–104, 149
Barr, Michael, 192
Bartow, Jeff, 185, 194

Bay of Pigs invasion, 58
Beard, Anson, 140, 154, 155, 202
Beard, Charles and Mary, 28–29
Beard, Patricia, 95, 204
Beard, Peter, 140
Bear Stearns, 207
Beck, Glenn, 251
behavioral economics, 120–21, 133
"Being a Leader" (Jensen and Erhard), 100–101, 127, 130–33, 134–35
Bell, Daniel, 77–78
Bennington College, 71
Bentley, Arthur, 256–58; on pluralism, 257, 258–63, 268
Berkshires, 33, 34, 35, 36, 44, 46, 55, 68
Berle, Adolf Augustus, Jr., 22, 23–69, 97; airline regulation and, 56, 61, 146; background of, 24–28; at Columbia, 44, 71; corporations embraced by, 58–64, 228, 252–53, 254; critiques of, 64–69, 111, 113, 138, 148; death of, 24, 68, 69; ego of, 24, 32, 36, 44, 50, 56; on financial markets, 39, 40, 109; marriage of, 33–36, 44, 46–47, 55–56, 58, 68; *Modern Corporation* by, 36–43, 47, 58, 60, 72, 103, 111, 112, 114, 151, 222, 247; pluralism and, 261, 263, 267; post–Roosevelt administration career of, 57–58; revival of ideas of, 245; in Roosevelt campaign, 43–48; as Roosevelt's assistant secretary of state, 56–57; in Roosevelt's Brain Trust, 48–55, 59
Berle, Adolf Augustus, Sr., 24–25, 26, 27–28, 31, 69
Berle, Beatrice Bishop, 33–36, 44, 55–56, 58; diary entries of, 45, 48, 49–50, 111; work of, 36, 46–47, 68
Bernanke, Ben, 165, 209
Bernard, Lewis, 98–99, 154, 155–56, 202, 204
Bernstein, Peter, 104–105
beta, as economic term, 108
Biden, Joe, 80, 220–21
Big Business (Lilienthal), 62
Big Short, The (Lewis), 206
Bilderberg (conference), 238
Binger, Carl, 34
bin Laden, Osama, 221
Bishop, Amy Bend, 33–34, 55
Bishop, Cortlandt, 33–34, 55–56
Black, Fischer, 107–108, 126, 128

black Americans, discrimination faced by, 66, 85, 147, 253, 264, 266; in housing, 7–8, 10–16, 86–88, 184, 188, 197; in policing, 194–96, 199, 200
Black Monday, 159
Black Panthers, 226
Black-Scholes formula, 107–108
Blackstone, 128
Blagojevich, Rod, 188
Blankenbeckler, Frank, 218
Blankfein, Lloyd, 211
blitzscaling, 235, 238, 224
Bloom, Ron, 214
Bloomberg, Michael, 205, 239–40, 241
Bohac, Ben, 85–86
bonds, 89, 96, 142–43, 151, 208; as fixed-income, 141; high-risk, 115, 117, 151–52; in WWI, 40, 93
Booth, David, 153
Bork, Robert, 147, 273n59
Born, Brooksley, 171–74, 176, 177, 178, 210
Boyce, Neith, 257
Brandeis, Louis D., 26; as anti-bigness, 31–32, 42–43, 47–48, 52, 60, 62, 73, 146, 244, 262; on *Other People's Money*, 39–40, 89, 157; political maneuvering by, 51–52, 53, 146; revival of ideas of, 266; taxation advocated by, 59
Branson, Richard, 235
Breyer, Stephen, 146
Brin, Sergey, 236
broadcasting, regulation of, 61
Brody, Ken, 163
Bryan, William Jennings, 28, 30, 145–46, 163
Buddhism, 242
Buffett, Warren, 104, 120, 210
Buick, 4–10, 73, 215, 219, 220
Bullitt, William, 26
bureaucrats, 109–10; accountability to market, 111, 114–15; as ruling class, 39, 71, 72, 88, 96; suspicion of, 148; *see also* executives
Burke, Edmund, 242
Burke, Edward, 184
Burnham, James, 70–71
Bush, George H. W., 136
Bush, George W., 136, 178–79, 213
Bush, Jeb, 248

business schools: corporate managers trained by, 78–79, 95; financial economics' influence on, 119; *see also* Harvard; University of Chicago; University of Rochester

CAB (Civil Aeronautics Board), 61, 146–47
CalPERS, 139
Capital Ideas (Bernstein), 104–105
capitalism, 3–4; as disaster, 71; dynamism of, 149, 151; embraced by liberals, 145–48, 160–78, 211, 254; shareholders changing role in, 97–99; without capitalists, 36–37, 39, 41, 61, 88, 96
Capitalism, Socialism, and Democracy (Schumpeter), 70
capital pools, 96, 103–104, 119, 137, 139, 149, 154, 211, 224, 253
Cards Against Humanity, 249
Carnegie, Andrew, 36, 82
Carnegie, Dale, 125
Carter, Jimmy, 147, 150
Castro, Fidel, 58
Catholic Church, 6, 7, 85, 130, 184–85, 189–90, 193–94
Celler, Emanuel, 59
Celler-Kefauver Act of 1950, 59
Center for Research in Security Prices, 103, 106
Cerberus, 213
CFTC (Commodity Futures Trading Commission), 170–74, 178
Chambers, Whittaker, 56
Chandler, Alfred, 109
Chaosium, 226–27
charter schools, 255
Chase, *see* J.P. Morgan Chase
Chevrolet, 73, 74
Chicago: Board of Trade in, 108, 170–72; Democratic political machine in, 6, 8, 85, 184, 256–57, 261; immigrants in, 6, 10–11, 84; murders in, 14–15, 195–96, 201; personal connections in, 85, 194; public housing in, 194–95; racial geography of, 7, 10–11, 86–88; South Side of, *see* Chicago Lawn
Chicago Board Options Exchange, 108, 170
Chicago Lawn, 4–16, 83–88, 182–201; abandoned houses in, 7, 87, 187, 189–90, 193, 196, 199; auto dealers in, 4–10, 83, 182, 215, 219–20; Catholic Church in, 6, 7, 85, 184–85, 189–90, 193–94; community

organizing in, 184–85, 187–94, 197–200, 261; corporate employers in, 7, 84–85, 182–83, 184, 193; gangs in, 14–16, 187, 189, 194–96, 197–201; in larger context, 22, 85, 108, 198; Martin Luther King in, 10–12, 88, 196; mortgages in, 14, 85–86, 183–93, 199; name of, 83–84; police in, 194–96, 198–99, 200; racial dynamics of, 7–8, 10–16, 84, 87–88, 184–85, 194, 196–99
China, 6, 118, 162, 208, 235, 241
Christian Mingle, 229
Chrysler, 77, 189; bankruptcy of, 5, 213–16, 221; dealers for, 80, 82, 220
Church of God, 75
Citigroup, 168–69, 177, 193, 208
Civil Aeronautics Board (CAB), 61, 146–47
civil rights movement, 10–12, 66, 145, 264
Clash of the Titans liberalism, 29–31, 40–55, 59–61, 254
Clayton Act, 32
Clinton, Bill, 80, 160–78, 190, 241; Community Reinvestment Act and, 167; deficit under, 160, 161, 163, 170; first term of, 160–62; impeachment drama of, 164–65; regrets of, 210; second term of, 162–77; Whitewater and, 165, 167
Clinton, Chelsea, 164
Clinton, Hillary, 164, 167, 183, 208, 248, 250
Coase, Ronald, 110, 113, 246
Columbia University, 33, 44, 64, 263
Commerce Clearing House, 42
commercial banks, investment banks vs., 50, 156, 169, 180–81, 203, 205, 207, 209
commissions, fixed, 149
Committee to Restore Dealer Rights, 217–19
Commodity Futures Modernization Act, 178, 210; process behind, 170–78
Commodity Futures Trading Commission (CFTC), 170–74, 178
communism, 50, 56, 70; failure of, 118, 163; rejection of, 24, 57, 76, 78
community organizing, 184–85, 187–94, 197–200; *see also* interest groups
Community Reinvestment Act, 167, 185
Comptroller of the Currency, 145
computers, 152, 163, 224; in investment banking, 104, 105, 108, 153, 154, 159, 202, 212; *see also* Silicon Valley
Concept of the Corporation (Drucker), 72–78, 81

conformity, 16–18, 64–66

conglomerates, 109–10, 116, 168; *see also* leveraged buyouts; mergers and acquisitions

Congregationalist church, 25, 37

Congress: auto dealers and, 8, 9–10, 81, 215–16, 217–19; bailout authorized by, 213, 215; banking regulated by, 49, 89–90, 166–70; campaign contributions to, 81, 160, 164, 169, 170, 190, 217; confirmation hearings by, 26, 74, 147; corporate oversight by, 28, 31, 59, 116, 118; deregulation by, 149, 151, 159–61, 166–70, 171, 174, 176, 178; housing regulated by, 11, 192; lobbying of, 9–10, 144–45, 146, 190, 210, 241

consumers, 31; corporations held accountable by, 63, 262; deregulation for, 146–48, 149, 166–67, 170; manipulation of, 62, 68

Coordination, Control, and the Management of Organizations (class), 119

Corporation in Modern Society, The (Mason), 68–69

corporations, 23–24, 28–29, 36–40, 60, 61, 72–73, 91; advertising used by, 62–63; as autocratic, 47, 262; big government as counter to, 24, 29–31, 40–55, 59–61, 63, 71, 78, 96–97, 111, 145, 222, 253, 262; as black box, 113; boards of, 40, 89, 113, 114, 118, 129; conservative critiques of, 112–15; converted to pure market entities, 19, 109–20; debt of, 105, 114–15, 117; executives of, *see* executives; finance vs., 95, 109, 119, 144, 150, 211, 253; founders of, 36–37; jobs lost at, 116, 182, 203; liberal acceptance of, 24, 58–64; liberal critiques of, 112, 262; lifetime employees of, 16–18, 116, 150, 233, 253; regulation of, 23–24, 29–30, 40–55, 59–61; research labs of, 68–69, 112, 233; shareholders of, *see* shareholders; in Silicon Valley, 246–48; as social institutions, 37, 41, 42, 61, 62, 64, 67, 72, 73, 75, 77, 78, 97, 111, 112, 116, 147, 150, 245, 253; start-ups vs., 223–25; trustbusting as counter to, 30, 31–32, 42, 53, 59; as unforeseen by founders of U.S., 23, 28, 47; in web of related institutions, 81, 85; *see also* General Motors; institutions; Organization Man

corruption, 50, 244, 257, 261

Council of Economic Advisers, 67, 165, 176

countervailing power, 18, 63, 164, 253

Countrywide, 183, 188, 191, 206

Cowles, Alfred, 103

Cowles Commission for Research in Economics, 103–108

crime, 14–16, 187, 189, 194–96, 197–201; white collar, 100, 135, 152

Croly, Herbert, 30, 163, 265*n*

Cruz, Zoe, 205–206

Cuba, 58

Daley, Bill, 190–91

D'Andrea, Amy, 6–7, 9, 84, 219

D'Andrea, Nick, 4–10, 18–19, 215, 218, 219–20

Darvish, Tamara, 9, 216–17, 218

Davis Polk, 91

Debreu, Gerard, 67

Debs, Eugene, 75

debt: in auto industry, 5, 212, 220; corporate, 105, 114–15, 117; derivatives and, 154–55; foreign, 164, 170; hedge funds and, 154, 175, 208; interest rates and, 160, 179; of investment banks, 141, 155, 181, 191, 204, 206, 207, 208; junk bonds and, 151; in leveraged buyouts, 117; risk magnified by, 155, 175; *see also* mortgages

democracy, 3–4, 45, 59, 64, 261–63, 267–68; threats to, 21, 30–31, 57

Democratic Party: in Chicago, 6, 8, 85, 184, 261; databases of, 250; deregulation by, 145–48, 149, 160–78, 211, 254; Silicon Valley and, 240–41, 248–51; Wall Street donors to, 163, 164, 169, 215

Department of Labor, 149

deposits, insurance of, 43, 50, 144, 145, 151, 159, 165, 166, 177, 180

deregulation, 143–51, 158–78, 202, 207, 253, 254, 268; by Democrats, 145–48, 149, 160–78, 211, 254; globalization and, 148, 205; interest rates and, 147, 151, 155; of mortgages, 180, 183–84; in 1970s, 144–48; skeptics of, 159–60, 167–68, 177, 180, 205

derivatives, 107–108, 153–55, 157, 206, 210; fight to keep unregulated, 167–78, 207; regulated by EU, 181; risks of, 175; skepticism about, 168, 178; volume of, 171, 178, 181; *see also specific financial instruments*

D. E. Shaw, 208

Desoer, Barbara, 191

Deutsche Bank, 190, 193

Dewey, John, 252, 258
dialog (conference), 238
Dicey, Albert Venn, 259
Different Worlds (magazine), 227
Dillon Read, 92
Director, Aaron, 103, 110, 147
Disciples (gang), 194
Dodd, David, 104
Dodd, E. Merrick, 41–42, 61
Dominican Republic, 56, 58
dot-com bust of 2000, 179
Drexel Burnham Lambert, 117, 151, 152
Drift and Mastery (Lippmann), 30
Drucker, Peter, 70–81 passim, 97–98, 116, 149
Dulles, Allen, 26
Dulles, John Foster, 26
Dungeons & Dragons, 226
DuPont, 91, 111
Durant, William, 74
Durbin, Richard, 10, 190, 192, 218
Duvall, Jeff, 218
dynamic modeling, 108

East Asia, debt in, 164; *see also specific countries*
East Garfield Park, 11–12, 13
eBay, 229, 230, 237
economics, academic, 53–55, 66–67, 102–23; on competition, 232; macroeconomic approach adopted by, 55, 113–20; statistical approach adopted by, 103–109
Economics and the Public Purpose (Galbraith), 96
economy, ways of organizing, 16–22, 252–55; *see also* corporations; investment banking; networks
Edison, Thomas, 36
efficient market hypothesis, 105, 120, 129
Ehrenhalt, Alan, 86
Einstein, Albert, 258
Eisenhower, Dwight, appointees of, 74
Electric Storage Battery, 137–38
elites, 22, 212; corporations founded by, 36–37, 82; at Morgan Stanley, 90–91, 94, 98, 137, 140, 153; Silicon Valley and, 238
Elmendorf, Doug, 176–77
El Rukns, 194
End of Ideology, The (Bell), 78
energy, regulation of, 61
Englewood, 7, 11, 86–87, 197
Enron, 127, 171

environmental movement, 145, 243, 264, 267
Erhard, Ludwig, 125
Erhard, Werner, 101, 123–27; in collaboration with Jensen, 100–101, 126–27, 130, 131–33, 134–35
Erhard-Jensen Ontological/Phenomenological Initiative, 100–101, 132–33, 134
est, 101, 123, 124–26, 131
European Union, 181
eWorld, 228
executives, 81, 109–13, 114–15; charges against, 100, 152, 211; compensation of, 114, 115, 118, 129, 162, 202, 204; decision-making by, 39, 41, 69; firing of, 138, 203–204, 214; pressures on, 129, 142; selection of, 112, 113; social responsibility of, 78; subjected to market, 41, 112, 114, 116–17, 118, 128–30, 133, 134, 142; *see also* bureaucrats
"Existence of an Equilibrium" (Arrow and Debreu), 67

Facebook, 222, 224, 237, 246–48; acquisitions by, 224–25; founders of, 232, 236, 247; LinkedIn vs., 233, 235; misleading information on, 250
factories, 14, 75–78, 85, 182–83
Fairchild Semiconductor, 223
Fair Deal, 67
Fair Housing Act, 11
Fama, Eugene, 119, 120, 121, 126, 153; efficient market hypothesis of, 105, 120, 129; journal edited by, 109, 114
fascism, 50, 59, 78
Fed, *see* Federal Reserve Board
Federal Communications Commission, 61
Federal Deposit Insurance Corporation, 43, 50, 144, 145, 151, 159, 165, 166, 177, 180
federal government, 21; corporations regulated by, 29–31, 40–55, 59–61, 63, 71, 96–97, 145, 262; deficit of, 160, 161, 163, 170, 179; deposits guaranteed by, 43, 50, 144, 145, 151, 159, 165, 166, 177, 180; finance deregulated by, 143–51, 158–78; liberal suspicion of, 148; markets regulated by, 115, 121, 254; in 2008 financial crisis, 190–91, 192, 208–11, 213–14, 217–19, 220–21; *see also* Congress; *specific administrations and agencies*
Federal Housing Administration, 86, 184

"Federalist Number 10" (Madison), 264–65, 266
Federal National Mortgage Association, 86
Federal Power Commission, 61
Federal Reserve Board, 32, 61, 166; Bear Stearns and, 207; under Bernanke, 209; under Greenspan, 159–81 passim, 210; New York branch of, 205; time prior to, 89, 90, 145; under Volcker, 150–51, 152
Federal Savings and Loan Insurance Corporation, 86, 145
Federal Trade Commission, 32
Feminine Mystique (Friedan), 18
feminism, 18, 145, 264
Fidelity Investments, 139
Financial Crisis Inquiry Commission, 210–11
financial economics: critiques of, 116, 118–19, 120–21, 127–30, 133–35; paradigm shift in, 102–109, 112–19, 131; Wall Street's marriage to, 153
financial institutions: closings of, 136, 158–59, 165; competition for talent between, 158, 205; growth of, 108, 115; limitations on, 95; in Silicon Valley, 223–25, 229; *see* banking; investment banking; savings and loans
financial panic of 1907, 89
Financial Services Modernization Act of 1999, 165–70
financial systems: computerization of, *see under* computers; deregulation of, *see* deregulation; failures in, 38, 48, 159, 174, 179, *see also* 2008 financial crisis; fragility of, 207; globalization of, *see* globalization; new techniques of, 115–20; reregulation of, 209, 211; *see also* capitalism; investment banking; Jensen, Michael
First Boston, 92
Fisher, Irving, 44
Fisher, Richard (Dick), 94, 138–39, 141; as head of Morgan Stanley, 156, 169, 201–202, 203
Fitzgerald, Jack, 216, 217
fixed-income investments, 141, 151, 205
FOO (conference), 238
Ford, 10, 80, 82–83, 168, 201
Ford, Henry, 82
foreclosures, 14, 186–93, 199
Fort, Jeff, 194
Fortune, 77–78
Fortune 500, 116
foundation endowments, 103–104, 149, 211, 224

401(k) plans, 149–50
France, conglomerates from, 182
Frankfurter, Felix, 52–53, 54, 56–57, 61–62
Franklin, Aretha, 219
free-market purism, 24, 44, 59, 64, 67, 76, 102–22; defection from, 127–30, 133–35; liberal conversion to, 144–48, 160–67, 254; pluralism and, 266, 267; *see also* Greenspan, Alan
free trade, 118, 161
Friedan, Betty, 18
Friedman, Milton, 102–103, 105, 112–13, 147
Fujitsu, 228
Future of Industrial Man, The (Drucker), 72
futures market, 108, 170–74, 178, 210

Galbraith, John Kenneth, 18, 19, 67, 72; on corporations, 62–64, 67, 96, 116, 147
Galton, Francis, 259
gangs, 14–16, 187, 189, 194–96, 197–201
Gates, Bill, 235
Geithner, Timothy, 205, 209
General Accounting Office (GAO), 168, 176, 177
General Electric, 17, 39, 59, 91, 109
General Motors, 22, 39, 72–83, 110; acquisitions of, 152; bankruptcy of, 4–10, 212–21, 261; Berle and, 42; credit company of, 5, 9, 80, 89, 213, 216, 220; dealerships for, 4–10, 79–82, 215–21; debt of, 212; decentralized management of, 73, 74; Drucker embedded at, 72–78, 81; as immune to markets, 109; Japanese competition with, 8, 115, 142, 214; management of, 73–75, 111, 142; Morgan Stanley and, 89, 91–92, 94, 99, 142, 152; Organization Man at, 17, 19; other industries tied to, 81–82; research lab at, 223; safety and, 146; size of, 73, 95, 224; workers' rights at, 75–78, 97–98, 214–15; during WWII, 55, 75
General Theory of Employment, Interest, and Money, The (Keynes), 54
Germany, 190, 256
G. H. Walker and Company, 136, 139
Gibson Greetings, 171
gig economy, 246, 255
Gilbert, Seymour Parker, III, 156, 202, 203–204

Glass-Steagall Act, 90, 148, 209; dismantling of, 165–70, 180, 202–203, 205, 207, 210

Glengarry Glen Ross, 233

globalization, 20, 164, 190, 212; deregulation and, 148, 205; of mergers, 182, 208; at Morgan Stanley, 148, 154, 171, 181, 202, 208, 209; parochialism despite, 268; prosperity and, 264; technology and, 3, 205, 245–46, 249; of trade, 161–62, 170, 182, 183

GMAC, 5, 9, 80, 89, 213, 216, 220

Goldman Sachs, 92, 128, 153, 181, 205, 208, 209, 211; former employees of in government, 161, 163, 169, 177

Google, 202, 222, 237, 246–48; employees of, 236, 238, 247

government, *see* federal government

Governmental Process, The (Truman), 263

Graham, Benjamin, 104, 119–20

Gramlich, Edward, 180

Gramm, Phil, 167, 168, 171, 178

Gramm, Wendy, 171

Granovetter, Mark, 231

Gray, Edwin, 159

Great Depression, 38, 48–49, 86, 181; anti-bank sentiment during, 144, 165; as ended by government, 55, 59, 64, 65

Greater Southwest Development Corporation, 185

Great Migration, 11, 87

Great Transformation, The (Polanyi), 71

greed, 47, 119, 144, 229

Greenhill, Robert (Bob), 137–38, 139, 156

Greening of America, The (Reich), 65

Greenspan, Alan, 159, 210; Clinton and, 160–61, 164; Glass-Steagall revision and, 168, 169, 172, 173; housing and, 179, 180

Greylock, 236–37, 245, 246

groups, *see* interest groups

Gulf and Western, 109

Gun Gospel (Hoffman), 226

Hamilton, Alexander, 30, 49, 163

Hapgood, Hutchins, 256, 257, 258

Harlan, John Marshall, 23–24

Harper's Magazine, 39–40

Hart, Dennis, 87–88

Harvard: Berle at, 25, 26, 29, 52–53, 78–79; Business School of, 38, 78–79, 95, 119, 120, 127, 139; faculty of, 41, 52–53, 62, 68; students at, 37, 232

hatred, as national culture, 15–16

Hayden, Tom, 18, 65

Hayek, Friedrich, 64, 70, 71, 102, 103, 105

health insurance: via employers, 17, 77, 215, 253; federal, 43, 67, 194, 240

hedge funds, 19, 154, 174–77, 180, 207–208

Heidegger, Martin, 132

Heisenberg, Werner, 125

Henry Street Settlement, 28, 35

Hewlett, William, 223

Hewlett-Packard, 223

Hill, James J., 140

Hill, Napoleon, 125

Hoffman, Bill, 225, 226

Hoffman, Reid, 22, 225–51; background of, 225–28; gaming and, 226–27, 228, 230, 234, 239, 244, 249; as investor, 236–37, 242; at LinkedIn, 230–31, 233–36, 240–41, 245–48; networking by, 236–39; at PayPal, 229–30; political involvement of, 239–46, 248–51; religion and, 242; at SocialNet, 228–29; suspicion of ideas of, 255, 267; wealth of, 236, 248

Hoffman, W. D., 225–26

Hofstadter, Richard, 32–33, 145

Holy Cross Hospital, 85, 193–94

home equity loans, 183, 186, 199

Honda, 214

H-1B visas, 241

Hong Kong, 205

Hoover, Herbert, 66

Hoover, Larry, 194

Hopkins, Harry, 57

hostile takeovers, 137–38; *see also* leveraged buyouts

House of Mirth, The (Wharton), 33

housing: abandoned, 7, 87, 187, 189–90, 193, 196, 199; discrimination in, 10–12, 87–88; price of, 179, 186–87; in projects, 13, 14, 187, 194–95; *see also* mortgages

How to Win Friends and Influence People (Carnegie), 125

Hoyer, Steny, 217, 218

Hubbard, L. Ron, 126

Hubler, Howie, 206

Huffington, Arianna, 235

Hyde Park, 197

Iacocca, Lee, 189

IBM, 17, 109, 111, 142–43, 223

Icahn, Carl, 115

identity politics, 145, 266
Illinois legislature, 86, 184, 188
immigrants, undocumented, 187, 189
index funds, invention of, 107, 108
India, 118
individualism, 18, 20, 47–48, 66; end of, 16, 39, 64, 69
Industrial Revolution, 28, 71, 266; corporate revolution compared to, 39, 72–73
inequality: economic, *see* wealth, concentration of; racial, *see* racism
inflation, 115, 163, 170; interest rates and, 144, 149, 150, 152; wages and, 75–76
information asymmetry, 120, 176
Inner-City Muslim Action Network, 185, 190
Instagram, 225
institutions: individualism vs., 16–19, 48, 66; loss of faith in, 222, 254–55; as mature groups, 18, 260; as necessary for pluralism, 267–68; transaction-based order vs., 19–22, 253, 255; *see also* corporations; federal government; Organization Man
insurance companies, 96, 103–104, 224
Intel, 223–24
Interest Equalization Tax, 148
interest groups, 258–68; desire to eliminate, 20, 260–61; successes of, 261, 264; types of, 259–60
interest rates, 54, 86, 212, 254; deregulation and, 147, 151, 155; Greenspan and, 160, 179; inflation and, 144, 149, 150, 152; on mortgages, 14, 190, 199
Internal Revenue Service, 149
International Nickel, 137–38
International Typographical Union, 101, 102, 122
Internet, 3, 163, 224, 246; bubble of 2000, 127; early conceptions of, 232; financial industry on, 205; as predicted in fiction, 228; regulation of, 241; *see also* networks; Silicon Valley
interstate banking, 161
Interstate Commerce Commission, 61
Investing in US, 250
investment banking, 88–99; academic paradigm shift in, 102–109, 112–20; antitrust suit against, 92–94; changes to in 1970s, 136–43; commercial banking vs., 50, 156, 169, 180–81, 203, 205, 207, 209; computerization of, 104, 105, 108, 153, 154, 159, 202, 212; deregulation of, *see*

deregulation; diversified portfolios in, 104; Glass-Steagall Act and, *see* Glass-Steagall Act; SEC and, *see* Securities and Exchange Commission; shifting clients of, 95–99; *see also* Morgan Stanley; *specific financial instruments*
Irish Americans, 6, 11, 84, 87, 184
Italian Americans, 6, 7, 10, 84
Itô, Kiyosi, 108
ITT, 109

Jackson, Andrew, 145
Jackson, Jesse, 12, 167
Jackson, Mahalia, 12
Jacobs, Irwin, 115
Japan, 117, 154, 182, 230; auto industry in, 8, 115, 142, 209, 214
Jdate, 229
Jefferson, Thomas, 30, 46, 47, 66
Jensen, Michael, 22, 100–109, 112–35; as advocate for free markets, 115–19, 138, 253, 267; background of, 101–102; character of, 106, 120–24, 130; corporations studied by, 112–15, 130; at Harvard, 119–20, 127; on integrity, 101, 130–31, 133–35; in Landmark, 123–24, 126–27; mind shift of, 100–101, 127–30, 135, 222; at Rochester, 109, 113–15, 119, 120, 126–27; at University of Chicago, 102–109
Jensen, Stephanie, 123
Jews, 26, 27, 34, 35, 193, 242; in finance, 98, 138
Jhering, Rudolf von, 259
Jobs, Steve, 152
Johns Hopkins University, 256, 257
Johnson, Earl, 197–201
Johnson, Jonathan, 200–201
Jones, Doug, 250
Journal of Applied Corporate Finance, 135
Journal of Financial Economics, 109, 114, 129, 134–35
J.P. Morgan Chase, 168, 190, 191, 193, 207, 208, 209, 233
Judge, Mike, 239
junk-bond market, 115, 151–52
"Just Say No to Wall Street" (Jensen), 129

Kahneman, Daniel, 121
Karan, Donna, 153
Kennedy, Edward, 146–47
Kennedy, John F., 58, 148

Keynes, John Maynard, 26, 54–55, 63, 66–67; in imaginary conversation, 121–22

King, Martin Luther, Jr., 10–12, 88, 196

Kintner, Robert, 56

Knee, Jonathan, 158

Kohlberg Kravis Roberts (KKR), 117, 128, 152, 183

Kool-Aid, 84, 182

Kraft, 182

Kravis, Henry, 117, 156

Kuhn, Thomas, 105

Kuhn Loeb, 92, 136

Ku Klux Klan, 11

La Guardia, Fiorello, 49

Landmark Forum, 123–27, 130–31

Latin America, 56, 164

Latin Kings, 189

Latinos, in Chicago Lawn, 184, 185, 186, 187, 189, 194

Law of the Lash (Hoffman), 226

Leach, James, 159–60, 167–68, 169–70, 176

Lee, Tyshawn, 195–96

Lehman Brothers, 207

Lenin, Vladimir I., 26

leveraged buyouts, 115, 117, 149, 152; *see also* mergers and acquisitions; private equity

Levin, Carl, 211

Levitt, Arthur, 172–74, 210

Lewis, Michael, 206

Liang Qichao, 29

liberalism: differing economic visions within, 29–32, 252, 253–54; markets embraced by, 163–64, 211, 254; pluralism critiqued by, 263–64; shifting focus of, 145–48

Liberal Party of New York City, 58

Lilienthal, David, 61–62

Ling-Temco-Vought, 109

Linguistic Analysis of Mathematics (Bentley), 258

LinkedIn, 230–31, 233–36, 239, 240–41, 245–48; Economic Graph of, 235, 246; Facebook vs., 233, 235; IPO of, 236

Lippmann, Walter, 26, 30, 163

Lithuanian Americans, 7, 10, 84, 85, 188, 190

Lloyd, Henry Demarest, 146

London, 205

Lonely Crowd, The (Riesman), 16, 64, 74

Long-Term Capital Management, 174–77

Lost City, The (Ehrenhalt), 86

Luce, Henry, 71

Lugar, Richard, 171

Macalester College, 102

Mack, John, 141, 153–54, 156, 157, 201–209

macroeconomics, 54–55, 113; *see also* free-market purism

Madigan, Lisa, 8

Madigan, Michael, 184, 188, 193

Madison, James, 264–65, 266

Mailer, Norman, 65

Main Street and Wall Street (Ripley), 38

Makers Users and Masters (Bentley), 261–62

management, *see* bureaucrats; executives

Managerial Revolution, The (Burnham), 70–71

Mann, Thomas, 258

Manne, Henry, 110–11, 119, 138

Manyika, James, 242–43

Maples, Mike, Jr., 251

Maria High School, 85, 193

markets, *see* free-market purism; investment banking; *specific financial instruments*

Markowitz, Harry, 104–105, 120

Marx, Karl, 41, 88, 97, 112, 259

Marzullo, Vito, 6

Maslow, Abraham, 125

Mason, Edward, 68–69

McCain, John, 215

McDonald, Colleen, 218

McDonald, Laquan, 15, 195

McKinsey & Company, 242

Means, Gardiner, 37, 38, 54, 62, 67, 103

Meckling, William, 109, 113–14, 119, 120

Medina, Harold, 93–94

Meeker, Mary, 202

Mellon Bank, 208

mergers and acquisitions, 19, 115–19, 129, 149, 151, 168–69; by banks, 166, 183; in Chicago Lawn, 182–83; globalization of, 182; at Morgan Stanley, 137–38, 142, 151, 152, 203

Merrill Lynch, 92, 143, 171

Merton, Robert C., 108, 109, 114, 126, 174, 210

Metcalfe, Bob, 232–33

Metcalfe's law, 232–33

Mexico: factories moved to, 182, 183; immigrants from, 187, 195 microeconomics, 55, 113; *see also* corporations

Microsoft, 168, 230, 246–48

middle class, 158, 245; corporations as benefit to, 17, 38, 66; corporations as hindrance to, 16, 52; regulation to support, 50, 160; as stockholders, 97; *see also* Chicago Lawn

Middle-earth liberalism, 31–32, 42, 53, 59, 262

Milgram, Stanley, 231

Milken, Michael, 115, 117, 151–52, 156

Miller, Merton, 105, 120

Mills, C. Wright, 64–65

Mind Dynamics, 125

MIT, 107, 108, 153

Mitsubishi, 209, 212

mobile devices, 237

Modern Corporation and Private Property, The (Berle and Means), 36–43, 47, 58, 60, 72, 103, 111, 114, 247

Modigliani, Franco, 105, 120

Moley, Raymond, 44

Mondelez, 183

money market funds, 212

money trust, 32, 40, 89

Mont Pelerin Society, 103

Moreno, Jacob, 231

Morgan, Henry, 90, 94, 136–37, 156

Morgan, J. P., 31, 36, 40, 59, 136, 140, 156; Morgan Stanley and, 89–90, 91, 209

Morgan, J. P., Jr., 89, 90–91, 158

Morgan Stanley, 89–96, 98–99, 136–43, 152–58, 201–10; bailout of, 135, 191, 213; board of, 203; changes to in 1970s, 136–43; commercial banks vs., 156, 169, 209; compensation at, 156, 157, 158, 202, 203, 204–205; in competition with its clients, 142; corporate clients of, 91, 94, 96, 99, 137, 142–43, 150, 202; debt of, 141, 155, 157, 178, 181, 204, 206, 208; deregulation and, 148–52, 202, 207; derivatives and, 153–55, 178, 202, 206, 207; diversity at, 153, 205; elitism of, 90–91, 94, 98, 137, 140, 153; expansion of, 202–203; fixed-income department at, 141; founding of, 89–90; as global company, 148, 154, 157, 181, 202; government employees from, 214; IPO of, 156–58, 202; Jensen honored by, 135; junk-bond department of, 152; largest loss at, 205–206;

mergers and acquisitions at, 137–38, 142, 151, 152, 203; mortgaged-backed securities and, 152, 206; price setting by, 91, 103, 105, 108, 139; prime brokerage at, 154, 207–208; research department at, 140, 142; shareholders as clients of, 99; Silicon Valley and, 152, 202; size of, 95, 203; syndicate system at, 91–96, 103, 136, 140, 143, 149, 150; trading at, 138–42, 150, 153–54, 202, 205–206; in 2008 financial crisis, 207–12

Morison, Samuel Eliot, 26

mortgages, 85–86, 183–84, 185–93; adjustable-rate, 151, 179–80; collapse of subprime market of, *see* 2008 financial crisis; federal involvement in, 184, 190–91, 192; loan modifications for, 191–93, 199, 200; predatory, 14, 185–87; racial politics of, 184, 185, 186, 188, 189; securities backed by, 108, 152, 179–80, 183, 192, 206–207, 211; state regulation of, 188; as unregulated, 183–84; *see also* 2008 financial crisis

Moss, John, 149

Musk, Elon, 229, 241

mutual funds, 97, 99, 139, 149–50, 157; inflation and, 144; statistical study of, 106–107, 108

My Years with General Motors (Sloan), 95

Nabisco, 7, 84–85, 152, 182–83

Nader, Ralph, 146, 147

Napster, 230

Nashashibi, Rami, 185, 196

Nation, The, 27, 28

National Automobile Dealers Association, 81, 215, 216

National Economic Council, 161, 166, 214

National Industrial Recovery Act (NIRA), 51–52, 53, 54

National Labor Relations Board, 54

"Nature of the Difficulty, The" (Berle), 43–44, 45, 48, 54

"Nature of the Firm, The" (Coase), 110, 113, 246

Nazis, 59, 64, 70, 263; in U.S., 11, 88

NBC, 232

Neal, Ann Collier, 11–16, 18–19

Neal, Richard, 13

Neighborhood Housing Services of Chicago, 185, 189–90, 198, 199, 200

net neutrality, 241
Netscape, 202
networks, 228–36; academic study of, 231; as
    alternative to institutions and transactions,
    21, 22, 222, 228; as disruptive, 237;
    human need and, 228, 229, 234; inequality
    maintained by, 255, 267; political
    application of, 240–42, 244, 246, 250–51;
    pre-digital, 233; users vs. income of,
    229–30, 231–33, 234
New Century, 183, 206
New Deal, 22, 43–55, 90, 95–97, 143–44;
    dismantling of, 144–45, 158, 161, 184;
    repudiation of, 102, 163
New Democracy, The (Weyl), 30
New Freedom, 31–32, 42, 53, 59, 262
New Nationalism, 29–31, 40–55, 59–61, 262
New Republic, The, 28, 30
New York, 28, 44, 49, 58
New Yorker, The, 36, 56
New York Times, The, 112–13, 221
Nicklaus, Jack, 139
NIRA (National Industrial Recovery Act),
    51–52, 53, 54
Nissan, 214
Nixon, Richard, 147, 148
Nobel laureates in economics, 105, 108, 110,
    123, 153, 177, 245
Nonzero (Wright), 244
normative, as economic term, 134
Nortel, 127
North American Free Trade Agreement, 161,
    182, 183
nouveau riche, 33
Nudge (Thaler), 133

Obama, Michelle, 220
Obama administration, 188, 190, 194; auto
    industry and, 4–5, 9, 214–21; donors to,
    190, 215, 240; during 2008 crisis, 134,
    192, 210–11; tech industry and, 240–41,
    248–50
Obamacare, 194, 240
Obama Foundation, 240–41, 248
Oberlin College, 25
Office of Management and Budget (OMB),
    165
oil prices, 144, 214
old money, 33
O'Neill, Eugene, 257
online dating, 229

ontology, 132
"Open Letter on the Digital Economy," 245
open marriage, 257
options market, 107–108, 170, 171
Orange County, CA, 171
O'Reilly, Tim, 238
Organization Man, 16–19, 65; rebellion
    against, 116, 224; replaced by network
    model, 233, 247; replaced by transaction
    model, 116, 158, 211, 253–54; see also
    corporations; General Motors; institutions
Organization Man, The (Whyte), 16–18,
    19, 65
"Organization Study" (Sloan), 74
OTC market, 173; see also derivatives
overnight lending systems, 208, 212–13

Packard, David, 223
Page, Larry, 236
Painter, Patrick, 218
Palmer, Arnold, 139
PalmPilot, 229
Panetta, Leon, 162
paradigm shifts, 105; in economics, 102–109,
    112–20
Park Forest, IL, 16–17, 20
Partnoy, Frank, 158
Patil, DJ, 240
Patriot Act, 230
Paulson, Henry, 205, 209, 212, 213
PayPal, 229–30, 236
Pearl Harbor, 56
Pecora hearings, 89–90, 91, 95
Peltz, Nelson, 182
Penn Central Railroad, 149
pension funds, 17, 18, 76–77, 112, 253;
    economy changed by, 97–98, 99; 401(k)s
    vs., 149–50; investing of, 103, 119, 139,
    140, 149, 150, 211, 224; maintained by
    corporations, 116, 122, 225, 233, 246
Perot, Ross, 152
Perrin, Steve, 226
Peterson, Rafi, 187, 198
Petito, Frank, 98
Pfleger, Michael, 8
phenomenology, 132
Phibro, 155–56
Pickens, T. Boone, 115
Pincus, Mark, 230, 232, 243; political goals
    of, 239–40, 244, 250, 251
Pioneers of Finance (video), 128

Pizzo, Tony, 185, 189–90, 191, 194
planned economies, 59
Plepler, Andrew, 191, 192
pluralism, 255–68; Bentley on, 256–63;
    conception of politics in, 261, 265–67;
    critiques of, 253–64; faux, 263, 267;
    humility and, 264–65
plutocracy, 30, 36
Polanyi, Karl, 70–72
police, 6, 189, 194–96, 198–99, 200;
    conservative empowerment of, 147; racism
    of, 15, 195–96, 199, 200
Polish Americans, 7, 84
politics: economics and, 4, 21, 96–97,
    144–48, 158–81, 219; pluralistic conception
    of, 255–68; Silicon Valley and, 239–46,
    248–51; suspicion of, 20, 148; Transaction
    Man mentality in, 254–55; violence
    in, 262–63, 265; see also community
    organizing; Congress; federal government;
    specific administrations; political parties
Pontiacs, 5, 220
Port Huron Statement (Hayden), 18, 65
positive, as economic term, 134
Positive Theory of the Normative Virtues, A
    (Jensen and Erhard), 131
Power (Berle), 40
predatory lending, 14, 185–87
price setting: by corporations, 63, 75, 79; by
    government, 51, 55, 59, 62, 67; by unions,
    76, 77
prime brokerage, 154, 207–208
Prime Reserve Fund, 212–13
Princeton, 98
principal-agent problem, 41, 112, 114, 116–17,
    118, 128–30, 133, 134, 142
Priorities USA, 240
private equity, 19, 115, 117, 149, 214, 219,
    221; GM and, 213; gone public, 128;
    Morgan Stanley competing with, 205;
    mortgaged-backed securities and, 180;
    takeovers by, 182, 183
Process of Government, The (Bentley), 257,
    258–63
Procter & Gamble, 171
Promise of American Life, The (Croly), 30,
    265n
prudent man rule, 149, 224
public schools, 249, 254–55
Pujo, Arsène, 89, 95
Purcell, Philip, 202–204, 205

Putney School, The, 227
"Putting Integrity into Finance" (Jensen and
    Erhard), 131

racism, 66, 85, 147, 253, 263–64, 266; in
    housing, 7, 10–16, 86–88, 184, 188, 197;
    in policing, 194–96, 199, 200
railroads, 36, 149, 267; regulation and, 29,
    147
Ranieri, Lewis, 152
Rattner, Steven, 4–5, 9, 214–16, 218–19, 221
Reagan, Ronald, 116, 151, 160, 162
Reardon, Mike, 185, 189–90, 192, 199
Reed, John, 169
regulation: of corporations, 23–24, 29–31,
    40–55, 59–61; of finance, 43, 44, 49, 50,
    61, 86, 89–90, 266; of Internet, 241; post-
    2008, 209, 211; as Socialist, 76, 112;
    see also specific agencies
Reich, Charles, 65
Reich, Robert, 161, 162, 164, 210
Republicans: Clinton and, 160–64, 167,
    171–78; deregulation and, 145, 147, 148–51,
    159–60, 178–79, 254; donors and, 215,
    249, 251; liberal, 58, 102, 112
repurchase market, 208
research labs, corporate, 68–69, 112, 223
retirement benefits, see pension funds; Social
    Security Administration
Reuther, Walter, 75, 76, 77
Rheem, 182
Riesman, David, 16, 17, 18, 64, 74
Riggs, Austen, 34
Ripley, William Z., 38
RJR Nabisco, 7, 84–85, 152, 182–83
Road to Serfdom, The (Hayek), 70
robber barons, 36, 46; see also specific people
Robert Taylor Homes, 195, 197, 198
Rock, Arthur, 223–24
Rockefeller, David, 233
Rockefeller, John D., 23, 33, 36, 82
Rockefeller, Nelson, 58
Rockwell, George Lincoln, 88
Rogers, Carl, 125
Romney, Mitt, 221
Roosevelt, Franklin, 44–57, 86, 146; Brain
    Trust of, 22, 49–55; campaign of, 44–48;
    inauguration of, 48–49; Morgan Stanley
    and, 89–90; Supreme Court and, 51–53;
    unknown views of, 44, 46, 49, 51
Roosevelt, Sara, 45

Roosevelt, Theodore, 29–31, 89
Rosenberg, John Paul, *see* Erhard, Werner
Rothman, Simon, 237, 246
Rubin, Robert, 210, 211; at Goldman Sachs,
    128, 161, 163, 169; on National Economic
    Council, 161, 166; as secretary of the
    Treasury, 162, 168–74 passim, 177–78
Rule 415, 150
Rush, Bobby, 8
Russell, Bertrand, 257
Russia, 26–27, 164, 250, 260
Rutter, Deanna Ruth, 226

St. Rita of Cascia, 7, 84, 185, 189, 191
Salomon Brothers, 143, 152, 153; former staff
    of, 174, 205
Samuelson, Paul, 67, 177
Sanders, Bernie, 250–51
Sarnoff's law, 232
savings and loans: in Chicago Lawn, 85–86,
    183, 191; deregulation of, 151, 159; failures
    of, 159, 165; federal insurance on, 86,
    143–44, 145, 151; Whitewater and, 165, 167
Schmidt, Eric, 238
Scholes, Myron, 107–108, 129, 153, 174
School in the Home, The (Berle), 25
Schumer, Chuck, 208
Schumpeter, Joseph, 70
Schwarzman, Stephen, 128
Scientology, 125, 126
Sears, 7, 85, 182, 202–203
seasteading, 243
Second Bank of the United States, 145
Securities and Exchange Commission, 90,
    91–92, 96, 144, 165; creation of, 43, 50, 51,
    53, 54; derivatives and, 155, 172, 173, 174,
    178, 210; fixed commissions and, 148–49;
    risk monitored by, 181, 204, 207; Rule 415
    of, 150; short selling halted by, 209
Security Analysis (Graham and Dodd), 104,
    119–20
September 11, 2001, 3, 179, 230
Settlers of Catan, 244
shareholders: on boards, 114; empowerment
    of, 97–99, 111, 152, 204, 253; executives
    removed by, 74; executives selected by, 112,
    113; in hostile takeover, 137–38; lack of
    accountability to, 37, 38, 39, 41, 61, 68, 69,
    72, 96, 247; typical behavior of, 139; war
    bonds as gateway to, 40; *see also* principal-
    agent problem

Sharpe, William, 104–105, 120
Sherman Act, 23, 28
Shockley, William, 223
short selling, 51, 206, 208–209
Silicon Valley (show), 239
Silicon Valley, 222–51; big corporations in,
    224–25, 233, 244, 246–48, 255, 266, 267,
    268; founding of, 223; globalization of,
    237–38, 241; Hollywood vs., 241; lobbying
    by, 237, 241; Morgan Stanley and, 152,
    202; online networks and, *see* networks;
    political vision of, 238–46, 248–51;
    start-up culture of, 223–25; Transaction
    Man in, 20, 22; venture capital in, 223–25,
    236–37, 247; workers' rights in, 225, 255
simulation hypothesis, 243
Sinai Health System, 193–94
singularity, 243
Sisters of St. Casimir, 8, 85, 188, 193–94
Six Degrees (program), 230
six degrees, as term, 231
60 Minutes, 124, 126
Sloan, Alfred P., 73–74, 75, 76, 81, 95, 110
small businesses: liberal defense of, 145–46,
    262; obsolescence of, 28, 31, 63, 69, 147;
    as part of corporate ecosystem, 79; *see also*
    auto dealers
Smith, Adam, 39, 41, 88, 109
Smith, Roger, 142
Snow Crash (Stephenson), 228
social entrepreneurs, 242
socialism, 75, 97–98; regulation equated
    with, 76, 112; rejection of, 20, 24, 48, 58,
    60, 78
social movements, 10–12, 66, 145, 264
SocialNet, 229
"Social Responsibility of Business Is to
    Increase Its Profits, The" (Friedman),
    112–13
Social Security Administration, 43, 54,
    76–77
South Korea, 157
Southwest Catholic Cluster Project, 185
Southwest Organizing Project, 185, 186, 192,
    193, 194, 195, 198
Soviet Union, 3, 57, 58, 59, 66, 70, 263
SpaceX, 229
Spark Networks, 229
Spencer, Herbert, 259
Sperling, Gene, 166–67, 169
Spits, Gonneke, 125

Spitzer, Alan, 215, 216–18, 220, 221
Spitzer, Alison, 221
Spitzer, Delbert (Del), 82–83
Spitzer, George, 82
Spitzer, John, 82–83
Spitzer, Pat, 217–18
Standard Oil, 23, 30, 82, 91, 146
Stanford University, 223, 224, 231; Hoffman at, 227, 238, 242, 244
Stanley, Harold, 90, 93–94, 156
Star Citizen, 239–40
Start-Up of You, The (Hoffman), 234
start-ups, 223–25, 236–37, 241, 242, 246; buyouts of, 247; see also specific companies
State Department, 56
steel industry, 30, 36, 55, 59, 82, 89, 91, 214
Stefanos, Leo, 84
Steffens, Lincoln, 257
Stein, Gertrude, 257
Stephenson, Neal, 228
Stevenson, Adlai, 58
stockholders, see shareholders
stock market: 1929 crash of, 38, 48; statistical study of, 103–109; see also investment banking; Jensen, Michael; Morgan Stanley; Securities and Exchange Commission shareholders; stocks
stocks: bonds vs., 96, 141; classes of in Silicon Valley, 247; executives compensated in, 114, 115, 162; new instruments outpacing, 108, 141, 171; online sales of, 241; on margin, 51, 155; see also stock market
Story of a Lover, The (Hapgood), 257
"Strength of Weak Ties, The" (Granovetter), 231, 233
Strickland, Ted, 220
strikes, 75, 76, 77
Strober, Sue, 126, 134
Structure of Scientific Revolutions, The (Kuhn), 105
Stuart, Harold, 93
subprime auto loans, 212
subprime mortgages, see mortgages
Subud, 125
suburbs, 16–18
suffragists, 264
Summers, Lawrence, 173–74, 177–78, 208, 210, 214

Supreme Court, 23, 146, 147, 209; Brandeis on, 32, 51–53
Sutton, Betty, 217
swaps, financial, 108, 171, 173
syndicate system, 91–96, 103; decline of, 136, 140, 143, 149, 150

Taft, William Howard, 25, 30
Taft-Hartley bill, 76
Talman Federal Savings, 85–86, 183, 191
Tamayo Financial Services, 186
Tarbell, Ida, 146
TaskRabbit, 246
Teaching in the Home (Berle), 25
Team Auto, 214–16, 218–19, 221
Tea Party, 266
technology, see computers; Internet; networks; Silicon Valley
TED (conference), 238
Temporary National Economic Committee, 59
Ten Step Sales Procedure (Spitzer), 82–83
Tesla, 229, 241
Thaler, Richard, 121–22, 123
"Theory of the Firm" (Jensen and Meckling), 113–15, 119, 131, 135
Thiel, Peter, 227, 228, 229, 231, 232, 238; as provocateur, 233, 249
Think and Grow Rich (Hill), 125
Time-Life, 71
Tokyo Stock Exchange, 154
"too big to fail" doctrine, 175, 176, 177, 209
totalitarianism, 64, 76, 263
Toyota, 214
trading: largest loss in, 205–206; rise of, 138–43; see also investment banking; Morgan Stanley
Transaction Man, 19–22; institutional model replaced by, 21, 158, 211, 253–54; loss of faith in, 222; paradigm applied to social issues, 254–55; pluralism and, 267–68; see also financial economics; investment banking; Morgan Stanley
Treasury Department, 181, 192; under Paulson, 205, 212; under Rubin, 162, 166, 168–78 passim; under Woodin, 48, 49
Treaty of Detroit, 75–78, 97–98, 118, 214, 225
"Treaty of Detroit, The" (Bell), 77–78
Troubled Asset Relief Program, 221

trucking, 61, 147
Truman, David, 18, 263
Truman, Harry, 67
Trump, Donald, 15–16, 183, 249–51
trustbusting, 30, 31–32, 42, 53, 59, 62, 89;
    GM's strategy against, 73; of Morgan
    Stanley, 92–94; obsolescence of, 116, 147,
    151; of tech firms, 143, 230
Turner, Frederick Jackson, 29
Tversky, Amos, 121–22, 123
2008 financial crisis, 3–4, 133–34, 207–21;
    automotive industry during, 4–10, 212–21;
    in Chicago Lawn, 188–93, 199–200; credit
    markets frozen during, 5; government
    bailouts during, 5, 135, 191, 208–10, 213;
    lead-up to, see deregulation; derivatives;
    mortgages

Uber, 237, 246
underwriting, 90–96, 103, 136–37; by banks,
    165–66; decline of, 142–43, 150, 153, 157
unions, 8, 13, 59, 101, 112, 118, 147; criticism
    of, 20, 116, 225, 249; government support
    for, 54, 85, 214–15, 262; as interest groups,
    18, 20, 63, 264, 266; pensions from, 97–98,
    122, 211; Treaty of Detroit by, 75–78
United Auto Workers, 75–78, 98
United Nations, 239
United States: core institutions of, 254–55;
    corporations unforeseen by founders of, 23,
    28, 47; global influence of, 3, 161–62, 164,
    249; national character in, 15–22
United States of America v. Henry S. Morgan,
    Harold Stanley, et al., 92–94
United Steelworkers, 214
universal basic income, 245
university endowments, 96, 103–104, 119,
    149, 211, 224
University of Berlin, 256, 257
University of Chicago, 256; economics
    paradigm shift at, 64, 102–109, 110, 121,
    147; graduates of, in finance, 153
University of Rochester, 109, 111, 113–15,
    119, 120, 121, 126–27
Unseen Revolution, The (Drucker), 97–98
U.S. Steel, 55, 82, 89, 91

Vanderbilt, Cornelius, 33, 36
Van Dyke, Jason, 195
Van Susteren, Greta, 216
Van Tiem, Katie, 192, 199

Vassar, 33, 35
Veblen, Thorstein, 37–38
venture capital, 223–25, 236–37, 242,
    247
Vietnam War, 58
Visa, 229
Visible Hand, The (Chandler), 109
Volcker, Paul, 210
Vorberg, Amy, 6–7
Vorberg, Elaine, 9, 218, 219, 220

Wachovia, 208
Wagoner, Rick, 214
Wald, Lillian, 28, 35
Wall Street, 19, 20, 22, 116, 138; Berle's work
    on, 27, 28, 36, 56; corporations vs., 95,
    109, 119, 144, 150, 211, 253; criminality
    of, 100, 135, 152; political giving by,
    163, 164, 169, 215; see also investment
    banking; Morgan Stanley; specific financial
    instruments
Wall Street Journal, The, 92, 156, 204
war, 3
Watergate, 147
wealth, concentration of, 20, 30, 38, 158,
    254, 262, 266; during New Deal, 253;
    pre–New Deal, 21, 30, 254, 262; Silicon
    Valley's solution to, 245–46
Weekend to Be Named Later, The
    (conference), 239
Weill, Sanford, 168–69, 172, 177, 210
Weinberg, Nat, 77
Weiner, Jeff, 235, 236
welfare states, 67, 78; corporations as, 67–68,
    77, 150, 267
Wells Fargo Bank, 108, 193, 229
Westinghouse Electric, 39
West Wing, The, 250
Weyl, Walter, 30
Wharton, Edith, 33
WhatsApp, 225
Whedon, Joss, 239
White, William Allen, 30–31
White Collar (Mills), 64–65
white flight, 7, 11, 13, 87–88, 197
white nationalism, 4, 11, 12, 87–88
Whitewater, 165, 167
Whitman, Walt, 62, 262
Whittemore, Frederick, 94–95, 96
Whyte, William H., 16–18, 19, 65, 79,
    254

Wilson, Charles, 74–78, 97–98
Wilson, Woodrow, 26, 46, 47; as antitrust, 29, 31–32, 146, 262
Win the Future, 250
Witter, Dean, 202–203
Wolfe, Tom, 125
women's labor, 17–18
Woodin, William, 48, 49
Woodward, Bob, 161, 164
workers, 75–78; as uncollared, 246, 247, 255; worldwide wages of, 118; *see also* pension funds; unions
Working Group on Financial Markets, 165, 168, 172–73, 176–78
World Bank, 91
WorldCom, 127
World Economic Forum, 238
WorldsAway, 228
World Trade Organization, 161–62
World War I, 26–27, 40, 46, 93

World War II, 55, 56, 57, 59, 62, 70, 75
Wright, George Frederick, 25
Wright, Mary Augusta, 25
Wright, Robert, 244
Wright brothers, 33

Xerox, 109
Xi Jinping, 241

Yale, professors at, 44, 65
Yee, Michelle, 227, 241, 242
Yellen, Janet, 176–77
York, Duke of, 239
Young, Andrew, 12

Zaffron, Steve, 124, 126, 130
Zen Buddhism, 125
Zionism, 31
Zuckerberg, Mark, 232, 236
Zynga, 230, 244

PRAISE FOR *TRANSACTION MAN*

"Lemann, a *New Yorker* staff writer and former dean of the Columbia Journalism School, has a skill for making grand stories about American life feel human. He did it in two earlier books, *The Promised Land*, his 1991 account of the great black migration, and *The Big Test*, about the SAT and meritocracy, which was published in 1999. Anyone who read those books when they appeared would have been better prepared for some of the political and cultural debates that followed. I suspect the same will be true of *Transaction Man*, given the present focus on economic inequality and corporate America's role in creating it."

—David Leonhardt, *The New York Times Book Review*

"Clearly, *something* has happened to make us sour on the American corporation . . . Exactly what went wrong is well documented in Nicholas Lemann's excellent new book, *Transaction Man* . . . Lemann's book is more than worth the price of admission for the perceptive history and excellent writing."

—Ryan Cooper, *Washington Monthly*

"[Lemann] is clearly well-versed in the financial, economic, and political histories of his Institution and Transaction Men . . . [His] writing . . . might be essential."

—Bradley Babendir, NPR

"*Transaction Man* anchors three periods of American capitalism to mini-bios of New Deal brain-truster Adolf Berle, conservative economist Michael Jensen, and LinkedIn tech guru Reid Hoffman . . . [Lemann performs] the impressive feat of elucidating complex and significant developments in under 400 lively pages."

—Robert Christgau, *Bookforum*

"[An] excellent and unusually framed economic history . . . This concise and cogent history of the theories that have transformed the American economy makes a potentially dry subject fascinating."

—*Publishers Weekly* (starred review)

"A fresh account of the magnitude of inequality in America and how it came to be . . . Lemann relies on his well-developed skills as a longtime journalist to weave the specific and the abstract into a narrative that is intellectually challenging."

—*Kirkus Reviews*

"Through the stories of individuals, often from varied neighborhoods, businesses, and corporations, Lemann makes these experiences come alive . . . [An] insightful business history."

—Caroline Geck, *Library Journal* (starred review)

"A thorough, impressive and hard look at the American economy and the people who most influenced its arrival in the present moment."

—*Literary Hub*

"With his characteristic fluidity of thought and of expression, Nicholas Lemann has written a powerful book about how America really works—and doesn't. Part history, part reportage, part argument, *Transaction Man* is original, compelling, and illuminating."

—Jon Meacham, author of *The Soul of America*

"Every so often there comes along a book that forces you to reconsider what you thought you knew. Nicholas Lemann's *Transaction Man* is one of these books. Focusing our attention on short-term visionaries and disrupters, activist professors, rogue economists, and Silicon Valley lifers, Lemann revisits and revitalizes the economic history of America since the New Deal."

—David Nasaw, author of *The Patriarch*

"Brilliant and incisive, *Transaction Man* illuminates America's economic history through colorful stories of the thinkers whose ideas benefited a succession of wealthy elites while failing ordinary people. For anyone who thinks Wall Street has too much power, this book explains how that power grew."

—Rosabeth Moss Kanter, Ernest L. Arbuckle Professor at Harvard Business School, founding chair and director of the Harvard Advanced Leadership Initiative, and author of *Move: Putting America's Infrastructure Back in the Lead*

"A brilliant, essential, and rollicking read. Nicholas Lemann deftly guides the reader on a fascinating excursion. Blending incisive commentary with deliciously salacious detail, *Transaction Man* thrums with whiz-kid New Dealers and postwar management gurus, New Age Svengalis and Great Recession financial prestidigitators, free-market mavens and Silicon Valley techno-titans."

—David M. Kennedy, author of *Freedom from Fear*

ALSO BY NICHOLAS LEMANN

The Promised Land: The Great Black Migration
and How It Changed America

The Big Test: The Secret History of the American Meritocracy

Redemption: The Last Battle of the Civil War

NICHOLAS LEMANN

TRANSACTION MAN

Nicholas Lemann is a staff writer at *The New Yorker* and the Joseph Pulitzer II and Edith Pulitzer Moore Professor at the Columbia University Graduate School of Journalism, where he also served as dean. His previous books include *The Big Test: The Secret History of the American Meritocracy*, *The Promised Land: The Great Black Migration and How It Changed America*, and *Redemption: The Last Battle of the Civil War*.

TRANSACTION MAN